JAWAHARLAL NEHRU

A Biography

VOLUME THREE

1956–1964

by the same author

JAWAHARLAL NEHRU

A Biography

Volume One: 1889–1947
Volume Two: 1947–1956

Sarvepalli Gopal

JAWAHARLAL NEHRU

A Biography

VOLUME THREE

1956–1964

Harvard University Press
Cambridge, Massachusetts
1984

Printed in Great Britain
10 9 8 7 6 5 4 3 2 1

Library of Congress Cataloging in Publication Data

Gopal, Sarvepalli.
Jawaharlal Nehru: a biography.
Includes bibliographies and indexes.
CONTENTS: v. 1. 1889–1947.—v. 2. 1947–1956.—
v. 3. 1956–1964.
1. Nehru, Jawaharlal, 1889–1964. 2. India—Politics
and government—20th century. 3. Prime ministers—India
—Biography.
DS481.N35G66 1976 954.04′2′0924 [B] 75-33411
ISBN 0-674-47310-8 (v. 1)
ISBN 0-674-47311-6 (v. 2)
ISBN 0-674-47312-4 (v. 3)

TO
' . . . NUMERO UNO . . . '

Preface

This third and last volume of the biography of Jawaharlal Nehru covers the years from the end of 1956 to Nehru's death in May 1964. As in the earlier volumes, the study of the personality branches out to take into view general forces and trends which affected, or were influenced by, him.

I am grateful to Shrimati Indira Gandhi for granting me access to Nehru's private papers. I have also been permitted to consult some official files of these years.

I have, as usual, taken full advantage of the learning and consideration of my colleagues at the Centre for Historical Studies in the Jawaharlal Nehru University.

Contents

Abbreviations

A.I.C.C.	All-India Congress Committee
A.I.R.	All-India Radio
C.I.A.	Central Intelligence Agency
C.P.I.	Communist Party of India
NEFA	North-East Frontier Agency
N.M.M.L.	Nehru Memorial Museum and Library
P.I.B.	Press Information Bureau
P.M.S.	Prime Minister's Secretariat
SEATO	South-East Asian Treaty Organization

Illustrations

Acknowledgments

The author and publishers are grateful to those listed below for permission to reproduce copyright material. The extract on p. 267 is taken from 'Stopping by Woods on a Snowy Evening', from *The Poetry of Robert Frost*, edited by Edward Connery Lathem; copyright 1923, © 196–9 by Holt, Rinehart & Winston; copyright 1951 by Robert Frost; reprinted by permission of Jonathan Cape Ltd and Holt, Rinehart & Winston, Publishers. The cartoons on p. 268, 'Give me the supreme faith of love' (*Evening Standard*, 27.5.64) and on p. 270, 'Storm over Asia' (*Evening Standard*, 28.5.64), both by Vicky, are copyright © 1964 by *London Evening Standard*. The cartoon on p. 96 by Sir David Low, 'Just an old Indian custom', first appeared in the *Guardian*, September 1959, and is reproduced by permission of the *Standard*. The cartoon on p. 47 by Herblock, 'How True', is copyright © 1957 by Herblock in the *Washington Post*.

1

The Domestic Scene

ONE

After Suez and Hungary, it was the domestic scene that demanded attention. A rather casual import policy, taken along with a general inflationary trend in world prices, the closure of the Suez Canal and growing expenditure on defence, precipitated a crisis in foreign exchange. The Second Plan had envisaged a withdrawal of Rs 2,000 million over five years from India's sterling balances; in fact, in the first nine months, Rs 2,180 million had been spent. So imports were reduced to the minimum and fresh projects in both the public and the private sectors were vetoed.[1] 'Because of this foreign exchange difficulty we have been cutting our plans and projects down to the bone, and sometimes a bit of the bone is taken off too.'[2] The requirement of foreign assistance from October 1957 to March 1961 was estimated at about Rs 7,000 million, and much of it would be needed in the next eighteen months. So Krishnamachari, who had taken over from Deshmukh as Finance Minister, went to Washington in search of loans. This economic pressure, rather than any direct effort by other countries, led to a reduction of interest in world problems and, without any change in basic policies, a reluctance to appear 'as a crusader on the world stage'.[3]

The situation was aggravated by the fact that the import of foodgrains could not be suspended. With drought in certain parts of the country and floods in some others by the end of the year, the food shortages became intense. Production of foodgrains fell by almost 10 per cent from 1956–7 to 1957–8, and prices of grain rose by 50 per cent from October 1955 to August 1957.[4] For equitable distribution of grain and control of prices,

[1] Prime Minister's note to Cabinet Ministers, 9 January 1957. File 37(35)/56–59–P.M.S., Vol. 1, S. 23A.

[2] Nehru to Vijayalakshmi, 17 September 1957.

[3] Nehru's telegram to Krishna Menon, 18 September 1957.

[4] F. R. Frankel, *India's Political Economy 1947–77* (Delhi, 1978), p. 142.

Nehru decided to rely at this stage, till increased yields became available, on compulsory procurement.[5]

These pressing short-term requirements had to be set against the background of long-term planning. Nehru drew comfort from the belief that these immediate difficulties were, in a sense, the growing pains of a healthy economy. By the summer of 1956 India had apparently come to the parting of the ways in her economic life. If the Second Plan were successfully implemented, the road to the future would be clear, even if the journey be difficult and tremendous; otherwise India would be dragged back by the past.[6] Thinking two or three generations ahead and planning for a break-through into self-sustained economic growth, he placed his faith in heavy industry and machine-building in the industrial sector and cooperative farming in agriculture. 'It is a basic fact that if you want to progress, you have to progress by having more steel and by making machines yourself.'[7] In the ultimate analysis no foreign country could be relied upon and India should, as soon as possible, cease to look to any of them for assistance in the building of machinery. Only if this were done within ten years could India expect to maintain her independence and fulfil the hope of high standards of living roused by the attainment of political freedom. The world was becoming more and more a technical civilization, and living standards could not be raised without using the latest techniques. Even for survival the country had to be technologically advanced.

> It is a difficult world, not a very gentle world; it does not care too much for the weak. And you have to be strong, in mind, in heart, in character and in technique and in the modern ways of life. Otherwise you go down. I have no doubt about it.[8]

All future industrial development revolved, therefore, round the production of heavy machines, and the sooner India set about this, the better.[9] The Second Plan envisaged an annual increase in steel production from 1·5 to 6 million tons. Till such heavy industry went into production, the nation would have to bear the burden of building such industry without recompense.

However, Nehru was by now also beginning to realize the 'utter, absolute and basic importance' of agriculture. As he later confessed, he had learnt this lesson slowly and painfully;[10] but after 1956 he was no longer taking it for granted that industrial progress would automatically result in greater agricultural production. Planning had become a problem of balancing, of finding equilibria between industry and agriculture, between heavy industry and

[5] Nehru to A. P. Jain, Food Minister, 31 July 1957. File 17(206)/56–66–P.M.S., No. 18A.

[6] Speech at the National Development Council, 2 May 1956, Planning Commission file Plan/69/55. Plan Coordination; address to the Congress Parliamentary Party, 14 May 1956. Tapes M-17/C(i) and (ii).

[7] 30 May 1957. Lok Sabha Debates, Second Series, Vol. 2, pp. 2,935–59.

[8] Nehru in the Lok Sabha, 13 September 1956. Debates, Part II, Vol. 8, pp. 7,126–44.

[9] Nehru to T. T. Krishnamachari, Commerce Minister, 1 April 1956. File 17(138)/56–57–P.M.S., No. 2A.

[10] 21 August 1958. Lok Sabha Debates, Second Series, Vol. 18, pp. 2,247–57.

light industry, between light industry and cottage industry; and there was also the need to balance between the present and the future, to give the people enough to carry on with while working for the better days to come.[11]

As clearly there would be no industry, big or small, without a stable agricultural foundation, it demanded separate attention, and he placed his faith for long-term returns in cooperative farming. Its basis could be the community development programme, which Nehru still regarded as the most revolutionary process then operating in India and more important than even the building of industrial plants. It had already spread out to 220,000 villages or nearly half the total number and, in the next five years, was expected to cover the whole country and touch almost every activity in the rural areas. But the efficacy of this programme was to be measured not so much by statistics, satisfactory as these appeared to be, as by its effectiveness in pulling the peasantry out of the rut in which they had lived for so long. It had not met with equal success everywhere, but the organization existed and could be energized. The network of community development should give rise to a large number of young men and women trained to undertake intensive and organized work in building not just roads and schools and hospitals, but 'something bigger and deeper, that is, the building up of the innumerable human beings in villages'. Special attention should be given to this programme, which would provide for cottage and small-scale industries, improved agricultural production and, above all, non-official village cooperatives and close contact with *panchayats*. 'I am getting a little tired of officializing everything.'[12] A self-reliant peasantry, persuaded to adopt new ways of thought and action without forsaking its traditional culture, taking voluntarily to improved methods of cultivation and cooperative farming and governing itself through *panchayats*, would promote the development of the individual as well as social cohesion and create a democratic and socialist structure in India. It was only with the enthusiasm and dynamism generated by the social changes effected by this programme that agricultural production could be improved. The crux of the problem was approaching each village and each farmer, placing the responsibility on the *panchayats* and the cooperatives which should form the basis of both the political and the economic structure of India, and utilizing the services of those trained for village work.[13] The cooperative, the *panchayat* and the school might together promote a climate of rural change. The ultimate aim in education was free and compulsory schooling for all boys and girls from seven to fourteen years of age, with a free supply of books and stationery and a free meal.[14]

[11] Addresses to the Congress Parliamentary Party, 19 July and 12 August 1957. Tapes M-25C(ii) and M-26C(i) respectively.

[12] To H. V. R. Iengar, 13 August 1957. File 37(51)/57–P.M.S., No. 3A.

[13] To B. G. Kher, 5 March, and to Chief Ministers, 21 March 1957; address to the All-India Manufacturers' Organization, 13 April, *National Herald*, 14 April 1957; note 27 April 1957, File 17(28)/57–P.M.S., Serial 21A.

[14] Nehru to H. R. Ratna, 29 May 1958.

> But, above all, we must give up the office and bureaucratic approach and go down to mother earth . . . It is not our mistakes that harm us much because we can recover from mistakes. It is ignorance and inertia that come in our way – ignorance of the scientific approach and even more so of the human approach, inertia which always sits heavily on a country if we work through routines and out-of-date methods. But even more depressing are some of our social customs which come in our way.[15]

Old practices which had no relation to facts or present-day living conditions should be discarded as being really a degradation of culture, and a 'basic cultural climate' suited to the modern age should be developed.[16]

With the available resources at least four million additional acres could be cultivated, and production would then be more than sufficient to meet the country's requirements. Not grandiose schemes, as he had earlier been inclined to place his faith in, but local effort seemed to be the prime need. The masses of water collected by the large river-valley projects lay idle without irrigation channels to carry them to the fields. Many tanks were in disrepair, and tube-wells sunk in large numbers were mostly out of use because the water rates were too high. Soil conservation was in neglect, and there was room for model seed farms. 'Democratic decentralisation' – heavy and unlovely words, but describing an indispensable driving force – could alone transform the Indian countryside.[17]

The world was changing, and one's thinking had to keep pace with the change. 'You have to go forward. You cannot sit down in the middle of a river.'[18] Obsolescence of the mind, living in a world of ghosts and spectres and shouting old, irrelevant slogans were all as dangerous as frozen dogma. Political and social thinking had to keep pace with technological advance and encourage a scientific attitude. Two books which he read at this time, John Strachey's *Contemporary Capitalism* and Gunnar Myrdal's *Economic Theory and Under-developed Regions*, confirmed Nehru's view that the nature of capitalism in the West had changed and was no longer that which Marx had analysed. Far from dying out, capitalism had prospered and even resulted in higher standards for the industrialized communities of the West. The under-developed countries should also think for themselves, exorcize the ghosts of Adam Smith and Marx and go beyond both classical economics and Marxism. India could only progress if her people, while both keeping their strong roots in the soil and learning from others, decided for themselves what was best suited for them in the prevailing circumstances. The need was for an Indian model of development. The new thinking would have to preclude violence if

[15] Nehru to Chief Ministers, 24 November 1957.

[16] Speech in the Lok Sabha, 13 September 1956, Debates, Part II, Vol. 8, pp. 7,126–44.

[17] To Chief Ministers, 23–4 January 1958. Nehru later commented on democratic decentralization: 'I am all in favour of it, but that name will kill anything.' Speech at the A.I.C.C., 16 January 1960.

[18] Address to the annual session of the Federation of Indian Chambers of Commerce and Industry, 23 March, *National Herald*, 24 March 1957.

only because there was in the atomic age no limit to the effect of violence; and technical development would have to be in accord with moral values. Scientific thinking should also have an ethical dimension.

Nehru emphasized the importance of setting economic programmes in a larger context. A better standard of living should not be achieved at the expense of the spirit of man, of his creative energy and adventurous spirit, 'of all those fine things of life which have ennobled man throughout the ages'. But it was not only general values of which Nehru was thinking; he was now concerned with what he termed India's 'national culture', with its deep roots in India's soil and in her history. The effort should be to move away from the 'bullock-cart mentality' without turning one's back on the best of a past of ten thousand years. The pace of change, however fast, had to be subject to the principle of continuity. Without change, a society would be static and half dead; without continuity, a society would lose its footing.

A 'paper approach' to socialism, based primarily on European experience, would not help. The 'doctrine of socialism should be adapted to the facts of the Indian situation and the background of her people; the tremendous achievements in science and technology should be utilized but brought in line with the experience of India. One could not live in the past, but one could also not deny it; nor could one import someone else's past. If socialism were to succeed in India, it could not be a carbon copy of European socialism but should fit in with the basic Indian philosophic outlook.[19] His study of Indian philosophy during the long imprisonment in Ahmednagar fort had brought him round to the view that the essential basis of ancient Indian thought was in accordance with the scientific temper and approach.[20] Nehru was still an agnostic, but a Hindu agnostic.

In contrast to his ringing declaration in 1929 that he was a scientific socialist, Nehru now conceded the attractions of a utopian socialism with no attachment to any particular doctrine but a broad commitment to everyone in society being well-off and equal. The nearest definition he would give of socialism was the creation of equal opportunity for all of India's population, leading on to the raising of the level of progress equally for all.[21] The moral basis of socialism was to Nehru beyond argument; it was the gospel of Tawney rather than of Marx, but Tawney with an ethical commitment replacing the core of Christian faith. He was now, as in the early 1920s, deeply concerned that Marxist communism was wedded to violence and gave more importance to the ends than to the means. 'It has always seemed to me more important to

[19] Speeches at the A.I.C.C., 3 and 4 January, *The Hindu*, 4 and 5 January 1957; speech at Bangalore, 23 February 1957, A.I.R. tapes; speech at the International House, Tokyo, 13 October 1957; speech at the A.I.C.C., 12 May, *The Hindu*, 13 May 1958; address at convocation of Delhi university, 6 December 1958, A.I.R. tapes.

[20] See J. Nehru, *The Discovery of India* (Calcutta, 1946), pp. 620–7.

[21] Address to the General Conference of the Technical Cooperation Mission, 20 November, *The Hindu*, 21 November 1957; address to annual session of Associated Chambers of Commerce and Industry, 14 December, *The Hindu*, 15 December 1957.

do anything in the right way than even to do the right thing in the wrong way.'[22] He still recognized the existence of a class war, but believed that it need not be resolved by force, for it could be dissolved by the democratic apparatus. Conflict might not be avoidable but it need not be waged with violence and hatred. Gandhi had not believed in the existence of a class war; Nehru recognized that it did exist, but hoped to wage it in the Gandhian way, with an adherence to principle and always proffering the hand of friendship.

Socialism could obviously not be introduced into India all of a sudden by magic; it would have to develop slowly by trial and error, keeping certain goals in view but without being closely tied to any doctrine. It was, in the words he had used even in the 1940s before India became independent, 'progressive socialism'[23] that he envisaged. Great differences in the economic condition of the people were unjustifiable and, in one of his favourite phrases, even a little vulgar; but a mere increase of taxes and despoliation of the rich would not lead to socialism and was a childish way of thinking. Any attempt at quick equalization would produce conflicts and perhaps also a slowing down of production which was harmful to the elimination of poverty. Socialism in India would have to be a combination of priorities in production and distribution. The first objective was production, even at the cost of equality, for socialism was a function of abundance and not the distribution of poverty. Social justice was of manifest importance, but there would be little of it in an environment of poverty and under-development. Production was basic, whatever the particular policy, communist, capitalist or socialist; and in every society, irrespective of ideology, increased production was the result of improved techniques based on scientific advancement. The state should control the principal means of production and strategic points of the economy; private interests should not exploit the community; the private sector should not overwhelm the public sector; and, more particularly, foreign interests should not gain a grip on the economy. But in the drive for production, which was the great, national cause, the private sector was as much a national sector as the public sector. Industrial progress and socialism would have to develop together, step by step, on parallel lines, and a whole complex of circumstances be created, pulling the Indian people out of poverty. Keeping a growing population fed even while striving to raise the standards of living and increasing the capacity for production implied integrated planning and the maintenance of advance at various levels. Economic growth and social justice had to promote rather than weaken each other, and heavy taxation in the form of novel levies on wealth and expenditure, which made India one of the most heavily taxed countries in the world, could not be permitted to reduce incentives for greater production.

[22] To B. Gopala Reddi, 29 October 1956.

[23] Interview to the press, 8 July 1945. *Selected Works of Jawaharlal Nehru*, Vol. 14 (New Delhi, 1981), pp. 35–6.

'The fact is our little heads have to bear many, many headaches at the same time . . . and sometimes one is surprised that a little head can contain so many headaches at one and the same time.'[24]

The task was made more difficult by Nehru's unwillingness to abandon the democratic path even though it might mean a slower pace, for to him this was the only way of strengthening the roots of socialism. The Indian 'caravan of crores' should advance towards socialism by democratic and peaceful methods. To Nehru the end and the means were inextricably linked; socialism would endure only if the approach were democratic, and there was increasing conflict between the idea of parliamentary government and full-blooded private enterprise. What India required was not merely an economic programme but a recasting of society and a revolution in thought; and if these were to endure they needed to be based on popular acceptance and would take time to achieve. 'We are not building a house with bricks and mortar. Our materials are human beings. Only with their willing cooperation can we build our society.'[25]

These were all high aspirations, but Nehru was optimist enough, especially in the light of the experience of the ten years since 1947, to believe that they could be fulfilled. India's efforts in all spheres converged on common objectives and these were not beyond reach. Foreign and domestic policies were parts of the same pattern, strengthening each other and leading to the common goal of self-reliance. 'I say it with a challenge that even if Jawaharlal Nehru were to go mad, the Congress and the country will not depart from this policy of non-alignment and socialism.'[26] The rapid progress in the extension of community development, in particular, he found 'most exhilarating'. He knew, of course, that there was a darker side to the picture, but was inclined to ignore the shadows on economic development in the brave hope that they would soon lift. He could not but recognize that land reforms, a drastic revision in tenures and agrarian relations, had not been achieved; and, as a first step, he wanted the eviction of tenants to be stopped.[27] A more positive measure appeared to him to be cooperative farming and he hoped that, with its extension, the tiller would secure confidence, incentive and opportunity. He would then, as Nehru later described it, catch *kismat* (fate) by its neck, bring it under his control and utilize it for his work.[28] It was a pity that, in addition to Strachey and Myrdal, he did not also read Paul Baran, who, on a visit to India in 1956, had argued that nationalization of land and annulment of rural indebtedness were indispensable.[29] No action having been taken on these lines, Baran wrote a year later of the 'vacuous socialist phraseology' in India

[24] Address to the Congress Parliamentary Party, 12 August 1957. Tape M-26C(i).

[25] Speech at the A.I.C.C., 4 January, *The Hindu*, 5 January 1957.

[26] Speech at the Congress session, Pragjyotishpur, 19 January, *The Hindu*, 20 January 1958.

[27] Speech at the A.I.C.C., 1 September 1957, A.I.C.C. papers, File C23(A); letter to Chief Ministers, 5 September 1957.

[28] Speech at New Delhi, 13 April, *The Hindu*, 14 April 1958.

[29] Paul Baran, 'On the Strategy of Economic Development of India', 4 March 1956 (mimeographed paper of Indian Statistical Institute).

and concluded that the Government was incapable of providing genuine leadership in the battle for industrialization, did not dare to offend the landed interests, and was powerless to mobilize the enthusiasm and the creative energies of the masses.[30] Nehru would not have agreed, but from Baran he would at least have gained a keener awareness of the formidable obstacles on the path.

TWO

The political side of the battle for democratic socialism looked brighter. In the general elections in the spring of 1957, Nehru's tours were much shorter than in previous campaigns, though enlivened by an incident when only the pilot's presence of mind averted an explosion in the air, after one of the engines of the aircraft had caught fire. The Prime Minister was still the centrepiece in the appeal of the Congress. This is not surprising, for Nehru was at this time at the summit of his powers. The *Guardian*, for example, which had thought that Nehru was losing his grip, that his judgment was a little less sure than it used to be, that his recent ideas lacked his former imaginativeness and that he was showing an insensitiveness of touch, changed its mind after a first-hand encounter at a press conference in London.

> A hundred men and women of the West were being given a glimpse of the blazing power that commands the affection and loyalty of several hundred million people in Asia. There is nothing mysterious about it. Mr. Nehru's power is purely and simply a matter of personality. It is as intangible as that. Put in its simplest terms, it is the power of a man who is father, teacher and older brother rolled into one . . . The total impression is of a man who is humorous, tolerant, wise and absolutely honest.[31]

This magnetism of the leader in itself would carry the Congress to victory in any election; but Nehru sought to underplay the force of his own personality and was willing to let the record of ten years in office speak for itself. This was impressive enough. The Second Five Year Plan was, despite short-term worries, shaping well and the hurdle of linguistic provinces had been crossed. Abroad, the nagging activities of China were more than balanced by Nehru's *rapport* with both Eisenhower and Khrushchev; non-alignment had become respectable and the place which India had secured for herself in the forefront of international affairs was generally welcomed. But Nehru asserted that he did

[30] Paul Baran, *The Political Economy of Growth* (New York, 1957), pp. 222, 226.
[31] See the editorials in the *Guardian*, 28 May and 5 July 1957.

not care very much about victory or defeat in the elections.[32] Success for the Congress at any cost was not his objective, and he frowned at suggestions of an alliance with the Muslim League in Kerala in order to keep out the communists. Any arrangement which ran counter to basic policies would lower the reputation of the Congress all over India and the party would then deserve to lose.[33] In the event, the Congress did relatively well throughout the country except in western Maharashtra, where public opinion was not reconciled to the composite state, and in Kerala, where the communists were returned as the largest single party.

Nehru himself was pleased with the elections, because they demonstrated the success of the democratic experiment being conducted on a vast scale and showed that the voters generally exercised the franchise intelligently and were not being pushed in any direction against their will.[34] But he recognized that the results could afford no satisfaction to the Congress. It had won a large number of seats because of its central leadership, its prestige and its nationalist appeal; but clearly the party had lost its grip. It had no real hold on the public mind, the intelligentsia and the students were generally opposed to it and peasant support, on which it relied so heavily, was being broken up by caste and was threatened by class interests. Its organization hardly existed except in some places at the top layers, and even this was weakened by faction and intrigue. It lacked the vital urge, 'the developing ideology of a living and progressive movement', and was unable to keep pace with the forces which its very success in earlier years had let loose. The Congress was in danger of losing the willing and affectionate allegiance of the people, and this was a more important matter than winning elections.[35]

However, while Nehru was concerned about the Congress, he was not impressed by the performance of the other parties which he had castigated, even before the elections, as 'museum pieces'.[36] The communists appeared to him to have become out of date and the captives of phrases; the splinter socialist party led by Ram Manohar Lohia he could hardly take seriously because of its adventurist tactics and obsession with personalities; and the Praja Socialist Party, which still claimed to represent the main stream of socialist thought, was floundering in contradictory ideas and at times even equating democracy with private enterprise. Jayaprakash Narayan in particular seemed to Nehru, even before the elections, to be saying and writing

[32] 'How to Approach the Electorate', address to the Congress Party in Parliament, 5 January 1957, *A.I.C.C. Economic Review*, Vol. 8, pp. 5–6.

[33] To B.Ramakrishna Rao, Governor of Kerala, 15 January 1957.

[34] See his letters to Barbara Wootton, 1 March, and to M. C. Chagla, 13 March 1957.

[35] Nehru to Sampurnanand, 5 April, and to U.N. Dhebar, Congress President, 7 April and 7 June 1957; address at the meeting of Presidents and Secretaries of pradesh Congress committees, *A.I.C.C. Economic Review*, Vol. 9, 1 May 1957; address to the Congress Parliamentary Party, 13 May 1957. Tape M-24/C.

[36] Speech at Pune, 1 February, *The Hindu*, 2 February 1957.

'things which have little to do with socialism and which have much to do with nonsense'.[37]

The election campaign itself saw Nehru and Jayaprakash criticizing each other repeatedly and with vehemence. To Nehru it seemed that Jayaprakash had gone back on his decision to retire from politics and was willing to join forces with any group in order to defeat the Congress. So, when Jayaprakash suggested to him that he should function as a national rather than a party leader and also help to build up a strong opposition to the Congress, Nehru reacted sharply. If by functioning as a national leader it were meant that he should form a coalition Government, this assumed a common dominant purpose among the parties, and he could not find any such feeling. If Jayaprakash were hinting that Nehru was sacrificing some essential policy by being a party leader, then Nehru thought he was wrong, for Nehru believed that in both domestic and foreign affairs he had been trying to eschew partisan policies. As for Jayaprakash's suggestion that he should encourage the growth of an opposition, he had in fact given every opportunity for an opposition to function; were he to go further and give it a protected position, it would immediately lose weight with the people. What the Congress had done in the last ten years constituted 'a remarkable and almost spectacular record of work for the progress of the country'. In particular, it had helped, in Nehru's view, to strengthen the foundations of democracy and check the tendencies to instability and disruption. Those formed the real opposition and a tremendously strong one. Since 1947 it had been a fight for survival in the domestic and the international spheres, and India had come through.[38] But, as the elections had shown, the fight was not over; and India was still far from achieving full social cohesion. 'Personally, I feel that the biggest task of all is not only the economic development of India as a whole, but even more so the psychological and emotional integration of the people of India.'[39]

To Jayaprakash's very angry reply, addressing Nehru not as *Bhai* (or brother) as he was accustomed to do but 'Dear Sir', and charging Nehru with having deteriorated from a national leader to a partisan of the Congress,[40] Nehru sent a soft answer couched in affectionate terms but without dealing with Jayaprakash's points of substance.[41] Thereafter personal relations were restored, by efforts on both sides, to the old footing; but there was not again any prospect of cooperation in public matters save on such non-political issues as community development. Particularly as the rebellion in Tibet developed, Jayaprakash was in sharp variance with Nehru on support to the Dalai Lama. To Nehru, on the other hand, Jayaprakash seemed to be functioning in a way which was not at all Gandhian; he blessed the conservative Swatantra Party, he

37 Nehru to H. K. Mahtab, 12 October 1956.

38 Nehru's speech at Madras, 31 January, *The Hindu*, 1 February 1957; Nehru to Jayaprakash Narayan, 3 April 1957.

39 Nehru to C. P. Matthen, 5 May 1957.

40 14 July 1957.

41 18 July 1957.

encouraged the Hindu communalists, and he condemned the Congress Governments repeatedly.[42]

THREE

Opposition to Nehru and the Congress was also developing on the right wing, and here the main question, at the start, was the official policy on language. On the rival claims of Hindi, English and the other languages of India Nehru saw little room for dispute. Hindi would obviously become more and more the language of education and administration, except in certain parts of India where the regional languages would be principally used. The medium of instruction would be Hindi or the regional language; but English should continue to be taught as an additional language and its knowledge should be encouraged. It was one of the principal languages of the world, and, if India were to develop and become an industrial nation, a wide and sound knowledge of English was indispensable.

> Also, if I may say so with all respect, we are a narrow-minded people and apt to live in our own shells. There is the danger of our getting cut off from the world of thought in all its aspects and becoming complacent in our own little world of India. For this reason also contacts with foreign languages are essential.

English could not take the place of Hindi as the national language; only a select elite knew English, and a linguistic caste system could not continue as in the days of the raj. But the change-over from English to Hindi should be gradual and not rushed. Apart from the possibility of English being then replaced not by Hindi but by the regional language, haste in official support of Hindi might well split the country. As the agitation over linguistic provinces had shown, India was yet to develop into a unified nation, and it would be rash to encourage further the forces of disintegration by pushing through a language policy. The use of Hindi should be promoted only with the consent of the non-Hindi-speaking people. Moreover, some regional languages had developed more than Hindi and their further growth should not be prejudiced.[43] For these reasons, Nehru turned down the suggestion of the President that Hindi, as well as English, be permitted as the language for Civil Service examinations.[44]

The controversy over languages was significant not only in itself but as an

[42] Nehru to K. L. Shrimali, 29 March 1960.

[43] Nehru's evidence before Official Language Commission, 19 February 1956; Nehru to Chief Ministers, 10 May, to Maulana Azad, 26 August, and to R. S. Dinkar, 9 September 1956; note on Hindi, 8 September 1956.

[44] Nehru to G. B. Pant, 12 June 1956.

indication of the strength of disruptive tendencies in the country. Nehru never ceased to stress the importance of curbing such tendencies for, if social cohesion weakened, even economic progress would not be advantageous; 'the social fabric disintegrates and society may consist of wonderful people, geniuses in every line but they are all geniuses going in different directions'.[45] But, during 1957, acute differences on the language issue developed in various parts of India. In the Punjab there was an agitation for the more vigorous spread of Hindi and, in contrast, in the south there was a growing insistence on an explicit commitment to continuance of English. Rather than expressing his views on specific demands, Nehru laid down the principles which should govern policies on language. Decisions should be reached by consent and not according to the dictates of majority or minority opinion. Every language in India should be given full scope and, in recruitment to official employment, persons from non-Hindi-speaking areas should be at no disadvantage. English could not be the all-India language for all time, but its study should be encouraged, and it could continue alongside Hindi as the linking language between different states for official purposes. In any event, there was no reason to hustle decisions or to fix strict time limits.[46] If quiet, flexible, objective and pragmatic approaches were sought, the problem would cease to bristle.

Rajagopalachari, already sore with Nehru and described by T. T. Krishnamachari as having attained by now a mood of 'aggressive senility',[47] placed himself at the head of the agitation in southern India in favour of English. When the Congress passed a resolution along Nehru's lines of thinking, he wrote to the Prime Minister, 'as a faithful servant of the nation', urging that the Constitution be amended so as to make English indefinitely the language of the central administration and for inter-state purposes. To assume that objection was being taken only to the timing of the replacement of English by Hindi appeared to Rajagopalachari to be wholly erroneous. Hindi and the other Indian languages could be no more than the media for official work within the states. Nehru replied that Hindi would not replace the regional languages, which would develop as media of instruction and for provincial administration. The only problems were about the central administration and relations between the states and with foreign countries; and in these areas English could not be given the status of the sole official language. It could never become the language of the masses, and its retention suggested a lack of real freedom and an acceptance that Indian languages lacked vitality. But knowledge of English would be encouraged in India, steps would be taken to ensure that candidates not knowing Hindi would not be handicapped in recruitment to official services, the change-over from English to Hindi would

45 Address to the National Council for Training in Vocational Trades, 30 July 1957. P.I.B., Delhi.

46 To Chief Ministers, 31 December 1957; speech at the A.I.C.C., 16 January, *The Hindu*, 17 January 1958.

47 Letter to Nehru, 18 June 1956.

only be by common consent and, even after the change-over, English could continue as the supplementary official language for as long as required. There would be no hustling in this matter and the approach would be a flexible one, adapted to changing circumstances.[48]

Dissatisfied with such assurances, Rajagopalachari continued his agitation, even hinting support for secession of the southern states and causing Nehru to complain that Rajagopalachari 'appears to have lost his head completely' which made rational argument with him quite impossible.[49] When Nehru spoke of the 'cold war' being promoted by Rajagopalachari,[50] the latter protested that he was only giving the 'unambiguous warning' due from an elder brother and had been obliged to speak out because he had recently found that Nehru was not influenced by private advice but only by public opinion and pressures. Nehru accepted that there seemed little prospect of either of them convincing the other, but what he regretted deeply was the approach to this problem and the general manner of dealing with it. 'I hope you do not consider it impertinent of me to say so, but this whole manner has appeared to me not aimed so much to convince and to win over but rather to coerce. Inevitably this produces contrary results. That is why I described it as some kind of "cold war".' The danger to India was from fissiparous trends. In the south a well-organized group was talking about independence.

> Anything more foolish I cannot imagine. Any attempt to bring this about will not only create disruption but civil war because I think that any further division of India will never be tolerated by the great majority of our people . . . But I do not remember your raising your powerful voice against it in the way you have raised it about the Union language. I am constrained to think that you are so angry with our Government and its policies as well as the National Congress that this colours many of your views on other subjects.[51]

All that Rajagopalachari could say in reply was that he did not wish to give recognition to the 'silly' agitation for secession by opposing it.[52]

Nehru was still writing to Rajagopalachari with deference and trying to be persuasive; but his tone changed when Rajagopalachari publicly criticized Nehru's reference to a 'cold war' as an indication of authoritarianism and Nehru's difficulty in accepting any criticism.[53] He curtly pointed out to Rajagopalachari that he had not replied publicly to Rajagopalachari's many speeches except for that one brief reference in Parliament and, in fact, had

[48] C. Rajagopalachari to Nehru in January and Nehru's reply, 17 January 1958; Nehru to Mirza Ismail, 6 March 1958.

[49] Nehru to Vijayalakshmi, 9 February 1958, and to H. K. Mahtab, 9 March 1958.

[50] 18 March 1958. Lok Sabha Debates, Second Series, Vol. 13, pp. 5,399–435.

[51] C. Rajagopalachari to Nehru, 21 March, and Nehru's reply, 26 March 1958.

[52] C. Rajagopalachari to Nehru, 28 March 1958.

[53] Speech at Madras, 27 March, *The Hindu*, 28 March 1958.

sought to take Rajagopalachari's views into account when formulating the Government's policy.

> It is not for me to judge, of course, as to what my failings are, as they are many, but I have found it a little difficult to understand where authoritarianism comes into the picture, in so far as I am concerned. Nor have I been able to follow how this illustrates my being blind to criticism. I shall be glad if you will kindly enlighten me . . . Do you think it helps or clarifies issues by saying that a person who does not agree is authoritarian or blind to criticism? Surely I would not be justified in saying this about you, even though you do not agree with me.[54]

It was widely thought that Rajagopalachari's general opposition to the Government of India and the Congress could be traced to lack of office;[55] and it was to provide Rajagopalachari with a job that Sri Prakasa suggested that he be offered the Vice-Chancellorship of the university at Banaras. Though Nehru's immediate reaction was favourable, on reconsideration he felt it would be unwise; and Pant and Morarji Desai, whom he consulted, were wholly opposed. The students, and many others, at Banaras would find the appointment unacceptable; nor would Rajagopalachari fit in.

> Rajaji, with all his ability and intelligence, has gone off the rails completely in every matter almost. I am amazed at his irresponsibility and his pettiness. His governing passion seems to be dislike of people. I have struggled against this growing impression of mine, but I have not been able to get rid of it.[56]

FOUR

In the long run, the most significant aspect to Nehru of the language problem, even more important than the role of Hindi or English, was the future of Urdu, for it was tied up with the place of the Muslim minority in India. Nehru was concerned by his growing impression that both the Government and the Congress Party were losing touch with Muslim opinion. Azad and other Muslim leaders in the Congress seemed to have little influence, and the right type of Muslim was not being chosen for contesting elections on behalf of the Congress. Even worse was the prevalent attitude that the Muslims were an extraneous group to be appeased when votes were required.[57] In India, with its great variety of people and the effort being made to build a democratic system,

[54] Nehru to Rajagopalachari, 28 March 1958.
[55] e.g., by Escott Reid, Canadian High Commissioner in India, *Envoy to Nehru* (Delhi, 1981), p. 201.
[56] Nehru to Sri Prakasa, 8 August 1958.
[57] Nehru to Lal Bahadur, 7 January 1957.

it was particularly necessary to give constant thought to the needs and complaints of the minority communities. The real test 'is not how we feel about it, but how they feel'. They should have no sense of grievance about the use of their language or about employment, and the Government should make sure that official policy was implemented at all levels. Nehru instructed the Chief Ministers to send him quarterly reports of official recruitment, particularly when this was done without examinations, and to give special attention to employment of members of the minority communities in the private sector.[58] He also drew the Home Minister's attention to the manner in which Urdu, a language recognized by the Constitution, was being gradually edged out in Delhi city, where Urdu had once enjoyed a proud and famous place;[59] and he instructed the Chief Minister of Uttar Pradesh to declare Urdu a regional language in those areas where its use was prevalent and elsewhere to continue to grant it the normal privileges of a minority language. The future of the Urdu language was integral to the promotion of the emotional unity of the people, which perhaps was the greatest problem before the country. 'If we cannot forget these caste and communal weaknesses, which erupt in us at the slightest provocation, and cannot tolerate other communities, then to hell with *Swaraj*.'[60] But there was also a more partisan interest. As the opposition parties had taken up the cause of Urdu in order to inveigle the Muslim vote, for the Congress it had now become a question 'not only of doing the right thing and the just thing, but also the politically correct thing'.[61]

As the Home Minister showed no enthusiasm for strengthening the place of Urdu for fear of communal trouble, Nehru was obliged to bring the matter up in Cabinet. In an implied rebuke to Pant, he made clear that he would face communal disturbances rather than do the Urdu-speaking people a manifest injustice; for this was not a personal or a sentimental matter but one of vital significance for the future. Though others than Muslims spoke Urdu, opposition to it had acquired a communal colouring, while to Muslims recognition of Urdu had become a symbol of their status. If the use of Urdu were officially discouraged or the impression of such an attitude strengthened, Muslims in India would feel that they were citizens only in name and not as of right and there was no future for them in this country. To create such frustration was to go against accepted policy and to endanger the state, for it would spread from the largest minority community to other groups like the Christians. 'The great question that faces India today is how far the different communities can learn to live with others as equals. In other words, it is a question of peaceful and cooperative coexistence. We talk about this in the international sphere but we have not realized it within the nation.'[62] The Cabinet considered the problem and issued a statement, intended to stress that

58 To Chief Ministers, 26 March 1958.

59 Nehru to G. B. Pant, 30 March 1958.

60 Speech at the A.I.C.C., New Delhi, 11 May, *The Hindu*, 12 May 1958.

61 Nehru to Sampurnanand, 19 May 1958.

62 Nehru to Pant, 9, 10, 12 and 24 June 1958.

all languages would be encouraged to the extent possible and to emphasize the need for friendly feeling between the various national languages. But the gulf between resolution and implementation yawned as wide as ever.

FIVE

The other minority community that demanded attention was that of the Nagas in north-eastern India. In the summer of 1956, Nehru was more worried about the unrest in the Naga areas than even about the growing Chinese strength in Tibet. This was understandable for, after the Naga National Council had declared the formation of a Federal Government in March 1956, the army had to be put in charge of operations; and any Government would be seriously concerned by the necessity of having to employ its troops for months to deal with people said to be its own citizens. Nehru persevered with his policy of willingness to discuss the situation if methods of violence and thoughts of independence were abandoned. The Assam Rifles, the local militia, were ordered to hit hard and swiftly at Phizo and his armed bands. Suppression of open rebellion was a matter with which there could be no interference. Nor could promises or assurances of any kind be made to the Naga National Council; and no political and other changes would even be considered till peace had been restored. But thinking had to begin as to the best way to make the Nagas feel at home in India without encouraging the hostile elements or ignoring the sentiments of the people of Assam. Nehru himself was prepared to separate the Naga hills district from Assam, add it to the Tuensang frontier division as part of NEFA and place the whole under central administration; but he did not wish to press immediately for this.

On his visit to London for the Conference of Commonwealth Prime Ministers, Nehru realized that the Naga problem, along with Kashmir, was hurting India's interests. The Government had clearly not acted effectively or indeed even come to grips with the situation. The army seemed to be getting nowhere and was gaining a bad reputation; and this failure, combined with a lack of thinking on the political plane, was alienating many even of those Nagas who were opposed to Phizo. It was not good enough to carry on indefinitely in a manner which promised no speedy results.[63]

These years formed, in fact, a 'black and senseless period' with mutual brutality sowing the seeds of bitterness.[64] But the Prime Minister was optimist enough to believe that the situation was all the time improving psychologically.[65] By the end of 1956 the back of the armed resistance appeared to have

[63] Nehru to Defence Minister, 24 July, and note, 25 July 1956.

[64] N. Rustomji, *Imperilled Frontiers* (Delhi, 1983), p. 31. Rustomji served for many years as a senior official in the north-eastern borderlands.

[65] Nehru's statement at press conference at Delhi, 25 October, *National Herald*, 26 October 1956.

been broken and political decisions, to be taken after the general elections, could be considered. That the Nagas were now engaged in fighting more with each other than with Indian troops and that Phizo had fled to Europe were indications that moderate opinion among the Nagas was gaining ground. But how the Government of India should deal with an improving situation was not clear.

> About the Nagas, I am much worried. This worry is not due so much to the military or other situations but rather to a feeling of psychological defeat. Why should we not be able to win them over? I do not like being pushed into repressive measures anywhere in India . . . this long-drawn out business has a bad effect, both internationally and nationally and, if I may say so, personally on me. I am, therefore, prepared to consider any reasonable approach to this problem which promises a settlement.[66]

As first steps towards such a settlement, Nehru authorized the Governor to let it be privately known that the Government of India would proclaim a wide amnesty and be prepared to divest the Assam Government of the administration of the Naga areas. People fighting in the Naga areas for what they considered their freedom could not be treated on a par with ordinary criminals in the settled parts of India and would be pardoned, with only serious cases being referred to a Naga council. As for central administration, the Constitution could be amended for this purpose; but the Nagas would be allowed to elect representatives to the Assam Assembly and a hope could be indicated at the same time that these centrally administered areas might, at a later stage, form part of a larger Assam.[67]

By May 1957, a political settlement of the Naga problem had become not only opportune but urgent. With the world drifting towards war and a crisis developing in relations with Pakistan, it was risky to tie up a considerable portion of the army in the Naga area. Nehru wanted the central Government to take over immediately the administration of the Naga hills district. This would have a psychological impact on local opinion and particularly on that section which was hostile; and 'essentially a settlement must be made with those who are opposed to us and not with those who are with us'.[68] Such a settlement would also enable a withdrawal of troops without loss of prestige and indeed appear as a gesture of confidence in the Nagas.[69] But the Governor and Ministers of Assam preferred to wait till the situation crystallized further and the leaders of the Naga hostiles themselves made overtures for a settlement, for any initiative taken by the Government might be regarded as a sign of weakness. The Chief Minister also threatened to resign if the

66 Nehru to S. Fazl Ali, Governor of Assam, 22 January 1957.
67 Ibid., 9 and 22 February 1957.
68 Nehru to B. R. Medhi, Chief Minister of Assam, 16 May 1957.
69 Nehru to Fazl Ali, 23 May 1957.

administration of the Naga hills district were taken away from the Assam Government.[70]

Despite this provincial resistance, Nehru announced that the Government of India had no wish to be vindictive and would take as lenient a view as possible even of criminal offences. They would also be willing, in consultation with Naga opinion, to amend the Constitution so as to grant the maximum autonomy to the Nagas; and help would be provided for self-development rather than any effort made at imposition of reforms.[71] The Naga response was not slow in coming. A Naga People's Convention, with representatives from every tribe, met at Kohima and sent a delegation with the proposal that the Naga hills district be merged with the Tuensang frontier division and the whole unit placed under central administration. Accepting the suggestion, which was in line with his own thinking, Nehru agreed to sponsor the necessary amendment of the Constitution. He also announced an amnesty for all offences against the state.[72]

This agreement seemed to Nehru to be the turning-point, for it took the sting out of the problem and enabled gradual progress to be made in the right direction.[73] So when, after the necessary statute had been enacted by Parliament, the Naga hills–Tuensang district came into existence on 1 December 1957, he felt more confident about the future. 'The steps we have so far taken are, I have no doubt, the correct ones and, once a correct step is taken, then the mind is more or less at ease, though it should always remain wide awake.'[74] Even abroad, where there had always been an interest in the Naga problem, considerable satisfaction was shown at Nehru's 'wise' decision in solving the Naga problem on 'a sensible and humane basis' without yielding to the unrealistic demand for independence.[75] Visiting the area, Nehru found that the atmosphere was, on the whole, peaceful. He repeated that there was no question of independence. 'Not a yard of India is going to go out of India.'[76] This seemed to echo the prevalent opinion, for the hostile remnants suspended fighting for two months, thus implicitly recognizing that the creation of an administrative unit had isolated them and strengthened the moderates. So attention could now be given, after years of unrest, to relief and rehabilitiation. Nehru directed that a few able officers be posted in the area with instructions to concentrate on communications, health and education and the consequent creation of a climate in which the Nagas could develop self-reliance and be integrated in mind and spirit with the rest of India. The chief danger was over-administration. There should not be too rapid a break from

70 Medhi to Nehru 22 May, and Fazl Ali to Nehru, 25 May 1957; Nehru to Fazl Ali, 2 June 1957.

71 23 July 1957. Lok Sabha Debates, Second Series, Vol. 3, pp. 4,818–33; message to Nagas for Independence Day, *The Hindu*, 13 August 1957.

72 Statement of Government of India, 25 September, *The Hindu*, 26 September 1957.

73 Nehru's telegram to Krishna Menon, 25 September 1957.

74 Nehru's note to Foreign Secretary, 12 December 1957.

75 Editorial comments in the *New York Times*, 28 September and 16 December 1957.

76 Speech at Shillong, 30 December, *The Hindu*, 31 December 1957.

the past or a feeling fostered among the Nagas of being uprooted from their traditional beliefs and customs.[77] 'The idea that by putting them in shorts we have civilized them seems to me mistaken.'[78]

Nehru's optimism, however, proved premature. Hostile activity, though diminished, was not extinguished and took advantage of the amnesty. It was known that assistance was being sought from Pakistan. So the Government of India authorized the army to seize weapons held without valid permits and to undertake intensive patrolling in specified areas if requested by the civil authorities.[79] It was also made clear that hostile elements could not exploit the amnesty to strengthen their position or indulge in criminal acts. But large-scale military operations were ruled out.[80] In fact, a large number of regular battalions were withdrawn and their work taken over by the Assam Rifles. Nehru claimed that he was not aware of any instance in any country where a Government had acted with such friendliness to win over an insurrectionary group.[81] But this policy of combining firmness with gentleness did not prove very effective. The militia took little action, for the Chief Commissioner was concerned about political repercussions; and the spectacle of soldiers standing by while the initiative passed to about 1,500 armed Nagas created a general impression of weakness.[82]

[77] Nehru's notes written in Shillong, 30 December 1957.
[78] To Lakshmi N. Menon, 6 June 1958.
[79] Nehru to Fazl Ali, 13 March 1958.
[80] Ibid., 12 September 1958.
[81] 28 August 1958. Rajya Sabha Debates, Vol. 22, pp. 1,470–4.
[82] Nehru to Fazl Ali, 15 and 24 November 1958.

2

The World Outside

ONE

By the end of 1956 the crises in Suez and Hungary had passed their peak and, in the process, weakened both colonialism and international communism. Yet the world situation was generally uneasy and seemed to be moving back to an intense phase of the cold war. The sharper delineation of the two opposing groups did not produce a state of mind conducive to peace or to the development of an atmosphere for solutions. 'I do not like the look of things in the world today. I cannot mention any particular thing – we have had of course many things but at the present moment I cannot mention any particular thing – but the whole look of it and many small things taken together produce a feeling of grave anxiety in my mind.'[1] A creeping sickness, a slow disintegration of the collective mind, seemed to be leading mankind gradually to its final destruction. While scientific advance stressed the need for disarmament, human fears propelled the armament race. That in such an atmosphere India should be celebrating the 2,500th anniversary of the birth of the Buddha was an obviously ironic contrast. 'So we hover between war and peace, between the atom and the Buddha. I find some comfort in thinking of the maxim of the Gita that we should do our duty to the best of our ability and try to stick to the right path without worrying too much about the consequences.'[2] In foreign policy this meant to Nehru not being pushed around by others or being swept by gusts of passion but trying to find one's way according to the light of one's own reason and developing what he termed a world mind, or a world approach to world problems. This would be possible if the concepts of the cold war, of dividing the world into communist and non-communist, did not dominate one's thinking and there was no assumption that one could be friends only with those with whom one agreed. Without losing sight of national interests, one should seek to be friendly with

[1] Speech to the Congress Parliamentary Party, 27 November 1956. Tape M-22/C(ii).
[2] Telegram to Krishna Menon, 23 November 1956.

all countries.[3] Friendship was not monogamous.[4]

Such an effort seemed to meet with general recognition except with regard to Pakistan. Differences over Hungary caused no permanent damage to cordial relations with the Soviet Union. As one means of averting the drift to war, Nehru suggested to Bulganin that the Soviet Union might take the initiative in stopping the testing of nuclear weapons. Such a move, rather than compromise proposals for the limitation or registration of such tests, would have a spectacular effect and compel other powers to do the same.[5] With China the question of the border was forcing itself on Nehru's attention, but not yet to an alarming degree. Basing himself on the view that India's northern frontier was a traditional one and that there was no doubt as to where it lay, Nehru had decided in September 1954 – soon after the treaty with China about Tibet had been signed – that the whole boundary should be shown on maps as a continuous line and no reference need be made to undemarcated areas. But, unfortunately, no map on a larger scale than 1 inch: 70 miles could be issued because of lack of finality in three minor areas. On the other hand, China had been issuing maps of varying scale showing boundary alignments which were never the same, but which included Aksai Chin, NEFA and various little pockets of Indian territory within China. When India objected to these delineations of the frontier, the Chinese authorities took the line that they had made no surveys and had not consulted neighbouring countries and were merely following Kuomintang maps. This was a weak argument, especially as their maps had been showing redrawn boundaries in other sectors, in one case to 'restore' considerable territory to Burma and in another to cede some areas to Mongolia. The pretension to innocence was further damaged by the Chinese distribution in Sikkim and the Himalayan regions of thousands of copies of a map showing Tibet and China as the palm of a human hand, and Ladakh, Nepal, Sikkim, Bhutan and NEFA as its five fingers.[6]

Moreover, Chinese claims to Indian territory were, in a few areas, not solely on maps. By May 1956 the Government of India had had reports that the Chinese were using the caravan route from western Tibet to Sinkiang that runs through Aksai Chin. Chinese patrols were also regularly visiting southern Demchok, a village in Kashmir near the Tibetan boundary; and a party of Chinese soldiers was seen in 1956 in the Nilang area in Uttar Pradesh. The Chinese Government had been seeking too since 1954 to assert their claims to Bara Hoti, two miles south of Tunjun La, recognized as a border pass by the 1954 agreement. When the Government of India protested about this, China agreed to the despatch of a joint investigation team to determine whether Hoti plain was north or south of the pass, but showed no anxiety to implement this proposal to solve a particular dispute.

[3] 4 December 1956. Rajya Sabha Debates, Vol. 15, pp. 1,527 ff.; address to the International Tuberculosis Conference, Delhi, 10 January, *National Herald*, 12 January 1957.

[4] Press conference in London, 5 July, *The Hindu*, 6 July 1957.

[5] Foreign Secretary's telegram to K. P. S. Menon, 12 May 1957.

[6] A. Pant, *Mandala* (Delhi, 1978), p. 71. Pant was Indian Political Officer in Sikkim at this time.

Nehru began now to wonder whether it had been wise to have desisted from raising with China in 1954 the question of the frontier alignment. Not much had been done on the Indian side regarding the establishment of checkposts along the boundary and the building of communications, while the Chinese were going ahead rapidly with the construction of roads and airfields in Tibet. This in itself did not imply any hostile intention towards India but, taken with the regular reprinting of their maps and the intrusions at various points on the border, it produced in Nehru 'a sense of disquiet'.[7] Yet he was dissuaded by his officials from raising, even at this stage, the general question of the boundary alignment with China. His concern at the persistence with which the Chinese showed on their maps delineations which incorporated large parts of India in China was also alleviated by his conviction that, for a considerable time to come, China would be too preoccupied internally to indulge in any aggression against India.[8] Even while warning his supporters against mental unpreparedness for whatever contingency might arise,[9] Nehru was insufficiently alert to possible Chinese encroachments on a major scale. Curiously, the reported presence of Chinese personnel in Aksai Chin, and the defiance of Indian sovereignty that this implied, roused no marked reaction in Delhi. Infiltration elsewhere was thought to be the greater danger, and it was planned to deal with this by methods other than confrontation.

> I am not at all sure of what China may do ten or twenty years hence. But to protect ourselves against possible developments, we have to do other things and not try to put up a useless Maginot Line. In particular we have to have peace, quiet and contentment on our side of the border. I am worried more about the Naga trouble from this point of view than about anything that the Chinese may do.[10]

It was, however, more than merely a matter of internal developments or even of bilateral relations. The problem of China had to be seen with reference to Nepal and Burma as well. The efforts of the Nepal Government to secure the establishment of a Soviet Embassy at Khatmandu suggested a desire to loosen their ties with India and to develop closer bonds with other countries, including China. Soon word came about various proposals for a Sino-Nepalese treaty; and it was from Zhou Enlai that Nehru heard that Nepal had been exchanging notes on various matters with the United States. The Nepal Government were, of course, acting fully within their sovereign rights; but the discourtesy to a traditional friend rankled.

> The policy of thrusting help in the hope of winning goodwill is always unsafe and sometimes leads to harmful reactions. The other country

[7] Nehru to Krishna Menon, 6 May 1956.

[8] Nehru to Foreign Secretary, 12 May, and remarks at Commonwealth Prime Ministers' Conference, 2 July 1956.

[9] Address to the Congress Parliamentary Party, 15 November 1956. Tape M-22/C(i).

[10] Nehru to K. N. Katju, Defence Minister, 28 July 1956.

> thinks that we are trying to buy their goodwill. Instead we get their ill-will. Anyhow, we can neither afford to help them much nor do we desire to do so in existing circumstances. They are perfectly free to go their own way and we shall go our own way.[11]

But, in fact, Nehru went further than standing aloof in displeasure; he informed the Chinese Government that the signing by them of a treaty of friendship with Nepal would, from India's viewpoint, be inopportune.[12]

If Nepal was seeking to move closer to China as a means of shoring up her independence against possible Indian encroachments, Burma became increasingly nervous of China's imperialist designs. 'I fear to find myself entering the SEATO alliance in spite of myself.'[13] Whatever Nehru's own concern about possible Chinese plans, he had no wish to see his design for peace in Asia founder on Burma's differences with China; and, as the developments in Nepal showed, he still commanded influence in Beijing. So he encouraged U Nu to go to China and talk matters over informally with Zhou and, while he thought it better that he himself should not participate in those talks,[14] he requested Zhou to be accommodating. 'I would like also to mention that, by and large, in these sparsely inhabited frontier mountain areas, frontiers and positions which are based on previous agreements and have also been accepted by usage, custom and tradition for appreciable periods, should not be disturbed or altered except by friendly agreements.'[15] Clearly Nehru was laying down a principle which, in his opinion, should govern China's frontier not just with Burma but with India as well. So he could not have been undisturbed when informed that Zhou had told U Nu that his Government regarded the McMahon Line as 'immoral' because it was based on an unequal treaty but, for the sake of an agreement, they would be prepared to accept it as a *de facto* frontier.[16]

The Chinese, on their part, were concerned at signs of unrest in Tibet and their first inclination was to direct the Dalai Lama and the Panchen Lama to decline the invitations to attend the celebration of the Buddha Jayanti[17] in India in the winter of 1956. Apart from the possibility of hostile demonstrations by Tibetans in exile in India, there was the fear that the Dalai Lama, once in India, might refuse to return to Lhasa. But ultimately the Chinese Government decided to take the risk. India's friendship, though not apparently as important to them now as in earlier years, was still perhaps regarded as of some value; and, as Zhou himself planned to be in and out of India in the course of his various journeys to the Soviet Union, Eastern Europe,

[11] Nehru's telegram to B. Sahay, Indian Ambassador in Nepal, 2 September 1956.
[12] Foreign Secretary's telegram to Indian Ambassador in China, 4 August 1956.
[13] U Nu to Nehru, 29 August 1956.
[14] Nehru to U Nu, 4 September 1956.
[15] Nehru to Zhou Enlai, 12 September 1956.
[16] Telegram to Nehru from Indian Ambassador in Beijing, 28 October 1956.
[17] The birth anniversary of the Buddha.

Pakistan, Afghanistan and Nepal, he would be able to keep an eye on the Tibetan leaders and ensure that the Government of India would prevent any embarrassing developments. Zhou told Nehru that Tibet, although always a part of China, had enjoyed autonomy and had never been an administrative province of China; and the People's Government wished to continue this tradition and to respect the religion of Tibet. It was because they were keen on maintaining the religious and cultural contacts between Tibet and India that they had allowed the Dalai and the Panchen Lamas to come to India. But the Chinese disapproved of the reception, almost on the same scale as that to a visiting head of state, given to the Dalai Lama in India; and Zhou made it clear that he expected the Government of India to prevent disturbances or demands for independence by Tibetans at Kalimpong or elsewhere. Nehru replied that there was no reason why there should be any trouble if an assurance were given that Tibet would have full internal autonomy.

In his talks with the Dalai Lama, Nehru advised him to press for such autonomy and not to talk about independence. He had signed a treaty to this effect and any effort on his part to break it would result in a major conflict and much misery to Tibet. In an armed struggle, Tibet could not possibly defeat China and could expect no assistance from India, which had recognized China's rights in Tibet. In fact, the Dalai Lama, far from devoting his attention to the building of autonomy in Tibet, was giving serious consideration to opting to stay in India. Although Zhou declared airily to Nehru that the Dalai Lama might stay in India as long as he abided by the Indian Government's regulations, Nehru recognized the concern behind this seeming indifference and persuaded the Dalai Lama to accept Zhou's assurances and return. A decision to remain in India would be the height of folly; his place was in his own country and he should give a lead to his people. 'I am', pleaded the Dalai Lama, 'a very young man. I do not know which way to look. The medicine that the doctor [Nehru] is proposing for my weakness seems to be bitter and unpalatable. I do not know whether I would really get well with that medicine.'[18] But he was finally persuaded that to precipitate matters at this stage would be to 'make a Hungary of Tibet'; and both the Dalai and the Panchen Lamas returned to Lhasa.

In this matter, therefore, Nehru had not let Zhou down; but he secured little in return. On Krishna Menon's advice, he raised the question of the boundary alignment, Zhou replied that he had known nothing about the McMahon Line until the Chinese Government had begun recently to study the border problem. Although China had never recognized that alignment, the Chinese felt they should recognize it because it was an accomplished fact and because of their friendly relations with India; they had not consulted the Tibetan Government and proposed to do so. For Nehru to regard this oral commitment as a 'quite clear and precise'[19] acceptance of the McMahon Line

[18] Quoted by A. Pant in his note on conversations with the Dalai Lama, 31 December 1956.
[19] To U Nu, 22 April 1957.

and to conclude that the major border issue had been settled for all practical purposes[20] was to be over-optimistic. When Nehru suggested that, apart from the McMahon Line, the two sides should agree on some principles, such as previous established practice and the watershed, on which bases the minor boundary disputes that existed could be settled, Zhou went no further than to say that the question could be solved or should be settled early. Once again, as in 1954, it would have been more prudent to have committed Zhou in writing in a joint communiqué; but Nehru had still faith in Zhou's word and trust in Zhou's friendship. He did not realize as yet that such faith and trust were heavily one-sided.

Nor was Zhou flexible and accommodating on other matters. On Hungary, he generally supported the Soviet position and contended that, once Nagy had asked the Western Powers for help, the Soviet Government had no option but to intervene. Nehru argued at length that, whatever Nagy's errors, the Soviet domination of Hungary could not be justified and had produced a strong reaction in many countries of Asia and Europe against the Soviet Union. 'Compulsory socialism' had no hope of success and any conflict between nationalism and socialism could mean only the weakening of the latter. But Zhou adhered to the Soviet line and the two Prime Ministers agreed to differ.

Nehru, who visited Washington in between Zhou's visits to India, was also eager to promote Sino-American relations. Thirty-four American prisoners in China had been released in the past eighteen months; but the Chinese refused to release the ten Americans who were still in detention on the grounds that the United States had not responded to their gesture and all but two of the Americans were not prisoners of war but spies. The number was too small to be more than an irritant to American opinion, but it was adequate to prevent headway in thawing relations between the two countries. Urged on by Krishna Menon, Nehru pressed Zhou to release them before he went to Washington; but Zhou insisted that the Americans agree in return at least to an informal meeting of Foreign Ministers and to expedite the return of Chinese students.[21] The reaction of Dulles was that any one who wished to leave the United States was free to do so. Eisenhower said that there was such strong feeling in the United States about the ten prisoners that he could take no forward step as regards China till these men had been released. Although American opinion had forgotten the great losses in the Second World War, it still remembered the losses in the Korean War. But if the prisoners were released, Americans would be permitted to go to China and their reports might bring about a change in the American outlook and help towards normalization. Zhou's reply to this was that the Americans could not forget the Korean War because victory had been denied to them; but China also had

[20] To Sampurnanand, 14 May 1957.

[21] Krishna Menon's telegram to Nehru, 3 December, Nehru's telegram to Krishna Menon, 5 December, Nehru to Zhou Enlai, 5 December, Nehru's telegram to Zhou, 7 December, and Zhou to Nehru, 9 December 1956.

strong feelings. She could not agree to the American demand that it was China which should throughout make concessions and, there being no sense of reciprocity in the American position, relations between the United States and China would probably remain as they were for a long time.[22]

However, though Nehru had found Zhou unyielding on every issue, the Chinese seemed to attach importance to the 'friendship of a thousand million'[23] and, for some months after these conversations with Zhou, relations between the two countries remained on a comparatively even keel. Nehru's policy was clear. He had no doubt that the Chinese were intensely nationalist. As he once expressed it, the Chinese were more Chinese than even the Indians were Indians.[24] They were masters of their own policies and were potential rivals rather than subordinates of the Soviet Union. They were toiling hard to become a major industrial power and their territory was so vast and their numbers were so rapidly increasing that even a nuclear attack would not destroy their organized life. Other powers, therefore, had either to seek deliberately to contain or even to destroy China, which would prove both a disastrous and an impractical task, or try to develop closer relations and thereby to encourage such tendencies as might exist in China towards more liberal and progressive policies. He was not discouraged by the growing rigour in the domestic and foreign policies of that country. He was aware, too, that in the particular setting of relations between India and China, points of conflict were developing. The Indian Ambassador in Beijing and the Consul-General in Shanghai reported, in the summer of 1957, that a coolness was growing on the part of the Chinese authorities. On Kashmir, the Chinese press tended to equate Pakistan and India and in June Zhou, in his address to the National People's Congress, minimized India's part in world affairs and mentioned her as but one of the countries playing a greater role in developing world peace. In September, the Chinese announced the completion of a road which seemed to run across the eastern extremity of Aksai Chin. But Nehru was determined to strive to work with China rather than to regard her as a potential foe, for he was convinced that this was the more worthwhile, and perhaps the only feasible, policy. The building of the road across Aksai Chin was a violation of Indian sovereignty, but as the Chinese map on which this road was depicted was on too small a scale for India to be certain of its alignment, Nehru decided to despatch reconnaissance parties in the summer before taking any action.[25] In public, he repeatedly expressed his faith in good relations with China. Although India and China each had their own way of public life and development, their cooperation could grow; and he continued to urge the importance of admitting the People's Republic of China to the United Nations.[26]

22 The preceding paragraphs are based on Nehru's notes of his talks with Zhou Enlai, Eisenhower and Dulles, December 1956–January 1957.

23 *People's Daily*, 12 December 1956.

24 Speech to the Congress Parliamentary Party, 19 July 1957. Tape M-26/C(i).

25 See Nehru's answer in the Rajya Sabha, 31 August 1959. Debates, Vol. 26, pp. 2,281–8.

26 27 March 1957. Rajya Sabha Debates, Vol. 16, pp. 723–41.

That the Chinese were nibbling at three points on the border concerned Nehru not so much in itself but as an indication of aggressive behaviour on the part of the Chinese; but he believed that Zhou had, in the winter of 1956, accepted the Indian alignment except for some minor disputes. So he instructed the Uttar Pradesh Government not to adopt an aggressive attitude in the disputed areas, for these matters were being settled in conference and there was no major border issue.[27] Nehru's view was that not only was the frontier with China not negotiable by India, but that China had accepted this and there was nothing to negotiate about. In Europe in the summer of 1957, he declared his confidence that relations between India and China would continue to be friendly. They followed divergent political and economic policies but there was no reason why they should interfere with each other. Their lack of agreement on many matters was no barrier to friendship.[28] There was no question of economic rivalry; only their approaches happened to be different and Nehru added that, in his view, the democratic way of India was sounder.[29] Such petty problems as existed he claimed that they had been able to solve by meeting together. The minor disputes on the frontier – and these to him were the only frontier disputes – they had not as yet settled; but these were very small areas in the high mountains on the Tibetan border, and were of no great value to either country.[30]

Nehru was also optimistic about conditions in Tibet and believed that the People's Government would respect its autonomy if other powers did not intervene. Indeed, he thought that, as a part of this process, the Chinese had, over the past six months, relaxed their control; many Chinese officials had been withdrawn, Chinese schools had been closed and Chinese troops, although still in effective occupation, were more unobtrusively deployed than before.[31] He later realized that there was continuing trouble in Tibet and that this was deepening the shadow on China's relations with India. When the Indian Political Officer in Sikkim visited Tibet in September, the Chinese authorities instructed the Dalai and Panchen Lamas to accord him no welcome, for Western imperialists were 'influencing' Nehru and he might side with them. Facilities granted to Indian trade agents in Tibet were also increasingly restricted. Yet these signs of distrust were not justified by any policy or action of India. Nehru had no intention of letting India be dragged into any rebellious activity undertaken by Tibetans and was inclined to side with the progressive social forces which China seemed to represent. 'Spirituality by itself, if widely acknowledged, may well be a strong shield.

[27] Nehru to Sampurnanand, Chief Minister of Uttar Pradesh, 14 May 1957.

[28] Press conference at Oslo, 22 June 1957. *Nehru in Scandinavia* (Information Service of India, Stockholm, 1958).

[29] Press conference at The Hague, 9 July, *The Hindu*, 11 July 1957.

[30] Nehru's reference to frontier disputes with China in his note on the Nepal–China frontier, 23 August 1957.

[31] Minutes of the Commonwealth Prime Ministers' Conference, London, fifth session, 28 June 1957.

Combined with primitive weapons, it ceases to be spiritual or effective.'[32] It was as part of this approach that he assured Parliament that there was not 'the remotest chance of a remote chance' of India having any kind of military conflict with Russia or China.[33]

TWO

Though, on the question of American prisoners in China, Nehru could not bring the positions of Eisenhower and Zhou closer, his visit to the United States in December 1956 was more fruitful than the earlier one in 1949. The broad cooperation in the Suez crisis prepared the ground for closer relations in other matters. It was reported to the Prime Minister, for example, that on problems of atomic energy the United States was far more flexible and understanding than other Western Powers. 'It seems clear to me that our *direct* relations with the United States should be strengthened and that our approach to them should not be made through or with the help of the United Kingdom.'[34]

Clearly the public both in the United States and elsewhere attached the highest importance to Nehru's visit. St Laurent told Eisenhower that it was a meeting of probably the two most influential statesmen in the world, the two whose influence radiated the most widely in the free world.[35] The United States Government showed Nehru the honours reserved for heads of state and embarrassed him with, for the first time in his life, a gun salute. But he himself did not expect too much from the visit and was concerned at the way in which the press in the United States boosted his planned talks with Eisenhower as almost in the nature of a world event. 'But how we are going to change the world's course of history in a day or two is more than I can understand.'[36]

In fact, in the talks extending over twelve hours, Nehru and Eisenhower, though not always in agreement, succeeded in evoking a general mood of understanding. Eisenhower, while accepting that the ultimatum and attack on Egypt were unjustifiable, found some of Nasser's actions and utterances objectionable; but he did not quarrel with Nehru's suggestion that a peaceful settlement in West Asia would be facilitated by a step-by-step approach. The Canal should first be cleared for traffic; then a long-term agreement on Suez could be attempted and in the more favourable atmosphere thus created the problem of Israel could also be settled in consultation with the Arab countries.

[32] Nehru's note on Tibet, 26 December 1957.

[33] 13 December 1957. Rajya Sabha Debates, Vol. 19, pp. 2,465–82.

[34] Dr Homi Bhabha, Chairman, Indian Atomic Energy Commission, to Nehru, 13 December 1956. Emphasis in original.

[35] Speech in Parliament, Ottawa, 9 January 1957.

[36] Nehru to Vijayalakshmi, 6 December 1956.

On Hungary, Nehru argued that Soviet action had been motivated by a sense of insecurity and the belief that Anglo-French aggression in Egypt had the approval of the United States. Liberalizing movements in the Soviet Union and Eastern Europe should be encouraged so that current fears would at least lessen, thus opening the door for peaceful solutions of existing problems. Even Dulles, speaking on this subject for the United States Government, agreed that the process of liberalization, which had happened sooner than he had expected, could not be reversed; but this in itself seemed to him to make war more likely, for the Soviet Union might prefer this to what she considered humiliations. On China, it was recognized in Washington that Nehru was striving, though in vain, to wrest concessions from Zhou, and was in sympathy with the American position. To Nehru's elaboration of India's case on Kashmir and the manner in which Pakistan was exploiting American arms in an effort to cow India, Eisenhower replied that it would be unwise to take any step in Kashmir which would upset the existing situation and create further difficulties – a comment in line with India's position. He also seemed to accept India's right to Goa and, while observing that the Portuguese authorities were very difficult to handle and his own Government had their hands full with major problems, promised to help in securing the release of Indian prisoners in Goa. He was as good as his word and, a few weeks later, the prisoners were released. Finally, when non-political matters were discussed, Eisenhower was enthusiastic in his promise of support for the Second Five Year Plan.[37]

It was clear that, specific issues apart, the talks had initiated a new phase in the relations between the two Governments to the extent that both Nehru and Eisenhower had gained a sympathetic appreciation of each other's position. Even before leaving Washington Nehru, to the delight of the State Department, announced that he now recognized that the policy of the United States was flexible and adapting itself to circumstances; the general approach seemed to him to be governed by an appreciation of a changing world and trying to fit in with those changing conditions. On their part, official circles in the United States were less inclined to believe that Nehru was a crypto-communist; and so considerable was the influence that he was known to have established that diehard opinion in the United States even feared that he might weaken American policy on China. 'In the current American mystique, the Indians have supplanted the British as the experts at stealing America's shirt.'[38]

To round off his visit, Nehru spoke at the National Press Club; and this session was televised live by all the networks and given a wider coverage than was usually accorded even to talks by the President. Introduced as 'the mystical man in the middle', he conveyed to his audience the overall

[37] Nehru's record of talks with Dulles, 16 December, report to Cabinet on talks with Eisenhower, 29 December 1956, and note on talks, 8 January 1957.

[38] Alistair Cooke in the *Guardian*, 17 December 1956.

impression of a man of 'warmth and candour and modesty and superb poise'.[39] A participant felt it to be as successful an exhibition of the art of diplomatic repartee as Washington could recall.[40]

The visit as a whole seemed to augur well for relations between the two countries; and developments immediately after the visit confirmed this growth in mutual understanding. The apprehension in the United States after Suez was that Soviet influence would fill the vacuum created by the elimination of British and French power in West Asia. Nehru had cautioned Eisenhower that the grant of economic aid by the United States to feudal and unpopular regimes was counter-productive and Eisenhower had agreed that there was some truth in this. But the announcement of the Eisenhower doctrine soon after Nehru's visit showed that recognition of the uncertain effects of economic assistance was leading to a heavier reliance on arms. Nehru was embarrassed, for he believed that this decision had given a wrong direction to the situation in West Asia, but he did not wish to criticize Eisenhower so soon after their talks. So he contented himself with an indirect reference and an expression of regret at the military approach, the brandishing of swords to make an impression on the world.[41] Eisenhower sent a personal explanation. He had resisted pressure to join the Baghdad Pact because of the views of Nehru and others; but the United States would have to assist those who might seek American help if attacked and, apart from the need for the consent of Congress in advance if procedural delays were to be avoided, a forthright statement might help greatly in diminishing the threat of aggression. 'I regret that our thinking on this matter had not, when you were here, developed to the point where we could discuss it.'[42] Nehru replied that, with the Soviet Union being too involved in Eastern Europe, he saw no danger of her committing aggression in West Asia. But, even otherwise, it was nationalism which was the strongest force in West Asia.[43] Though the countries of this region were backward and far removed from communism, the holding out of threats might in itself increase the possibility of Soviet intervention. Few would now question the validity of Nehru's attitude.[44] Yet in public Nehru's criticism continued to be mild. He said no more than that the treating of West Asia as a vacuum to be filled from outside was a dangerous and unreal approach; if the local populations were not left to themselves to develop their independence, the area would again become an arena for the rivalry of the great powers.[45]

39 Report of British Embassy to the Foreign Office in London, 22 December 1956.

40 Neal Stanford in the *Christian Science Monitor*, 20 December 1956.

41 Speech at the A.I.C.C., 6 January, *National Herald*, 7 January 1957.

42 Eisenhower to Nehru, 7 January 1957.

43 Nehru to Eisenhower, 11 January 1957.

44 cf. Professor D. C. Watt's description of the Eisenhower doctrine: 'a short course in how not to make policy in the Middle East'. *Times Literary Supplement*, 11 September 1981.

45 25 March 1957. Lok Sabha Debates, Vol. 1, Part II, pp. 651–71.

THREE

Such friendly expressions of differences of opinion between India and the United States did not, however, extend to Kashmir. Throughout the summer of 1956, India's relations with Pakistan had remained in the background. Nehru refused to discuss Kashmir even informally at the Commonwealth Prime Ministers' Conference, and thereafter Suez and Hungary monopolized attention. In October the two Prime Ministers were doing no more than exchanging notes and letters about the alleged harassment of minorities in the two countries.[46] But the next month the Pakistan Government returned to the question of Kashmir and protested about the enactment of a Constitution by the Kashmir Constituent Assembly and reports that Kashmir would now be integrated with India. Nehru took the line that the Constituent Assembly had been sitting for nearly six years and was competent to decide anything it chose in regard to the state. India was not bound to accept everything that that Assembly might decide, but the situation had changed considerably since India had made her commitments to the United Nations and the relations of Kashmir to India must be considered as finally settled.[47]

The atmosphere was worsened further by Suhrawardy, who had replaced Chaudhuri Mahomed Ali as Prime Minister, and the new Foreign Minister, Feroze Khan Noon. They made no secret of the fact that dislike of India was the driving force of their foreign policy; and it was in this mood that they raised once again the question of Kashmir at the Security Council. Krishna Menon, already in New York, advised that India retort by demanding of the Security Council that Pakistan's continuing aggression in Kashmir be ended. Nehru agreed to this, but the foreign affairs committee of the Cabinet, consisting of Azad, Pant, Katju and T. T. Krishnamachari, criticized Nehru and Menon for making what could appear to be an 'undignified and petty' proposal which might well harm India by reopening the whole question.[48] This was perhaps the only occasion in these heyday years when Nehru and Menon had to give way to their colleagues on an issue of foreign policy; and, in the event, it was proved that the Prime Minister would have been wiser to have insisted on formulating his own tactics. Menon had to content himself with arguing at great length before the Security Council that the real issue was vacation of aggression from an area which had acceded permanently to India. His marathon speeches stating India's position in detail from 1947 made little impact on his immediate audience, which included six military allies of Pakistan. The Kashmir question had got entangled with the cold war

[46] H. S Suhrawardy to Nehru, 9 October, note of Ministry of External Affairs to Foreign Ministry of Pakistan, 12 October, and Nehru's letter to Suhrawardy, 23 October 1956.

[47] *Aide-mémoire* of Pakistan Government, 22 November, and Nehru's record of talk with the High Commissioner of Pakistan, 22 November 1956.

[48] Krishna Menon's telegram to Nehru, 5 January, and Nehru's replies, 7 and 8 January 1957.

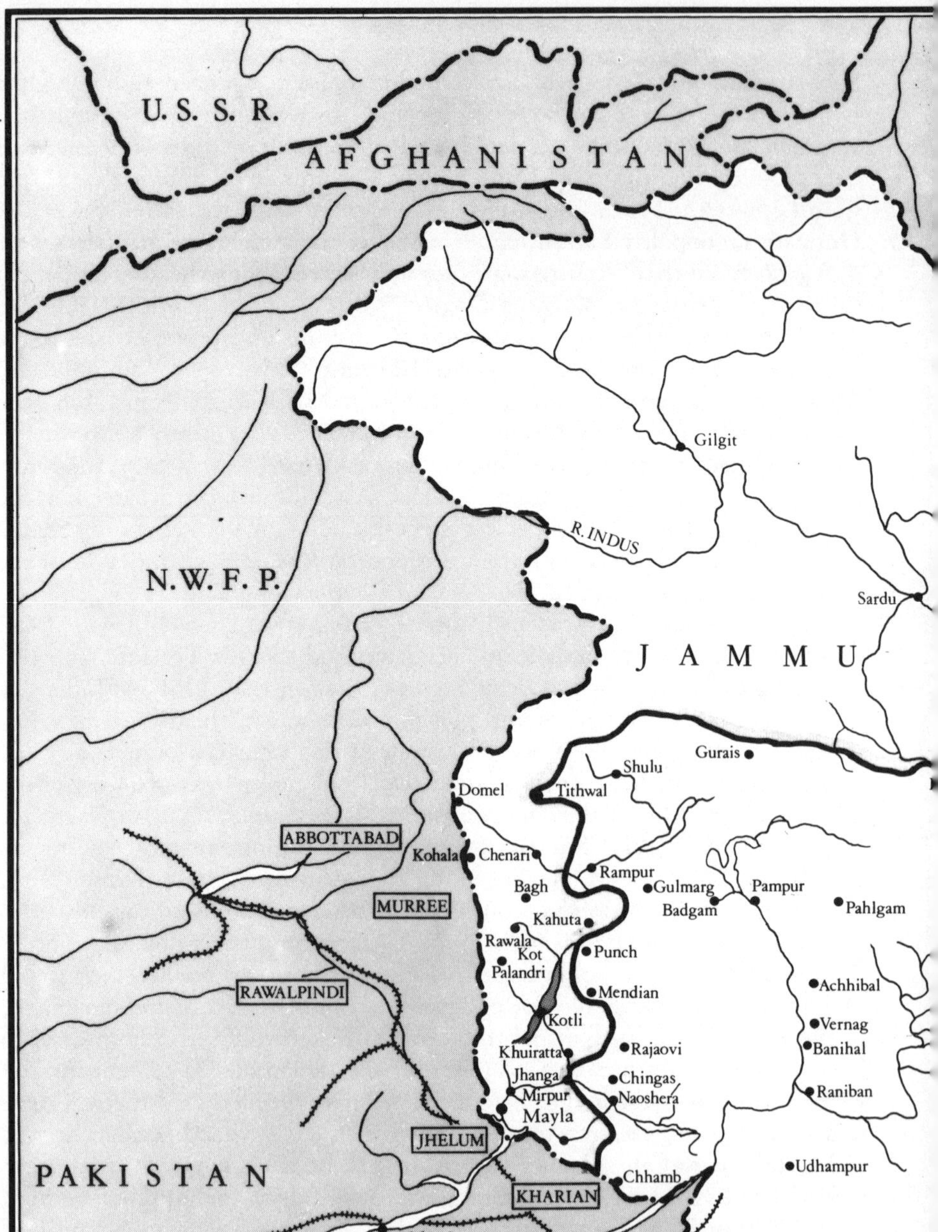

U. S. S. R.
AFGHANISTAN
Gilgit
R. INDUS
N.W. F. P.
Sardu
JAMMU
Gurais
Shulu
Domel
Tithwal
ABBOTTABAD
Kohala
Chenari
Rampur
Bagh
Gulmarg
Pampur
MURREE
Badgam
Pahlgam
Kahuta
Rawala Kot
Punch
Palandri
RAWALPINDI
Mendian
Achhibal
Kotli
Vernag
Khuiratta
Rajaovi
Banihal
Jhanga
Chingas
Mirpur
Naoshera
Raniban
Mayla
JHELUM
PAKISTAN
Udhampur
Chhamb
KHARIAN
Malakwai
Gujrat
SIALKOT
Ramgarh
R. JHELUM
R. CHENAB

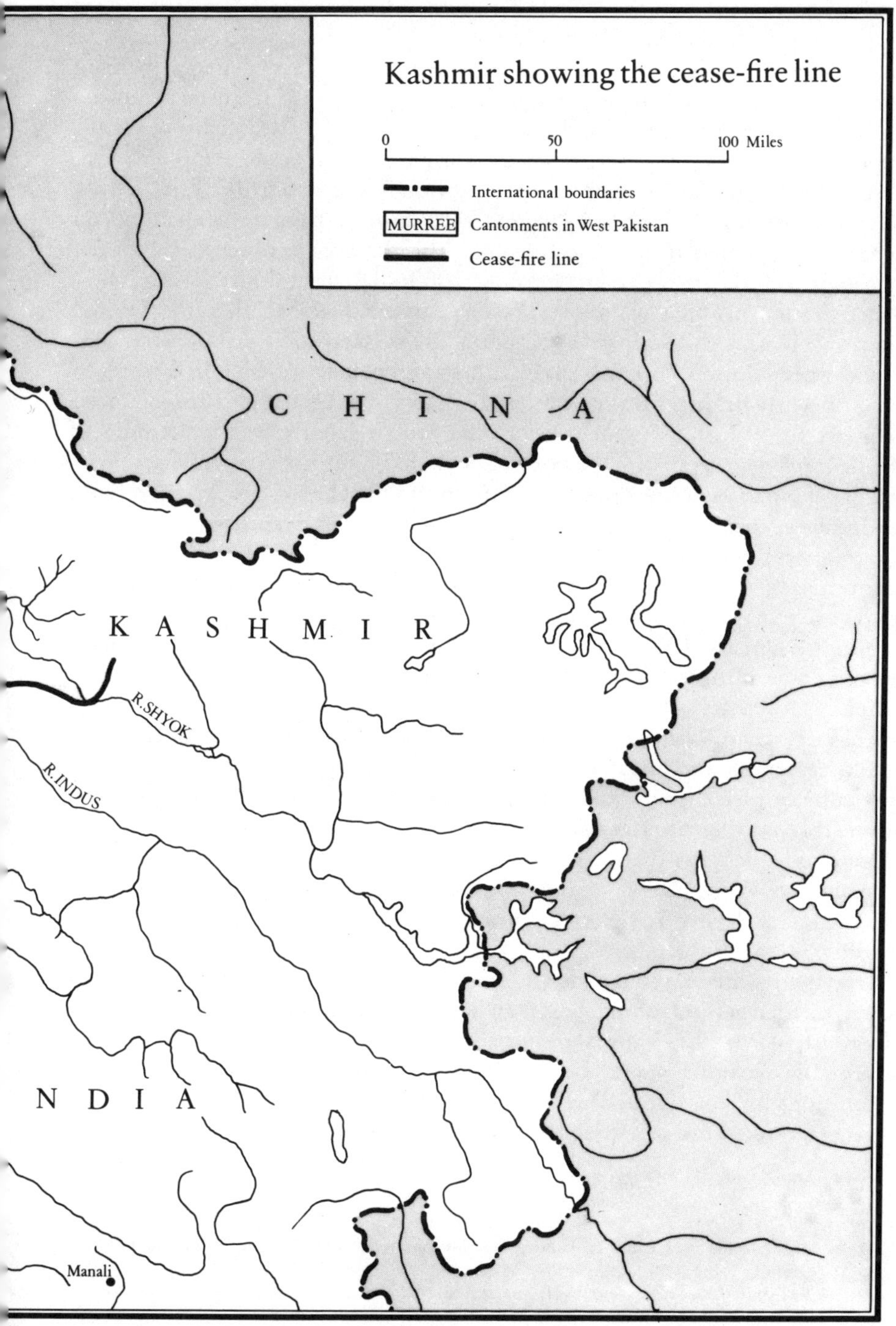
Kashmir showing the cease-fire line
0
50
100 Miles
International boundaries
MURREE
Cantonments in West Pakistan
Cease-fire line
C H I N A
K A S H M I R
R. SHYOK
R. INDUS
N D I A
Manali

and, as Menon warned the Prime Minister,[49] this was not a case India could hope to win. The dislike of Nehru and of his policies among British politicians was widespread; and even leading members of the Labour Party, barring Aneurin Bevan, were highly critical. The attendance at the official reception in London on Republic Day was significantly thin. 'It seems obvious', reported Vijayalakshmi,[50] 'that we are being punished for our stand on Suez.' Even the Eisenhower Government, despite all the goodwill promoted by Nehru's visit in December 1956 and the claim to have an open mind on Kashmir, appeared to be more influenced by the need for bases than by the substance of the issue or the prospect of India's friendship. Contrary to Eisenhower's implicit assurance, Dulles informed Nehru that the United States would have to support a plebiscite unless India and Pakistan agreed on some other solution.[51] Although Nehru was prepared for the United States to line up with Britain on this matter, he had not expected such pronounced support for Pakistan, while Krishna Menon declared that the attitude of Dulles 'makes me sick. He could at least have the courtesy to have kept quiet.'[52] Nor was public opinion in Britain and the United States sympathetic to India on this matter. So the most that India could expect in the Security Council was that the matter would be talked out. But Menon's dramatic performance in New York secured for him for the first time considerable popularity in India.

On 24 January 1957, two days before the new Constitution of Kashmir would come into effect, the Security Council passed a resolution which was intended as a rebuff to India. It reiterated the commitment to hold a plebiscite, asserted that no decision of the Constituent Assembly of Kashmir could determine the future of the state and, rejecting India's stand, spoke of the subject as a dispute and not a question. The Soviet Union abstained, ostensibly on the ground that, after the decisions taken by the Kashmir Assembly, there was no issue to discuss. Krishna Menon accepted this explanation;[53] but the Soviet attitude was doubtless intended also to convey displeasure at Nehru's policy regarding Hungary.[54] 'We get the worst of both worlds.'[55]

Having pointedly rebuked India, the Security Council continued to discuss what further action should be taken in the matter. Menon, with Nehru's approval, let it be known informally that the only operative proposal acceptable to India would be an invitation to both parties to honour all resolutions of the United Nations and seek peaceful ways of resolving difficulties in accordance with the Charter. Nehru was prepared to go a little

49 Telegrams to Nehru, 13 and 23 January 1957.

50 Telegram to Nehru from London, 28 January 1957.

51 23 January 1957.

52 Nehru's telegram to Menon, 24 January, and Menon's telegram to Nehru, 23 January 1957.

53 Telegram to Nehru, 26 January 1957.

54 See S. Gopal, *Jawaharlal Nehru*, Vol. 2 (London, 1979), p. 299.

55 Nehru to S. W. R. D. Bandaranaike, 21 January 1957.

Herblock's cartoon in the *Washington Post*, 29 January 1957

"How True"

further, if necessary, and agree to the Secretary-General being asked to deal with the matter in all its aspects with a view to arriving at a peaceful settlement. In theory a plebiscite could not be ruled out, but in practice it was unthinkable as it would lead to very grave consequences.[56] Krishna Menon, however, was unwilling to bring the Secretary-General into the picture. The British Government, claiming to seek a solution acceptable to both India and Pakistan, requested Nehru to make some gesture, after the general elections in India, which would help to allay Pakistan's sense of frustration; in the meantime, Britain would work for a 'holding' resolution which would keep Pakistan happy.[57] Nehru regarded this as a position slanted against India.

> From your message it appears that you consider that India is in the wrong and Pakistan was the aggrieved party and that therefore India must make some kind of a gesture to put itself right. I confess that I am wholly unable to understand this argument which completely ignores the facts of the case. Pakistan has undoubtedly been the aggressor and we have been the aggrieved party. Because of our desire to have peaceful settlements and friendly relations with Pakistan, we have made every effort not to lay too much stress on Pakistan's wrong-doing. That is now

[56] Nehru's telegram to Krishna Menon, 3 February, and telegram reporting conversation with Malcolm MacDonald, British High Commissioner, 4 February 1957.

[57] H. Macmillan's message to Nehru, transmitted on 8 February 1957.

> brought up against us . . . No government in India can possibly think of giving up what it considers right from every point of view, both legal and practical, and continue to exist.

Nehru even hinted, in conclusion, that Britain's seemingly unfriendly attitude might have repercussions on India's continuance in the Commonwealth.[58] But, to enable the issue to be removed at least temporarily from the supercharged political atmosphere, he was prepared to agree to a reference to the Hague Court of the legal issue of accession.[59]

Macmillan denied that Britain was forcing the pace or giving encouragement to Pakistan;[60] but, despite this personal assurance, in New York the British and American delegations informed India of their intent to sponsor a resolution requesting the President of the Security Council to examine quickly any proposals which would contribute to demilitarization or help towards a settlement, bearing in mind previous resolutions, the statements of the two parties and Pakistan's proposal for a United Nations force.[61] This, far from being a 'holding' resolution, virtually ignored India's standpoint on Kashmir and her determination, reiterated recently by the Prime Minister,[62] not to permit foreign troops on her soil. The failure to take the offensive at the Security Council, as suggested earlier by Menon and Nehru, had enabled Britain and the United States to try to push India into a corner on the Kashmir issue. Home informed the Indian Government that, if they disliked the draft resolution, there was little Britain could do to help; Pakistan would accept nothing less and, if the resolution were vetoed in the Security Council, would take the matter to the General Assembly.[63] But, faced with India's strong objections and knowing that the Soviet Union would no longer abstain but would permit passage of the resolution only if it were toned down, Britain withdrew the clauses regarding demilitarization and a United Nations force and suggested only that the President of the Security Council be asked to examine all proposals likely to contribute towards the settlement of the dispute, having regard to previous resolutions.

So, with the passage of such a resolution, for the time being the battle was suspended. Indeed, as the smoke cleared, the debates in the Security Council and the resolution adopted seemed to have been more important in darkening India's relations with the United States and Britain rather than those with Pakistan. Nehru gave voice to the general dislike of the Security Council resolution, describing it as 'perilously like collective aggression or collective approval of aggression';[64] and he charged the Western Powers with seeking

[58] Nehru to Macmillan, 8 February 1957.

[59] Nehru's telegram to Krishna Menon, 9 February 1957.

[60] To Nehru, 8 February 1957.

[61] Note given by British delegation to Krishna Menon and reported by him in his telegram to Nehru, 11 February 1957.

[62] Nehru's speech at Delhi, 3 February, *The Hindu*, 4 February 1957.

[63] Vijayalakshmi's telegram to Nehru, 13 February 1957.

[64] Interview to the Press Trust of India, 21 February, *The Hindu*, 22 February 1957.

deliberately to create trouble for India and humiliate her. 'I am not going to sell India's honour and freedom under any pressure from even the mightiest power on earth.'[65] Even more than at the time of Suez, there was a fairly general feeling in India that the Commonwealth connection was hardly worthwhile and, had Nehru weakened on this issue, there would have been a loud outcry all over the country to put an end to it. But Nehru had no intention of encouraging the criticism of the Commonwealth association, if only because such matters should not be dealt with in a huff;[66] and he informed Parliament that, with so many disruptive tendencies in the world, he was reluctant to break a relationship which did not impede India's independence.[67] But he added, on the lines of his message to Macmillan in February, that even he had felt for the first time since 1947 that the Commonwealth association might at some time or other require further consideration.[68]

In accordance with the resolution of the Security Council, its President, Gunnar Jarring of Sweden, visited Karachi and Delhi in the spring. He could have had little hope of securing major concessions from India, for Nehru, in the days before Jarring's arrival, had made clear that he could see no flaw in the strength and validity of India's case. Accession to India and aggression by Pakistan were to him the essential facts and he could find no international commitment made by India which she had violated or not fulfilled. Indeed, he saw the Kashmir issue as a basic conflict between the modern age and medievalism, progress and reaction, the welfare of the local inhabitants and their suppression.[69] Despite these declarations of firmness, Jarring asked Nehru to give some assurance, presumably of a plebiscite, which would enable Pakistan to implement the earlier resolutions of the Security Council by withdrawing from the territory she had occupied in Kashmir. Otherwise no progress seemed possible to him, for Pakistan would not withdraw on her own and Nehru had explicitly committed India not to use force to recover the occupied territory. Nehru's response was that he had not ruled out a plebiscite under any circumstances; but he could make no proposals unless the question of Pakistani aggression were first settled.[70] Jarring then went on to Karachi and, finding that the Pakistani Government insisted that they had implemented that part of the resolution of the Security Council of 1948 relating to a cease-fire, came back to Delhi with the suggestion that this point at least might be referred to international arbitration. Nehru did not object to this on its merits but feared that any such reference might divert attention from the major issues of accession and invasion.[71] There was also the wider danger that

[65] Speech at Kanpur, 4 March, *National Herald*, 5 March 1957.

[66] To Vijayalakshmi, 9 March 1957.

[67] 20 March 1957. Rajya Sabha Debates, Vol. 16, pp. 231–45.

[68] Speech in Lok Sabha, 25 March 1957. Debates, Vol. 1, Part II, pp. 651–71.

[69] Speeches in Rajya Sabha, 20 March. Debates, Vol. 16, pp. 231–45. And in Lok Sabha, 21 March 1957. Debates, Vol. 1, Part II, pp. 226–46.

[70] Nehru's note on discussions with G. Jarring, 27 March 1957.

[71] Nehru's note on discussions with Jarring, 6 April 1957.

acceptance of arbitration on even a minor aspect of the problem might open the door to referring the whole question to arbitration and converting aggression itself into a matter of contention. No country, as he later said,[72] accepts arbitration about its own territory. So it looked as if the whole matter would have to be referred back to the Security Council.

The report of Jarring was, from India's viewpoint, realistic in that, though he suggested arbitration on a specific issue, he did not recommend a plebiscite irrespective of other developments and in fact recognized that a plebiscite might cause grave problems. But few outside India seemed able or willing to grasp India's main point that, whatever might be her own rights and wrongs in Kashmir, Pakistan had no rights.

Meantime, the Ministers of Pakistan, Suhrawardy and Noon, spoke continuously of war and asserted publicly that their country had joined SEATO and the Baghdad Pact only to secure arms for use against India; and such arms continued to pour into Pakistan from the United States under a programme of military assistance which had been greatly expanded in return for a base for U-2 planes.[73] Although the United States Government had promised to let India know the type and quantity of such military assistance, the information was never precise. But it was known that the mechanized wing of the Pakistan army had now been equipped with tanks of the latest model and was in many ways much bigger and stronger than the Indian armoured divisions. Even greater was the disparity in strength between the two air forces, for Pakistan had secured in large numbers the latest type of fighter-bomber aircraft.[74] These developments obliged India to divert money from her development programmes and, while making no effort to compete with the aid being given to Pakistan by the United States, to purchase where she could sufficient equipment to save herself from being wholly at the mercy of any Pakistani military adventure. The United States was officially informed of these efforts and of what they might mean to India's relations with that country.[75] However, the Government did not intend to buy arms or military equipment from the Soviet Union, because of both the possible repercussions on India's relations with other countries and her basic policies, and the fear that the United States might use this to justify an unlimited supply of arms to Pakistan. So, if any offer came from the Soviet Government, it was decided to be non-committal without giving the appearance of cold-shouldering them. But the Soviet authorities were shrewd enough not to invite a rebuff. Khrushchev told an Indian military delegation that he understood India's delicate position in international affairs and had no wish to embarrass her Government. The initiative would always have to come from them. When

72 Press conference at Oslo, 22 June, *The Hindu*, 24 June 1957.

73 M. S. Venkatramani, *The American Role in Pakistan* (Delhi, 1982), p. 336.

74 Nehru to G. D. Birla and to Lord Mountbatten, 2 April 1957.

75 Nehru's note to Foreign Secretary authorizing communication to United States Ambassador, 4 April 1957.

they suggested training for some Indian officers in the Soviet Union, he and Marshal Zhukov promptly agreed.[76]

The matter of Kashmir came up again at the Commonwealth Prime Ministers' Conference in the summer of 1957. Suhrawardy indulged in bitter attacks on India on every possible occasion, making clear that Kashmir was a symptom more than a cause of Pakistan's ill-will towards India. Nehru himself was somewhat isolated at the conference, for Bandaranaike did not attend, Diefenbaker, though friendly, was relatively a stranger who could not automatically inherit the warm relations between Nehru and St Laurent, Nkrumah had no experience of these meetings, and Macmillan and Menzies could not wholly shake off the memories of Suez. So Nehru's vigorous pleading for a friendly attitude to China secured little response; and, even on India's need for large financial credits, expressions of sympathy were not transformed into specific commitments. It, therefore, seemed probable that on Kashmir too India would find little support. But Suhrawardy over-played his hand and the conference showed almost no interest. Macmillan, when he met the two Prime Ministers separately, was still keenly aware of the reactions in India to the earlier British attitude at the United Nations and contented himself with urging that some step forward should be taken on the question of the distribution of the Indus canal waters, the Kashmir issue itself being put in cold storage.[77]

Nehru did not conceal that he was still sore about the attitude of the Western Powers at the Security Council earlier in the year. He told Parliament that in his long experience he had seldom come across anything so astounding as their persistence in ignoring obvious facts.[78] Now, in addition to the earlier aggression, Pakistan was promoting acts of sabotage in Kashmir. Macmillan suggested that, instead of stressing aggression, attention might be given to implementing the two parts of the 1948 resolution.[79] Nehru replied that India was always ready to consider any suggestion for a constructive approach consistent with her own stability and integrity.[80] Despite this assurance, the British Government, realizing that Nehru was still sensitive on this subject, promised that, when the question came up again at the United Nations, they would not take the initiative.[81] Nehru, at this time on a visit to Japan, reiterated his opposition to any despatch of foreign troops to Kashmir, which was Indian territory; and he thought it monstrous that some powers should be adopting 'double standards' on Kashmir'.[82] But Menon passed on reports that

[76] Nehru's telegram to K. P. S. Menon, 24 July, and K. P. S. Menon's telegrams to Secretary-General, 25 July 1957.

[77] Nehru to Krishna Menon, 5 July 1957.

[78] 9 September 1957. Rajya Sabha Debates, Vol. 18, pp. 4,192–207.

[79] To Nehru, 15 September 1957.

[80] Nehru to Macmillan, 18 September 1957.

[81] Commonwealth Secretary's telegram to Menon, reporting talk with British High Commissioner, 6 October 1957.

[82] Press conference at Tokyo, 7 October, *The Hindu*, 8 October 1957.

the British delegation was active in mustering support against India.[83] Particularly unfriendly was the statement that the questions of accession and aggression had never been pronounced upon and therefore could be set aside. The draft resolution introduced by Britain and the United States, though watered down to avoid the Soviet veto, was, even as finally passed, unacceptable to India because of the suggestion that negotiations be resumed with Graham in continuance of the discussions of 1953. But, after an official protest from the State Department, Nehru rebuked Krishna Menon for attributing motives to Britain and the United States and asked him to make shorter speeches. A brief, dignified statement rejecting the proposal to continue talks with Graham on demilitarization would be enough.[84] Though he did not say so, he obviously agreed with Radhakrishnan: 'I am very sorry for Krishna Menon. He is a sick man and we should not impose a heavy strain on him. It hurts him and it hurts us.'[85]

Indeed, at least as far as the United States was concerned, Nehru did not lose his perspective and, by the end of the year, informed an American audience that the basic approach of the two countries, in spite often of hard criticism on both sides, was a friendly and appreciative one with a desire for improvement.[86] In fact, banking on his good relations with the Governments of both the United States and the Soviet Union, Nehru publicly appealed to them to suspend all nuclear explosions and tests and to turn to the ways of peaceful co-existence and to negotiations on the problems which divided them.[87] The Soviet Government were willing to cease nuclear testing if the Western Powers also agreed to do so; but Eisenhower was prepared for this only if the production of nuclear weapons was also prohibited.[88]

[83] Telegram to Nehru, 11 October 1957.

[84] Nehru's telegrams to Menon, 19 and 20 November 1957.

[85] To Nehru, 22 November 1957.

[86] Address to the U.S. technical cooperation mission, 20 November, *National Herald*, 21 November 1957.

[87] 28 November, *National Herald*, 29 November 1957.

[88] Bulganin to Nehru, 11 December, and Eisenhower to Nehru, 15 December 1957.

3

Kerala 1957–1959

When considering the setbacks to the Congress in the elections of 1957, Nehru was concerned more by the wave of emotion which had swept the electorate in Maharashtra and Gujarat than by the victory in Kerala of the communists, achieved by years of effort in strengthening their organization and building up, in sharp contrast to the local Congress, a reputation for sincerity and integrity. While some of the economic theories of communism were acceptable to Nehru, he did not approve of the methods of the Indian communists, which he regarded as motivated by violence and hatred, disruptive and often anti-national and based on extra-territorial considerations.[1] So the Communist Party appeared to him 'absolutely and completely out of place' in India.[2] In Kerala during the election campaign, he denounced the Indian communists as intellectually bankrupt and having apparently lost the capacity to think. 'The clock of the world has moved on while the clock of communist minds in India stopped long ago.' Their ideas appeared to him bookish, immature and negative, and to bear no relevance to the situation in India, to parliamentary democracy or to peaceful progress. He added that he found it difficult to deal with them because of what seemed to him their utter irresponsibility; they were always on the brink of disturbances and violence and looking abroad for inspiration.[3] But when, after the elections, the Communist Party was in a position to form a Government in the state, he was willing to give it a chance. The communists had contested the elections on a moderate programme, and a Government they formed could hardly be called a 'pure communist' one.[4] They had, for example, faced by the Prime Minister's firm objection to the nationalization of plantations owned by foreigners, retracted their commitment made during the elections.[5] The fact that ultimate authority lay with the central Government was an extra reassurance.

[1] See his letter to Jayaprakash Narayan, 3 April 1957.

[2] Speech at Madras, 31 January, *The Hindu*, 1 February 1957.

[3] Speeches at Ernakulam, 24 February, and Calicut, 25 February 1957, A.I.R. tapes.

[4] Comment to the press, 29 March, *The Hindu*, 30 March 1957.

[5] Nehru's statement, 1 February, and Namboodiripad's reply, 2 March 1957, quoted in G. K. Lieten, 'Progressive State Governments', *Economic and Political Weekly* (Bombay), 6 January 1979, p. 31.

Indeed, Nehru was subconsciously almost proud of the fact that it had been given to India to provide the world with the first instance of a Communist Party attaining power through democratic elections.[6]

The leaders of the Communist Party were keen on forming a ministry in Kerala for, although aware of the limitations of a state Government under the Indian Constitution, they saw office as a step in a war of position. It could be used to strengthen the party and its popularity among the people. When E. M. S. Namboodiripad, a leader respected throughout India for his dedication and intellectual sharpness, was invited to form a ministry, his first public comment was that his policy as Chief Minister would not be to establish a socialist society.[7] The communists in Kerala would only try to implement the promises which the Congress and the central Government had made but which the Congress Governments in the states had failed to carry out. But the first steps taken by the ministry did not suggest a conformist attitude. Death sentences were commuted, an amnesty was granted to all political prisoners, and evictions of tenants were banned. Also, certain declarations were made which did not seem to the central Home Ministry to be in accord with the letter, or at least the spirit, of the Constitution. Pant, the Home Minister, believed that the state Government were manoeuvring for position and would later blame the Government of India for failure to fulfil many of the promises made during the elections.[8]

Clearly Nehru would have to find a way of cooperating with the ministry in Kerala without being pushed by it along lines which seemed undesirable. A crucial role in such an effort would be played by the Governor, in touch with Delhi and representing an all-India viewpoint and yet in a position to advise his Ministers. At this time the post was held by Ramakrishna Rao, a conservative Congressman inclined to take the lead from Pant, who himself had no liking for the communists. So Nehru also had to ensure that his colleagues did not adopt too rigid a posture towards the Kerala Government. Namboodiripad was not slow to discern this difference in approach between Nehru on the one hand and Pant and Rao on the other and, within days of assuming office, took his case to the higher and more sympathetic court of Nehru. Writing, as he said, not so much as Chief Minister to Prime Minister but as a worker in the cause of national advancement to the most outstanding national leader in the country, Namboodiripad acknowledged that the experiment of a communist Government in Kerala could only succeed if he and his colleagues established with the central authorities relations which were not only correct constitutionally but of sincere cooperation. This they would try to do, but it would only be possible if Nehru took a personal interest in the matter, for Pant and Rao had already

[6] See his letter to Vijayalakshmi, 12 March 1957.
[7] Quoted in Lieten, 'Progressive State Governments', p. 31.
[8] Pant's note to the Prime Minister, 8 April 1957.

shown that they were lacking in the broad vision that was required.[9] Nehru replied promptly to this 'well worded' letter,[10] asserting as expected that, while he had no prejudice against the communist Government, he would stand loyally by his colleagues at the centre. They were all interested in cooperating with the Namboodiripad ministry; but the Communist Party had for long been associated with violent methods and had repeatedly declared its intention to break the Constitution. It was, therefore, difficult to be convinced that their promise to respect democracy was an article of faith and not a mere tactical device. It was against this 'background atmosphere' that the release of prisoners convicted for major crimes had to be considered. Apart from the legal and constitutional aspects of this decision, there were also issues of propriety and procedure. The central Government had a right to be consulted because other states were also concerned; and a unilateral decision on this subject implied discourtesy to the President and the Supreme Court. Moreover, how was a political offence to be defined? During the elections, in some states well-known gangsters with no political interests had sought the shelter of political parties.[11]

Yet, Nehru publicly made clear that he was keeping an open mind and, if the communist ministry was genuine about functioning within the terms of the Constitution, did not rule out the possibility of working with it in the pursuit of socialist objectives.[12] On the particular issue of the commutation of death sentences, a compromise was found. Pant, with Nehru's support, agreed to life imprisonment in place of capital punishment in three cases in which earlier the President had rejected mercy petitions; and Namboodiripad on his side promised that these prisoners would not be released before serving their full terms in gaol.[13] Nehru also quickly laid another ghost. Hearing that all decisions in Kerala were being taken not by the ministry but by the Party and that the Party planned to send a senior leader to Moscow for guidance, Nehru had the Soviet Ambassador reminded that there should be no interference in India's internal affairs; and the assurance came from Moscow that the Soviet Government would not encourage any communist leader from India visiting them to discuss Kerala.[14] In Europe that summer, Nehru was able repeatedly to testify that the Namboodiripad ministry was acting with extreme propriety and had abided by its promises to function strictly within the Constitution and to cooperate with the central Government.[15]

However, differences between the central and state Governments soon

[9] E. M. S. Namboodiripad to Nehru, 15 April 1957.

[10] Nehru to Ramakrishna Rao, 19 April 1957.

[11] Nehru to Namboodiripad, 17 April 1957.

[12] Press conference at Colombo, 19 May, *The Hindu*, 20 May 1957.

[13] Pant's note, 1 June, and Nehru's note, 8 June 1957.

[14] B. R. Rao to Nehru, 25 April, Nehru's note to Secretary-General, Ministry of External Affairs, 28 April, and K. P. S. Menon to Secretary-General reporting conversation with Kusnetzov, 5 June 1957.

[15] Press conferences at Helsinki, 19 June, Oslo, 22 June and London, 4 July 1957, *National Herald*, 21 June 1957, *Nehru in Scandinavia* (Information Service of India, Stockholm, 1958), and transcript of press conference at India House, London, respectively.

developed on other issues. The ministry introduced a Bill to regulate private educational institutions in Kerala. Pant warned them that certain clauses might be *ultra vires*, and the Bill as a whole might serve, if passed, to discourage the initiative of non-official agencies.[16] Nehru, on his return from Europe, did not think it advisable to intervene personally; he could hardly embark on a detailed analysis of the Bill on the eve of its enactment, and to deal with only a few points would imply his approval of the rest of the Bill.[17] But, taking advantage of a letter from Namboodiripad supporting Nehru's general attitude on planning and inviting him to Kerala to judge for himself whether criticisms of the state Government were justified, Nehru mentioned his concern at reports of the deterioration in the maintenance of law and order. As for the Education Bill, he had looked through it and found that much of it was good. Some provisions had struck him as unhappy and likely to lead to trouble, but he had not wished to interfere.[18] This was a far friendlier message than Pant's communication.

On their side, the Kerala Government continued, in Nehru's phrase, to put on the most proper and decorous constitutional clothing,[19] and even sent some Ministers to attend a conference convened by the Gandhian leader, Vinoba Bhave, and sign a statement pledging themselves to a 'truthful' and non-violent approach to the solution of the land problem. Within the state, apart from the controversial Education Bill, the communist Government adopted measures which served to strengthen their position but at which few could cavil. The salaries and allowances of subordinate officials were raised and 35 per cent of places in educational institutions and the services were reserved for the backward classes. While helping to maintain law and order to the satisfaction of the planters,[20] the Government intervened in labour disputes on the side of the workers and provided legal aid gratis to the poor. A heavy subsidy was given to the farmers and the rice secured from them was sold by the Government at a fair price. An administrative reforms committee, the first of its kind in any state, was constituted. The lawlessness of which Nehru had earlier complained, and which he still believed to be causing considerable apprehension among many people in Kerala,[21] was perhaps strengthened by communist pressure on the police and the magistracy; and Pant warned Namboodiripad against this.[22] But there was insufficient evidence to justify any general allegation against the ministry. Even the Governor, who resented the growing popularity of the Communist Party, had to admit that there

16 Pant to Namboodiripad, 5 July 1957.

17 Nehru's note, 17 July 1957.

18 Namboodiripad to Nehru, 29 July, and Nehru's reply, 31 July 1957.

19 Press conference at Tokyo, 7 October 1957, *Journal of the Indo-Japanese Association of Japan*, Vol. 6, No. 1.

20 See statement of the President of the United Planters' Association of South India in September, *The Planters Chronicle*, 1 October 1957, quoted in G. K. Lieten, *The First Communist Ministry in Kerala 1957–9*, (Calcutta, 1982), p. 109.

21 Press conference at Delhi, 21 October, *National Herald*, 22 October 1957.

22 Pant to Nehru, 21 November 1957. File 25 (82)/57–P.M.S.

seemed little chance of reversing this trend unless the ministry made a major mistake or lost its slender majority of two through defeats in by-elections.[23]

The Education Bill was passed by the Kerala Assembly on 2 September 1957 and forwarded to the President for his approval. The central Government, on the Attorney-General's advice, sought the advisory opinion of the Supreme Court as to whether the President should withhold his assent and refer the Bill back to the state Government for reconsideration of certain clauses.[24] Meantime the local Congress, which seemed to Nehru to be lacking proper guidance,[25] threatened to launch a mass campaign to encroach on Government land. Namboodiripad appealed to Nehru to countermand any such move, which would compel the local authorities to call on the police to take preventive action, and once more invited Nehru to visit Kerala to form his own judgment.[26] Nehru regretted that he could not go to Kerala for some time but made clear that he disapproved of unlawful actions by the opposition.

> I am clearly of opinion that our political work and agitations should be on a peaceful and decent level, whatever the party concerned might be. Whatever party might misbehave in this matter, I would disapprove of it. Certainly I do not want the Congress Party to do any such thing . . . It seems to me that if any party permits resort to violent methods, this will injure greatly our public life and not serve any good cause.[27]

He also informed the Chief Minister that he had asked Dhebar, the President of the Congress, to restrain his partymen in Kerala and call off demonstrations;[28] and Dhebar added his assurance that the local Congress would function as a responsible and constructive opposition.[29]

Unexpectedly, in view of his general sympathy with left-wing movements, Krishna Menon, after a visit to Cochin, reported that there was a considerable deterioration in the situation in Kerala. Far more sinister trends were developing than might be inferred from the seeming quiet on the surface and he expected conditions to become worse.[30] It is difficult to know what Krishna Menon had in mind; possibly this was part of his bid to consolidate his new-found popularity in the Congress. But clearly his evaluation, rather than the perennial complaints of the local Congress and the Governor's reports, influenced Nehru, and the new year saw the Prime Minister more critical than before of the Namboodiripad Government. He rebuked the Chief Minister for the criticism of the President said to have been voiced by the Kerala Communist Party for his reference of the Education Bill to the Supreme

23 B. R. Rao to the President, 20 September 1957.
24 Minutes of meetings of the Cabinet, 29 October and 13 December 1957.
25 Nehru to Pant, 25 November 1957.
26 Namboodiripad to Nehru, 2 December 1957.
27 Nehru to Namboodiripad, 4 December 1957.
28 Nehru to Namboodiripad, 13 December 1957.
29 Dhebar to Namboodiripad, 11 December 1957.
30 Krishna Menon's note to Prime Minister, 2 January 1958.

Court.[31] He continued to deprecate the recourse to violent methods by the opposition in Kerala, but now suggested that the state of tension and conflict was largely due to the attitude and activities of the Communist Party. It had set a bad example which apparently was being followed by others.[32] He was also once more reiterating his dislike of the communist approach, its promotion of class bitterness and hatred, the rejection of accepted standards of public behaviour and the proneness to seek guidance abroad.[33] It was now his view that the communists in Kerala were adopting the Leninist tactic of pretending to accept 'bourgeois' democracy as a legitimate move in the struggle to establish communist supremacy. 'I don't want communism here.'[34]

Namboodiripad denied that the Communist Party had passed any resolution criticizing the President, but adhered to the view that reference to the Supreme Court was a constitutional procedure without precedent which seemed to have been adopted because it concerned a communist Government. 'I think we have a right to expect from you an approach to such problems which is not strictly a Congressman's approach but an approach which would be non-partisan and national.'[35] Nehru did not react immediately and, on a visit to Kerala, was correct and non-committal. But he expressed his satisfaction at the Communist Party thinking more and more on nationalist lines; and Namboodiripad was appreciative.[36] It was, in a sense, as the chief custodian of public values rather than from any party viewpoint that Nehru chided Namboodiripad for the special grant reported to have been made to schools in a constituency where a by-election was pending and for the collection by the Communist Party over the past year of a sum too large to have been possibly secured by legitimate methods.[37] The reply of the Chief Minister that the Communist Party had adopted no coercive means and had collected little, and far less than the Congress, did not seem to convince him.[38] But both the Prime Minister and the Chief Minister took care not to drift into confrontation. Nehru requested his colleagues in Delhi to consider the various proposals for industrial projects submitted by the Kerala Government on their merits and without any prejudice. Curiously, what gave the planning commission concern was that the state Government appeared to be unduly favouring the private sector. The Birla group was given permission to set up a wood-pulp plant, and plans were drawn up to invite a private company to construct a refinery for the manufacture of lubricating oil, in contravention of

31 Nehru to Namboodiripad, 15 January 1958.

32 To V. R. Krishna Iyer, Law Minister of Kerala, 17 January and 28 February 1958.

33 Address to the annual conference of the personnel of the Technical Cooperation Mission, New Delhi, 20 November, *The Hindu*, 21 November 1957.

34 Interview to *Reynolds News* (London), 2 February 1958.

35 Namboodiripad to Nehru, 21 January 1958.

36 Nehru's speech at Trivandrum, 24 April, *National Herald*, 25 April 1958; Namboodiripad's comments to the press, 30 April, *The Hindu*, 1 May 1958.

37 Nehru to Namboodiripad, 13 May 1958.

38 Namboodiripad to Nehru, 19 May, and Nehru's reply, 21 May 1958.

the industrial policy of the Government of India.[39] There was, in fact, little that was communist in the official activities of the state ministry and even the Communist Party disapproved of some provisions of the agreement with the Birla group.[40] Namboodiripad, writing twelve months after assuming office, regarded as their main achievement not any radical orientation or policy but the evidence which they had provided to non-communists that the Kerala Government was national, democratic and socialist. They were breaking the prejudices which assumed that communism was alien to Indian traditions and values and that a communist Government would endanger religion, mark 'the beginning of the end of the nation' and would not respect the Constitution.[41] In the same vein, the Law Minister of Kerala wrote to the Vice-President a few months later that the authentic voice of India was 'not political but philosophic, and not Marxist but Vedantic'.[42]

Less placatory were the Chief Minister's reported objections to the activities of the opposition parties in Kerala. After a communist victory in the by-election which Namboodiripad claimed to be a fresh mandate from the people, the Chief Minister remarked that if the opposition persisted in its activities, these would divide the people and might lead to civil war as in China and with the Congress meeting the same fate as Chiang Kai-shek. Nehru sought a clarification. Would Namboodiripad ask the communists in other parts of India not to oppose? Would the communists hold on to power in Kerala even if they lost the elections? What was the justification for comparing India with China under Chiang Kai-shek?[43]

To blow up such stray remarks to this level of importance suggested that by now Nehru had given up his earlier sympathetic attitude and neutrality towards the communist effort at parliamentary government and was preparing for a public expression of his disapproval. He even hinted, in interviews to foreign journalists, that he felt that the days of the communist Government were numbered.[44] But Namboodiripad's answer to the reprimand was soft. He told the Prime Minister that his speeches in Kerala, with their emphasis on national unity, had reminded him of Nehru's call in 1936 for a joint front against the British. Now the programme was for national construction on socialist lines, and the Communist Party endorsed this heartily. But the

39 Nehru to A. P. Jain, Food Minister, 27 January, Namboodiripad to Nehru, 24 April, V. T. Krishnamachari, Deputy Chairman, Planning Commission, to Nehru (no date), and Nehru to Namboodiripad, 8 May 1958. Files 17(283)/58–59–P.M.S., 1A, 17(298)/58–P.M.S., 2A and 17(219)/57–61–P.M.S., 19A and 20A.

40 Lieten, *The First Communist Ministry*, p. 60.

41 Article in *New Age*, April 1958, quoted in J. Singh, *Communist Rule in Kerala* (Delhi, 1959), pp. 88–9.

42 V. R. Krishna Iyer to S. Radhakrishnan, 6 September 1958. Radhakrishnan papers.

43 Nehru to Namboodiripad, 15 June 1958.

44 'So far as the near future is concerned, the Communists, in my opinion, will be lucky if they manage to hang on to Kerala, let alone expand their hold anywhere else.' Interview in *Daily Telegraph* (London), 10 May 1958. 'None of us can see very far into the future, but in my opinion the Communists have to have a great deal of luck to be able to stay in power in Kerala much longer.' Nehru to Ralph Oppenheim, reported in *Politiken* (Copenhagen), 16 June 1958.

biggest obstacle to any such joint effort seemed to him to be the attitude of the Congress, which behaved as if it were the nation. This had led him to speak of the dangers of a policy of division which would, unless checked, result in national disruption and even civil war; but he had not compared existing conditions in India with those of China under Chiang Kai-shek. It was for Nehru, as the foremost national leader, to work out, in consultation with other political parties, a code of conduct for ministries and oppositions.[45]

However, Nehru was not to be appeased; and developments in the communist countries had a bearing on his approach to Kerala. He had been worried by the Soviet attitude towards Tito. It suggested a return to ideological rigidity and more of an ecclesiastical than a political approach.[46] Khrushchev had hinted that this was no concern of Nehru: 'We hope that India will permit us to settle ideological disputes in our own way.'[47] But, apart from the merits of the case, Nehru could not fail to take notice of this departure from non-interference in the internal affairs of another country. Then came the execution of Nagy in Hungary. Nehru's reaction was severe.

> I am afraid that it will be very difficult for the Soviet Government to outlive this black mark . . . Many people who believed in the bonafides of the Soviet Union for peace rather doubt them now. Because we restrain ourselves in our utterances, it should not be thought that we do not feel strongly on these subjects. All our moral sense has been deeply shocked.

This execution had almost put an end to the idea of real peace for a generation;[48] and Nehru turned away mentally not only from the Soviet Union, which he held responsible for this cold-blooded act, but generally from Communist Parties, including that of India, which supported the Soviet Government and their policies in Hungary and towards Yugoslavia. The reiteration by the Indian Communist Party at its latest session that it adhered to peaceful methods was washed out for him by its pro-Soviet position in foreign affairs. In fact, he saw in this proclaimed preference for the parliamentary system a dissembling of a basic difference, much worse than the open attitude of communists elsewhere. To send a congratulatory message to the Communist Party of Yugoslavia and then to criticize it on learning of the Soviet attitude was to him clear testimony that the thinking apparatus of the Communist Party of India lay outside the country.[49] So he wrote a long reply to Namboodiripad questioning his conception of unity, suggesting that they were frequently using words in different senses and defending fully the Congress position. He could envisage no joint front with the Communist

[45] Namboodiripad to Nehru, 23 June 1958.
[46] Nehru to Chief Ministers, 18 May 1958.
[47] K. P. S. Menon's telegram to Foreign Secretary, reporting conversation with Khrushchev, 16 May 1958.
[48] To K. P. S. Menon, 28 June 1958.
[49] Speech at the A.I.C.C. 12 May, *The Hindu*, 13 May 1958.

Party, which had its own ideology and policies in domestic and external affairs. Its first loyalty was to the Communist Party of the Soviet Union; its concept of joint fronts was to win state power through democratic processes in order to establish the dictatorship of the proletariat; and it would never renounce the possibility of non-peaceful methods. Policies apart, there was a widespread lack of faith in the bona fides of the Communist Party. Though India had a basic strength, to progress was going to be a hard task because of reactionary forces; and in this context the Communist Party was, despite its assurances, playing a reactionary role. There was also the fear, strengthened by the party's change of position on Yugoslavia, that it would often function at the dictates of an outside authority.[50]

Clearly, the increasing rigidity of Soviet and Chinese policies in the summer of 1958 had not only disappointed Nehru but influenced the rethinking on first principles which he had undertaken during his short holiday in Manali. Civilization appeared to him mentally exhausted and unable to cope with the rapid pace of change in human life. Science was advancing far beyond the comprehension of a very great part of mankind and posing problems which most persons were incapable of understanding, much less of solving. The disciplines of religion and social usage were fading away without giving place to other moral or spiritual disciplines. Rationalism too seemed inadequate, appearing to deal with the surface of things without uncovering the inner core. 'Science itself has arrived at a stage when vast new possibilities and mysteries loom ahead. Matter and energy and spirit seem to overlap.' Communism offered some kind of faith and discipline and succeeded, to an extent, in giving a content to man's life. But ultimately it failed, partly because of its rigidity but even more because it ignored certain essential needs of human nature. The suppression of individual freedom created powerful reactions and the resort to violence encouraged an evil tendency in man. The contempt of communism for the moral and spiritual side of life ignored a basic human element and deprived man's behaviour of standards and values.

In contrast, Gandhi's peaceful and tolerant approach seemed to Nehru more scientific, reasonable and civilized. It was also a more practical approach, for the world had reached a stage when any attempt at a forcible imposition of ideas on a large section of the people was bound ultimately to fail. Suez and Hungary were striking instances of this. In India an appeal to violence was particularly dangerous because of its disruptive character; but basically it was now, throughout the world, not just an ethical doctrine but a practical proposition that wrong means would not lead to right results.

Nehru now believed that democracy and socialism were not ends in themselves but means to achieve the good of the individual. Real social progress would come only when opportunity was given to the individual to

[50] Nehru to Namboodiripad, 30 June, and remarks at press conference at Delhi, 3 July, *National Herald*, 4 July 1958.

develop, provided the individuals did not constitute any particular group but comprised the whole community. So the touchstone of any political or social theory should be how far it enabled the individual to rise above his own self and think in terms of the common good. The law of life should be not competition or acquisitiveness but cooperation, the good of each contributing to the good of all. In such a society the emphasis would be on duties; and rights would follow the performance of duties. 'We have to give a new direction to education and evolve a new type of humanity.'

This line of thought was moving towards metaphysics, which normally Nehru shunned; but now he was attracted to it and willing to search for something basic underlying the physical world. He was drawn to the Vedantic conception that everything, sentient or insentient, had its place in the organic whole and to the belief that a spark of the divine impulse or the energy or life force which pervades the universe might help to get rid of some of the narrowness of race, caste and class and lead to more tolerance and understanding. Planning for socialism was important, for the barrier of poverty had to be broken by the utilization of modern techniques and new sources of power. But India had to evolve her own peaceful approach and seek the objective of individual improvement and the lessening of inequalities without forgetting the ethical and spiritual aspects of life which were the basis of culture and civilization and which gave some meaning to life; 'and perhaps we might also keep in view the old Vedantic ideal of the life force which is the inner base of everything that exists.'[51]

This was a new Nehru, or rather a reversion to the earlier Nehru of the 1920s, the conventional Hindu untouched as yet by rationalist ideas and the unquestioning worshipper of Gandhi, seeing in his master's philosophy and methods an ideology far superior to that of Bolshevism or Fascism. He was now a socialist but was seeking to mix his left-wing ideas with a sophisticated form of religious commitment. He had always favoured the method of non-violence; but, whereas in the 1930s and 1940s it had commended itself to him as the technique most suited to India, he was now persuaded of its intrinsic merit and considered it more important than even the objective. It was a curious amalgam of socialism, science and religion which he was now trying to evolve.

Against this Nehru, Namboodiripad had little chance. The Chief Minister sought to argue that the basic loyalty of the Communist Party was to the Indian working class. It followed a nationalist approach, believed in different ways to socialism and, while regarding the Soviet Union as a guiding star, would not slavishly copy what had happened in that country. As for conditions in Kerala he reported, not by way of complaint but 'just out of desperation', that the local Congress was by no means adopting a peaceful approach as elaborated by Nehru.[52] But Nehru had, in a sense, ceased to listen and now

[51] Note, 13 July 1958, printed as 'The Basic Approach', *A.I.C.C. Economic Review*, 15 August 1958.
[52] Namboodiripad to Nehru, 22 July 1958.

served what was virtually a charge-sheet on Namboodiripad. On the basis of complaints from a large number of persons and organizations in the state and reports of murders committed by communists, he believed that a very undesirable situation, full of violence, had developed; and the state Government appeared to be making matters worse by extending preferential treatment to communists. Many of them serving prison sentences had been released and cases against others had been withdrawn. A magistrate who had refused to oblige the Government by dropping a case against a communist had soon after had his powers curtailed; and some police officers were said to have been suspended because they had incurred the dislike of communists. 'Political parties sometimes come into conflict but the situation that has arisen in Kerala is something much deeper than that. It may be that the opposition parties have to shoulder part of the blame, but the ultimate responsibility must necessarily be that of the Government.'[53]

Nehru's main grievance against the Kerala Government was that they had created an atmosphere in which those critical of the Communist Party had little sense of security, and many had the feeling that the Government did not treat all parties and groups impartially. Although the local Congress was not wholly blameless and its incessant agitation and wild talk did not fit in with general Congress policy, the communists seemed to him to be deliberately encouraging violence in thought, word and action. But Nehru's democratic instincts had not been wholly submerged by his new antipathy to communist ethics and practices, nor did he forget his obligations as Prime Minister to a Government formed legitimately in one of the states by another party. So, though he minced no words in his private correspondence with Namboodiripad, he publicly refused to criticize and rejected the idea of intervention by the central Government.[54] It was, indeed, on Nehru's general sense of fair play and reluctance to reach conclusions without understanding all aspects of a problem that Namboodiripad cleverly played, by seeking his personal attention to a basic re-examination of the approaches of the Congress and the communists to each other.[55]

This situation, however, did not endure. In August, for the first time Nehru spoke publicly in terms critical of the Kerala Government, and declared that he had not been convinced by their answers to the charges.[56] He disliked the spiral of violent demonstrations leading to police firings and, though of the general view that the police should not carry firearms, sympathized with their predicament when surrounded by angry mobs. But he blamed the state Government for terrorizing people, a development which had nothing to do with communism and, though unclear as to what his Government should do, was clear that the situation could not be ignored. He

[53] Nehru to Namboodiripad, 29 July 1958.
[54] Press conference at Calcutta, 27 July, *The Hindu*, 28 July 1958.
[55] Namboodiripad to Nehru, 4 August 1958.
[56] Press conference at Delhi, 7 August, *The Hindu*, 12 August 1958.

was thinking vaguely of a thorough investigation or some other impartial and constitutional action.[57] The Chief Minister and the central committee of the Communist Party protested against Kerala being singled out for such an inquiry,[58] and Namboodiripad met the Prime Minister to state the case of the Kerala Government. It was also announced that the police had been instructed to ignore pressures from local communist leaders. The party militia too became more subdued; and there is no strong evidence that the communists brought about a breakdown of law and order.[59] But Nehru saw no reason to alter his thinking. A report by Krishna Menon on a visit to Kerala, which the state Government denounced as a 'conducted tour',[60] confirmed Nehru's attitude. Subsequent developments and information also lent support to his view that a considerable section of the people in Kerala had a feeling of 'political insecurity', in the sense that some political parties were being harassed and others protected.[61] The statement by the Communist Party that it had collected about forty lakhs of rupees in the state since it had come to power strengthened his belief that the Government was showing special favours to the Party.[62] So specific charges against the ministry in Kerala and his general distrust of communist attitudes fed on each other.

> What has distressed me for many years is a certain approach of the communist party which seems to me to have little to do with normal standards of behaviour. The ardent communist works for a cause, which is good. But, like the Jesuit of old, he thinks that every standard or value can be sacrificed for the good of the cause. I think this is a very harmful approach. Also, unfortunately, there is an association of violence, both in words and action. The result is a lack of faith even in assurances. When standards and values go, what remains?[63]

The consequence of this growing dislike of communist activities and approaches was a steady weakening of the reluctance to interfere, in an arbitrary manner, in Kerala. Nehru was justified in claiming that the Government of India had tried their best to deal with the Kerala ministry just as they had dealt with the Congress Governments in all the other states and that he personally had been 'bending over backwards' to maintain an impartial attitude.[64] But he was clearly finding it difficult to sustain this posture and to refrain from interfering in the state. The fact that the police had to open fire on

[57] Address to the Congress Parliamentary Party, 10 August 1958. Tape 36/C Part I.

[58] Namboodiripad's comments and resolution of the central committee of the Communist Party of India, 12 August, *The Hindu*, 13 August 1958.

[59] T. J. Nossiter, *Communism in Kerala* (Delhi, 1982), pp. 145, 158.

[60] V. R. Krishna Iyer to Prime Minister, 1 September 1958, and Menon's note in reply, File 25(82)/58–P.M.S., Vol. 2.

[61] Press conference at Delhi, 7 September 1958. File 43(73)/56–58–P.M.S., No. 10A.

[62] Nehru to H. C. Heda, 3 September, and to V. R. Krishna Iyer, 5 September 1958.

[63] To V. R. Krishna Iyer, 16 October 1958.

[64] 27 November 1958. Lok Sabha Debates, Second Series, Vol. XXII, pp. 1,707–12.

1 With U Nu, the Panchen Lama and the Dalai Lama, Delhi, 26 November 1956

2 With the Eisenhowers at the White House, 16 December 1956

3 With Zhou Enlai, Delhi, 1 January 1957

three occasions in the plantations on agitating labourers whose sympathies were with the communists sugested that the Government, while not influenced solely by party considerations, was losing control of the situation. So Nehru asked the Home Minister to secure more information from the local authorities and to consider ordering the army to move in.[65] Utilizing a representation made by the British High Commission on behalf of some British planters, Pant offered central assistance to the local Government in restoring law and order, and added that the situation would not have deteriorated if the Kerala Government had referred the demands of the labourers in the plantations to adjudication instead of justifying the strikes. Namboodiripad, not surprisingly, rejected the offer of central intervention, claimed that the situation was under control and suggested that Pant advise the planters to negotiate a settlement.[66] The Governor reported that the state administration was trying to assist the communist trade union organization to improve its position as against that of the unions supported by the Congress and was censuring the police officers who had attempted to control violence in these labour disputes. But Pant did not think the time had yet come for central intervention against the Namboodiripad Government.[67]

Nehru, therefore, held his hand. It was probably the communist Government in Kerala which he had in mind when he spoke of democracy as something deeper than voting, elections or a political form of government. 'In the ultimate analysis, it is a manner of thinking, a manner of action, a manner of behaviour to your neighbour and to your adversary and opponent.'[68] Yet, to avoid any feeling of discrimination against the Kerala Government or grievance that they were being unfairly denied help, he ordered that the matter of assistance for the Panniar hydro-electric project be looked into immediately.[69] Thereafter problems elsewhere, particularly events in Tibet, pushed Kerala to the back of his mind; and it was only in May 1959 that a letter from Namboodiripad again drew his attention to the state. Although the provision in the Education Act that teachers in all colleges should be chosen from panels drawn up by the public services commission had secured the support of all parties in the assembly, the managements of private institutions continued their agitation. The Chief Minister saw no scope for compromise and expressed his determination to deal firmly with such opposition, but sought an interview with the Prime Minister,[70] presumably as part of his effort to secure a peaceful solution.

Nehru had, even before the receipt of Namboodiripad's letter, denied the existence of a joint front of the opposition parties in Kerala and played down

[65] Nehru to Pant, 21 October 1958.

[66] Pant's telegram to Namboodiripad, 22 October, and the latter's reply, 23 October 1958.

[67] Pant to Nehru, 22 November 1958.

[68] Speech at the symposium on the prospects of democracy in Asian countries, Delhi, 12 December, *The Hindu*, 13 December 1958.

[69] Nehru to Hafiz Ibrahim, Minister for Irrigation and Power, 2 February 1959.

[70] Namboodiripad to Nehru, 14 May 1959.

the participation of the local Congress as being no more than the peaceful protests of certain individuals.[71] Nevertheless the Congress Party in the state intensified its participation in the agitation on the ground that the central authority of the party had not instructed them not to have any connection with the movement.[72] So the Congress was speaking with three voices: the members in Kerala active in violent agitation, the central leadership permitting such activity without approving it, and Nehru disapproving of it but taking no action to curb it. Not surprisingly the agitation accelerated and, when Nehru travelled south to Ootacamund in the first week of June, he grasped that the possibility of violent conflict was growing, with political rivalries drawing strength from religious, communal and caste feelings. It was, in fact, a Minister of the Kerala Government who informed him that the opposition was collecting 'Nehru crowds' – that is, crowds of the vast size which normally only collected to see and hear the Prime Minister.[73] Nehru, therefore, appealed to both sides, to the state Government to consider why this deep and widespread distrust of its bona fides had arisen, and to the opposition to renounce its methods. The Government should treat its opponents with consideration and even seek a measure of cooperation while the opposition, particularly the Congress, should function within the limits of democratic conventions. Certainly the Government of India would not support sectarian demands or the use of violence.[74]

As was to be expected, the statement satisfied no one. The Communist Party, hard-pressed in a state with a voluble democratic tradition and a powerful and hostile Church, criticized Nehru for not condemning the activities of the Congress in Kerala in a more downright manner;[75] and Congressmen, though smarting under his rebukes, were yet encouraged by his acknowledgment of a mass upsurge and made no effort to mend their ways. A further note of what could well have developed into personal embarrassment was introduced by the fact that Nehru's daughter, Indira Gandhi, had now become the President of the national Congress organization. For the first ten years of Nehru's Prime Ministership, Mrs Gandhi had stayed aloof from politics and served mainly as his hostess; but in 1956 and 1957 she had worked intensively in the election campaign. Her father thought she had become busier even than he and was rather overdoing it, but this was perhaps good for her in a psychological sense. She travelled round the country, and it seemed to Nehru, who saw very little of her for weeks at a time, that she had helped the Congress in the elections more than almost anyone else.[76] Her special interest

71 Press conference at Delhi, 14 May, *National Herald*, 15 May 1959.

72 R. Sankar, President Kerala pradesh Congress committee at Delhi, 23 May 1959. Quoted in H. Austin, *Anatomy of the Kerala Coup* (Delhi, 1959), p. 37.

73 Nehru's speech in the Lok Sabha, 19 August 1959. Debates, Second Series, Vol. XXXIII, pp. 3,137–65.

74 Statement to the press, 6 June, *The Hindu*, 7 June 1959.

75 Statement of Ajoy Ghosh, General Secretary of the C.P.I., 8 June, *The Hindu*, 9 June 1959.

76 Nehru to Dorothy Norman, 8 October 1956, and to Vijayalakshmi, 6 February, and to U Nu, 20 March 1957.

was the Allahabad constituency, which she organized 'like a general preparing for battle', and where she shook up, in particular, the women, especially Muslim women. 'Hardly eating and often carrying on with a handful of peanuts and a banana, she has been constantly on the move, returning at midnight, flushed, slightly gaunt but full of spirit and with flashing eyes.'[77] She was then, after the elections, nominated to the working committee of the Congress and, two years later, in January 1959, elected its President. Nehru had studiously refrained from influencing these decisions,[78] but obviously his daughter's role as leader of the party agitating for a change of Government was not a negligible element in the Kerala crisis. Many years later, the leader of the local Congress testified to Nehru's great reluctance to dismiss the communist Government, and believed that but for Mrs Gandhi's influence they would not have been able to convert the central Government to their way of thinking.[79] Namboodiripad also has attributed to her considerable responsibility for the agitation.[80] Mrs Gandhi herself has denied that her role was as decisive as has been sometimes suggested.[81]

For the time being, Nehru continued in public his political tight-rope walking. He talked of the growing feeling of unfair dealing that had developed in Kerala and emphasized that the true test of tolerance was to put up with what one disliked. These remarks were obviously made in criticism of the state Government. He also continued to be ambivalent about the activities of the local Congress and suggested that if some Congressmen were participants in the agitation, they were functioning more as Catholics than as partymen. To offset this quibbling and in fairness to himself and to his principles, he added that 'so far as I am concerned, I do not propose, intend, look forward to or expect governments to fall down except through normal democratic processes.'[82] In private he was even less hesitant. He warned the leader of the caste organization as well as the Governor that the state Government had the right to suppress the agitation and the central Government would, if necessary, come to their assistance.[83] He also advised the local Congress not to associate itself with the activities of the opposition. This would mean the abandonment of the party's principles as well as of democratic practices and would cause adverse reactions in both Kerala and elsewhere in India. To talk of pushing out the elected Government was to encourage civil conflict and to challenge the Constitution; and the Government of India, responsible in the final analysis for law and order, would have to suppress such direct action.[84]

77 Nehru to Vijayalakshmi from Allahabad, 12 March 1957.
78 Nehru to J. C. Moitra, 20 January 1959.
79 R. Sankar's testimony, 28 October 1970. Oral History Project, N.M.M.L.
80 E. M. S. Namboodiripad, *Conflicts and Crisis* (Bombay, 1974), p. 58.
81 *Ma Verité* (Paris, 1980), p. 124.
82 Statements at press conference at Delhi, 10 June, *National Herald*, 11 June 1959.
83 To M. Padmanabhan, President of the Nair Service Society and to B. R. Rao, 15 June 1959.
84 To R. Sankar, 15 June 1959.

Namboodiripad, still hopeful that he could avoid calling in the army, retained his faith in Nehru's democratic instincts and invited Nehru to visit Kerala. Though the Prime Minister had been positive and helpful in refusing to countenance any movement with a communal or caste complexion and in insisting that disputes should be settled peacefully, his reference to a popular upsurge had overrated, according to Namboodiripad, what was in essence an agitation of Nairs and Catholics.[85] The Prime Minister arrived in Trivandrum on 22 June. Namboodiripad wished him to make clear that the Government of India made no distinction between direct action against the state ministry in Kerala or elsewhere, while on their part the communist Government would do their best to resolve differences by discussions with the opposition.[86] But, after three days of long talks with the Governor and the Ministers and meetings with representatives of every shade of opinion, the impression grew upon Nehru that the situation was much worse than he had expected. The atmosphere was near hysteria with 'thick walls of group hatred' and little room for any effort at compromise. The tension was such as he had not seen anywhere before and for which even the reports he had received had not prepared him.[87] It was, as he described it later, like a merciless contest between two hostile countries, with almost everyone taking sides.[88] The sense of personal security was also rapidly declining, and many private citizens roamed the streets with knives. Nehru told the Congress and other opposition parties that, while they had a right to agitate, they should maintain norms of public behaviour and not encourage violent or vulgar activity. He also publicly expressed his disapproval of picketing, especially by children.[89] However, realizing that the immediate and total withdrawal of picketing might not be feasible, Nehru suggested that picketing of schools and buses be given up and that in front of public offices it be gradually replaced by other forms of peaceful agitation. On his return from Kerala, the Congress Parliamentary Board, at Nehru's initiative, permitted token picketing;[90] but it was expected that this too would be gradually withdrawn.

Of the Ministers, Nehru inquired 'by what alchemy' they had succeeded in making themselves so unpopular and creating so strong and widespread an opposition, in which even those normally not concerned with politics were now so active. A concentrated and accumulating fear of insecurity, of injustice, of not being treated fairly under the law had grown and covered practically every section of the population except those directly or indirectly associated with the Government and the Communist Party. His own explanation of this 'astonishing failure' was that the Namboodiripad ministry, in power with the support of only 35 per cent of the electorate, was guided too

85 Letter to Nehru, 13 June, and statement at press conference, 13 June, *The Hindu*, 14 June 1959.
86 Namboodiripad's note to Prime Minister, 22 June 1959. File 7(192)/59–P.M.S., Vol. 3.
87 Press conference at Delhi, 7 July 1959. File 43(73)/59–P.M.S., 9A.
88 Address to Congress Parliamentary Party, 2 August 1959. Tape M–44/C(ii), N.M.M.L.
89 Statement at Trivandrum, 25 June, *The Hindu*, 26 June 1959.
90 Statement of the Congress Parliamentary Board, 29 June 1959.

much by Party directives and external factors and tended to assume a posture of confrontation with non-communist elements. Rather than developing a 'progressive reasonableness', the Communist Party, when in power, got into bad odour with the people by ignoring them.[91] On the Education Act, for example, Nehru believed that the ministry should have been more accommodating on specific clauses and thereby avoided antagonizing the Catholic Church. He did not give sufficient weight to the element of wilful obstruction in the opposition which had been nurtured by the fact that the central and state Governments belonged to different parties.

The immediate concern, however, was to lower the tension. Nehru advised the ministry to discuss the controversial clauses of the Education Act with its critics. Namboodiripad was willing, but the Catholic bishops and the leaders of the Nair Service Society who, more than the Congress, were concerned with this matter, were not. The leader of the caste organization, Mannath Padmanabhan, had, as Nehru observed later,[92] not much political understanding and was behaving at this time 'most peculiarly as some kind of an incarnation of the deity'. The Prime Minister also proposed an independent judicial inquiry into the recent police firings. To this too the Chief Minister agreed, but obviously this was only a palliative. Nehru's main suggestion was that the Chief Minister should call for fresh elections. This would not only test the claim of the opposition, which to Nehru seemed credible, that the Government had lost much of its popular support; it would also, by providing for three or four months of campaigning, lead to disengagement in Kerala. Elections would not solve the problem but they would at least provide a new opportunity to disentangle the problem. But, while some members of the Communist Party saw the advantage of elections held while they were in office, the proposal was not acceptable to the leadership as a whole.[93] So, on Nehru's return to Delhi, the Congress in Kerala was secretly advised to demand elections rather than the dismissal of the ministry; the Namboodiripad Government were unlikely either to agree to this or to resign, and the Congress should then present a petition to the President asking for an inquiry into the charges against the Government.[94]

Nehru was now convinced that elections formed the only way of dealing with the situation; but he was still reluctant to intervene and preferred to watch developments, leaving the initiative with the Kerala Government. He also made clear his approval of the general principles of the agrarian legislation recently enacted in the state and refused to insist on the Education Act as a whole being held in abeyance. But he suggested to Namboodiripad that he make a further concession to the opposition and discuss every aspect of the

[91] Nehru in the Rajya Sabha, 25 August 1959. Debates, Vol. XXVI, pp. 1,759–62.

[92] Nehru to M. K. Vellodi, 6 October 1959.

[93] See K. Damodaran, 'Memoirs of an Indian Communist', reprinted in K. N. Panikkar (ed.), *Prospects of Left Unity* (Delhi, 1979), p. 127.

[94] Congress Central Parliamentary Board's confidential instructions to Kerala pradesh Congress committee, 26 June 1959.

Education Act and not only the disputed sections, with perhaps a reference to the Prime Minister for a solution if no agreement could be reached.[95] But the opposition was still not prepared to discuss the Act. Nehru regretted this, but concluded that the Act and other specific matters of controversy had been pushed into the background by the basic conflict.[96] There was, in short, no common ground between the Government and the other parties in Kerala; and it was the breakdown in political relations rather than the legal and constitutional aspects of the question which was to Nehru most worrying. The mutual consideration essential for the proper functioning of democracy had vanished. It was this which Nehru sought to impress on Namboodiripad when he invited him to Mashobra for private talks. The agitation could be suppressed, but this would be no solution. The Chief Minister seemed to agree. He had no remedy of his own to offer and, though opposed to elections under compulsion, promised to reconsider it.[97] In fact, he personally was willing to hold them.[98]

However, confident, as a result of his talks with the Prime Minister, that there was no possibility of the central Government's intervention in Kerala,[99] Namboodiripad, after consulting the National Council of the Communist Party, reported to Nehru that forcing mid-term elections in the one state administered by a party other than the Congress would smack of discrimination and strengthen the feeling that this would become the regular practice whenever any party opposed to the Congress formed the Government. It was also thought that the failure to carry out the instructions on picketing given by Nehru and the Parliamentary Board suggested that other sections of the leadership of the Congress were encouraging the agitation.[100] Meantime, whatever the inspiration, the agitation was mounting and each day, alongside intense police control, about five thousand persons were arrested, including a large number of women. Nehru assured Namboodiripad that any help he might seek from the central Government would be forthcoming, arranged for flag marches by the troops and ordered the naval garrison to take over the protection of petrol depots and other vital areas.[101] Namboodiripad's complaint that, though Nehru had given the state ministry whatever assistance had been sought at the governmental level, his 'moral authority' had been denied to them,[102] was also not justified. For Nehru once again, when the leader of the Nair caste organization met him, denounced in the severest terms picketing, direct action and propaganda to stir up hatred and

95 Statement to press at Delhi, 26 June, *The Hindu*, 27 June 1959; to Namboodiripad 30 June, and to Chief Ministers and to R. Sankar, 2 July 1959.

96 Nehru to Chief Ministers, 2 July 1959.

97 Nehru's note on conversations with Namboodiripad, 11 July 1959.

98 Private information.

99 Namboodiripad's remarks to the press at Delhi, 12 July, *The Hindu*, 13 July 1959.

100 17 July 1959.

101 Nehru to Namboodiripad, 26 July 1959.

102 Namboodiripad to Nehru, 29 July 1959. File 7(192)/59–P.M.S., Vol. 3.

violence, and urged the opposition to agree to discussions with the Government.[103] Further, on hearing that the Kerala Congress was calling on landholders not to cultivate as a form of protest, he asked Mrs Gandhi, as President of the organization, to issue clear directives against any such action.[104]

However, just as Nehru hoped that decisions would be taken in Trivandrum, the state Government had no wish to incur the odium of seeking military assistance and preferred the initiative to come from Delhi. What they desired was moral pressure from Nehru and the national leaders of the Congress on the local opposition parties to call off the agitation. Nehru contended that it was beyond his capacity to stop a movement which had developed such intensity. This was for him to underrate his own authority; certainly he made no effort to terminate the agitation and sought only to keep it in non-violent and constitutional channels. He was undoubtedly inhibited by his loyalty to the Congress and his antipathy to the methods and political outlook of the Communist Party. In this unprecedented situation of a local Government with a different political complexion from that at the centre, it was not easy to maintain logically impeccable postures. Nehru argued that had there been a similar crisis in a state governed by the Congress he would have acted much sooner. But it was also true that if the local Congress had agitated against a Congress Government, it would have been sternly and promptly ordered to desist. The Congress in Kerala was defiant and fiercely combative because it was confident of the sympathy, if not of the Prime Minister, of most of the other leaders in Delhi.

Towards the end of July, Ajoy Ghosh, the general secretary of the Communist Party, and A. K. Gopalan, one of its leading members who came from Kerala, discussed the situation with Nehru. They asked him what the central Government intended to do and were told that no decision had as yet been taken. They requested him to use his influence to cancel the mammoth demonstration being organized to take place on 9 August, if not to call off the agitation altogether. Nehru said he was unable to do this. In that case, replied Ghosh and Gopalan, 'the sooner you act the better'. It would have suited the Congress to allow the agitation to continue, for it increased the unpopularity of the Communist Party and demonstrated the helplessness of the state Government. But giving greater consideration to public security, on 30 July the Government of India, acting on the Governor's formal recommendation and recognizing that every political party and communal and caste group desired central intervention, dismissed the Namboodiripad ministry and took over the administration. 'We have been', Nehru told Namboodiripad,[105] 'most reluctant to have any kind of Central intervention, but we have felt that it is no longer possible to allow matters to deteriorate, leading to continuing

103 Nehru to B. R. Rao, reporting his conversation with M. Padmanabhan, 21 July 1959.

104 Note to Congress President, 21 July, and letter to R. Sankar, 22 July 1959.

105 30 July 1959.

conflicts and human suffering. We have felt that, even from the point of view of your government, it is better for Central intervention to take place now.' Ghosh and Gopalan, meeting Nehru again soon after the dismissal, virtually admitted that central intervention had become essential.[106]

However, Nehru did not conceal his unhappiness at a decision which he claimed had been 'hurled upon us by circumstances'. He argued that, confronted with a situation where they had to take action, the central Government had acted within the provisions of the Constitution to create another democratic situation and enable the democratic solution of elections.[107] But it was, as Nehru himself recognized,[108] a bad precedent which went against the democratic conventions which he, more than anyone else, was trying to establish in India. Even Rao, the Governor, whose sympathies lay with the opposition, recognized that it had never reconciled itself to the verdict of the elections.[109] Particularly after the Communist Party won a by-election in 1958, the local Congress leaders seem to have concluded that their only recourse was to secure the ousting of the ministry. Whatever the sins of the communist Government, the methods adopted by the opposition were not such as commended themselves to Nehru. Men and groups representing communal and reactionary elements had resorted to violent agitation and succeeded in involving the Congress. Speeches had also been made, hinting at a crusade against communism and international communism; these seemed to Nehru highly objectionable for they might well, if carried through, have put an end to India's non-alignment.[110] So, somewhat casuistically, Nehru informed Rao that the central Government had taken over the administration not because of agitation but because a certain situation had arisen; logically, therefore, there should be no large-scale release of prisoners but gradual releases of those who had served a large part of their term or paid part of their fine. The Agrarian Relations and Education Acts should also not be revised immediately.[111]

There is much to be said in justification of Nehru's policy towards the communist Government in Kerala. There were no models for him to follow in dealing with a ministry formed in one of the states by the Communist Party after winning a majority in the elections. He did not seek to deny them the prize and ensured that the central Government was scrupulously correct in considering their requests for assistance or support in economic and financial matters. When the agitation developed, he was confronted with a problem which was not only unprecedented but which accentuated the illogicality of the situation. His own party was gradually drawn in and ignored his pleas for moderation. He believed that agitation was a part of politics but was unable

[106] Nehru to B. R. Rao, 1 August 1959.
[107] Press conference at Delhi, 7 August, *National Herald*, 8 August 1959.
[108] Nehru to B. R. Rao, 30 July 1959.
[109] B. R. Rao to Nehru, 31 July 1959.
[110] Nehru to B. R. Rao, 30 July 1959.
[111] Nehru to Rao, 1 August, and telegram, 3 August 1959.

or, as it seemed to many, unwilling, to insist that such agitation be limited to moderate and constitutional activity. His obligations as Prime Minister and his inclinations as party leader came into conflict, and it became increasingly difficult to reconcile the two. Nor did the Communist Party make it easy for him. As Nehru saw it, the party had been given a chance in Kerala and had failed in that chance, for its members could not adapt themselves to the Indian context or fit easily into a democratic structure.[112] Their ways of governance were abrasive, they declined the responsibility of subduing the agitation and they urged the Prime Minister to avoid, in his turn, the decision of maintaining law and order by using his authority in his own party for their benefit and insisting that the agitation be terminated. In fact, Nehru in his private correspondence was stern in his reprimands to his partymen. But for once they were in a position to act against his wishes for they knew that they had the support of Nehru's colleagues both in the Government and in the party. So finally Nehru was driven into a decision, by the communists who passed on the initiative to him so that they could appear as victims and by the Congress who looked for undeserved and undemocratic advantages from a contrived crisis. Nehru knew that dismissal of the state Government could not be justified on principle and that he was being deliberately pushed into it. If he had acted earlier the situation might have been contained; but his strict adherence to a correct attitude of non-intervention led by the summer of 1959 to conditions in Kerala from which he could no longer stand aloof. Even then, if the Namboodiripad ministry had accepted his advice and ordered elections under their own auspices, the situation might have been retrieved. But there was no reason why the Communist Party should help him out of a quandary created by the Congress Party. So Nehru, acting as Prime Minister with ultimate responsibility, took what seemed to him an inescapable step. It could be faulted in theory and could be interpreted as inspired by narrow party advantage; but it appeared to him to be required in the public interest. He finally arrived at a decision which he knew to be wrong for what he believed were the right reasons.

The dismissal of the communist ministry in Kerala seemed to be justified by the results of the elections which followed, for the Congress won a comfortable majority. But it tarnished Nehru's reputation for ethical behaviour in politics and, from a long-term view, weakened his position. For his chief strength, both before and after independence, had been the influence he commanded in left-wing and radical circles and generally among thinking people who often had little interest in immediate political problems – an influence which enabled Nehru to force the Congress machine to move along paths of which it did not approve. Even when, in the early years of free India, the Communist Party had been severely critical of him and hostile to his Government, Nehru had retaliated sharply but had not allowed his measures against communist resistance to be swamped in general opposition to com-

112 25 August 1959. Rajya Sabha Debates, Vol. XXVI, pp. 1,759–62.

munist ideology and objectives. Thereafter the Communist Party had returned to the track of general cooperation with Nehru. But now, in the summer of 1959, Nehru allowed himself to be driven into action alien to his outlook and contrary to his general style of political functioning. This made it much more difficult for him, in the penultimate stage of his career, to achieve the goals of his economic and social policies.

4

Tibet, China and Pakistan 1957–1959

ONE

Towards the end of 1957, Nehru's role in foreign affairs seemed to enjoy the rare distinction of being of advantage to his own country as well as to the world. The denunciation of the *Daily Express* that he had 'started in sin and he has gone on in wickedness'[1] was an isolated view. *The Economist* believed that India was unrivalled in 'articulate detachment' and in possessing a 'genuine bird's eye-view';[2] and left-wing opinion was rapturous. 'Today on this centenary India stands in the forefront of the leading world powers honoured by all and exercising a powerful influence on the side of peace and national freedom and for the ending of colonialism, colour bar and cold war.'[3] Sharing this opinion, Mountbatten stated many years later that, if Nehru had died in 1958, history would have remembered him as the greatest statesman of the twentieth century.[4] Mountbatten saw that year as marking both the peak and the commencement of a downhill trend because it was from then that India's relations with China, already uneasy, began rapidly to deteriorate.

The influence which he commanded Nehru sought to utilize to give an impetus to the process of disarmament. There was little hope of progress at the United Nations on the topics of nuclear testing and the manufacture of nuclear weapons. The Disarmament Commission had broken up and there was no machinery for resuming discussions. Krishna Menon believed that it was not the United States but France and Britain which were opposed to talks.[5] So disarmament took precedence even over Kashmir in Nehru's talks with Macmillan at Delhi in January 1958. Messages were received from Bulganin urging a conference at high level on disarmament and Nehru favoured the immediate initiation of informal discussions which could lead to

[1] 15 August 1957.

[2] 16 August 1957.

[3] R. Palme Dutt, 'India's First Decade', *Daily Worker*, 15 August 1957. Palme Dutt presumably had in mind the centenary of the revolt of 1857.

[4] Interview with the author, 28 May 1970.

[5] Cabinet minutes, 20 December 1957.

a meeting of Foreign Ministers or Heads of Government. The very fact of such discussions would help to relax tension. It was in the same hope that he welcomed the proposals being mooted in various official and non-official quarters for some form of disengagement in Europe. But Macmillan was unwilling to consider any reply to Bulganin's suggestions which might not be approved by the United States; and Eisenhower, while not rejecting the proposal for a conference on disarmament, attached such conditions as to make it most unlikely.

Though disappointed by this negative attitude, Nehru did not allow it to push him into taking up Tito's idea of a joint statement by India, Sweden and Yugoslavia calling for a conference on disarmament.[6] He also turned down the suggestion of Zhou Enlai that he declare in favour of the conversion of Asia into a 'nuclear free' zone, for he thought it would be improper to do so without consulting such countries as Japan and Indonesia. It might also, by narrowing the problem, come in the way of an international conference at the highest level.[7] He preferred to continue his private and informal efforts to draw the United States and the Soviet Union closer towards negotiations on this question rather than appear to exercise public pressure.

A hopeful sign was the Soviet announcement in March, suspending nuclear tests and expressing willingness to consider control and supervision. A vital and psychological moment in the world's history seemed to Nehru to have arrived and he appealed to Eisenhower for the wise handling which could well make a great difference.[8] The American response was not as dramatic as Nehru would have liked; but their proposal that fissionable materials should only be produced for peaceful purposes was a step forward and Nehru believed that there was a good chance of a high-level conference in 1958. Khrushchev agreed to Eisenhower's proposal for a meeting of experts to work out means of ascertaining violations of any agreement to terminate nuclear tests; and, when the Soviet Government suggested that India should participate, Nehru expressed willingness to do so if it could be of help.[9]

The hopes being thus gradually built up received a setback with the sudden eruption of a fresh crisis in West Asia. A civil war had been raging for some time in Lebanon with the attendant danger of foreign intervention. Nehru thought the danger of such intervention had lessened with the visit of Hammarskjöld to the area and the efforts of the observer group of the United Nations;[10] but the crisis widened with the overthrow of the monarchy in Iraq. The United States promptly landed marines in Lebanon; and Britain despatched troops to Jordan. Nehru did not conceal from these two countries his disapproval of such armed intervention. To think in terms of communism and

[6] Nehru's reply to Tito, 26 January 1958.

[7] Telegram from Indian Embassy in Beijing, 1 February, and reply of Ministry of External Affairs drafted by Nehru, 5 February 1958.

[8] Nehru to Eisenhower, 2 May 1958.

[9] Press conference at Delhi, 4 June, *National Herald*, 5 June 1958.

[10] Press conference at Delhi, 3 July, *National Herald*, 4 July 1958.

anti-communism and ignore the feelings of the peoples of these countries was wholly to misread the situation.[11] But the immediate issue was the imminence of war and, with the world possibly taking 'a leap to suicide',[12] disarmament was becoming a dream with no reality. To make it easier for the United States and Britain to withdraw their troops, Nehru refrained from public condemnation but urged them privately to do so and allow the United Nations to deal with the situation. He did not favour a United Nations police force and thought a strengthening of the observer group would suffice. As the Western Powers thought this inadequate, Nehru felt it necessary to warn them that the slightest move towards intervention in Iraq would lead to India's recognition of the new regime.[13] At the same time he agreed to Khrushchev's suggestion of an immediate meeting of the Heads of Government of the United States, the Soviet Union, Britain, France and India, along with the Secretary-General of the United Nations.[14] The inclusion of India – and the significant exclusion of China – indicate Nehru's personal standing at this time as well as the cordiality of Indo-Soviet relations and mark a public disclosure of the rift between the Soviet Union and China. Significant too was the pointed silence, in Eisenhower's reply to Khrushchev, on the invitation to India. The reaction of the Western countries generally to such a small, high-level, meeting was not favourable and the issue was referred to the General Assembly.

A reduction of tension having been achieved at the United Nations, the United States and Britain announced that, after a while, they would suspend nuclear tests for a year. As the proviso was thought to imply immediate testing, the Soviet Government revoked their own suspension. At a conference convened to consider the matter, the Soviet delegation wished the issue of nuclear tests to be taken up on its own, whereas the United States contended that it could not be isolated from the general problem of disarmament. Eisenhower and Hammarskjöld sought Nehru's mediation as and when he thought proper. Particularly as Khrushchev had rejected inspection of Soviet sites by the Western Powers but was willing to accept inspection by India, the United States urged Nehru to intervene. 'I still hold', wrote Paul Hoffman, who represented the United States in the negotiations on disarmament, 'to the belief that the great address on the controlled limitation of armaments is yet to be made, and that you are the man to make it.'[15] But Nehru saw no role for himself in this matter, as neither side appeared really serious about stopping nuclear tests. 'If the cold war leads to an atomic or other war, there is no help for it.'[16] Then Eisenhower himself appealed to Nehru.

[11] Nehru's note to Foreign Secretary, 16 July, report of conversation with British High Commissioner, 17 July, letters to H. Macmillan and J. Diefenbaker, 17 July, and letter to Eisenhower, 18 July 1958.

[12] Nehru to B. C. Roy, 18 July 1958.

[13] Nehru's telegram to Vijayalakshmi, High Commissioner in London, 18 July 1958, and Foreign Secretary's telegram to Indian mission at United Nations, 20 July 1958.

[14] Khrushchev to Nehru, 19 July, and Nehru's reply, 20 July, *The Hindu*, 21 July 1958.

[15] To Nehru, 12 November 1958.

[16] Nehru to Krishna Menon, 26 November 1958.

> Universally you are recognized as one of the most powerful influences for peace and conciliation in the world. I believe that because you are a world leader for peace in your individual capacity, as well as a representative of the largest of the neutral nations, your influence is particularly valuable in stemming the global drift toward cynicism, mutual suspicion, materialistic opportunism and, finally, disaster.[17]

Yet Nehru was not to be tempted. While promising to take advantage of any opportunity when he could be of some service, he was hesitant to intervene unless convinced that such action would be helpful.[18] He also turned down Rajagopalachari's suggestion that he make a public appeal to the Governments concerned.[19] But he did, in response to a request from a Moscow journal for a New Year message, plead for disarmament by progressive stages, with the ending of nuclear tests as the first step. This could be linked with such measures of control as might be considered necessary and with some forms of disarmament.[20]

TWO

Nehru's disinclination to push himself forward in the negotiations on disarmament, even while he recognized their crucial importance, was based on a healthy sense of realism, a preoccupation with domestic problems of planning and development and an involvement with India's own concerns in matters of foreign policy. Relations with China were moving gradually nearer to the foreground of the picture. It has been suggested that, sometime between June and November 1957, China's domestic and external policies underwent a radical transformation and, with the United States developing an increasingly aggressive posture towards her, China's cautious, consolidating approach was giving way to a forward surge.[21] If so, it was not reflected immediately in the attitude to India. In January 1958, Zhou, forwarding the Dalai Lama's invitation to Nehru to visit Tibet, added that the Chinese Government would welcome the visit and he himself would accompany Nehru.[22] The Prime Minister was willing to go, and suggested the first fortnight of September.[23] Nehru also, as part of an effort to maintain relations with China on a correct level, sought to curb the political activities of the

[17] Eisenhower to Nehru, 27 November 1958.

[18] Nehru to Eisenhower, 3 December 1958.

[19] Nehru to Rajagopalachari, 4 December 1958.

[20] Answers to *Sovietskaja Roosiya*, 10 December 1958.

[21] D. Zagoria, *The Sino-Soviet Conflict 1956–1961* (Princeton, 1962), p. 66; M. B. Yahuda, *China's Role in World Affairs* (London, 1978), pp. 65–7.

[22] Telegram of R. K. Nehru, Indian Ambassador in China, to Prime Minister, 13 January 1958.

[23] Prime Minister's telegram to R. K. Nehru, 21 January, and Foreign Secretary's telegram to Embassy in Beijing, 11 February 1958.

Tibetan refugees in India. It was folly to think of defeating China by armed force and India could certainly provide no arms for this purpose. Change had become imperative in Tibet and, if the Tibetans themselves did not promote such change, it would come from outside. They should not challenge Chinese sovereignty but keep united and seek full autonomy.[24]

However, these indications from both sides of a desire for better understanding proved deceptive. In February, the Prime Minister suggested that a patrol might be sent in the spring to ascertain details of the road constructed across the Indian territory of Aksai Chin by China.

> I do not think it is desirable to have air reconnaissance. In fact, I do not see what good this can do us. Even a land reconnaissance will not perhaps be very helpful . . . I do not see how we can possibly protest about the alignment of the road without being much more sure than we are. What we might perhaps do is that in some communication with the Chinese government in regard to the points in dispute which have to be decided we should mention the Aksai Chin area. It is suggested that our maps should be sent to the Chinese. Certainly they can be sent through our embassy. But I think it would be better to do this rather informally.[25]

A similar, informal protest was decided upon when it was known that the Chinese Embassy in London was distributing maps with boundary alignments different from those on Indian maps.[26]

Yet, in contrast to Nehru's determination to react in a low key to Chinese acts of unfriendliness, to say the least, the Chinese did not appear to be in a mood to devote any attention to India. Nothing more was heard of the projected visit to Tibet. Unqualified support was given to the Soviet Union in its reversal of the trend of three years and denunciation of Yugoslavia's ideological nonconformity; and Nehru saw in this a breach by China of one of the five principles providing for non-interference in another country's internal affairs. The Soviet Union could argue that its interest in Yugoslav communism had a long history; but there was no ground for China's condemnation in violent language of developments in that country. If she could do that in Yugoslavia, there was no reason why she would not do so, if the occasion arose, in India; and her stiff attitude on the border indicated that such an occasion might not be far off. 'All this signifies that we have to be particularly careful in the future in what we say and do in regard to China especially.'[27]

However, although China stood by the Soviet Union on the Yugoslav question, the rift between China and the Soviet Union was widening. In March 1958 Mao was speaking in favour of Khrushchev; but in the same year,

24 Nehru's note to Foreign Secretary, reporting conversation with the Prime Minister of Tibet, 13 January 1958.

25 Nehru's note to Foreign Secretary, 4 February 1958.

26 Nehru's note to Foreign Secretary, 8 April 1958.

27 Nehru's note to Foreign Secretary, 15 June 1958.

as Mao said much later, China decided to give priority to self-reliance.[28] Nor could the Chinese have failed to notice that, to settle the crisis in West Asia, Khrushchev had suggested a five-power meeting, including India but omitting China. For her part, China too seems to have embarked on independent foreign and strategic policies.[29] According to a Soviet diplomat who defected to the West in 1959, a 'gentleman's agreement' between the Soviet Union and China, whereby South-East Asia would be in China's sphere of influence while India and areas west of India would be parts of the Soviet sphere, was ended in 1958 by Chinese 'intervention' in India.[30] As Sino-Soviet relations cooled, Nehru, more far-sighted in this matter than most of his colleagues and advisers, did what he could, without compromise of principle, to strengthen India's relations with the Soviet Union. Overruling the Finance Minister, Morarji Desai, who had taken over from Krishnamachari, the senior officials of the Ministries of External Affairs, Finance and Commerce and the Governor of the Reserve Bank of India, he approved acceptance of the Soviet proposals that India would export as much as she imported from the Soviet Union after setting off Soviet expenses in India and that both accounts would be maintained in rupees, involving a loss by India of foreign exchange. For he saw that there were larger issues involved than petty trade and fear of the rupee account being used for Soviet propaganda in India.[31] The decision of the previous year not to secure arms from the Soviet Union had also to be reconsidered, for Nehru was no longer keen on purchase of arms and equipment from the United States because of their insistence that India should not sell these arms to others. The condition was in substance unobjectionable, for India had no intention of resale and had, in fact, accepted such a condition in 1951; but now the very fact of conditions seemed to Nehru irksome.[32]

The sustained cordiality between India and the Soviet Union was paralleled by the increasing rift between India and China. In public Nehru did not disclose his awareness of the strain in Sino-Soviet relations and spoke of them in the same breath. He asserted that India would resist any attack from Russia or China, but added that he did not think that either Russia or China wished to attack India and, even if such aggression were intended, it would be very difficult for before that happened a world war would ensue.[33] But he could not shut his eyes to the growing unfriendliness of China. Pressed to fix a date for Nehru's visit to Tibet, the Chinese Government replied that he should postpone it.[34] A general deterioration of relations had clearly set in. In July

[28] Mao's speeches of 22 March 1958 and 30 January 1962, S. Schram (ed.), *Mao Tse-Tung Unrehearsed* (Penguin edn, 1974), pp. 114 and 178 respectively.

[29] Yahuda, *China's Role in World Affairs*, pp. 106–7.

[30] A. Kaznacheev, cited in R. H. Donaldson, *Soviet Policy towards India: Ideology and Strategy* (Harvard, 1974), p. 152.

[31] Nehru's note, 6 November 1958.

[32] Nehru's note to Foreign Secretary, 10 December 1958.

[33] Speech at Delhi, 31 July, *The Hindu*, 2 August 1958.

[34] Foreign Secretary's telegram to Indian Embassy, 11 July, and note of Chinese Government, 15 July 1958.

Chinese troops occupied Khurnak fort in Ladakh and *China Pictorial* once more published a small-scale map showing a large part of north-eastern India, some areas in Uttar Pradesh and considerable portions of eastern Ladakh within the 'approximate borders of China'. Apart from registering an official protest, Nehru repeated in Parliament that the boundary was a firm one requiring no more than a few minor adjustments. 'So far as the broad boundary, the international frontier between India and the Chinese state including the Tibetan region is concerned, it is not a matter of dispute so far as we are concerned. It is a fixed thing. There is nothing to talk about.'[35] On China's side, Nehru's support of their claim to the offshore islands, Quemoy and Matsu, appeared to be tempered by his desire that the matter be settled peacefully and by his obvious disapproval of their regular bombardment of the islands. Zhou spoke to the Indian Ambassador of the imminence of war; he had in 1950 given Panikkar advance information of major hostilities and he was doing so again.[36] But Nehru did not react with the same degree of involvement as he had shown in the Korean crisis, and a month later the Ambassador was informed that the Chinese had never intended to occupy the offshore islands as the American presence on them was useful for applying pressure. The problem of Taiwan and the islands was a long-term one and the Chinese were prepared to wait.[37] But the whole episode did not draw India and China closer.

There was Chinese concern, too, at the activities of Tibetan émigrés on the Indian side of the border. A formal Chinese protest led to an assurance that the Government of India would not tolerate such activities, and the Bengal Government were directed to take necessary action.[38] But this did not seem to satisfy the Chinese, and they watched sullenly as Nehru, denied an invitation to Tibet, proceeded to Bhutan after just touching their territory at Yatung. Even this brief glimpse gave Nehru the impression that Tibet was occupied territory whose people lived in fear of their masters and where the Khampas were in revolt.[39]

The visit to Bhutan itself was personally adventurous and politically fruitful. Trekking for five days on foot or on a pony along rough bridle-paths, crossing passes at a height of about fourteen to fifteen thousand feet and spending the nights, for the first time in his life, in a sleeping-bag, Nehru felt carefree, with the worries of his office dropping away at least temporarily.

> Somehow, the Himalayas give one a sense not only of peace but of permanence, and of something above and away from the follies of human

[35] 4 September 1958, Lok Sabha Debates, Second Series, Vol. XIX, pp. 4,629–32.

[36] G. Parthasarathi's telegram to Foreign Secretary after meeting with Zhou Enlai, 21 September 1958.

[37] G. Parthasarathi's telegram to Foreign Secretary after conversation with Chen Yi, Foreign Minister, 24 October 1958.

[38] Foreign Secretary to Chief Secretary, Bengal, 3 August, and Nehru to B. C. Roy, Chief Minister, 4 August 1958.

[39] Nehru's telegram to Krishna Menon, 5 October 1958.

beings. No doubt this is a false impression because nuclear warfare and radiation will not spare the Himalayas. In Hindu mythology, the gods had their abodes in these mountains; they chose well. But the old gods fade away and new gods of a fiercer kind take their place. Even so the peace of the Buddha still prevails here and if we can have some inner peace within ourselves, perhaps we might even be able to face the threat of the bomb which has been described to be brighter than a thousand suns.[40]

Descending into Paro, the capital of Bhutan, situated in a valley at 7,500 feet, Nehru drew the Maharaja's attention to the revival of Chinese expansionism under cover of communism. India could not have refused to recognize Chinese authority in Tibet, but she had urged the recognition of local autonomy. Now it was clear that the Tibetans were unhappy at the changes being wrought by the Chinese; yet violent rebellions would lead them nowhere. To seek help from abroad was a policy doomed to failure and India could not encourage anti-Chinese activities in her territory. As for Bhutan, while India would protect her internal independence, she could not be independent in the international sense of the word. From both the political and economic viewpoints, Bhutan would have to choose between India and China. Indeed, she had made the choice long ago and the world should know that any incursion into Bhutan from Tibet was an incursion into India and would involve a conflict with India. If this fact were well known, no incursion need be expected. This was not a matter of likes and dislikes but of the current position in the world and the possibility of a major conflict. The Maharaja and his Prime Minister expressed their full agreement with this analysis, and Nehru thought it important that his visit be followed up by the improvement of road communications between India and Bhutan. But it was not solely the official attitude in Bhutan which pleased Nehru and gave him confidence in the future. 'Above all, it is the people's affection here that has touched me.'[41] This, more than the beauty of the scene and the welcome of the authorities, led him to write on his departure that 'now Bhutan has become a living part of my mind and heart'.[42]

Such tightening of India's ties with Bhutan, of which the Chinese must have been aware, could have given them no satisfaction; and even the decision of the Government of India to prevent armed Khampas from crossing the border and, in the case of those who managed to cross over, to disarm them and to send them back to Tibet, did not help to stem the steady decline in relations. There were reports of strengthening of Chinese armed personnel in Hoti, in contravention of the understanding between the two Governments, and of Chinese infiltration across other parts of the frontier. Nehru asked the

[40] First draft of the Foreword to *A Bunch of Old Letters*, written at Gangtok, Sikkim, 16 September 1958.
[41] Nehru's notes on his visit to Bhutan, 26 September 1958.
[42] To the Maharaja of Bhutan, 27 September 1958.

Foreign Secretary to take up these matters informally with the Chinese Ambassador and to point out that India, regarding the boundary as broadly beyond dispute, was anxious to settle minor differences once and for all, so that friendly relations would not suffer because of petty incidents. The discussions on Hoti could be raised to a higher level. The Ambassador's attention could also be drawn to the continued publication by the Chinese Government of maps showing portions of Indian territory within China.[43]

'The general Chinese attitude to us', Nehru wrote to Krishna Menon,[44] 'in many small matters has not been at all friendly or even sometimes courteous. I realise that this is probably due to the petty officers, but there can be little doubt that the new turn in internal policy in China has had some effect on their external contacts.' The Government of India protested to China, on the basis of a report of a reconnaissance party, about the construction of a road across the northern part of Aksai Chin and the arrest of some members of an Indian patrol. The Chinese rejected the protest but pushed back across the border the Indians whom they had taken prisoner after detaining them for nearly a month.[45] Moreover, to make clear that to the Chinese Government it was now a wider issue than specific disputes and old maps, in their written answer to the Indian protest about the map in *China Pictorial*, in addition to the old plea about routine repetition of Kuomintang maps, they stated that they had not as yet undertaken a survey of their boundary nor consulted with the countries concerned and they would not make changes on their own.[46] In other words, they virtually repudiated, for the first time, the traditional alignment shown on Indian maps and implied that the boundary was an open issue which should be the subject of discussions. So Nehru decided to write directly to Zhou, expressing his surprise at the Chinese attitude, which was contrary to what he had been since 1949 led to believe, and asserting what he had repeatedly declared in Parliament. 'There can be no question of these large parts of India (shown as Chinese territory on Chinese maps) being anything but India and there is no dispute about them. I do not know what kind of surveys can affect these well-known and fixed boundaries.'[47]

THREE

In 1958, however, Nehru was still more preoccupied with Kashmir and Pakistan than with China. Few occurrences in India in the past few years had distressed him more than the continued detention of Sheikh Abdullah; so it

43 Nehru's two notes to Foreign Secretary, 8 October 1958.

44 To Krishna Menon in New York, 14 October 1958.

45 Note of the Indian Government, 18 October, reply of the Chinese Government, 1 November, and rejoinder of the Indian Government, 8 November 1958.

46 Memorandum of the Foreign Office of China, 3 November 1958. White Paper, I, p. 47.

47 Nehru to Zhou Enlai, 14 December 1958. White Paper, I, pp. 48–51.

was to his great relief that Abdullah was released on 11 January 1958. The Prime Minister hoped that, after Abdullah had given vent to his pent-up feelings of anger and frustration, it might be possible to talk to him about the future. Abdullah's speeches were as expected, critical of the Governments of India and Kashmir and likely to fan communal feelings. At the same time Abdullah sent three of his colleagues to meet Nehru and they sought to explain away some of his statements as the result of excitement and mental disturbance. Nehru's advice was that speeches should be avoided for a while; as for a meeting with Abdullah, it might be wiser to wait till both Abdullah and the situation had calmed down.[48] Despite this caution, Abdullah continued on what Nehru believed was 'a wrong and dangerous path'[49] and was back in prison on 29 April. Nehru had wanted the Kashmir Government to initiate judicial proceedings rather than detain him without trial, but Pant and the Chief Minister were opposed to a trial.[50]

Equally depressing was the fact that there seemed to be no change in the attitude of the Pakistan Government towards India. It was, Nehru had earlier remarked ruefully, a haunted world; there was hardly a country which did not carry its ghost about with it and, for India, it was the ghost of Pakistan. Behind that ghost lay the history not only of the past ten years but also of the many years preceding freedom. Relations with Pakistan appeared to be a continuation of the old communal conflict, and there could be no real solution till that basic conflict in the minds of the people in Pakistan and India was resolved. He did not claim that India was free from this communal temper, but it did not dominate everything else as in Pakistan. No Government in that country had had any policy except of fear and hatred of India and, till that ceased, the future was dark.[51] Little hope could be sustained of settling the Kashmir problem or any other issue between the two countries as long as Pakistan's approach on all matters was that of bitter dislike of India. But he did not exonerate himself and acknowledged his failure to win the goodwill of the Government of Pakistan.[52] There is corroboration, from the Pakistan side, of this spectre of suspicion smothering all efforts at improved relations; Noon, the Prime Minister, told Macmillan in Karachi in January 1958 that, India's intentions being evil, there was little hope of a settlement on Kashmir.[53]

The constant talk of 'holy war', the continuous migration of Hindus from East Bengal, the sporadic resort to firing without any provocation along the borders, and the numerous instances, for which Pakistan was thought to be responsible, of sabotage and bomb explosions in Kashmir formed varied

[48] Nehru's report to Bakshi Ghulam Mahomed of conversations with Abdullah's supporters, 15 February 1958.

[49] Letter to M. Magray in London, 14 April, quoted in *The Hindu*, 1 May 1958.

[50] Nehru to Bakshi Ghulam Mahomed, 16 April, and Pant to Nehru, 19 April 1958.

[51] Nehru to Chief Ministers, 1 November 1957.

[52] 18 March 1958. Lok Sabha Debates, Second Series, Vol. XIII, pp. 5,399–435.

[53] H. Macmillan, *Riding the Storm* (London, 1971), p. 392.

evidence of this ingrained attitude of basic conflict.[54] Nor did Graham's report in March 1958 help to improve matters. He was less sensitive than Jarring to the basic issues as well as to the changing situation; and he ended his report with the odd recommendation, rejected out of hand by India, that the Prime Ministers of India and Pakistan meet under his chairmanship. India could not accept the implication that the two countries were on an equal footing in this matter and should plead their cases before a third party. It was in this setting of stalemate that Pakistan went back to the Security Council with a fresh complaint, based mainly on Abdullah's re-arrest. The failure of the Kashmir Government to initiate promptly the conspiracy case of which they talked loudly, and the difficulties faced by the counsel defending the three supporters of Abdullah who had been arrested along with him, did not strengthen India's hand. But it was not the tarnishing of India's image which alone worried Nehru; he disliked the delay of justice and urged Bakshi Ghulam Mahomed to commence the conspiracy case and to give full opportunities to the defence.[55] Against the outside world, however, he closed ranks. The British Government were informed that India would not resort to force and her Prime Minister was willing to meet his counterpart from Pakistan; but such a meeting would serve no useful purpose until Pakistan gave up her bellicose attitude and accepted the basic position, as stated by India, on Kashmir.[56] Eisenhower's offer of 'friendly assistance' in bringing the Prime Ministers of India and Pakistan together to discuss all problems was also politely but firmly declined on the ground that no third party could intervene in a matter which would ultimately have to be settled directly by the two countries. India would like to have normal and friendly relations, but saw no hope of them in face of the policy of hatred which every Government in Pakistan since 1947 had adopted and of the aggressive intransigence which had been encouraged by military alliances and the attitude of the Western Powers in the Security Council.[57]

Nehru's resolve in this matter was probably strengthened by his contempt for the Ministers of Pakistan, Suhrawardy and Noon, and by the murder of Khan Sahib, the Chief Minister of West Pakistan and an old friend whom he respected as the one man of integrity in murky surroundings. There seemed to him to be a breakdown of the spirit of the people of Pakistan and 'the almost visible cracking up' of the structure of the country.[58] The replacement of Suhrawardy by Noon as Prime Minister was not to Nehru a marked improvement but, when Noon agreed to come to Delhi for talks on border issues, Nehru expressed the hope that if these could be settled it might help to break

[54] See Nehru to H. Macmillan, 10 April 1958, and remarks at press conference at Delhi, 4 June, *National Herald*, 5 June 1958.

[55] Telegram and letter, 9 May 1958.

[56] Nehru's note to Commonwealth Secretary, 13 May 1958.

[57] Eisenhower to Nehru, 14 May, Nehru's report of conversation with American Ambassador, 16 May, and Nehru to Eisenhower, 7 June 1958.

[58] Nehru to Chief Ministers, 18 May 1958.

down the 'solid wall of violent hatred' and create a better atmosphere for the discussion of major problems.[59] The two Prime Ministers agreed to rectify the border on the east by settling odd disputes and to exchange a number of enclaves. Nehru had been prepared for an exchange of all enclaves on the eastern border without asking for compensation elsewhere, although the extent of Indian territory involved was much larger than that of Pakistan; but no such general settlement could be reached. Nehru proposed to refer the border disputes which remained to an independent tribunal. For once, in the interest of goodwill, Nehru overcame his distaste for arbitration; but Noon refused to accept this process, as he said, on one particular matter – meaning presumably that he would like arbitration on all matters including Kashmir. So unsettled border issues were reserved for later consideration.[60]

Nehru also thought of a new approach to the question of the division of the Indus canal waters. Instead of India retaining all the waters of the Sutlej and paying large sums to Pakistan for developing alternate supplies, he was willing to provide them with all the water they had previously secured or with half that amount along with funds to build link canals.[61] But all these efforts at better relations were lost to sight with the overthrow of the democratic system in Pakistan and the declaration of martial law. Nehru's Government, like many others, immediately recognized the *de facto* authority of the regime of Mirza and Ayub Khan. Clearly the change had been received with relief by the people of Pakistan for they had grown tired of the corruption and intrigue of the politicians. But Nehru did not conceal his intellectual and emotional resistance to a military regime; nor could he resist pointing out the contrast between India, with its strong democratic tradition, and Pakistan, born of a negative attitude to Indian nationalism, rootless and lacking in positive content even after 1947.[62] 'Obviously we have to be alert and vigilant, but I think that Pakistan is going to pieces with extraordinary rapidity. What is more, the allies of Pakistan realize this, even though they may not say it.'[63] Nehru rightly forecast that the rule by soldiers would solve no problems except the maintenance of law and order in a narrow sense; and he drew from this the conclusion (wrongly as it turned out) that military rule would not last for more perhaps than a year.[64]

The ousting within weeks of Mirza by Ayub meant the establishment of full-blooded army rule and the paradoxical creation of a dictatorship within the Commonwealth – although the resilience of that association was sufficient to adapt itself even to this and Pakistan became a precedent for many other member-states. In foreign policy, Ayub's *coup* could be expected to

[59] 26 August 1958. Rajya Sabha Debates, Vol. XXII, pp. 1,047–55.

[60] Nehru to B. C. Roy, 18 August 1958; Nehru's statement on talks with Noon, 12 September 1958, Lok Sabha Debates, Second Series, Vol. XX, pp. 6,200–10.

[61] Nehru's note, 16 August 1958.

[62] Press conference at Delhi, 12 October, *National Herald*, 13 October 1958.

[63] Nehru to Krishna Menon, 14 October 1958.

[64] Nehru's note on talks with officials of the World Bank, 11 October 1958.

make little difference. For some years Pakistan had been a protegé of the United States, and the army would not have dared to act if it believed that its seizure of power would be disliked in Washington. But Mirza's removal did not seem to Nehru a good sign, for he might have functioned as a restraining influence especially as far as India was concerned.[65] When the people of Pakistan realized that a military regime was solving no problems, then the rulers might resort to some adventure to divert popular attention. Although assured by the United States that they had had no pre-knowledge of Ayub's action and that they would exercise every restraint on him,[66] Nehru remained uneasy in his mind. Nowhere else in the world was there such a naked military dictatorship and when that dictator pronounced that a war with India would be popular with his people and he would 'certainly, if necessary' go to war, it followed that India should at least remain vigilant. A Government ruling by martial law, with no checks on its authority and with heavy supplies of weapons from abroad, obviously threatened India more than ever before.[67] Eisenhower was more appreciative than Dulles of India's problem. He himself, he told the Indian Ambassador, was on the horns of a dilemma. He had to help Pakistan because she was an ally of the United States but he realized that the grant of such military assistance to Pakistan imperilled the the friendship of India.[68] Yet Nehru thought it necessary to state once more that any attack on Kashmir was aggression against India and would have to be met anywhere and everywhere.[69]

The treaty signed by Pakistan with the United States in January 1959, which was said to provide for the supply of 'non-conventional' weapons and the establishment of launching-sites for missiles, led Nehru to have a verbal protest made to the United States. The American Ambassador gave the usual assurances that no large-scale increase in military aid was contemplated under the new agreement and that the United States would not allow Pakistan to attack India. He added his belief that the new regime in Pakistan, being military, would certainly be more careful about such adventures.[70] But Nehru was inclined to think that the danger was in fact greater, for a soldier in political authority was accustomed to think in military terms. His fears seemed to be borne out by statements of Ministers and officials in Pakistan that the treaty was intended to protect Pakistan against all countries and not, as the United States claimed, only from any country controlled by international communism. Nor was Nehru assured by the description of the treaty as a defensive one, for there was no more than a mental line demarcating defence

65 Nehru's note on Pakistan, 28 October 1958.

66 Nehru's note on conversation with United States Ambassador, 31 October 1958.

67 Press conference at Delhi, 7 November, *National Herald*, 8 November 1958, and speech in Lok Sabha 8 December 1958. Debates, Second Series, Vol. XXIII, pp. 3,682–93.

68 M. C. Chagla's telegram to Nehru reporting conversation with Eisenhower, 8 December 1958.

69 15 December 1958. Rajya Sabha Debates, Vol. XXIII, pp. 2,254–69.

70 Nehru's notes to Secretary-General, Ministry of External Affairs, 4 and 16 January, and note of Commonwealth Secretary, 20 January 1959.

from aggression. It was obvious that the United States would be unable to prevent the utilization of these arms by Pakistan for an offensive action against India. Still, if only for the record, he sought an official clarification in writing from the United States that the interpretations being placed on the treaty in Pakistan were incorrect.[71]

FOUR

In a sense, this note to the United States was an appropriate prelude to later events, for Pakistan was now interested and became gradually involved, in search of her own advantage, in the sharp deterioration in relations between India and China. At the end of 1958, Nehru was assuring the Chief Ministers that he had noticed no marked tension in India's relations with China or the Soviet Union.[72] Soon after, that the problem of the boundary had become a major one was made clear by Zhou's reply of 23 January 1959, when China cast off the last traces of subterfuge and, contending that the boundary had never been formally delimited, laid claim to large areas of Indian territory. Then came the flight of the Dalai Lama from Lhasa in March 1959. For nearly three years the Khampas had been in revolt in areas east of Tibet province, and this unrest now spread to Tibet itself. In November 1958, when the Dalai Lama sought Nehru's advice as to whether he should agree to the Chinese suggestion that he proceed to Beijing, Nehru had been reluctant to give a categoric reply. All he suggested was that the Dalai Lama could say that his absence would remove a restraining influence on the situation in Tibet; but if the Chinese insisted there was little he could do.[73] From January, India was faced with the problem of numbers of Tibetan refugees wishing to cross over. Nehru, maintaining a strictly correct position, ordered that no Tibetan should be permitted into India, but the wounded and the sick should be given medical aid at the border outposts.[74] He also, when reports were received of fighting in Lhasa, refused to give any general commitment that refugees would be let in, for, as he said later, that would be to invite people to roll into India from all over the place.[75] But he decided to treat the Dalai Lama himself on a different basis[76] and, when overtures were made on his behalf, he was informed on 19 March by the Government of India that, if he requested asylum, it would be granted.[77]

71 Nehru's instructions to Commonwealth Secretary, 14 March 1959.

72 Nehru to Chief Ministers, 31 December 1958.

73 A. Pant's telegram 21 November, and Nehru's note, 26 November 1958.

74 Nehru's note to Foreign Secretary, 13 January 1959.

75 30 March 1959. Lok Sabha Debates, Second Series, Vol. XXVIII, pp. 8,461–8, 4 May 1959. Rajya Sabha Debates, Vol. 25, pp. 1,671–84.

76 Foreign Secretary's telegram to Indian Political Officer in Sikkim, 15 March 1959.

77 Foreign Secretary's telegram to Indian Consul-General at Lhasa, 19 March 1959.

Two days earlier the Dalai Lama had left Lhasa, and he crossed the Indian border on 31 March.

The flight of the Dalai Lama and his arrival in India placed, on the already brittle relations between India and China, a heavy strain from which they never recovered. While the notes exchanged on the border incidents had been growing in acerbity since 1954, it was India's reception of the Dalai Lama and other Tibetan refugees that intensified the language of Chinese protests. Nehru's decision to grant the Dalai Lama asylum had the near-unanimous support of public opinion in India, and Nehru himself had no hesitation or second thoughts about this humanitarian act, particularly appropriate in that the Dalai Lama was respected in India as a high priest of Buddhism.[78] Moreover, apart from the consideration for him as an individual, there was widespread sympathy for Tibet because of the 'cultural kinship', in Nehru's phrase, between India and Tibet. But the Chinese Government, who alleged that the revolt in Tibet had been instigated and assisted by American and Kuomintang elements,[79] regarded the grant of asylum to the Dalai Lama as an unfriendly act. In 1954 Zhou had told Nehru that Panikkar had said that if the Dalai Lama ever sought asylum the Government of India would have to grant it, and the Chinese Government had agreed; but in 1959 they took a different view. They were correct in assuming the involvement of the United States in events in Tibet, for it is now known that a radio operator trained by the C.I.A. accompanied the Dalai Lama and was in continuous touch with the American Embassy in Delhi.[80] Probably the Chinese knew this even then, for there were reports in New Delhi that they were intercepting these messages and were perhaps even tracking the Dalai Lama's movements.[81] It is also said that American aircraft provided cover for the Dalai Lama's party.[82] But there is no evidence to suggest that the Government of India were aware of American complicity in the flight of the Dalai Lama.

In what was clearly a critical point in India's foreign relations,[83] Nehru sought to work out a policy which would harmonize four seemingly conflicting objectives: to help the Tibetans while maintaining friendship with China and to ensure the security of India in a new context without casting off the anchor of non-alignment. He declined to recognize 'a free Government' of Tibet in India and requested the Dalai Lama to function with restraint and

78 Only Krishna Menon had doubts then and later; M. Brecher, *India and World Politics* (London, 1968), p. 145; S. Dutt, *With Nehru in the Foreign Office* (Calcutta, 1977), p. 150.

79 Telegram from G. Parthasarathi to Foreign Secretary, reporting conversation with Chinese Vice-Minister of Foreign Affairs, 21 March 1959.

80 H. Rositzke, *C.I.A.'s Secret Operations* (New York, 1977), pp. 173–4. Rositzke was the C.I.A.'s chief representative in India from 1957 to 1962.

81 W. R. Crocker, *Nehru* (London, 1966), p. 106. Crocker was Australian High Commissioner in Delhi at this time.

82 T. D. Allman in the *Guardian*, 19 January 1974.

83 cf. 'Like the United States of 1776, the independent India of 1947 tended to think of power politics as none of its business. As other newly independent nations have done before it, Mr. Nehru's India may be emerging from the age of innocence. In later years, the republic of India may look back upon this month as its moment of truth.' *The Economist*, 4 April 1959.

responsibility. India had gone as far as she could to help Tibet and neither she nor any other country could convert sympathy into more positive assistance. 'Let us face facts. One cannot bring heaven to the people in India even if I wish it. The whole world cannot bring freedom to Tibet unless the whole fabric of the Chinese state is destroyed.' Only a world war, an atomic war, could perhaps make that possible.[84] In the same vein, he disapproved of the emotional responses of certain sections of the Indian public to developments in Tibet. There was no question of India intervening in Tibet; the most that India could do 'in helping the Tibetans to have a square deal'[85] was to assist a situation gradually to develop which would induce the Chinese Government to moderate their policy in Tibet. So he rejected the President's suggestion that he denounce this 'new colonialism' publicly, for such action would have led to a rupture of diplomatic relations with China.[86] India could not put forward any demands to China on the situation in Tibet. Indeed, he made no direct approaches to China, not even informally, but contented himself with public expressions of India's concern and of her hope that Tibet would enjoy autonomy; and even these sentiments were always coupled with a stress on the importance of good relations between India and China. Once the isolation of Tibet had been broken down, social and economic changes were bound to come. It had been India's hope that these changes would come gradually and through Tibetan agencies; and the Chinese Government seemed to have appreciated this position and postponed the imposition of reforms. But the inherent contradictions of the situation made conflict in some form almost inevitable. 'The only possible way for us to be helpful in this situation is to continue to have some kind of a balanced outlook. The moment we leave that, nothing more can be done by us. I know that even otherwise we cannot do much.'[87] India should be wary of playing into the hands of those who wished to exploit the rebellion in Tibet as a weapon in the cold war. It would only harden China's attitude, and the Soviet Union, which till now had said very little about Tibet, would then support China fully.[88]

However, even this cautious and correct attitude, so deliberately framed, did not appease the Chinese Government, who, in Nehru's view, were becoming rigid and increasingly arrogant and were inclined to throw their weight about.[89] In an official statement, Kalimpong was described as 'the commanding centre' of the Tibetan rebellion;[90] and an immediate Indian contradiction appeared to give no satisfaction. At a meeting of the Chinese National People's Congress, although Zhou welcomed Nehru's statements and said there was no reason why the two countries should let their friendship

[84] Record of Nehru's meeting with the Dalai Lama, 24 April 1959.
[85] Nehru to Chief Ministers, 25 March 1959.
[86] Rajendra Prasad to Nehru, 29 March and 1 April, and Nehru's replies, 30 March and 2 April 1959.
[87] Nehru to C. Rajagopalachari, 8 April 1959.
[88] Nehru's oral message to the Dalai Lama, 9 May 1959.
[89] Nehru to C. Rajagopalachari, 8 April, and to Vijayalakshmi, 15 April 1959.
[90] 29 March 1959.

be shaken by a handful of rebels, other speakers condemned India's attitudes and actions as inconsistent with the Panch Sheela and charged Indian 'expansionists' with holding the Dalai Lama 'under duress'. The Government of India were later charged with encouraging the rebels and interfering in China's internal affairs.[91] As Nehru remarked sadly, terms like Panch Sheela had lost their shine and were being hurled about without meaning.[92]

Yet, despite these provocations, Nehru continued to maintain a moderate and courteous tone in his rejoinders and, while not concealing the 'full sympathy' for Tibet which was not an 'empty sentiment', asserted that he would not allow posterity to blame him for leaving behind a trail of bitterness towards China.[93] Parthasarathi, the Ambassador in Peking, reported that there was no meeting ground between the two countries on the Tibetan issue and India–China relations should be viewed no longer as an emotional matter; but, apart from Tibet, it was in the interest of both countries to be friendly, for if China's friendship was necessary for India, so was India's friendship for China.[94] Nehru decided to make this clear and, rather than increase the tension between the two countries, wait till China cooled down and saw reason. 'The time for any country to display arrogance in dealing with India is long past. We have still some remains of what we learnt from Gandhiji. We shall, therefore, continue to be polite and seek friendship and at the same time to hold firmly to the policy we consider correct.'[95] It was relatively easy to take up extreme attitudes, as China had done, and to talk without restraint. 'We have to follow a more difficult path.'[96]

In this setting of Sino-Indian tension, Ayub Khan proposed a meeting with Nehru, of whom he spoke in extravagant terms,[97] and envisaged better relations leading to common defence arrangements between India and Pakistan. The intent was to exploit the growing military strength of Pakistan and India's soured relations with China to push Nehru off non-alignment and lead him via military accord against China into major concessions on Kashmir. Writing later, Ayub virtually accepted this by clarifying that all that he had meant by common defence was a settlement of problems, i.e. Kashmir, with perhaps an understanding of neutrality if either party were engaged in war with a third power.[98] But Nehru was not easily frightened; nor had he given

[91] 'Some Indian statesmen and papers have been actively sympathising with the rebels and the Indian Government has done nothing to discourage them, quite the contrary . . . Will the Indian official circles henceforth perpetually intervene in China's internal affairs? What are Indian official circles thinking of?' Shih Ping in *People's Daily*, 24 April 1959.

[92] 4 May 1959. Rajya Sabha Debates, Vol. XXV, pp. 1,671–84.

[93] Speeches at Allahabad, 6 April, and Madras, 15 April, *The Hindu*, 7 and 16 April respectively.

[94] Telegram to Foreign Secretary, 20 April 1959.

[95] Nehru's telegram to Indian Ambassador in Beijing, 29 April 1959.

[96] Nehru to Apa Pant, 23 May 1959.

[97] 'I regard him as a very great man indeed. For Mr. Nehru I am prepared to do anything. Please assure him from me and give him my word as a soldier and an honest man that I am sincerely anxious to build up the best possible relations with India.' Report of R. Dayal, Indian High Commissioner in Pakistan, on conversation with Ayub.

[98] M. Ayub Khan, *Friends not Masters* (Oxford, 1967), p. 128.

up hopes of at least restoration of normalcy in relations with China. So he curtly turned down Ayub's offer. To give up non-alignment was to abandon one's moorings and to drift, to lose one's self-respect and to hang on to some other country. As for a common defence policy, against whom was this to be directed?[99] It would place India immediately in a military camp and give her policy both an anti-Soviet and an anti-Chinese stance. For the time being, till the mood of excitement in China passed, he would be content with no long-term decisions. Rather,

> maintaining our dignity, maintaining our rights, maintaining our self-respect, and yet not allowing ourselves to drift into wrong attitudes and hostile attitudes and trying to help in removing or in solving such problems as arise, we may help a little – they cannot be solved quickly – that is the very utmost that one can do in the circumstances or, at any rate, creating an atmosphere which may help in doing this. How far it will go, I do not know.[100]

It was a modest, yet realistic and positive, formulation of policy.

In practice, this policy took the shape of seeking to stem the further weakening of relations with China and resisting any unjustifiable compromise with Pakistan on the rebound. There were now over twelve thousand Tibetan refugees in India and efforts were made to settle them in various parts of India. Their very presence in India was seen by the Chinese as a continuous affront, and all Nehru could do was to try to tone down this resentment by dissuading the Dalai Lama and his followers from political activity. India too had cause to complain of the affront provided by Chinese maps; she too had her pride and self-respect and there was a widespread feeling in the country that the Chinese Government often acted as a bully. But Nehru decided to let matters remain as they were and leave the next step to the Chinese – a step which he did not expect to come soon.[101]

Believing that he had at least temporarily arrested the display of China's irritation with India and hoping that China's isolation in the world might have at least a marginal impact, Nehru took a firm line with Pakistan. He informed Ayub that, if only from the narrowest viewpoint of opportunism, he would like to see a progressive solution of problems with Pakistan and a reduction of the military burden though not an agreement on joint defence which went counter to India's wider policies. But, given the increased military assistance from the United States, the aggressive anti-Indian speeches of Pakistani leaders, the frequent violations of the cease-fire line in Kashmir, the regular firing across the border from East Bengal and the plan to build the Mangla dam in what was Indian territory in Kashmir, he declined to

[99] Nehru's speech in the Rajya Sabha, 4 May 1959. Debates, Vol. 25, pp. 1,671–84.
[100] 8 May 1959. Lok Sabha Debates, Second Series, Vol. XXXI, p. 15,925–39.
[101] Nehru's telegram to G. Parthasarathi, 9 May 1959.

be drawn, by soft words expressed in private, into a meeting with Ayub.[102] Personal discussions themselves would yield no results unless the situation, circumstances and all other factors had been brought to a certain pitch from which results could flow.[103] But such an unyielding attitude towards Pakistan was not helped by the Chinese. Suspicion continued to mount in Peking of the bona fides of the Nehru Government.[104] On 16 May, in a statement which, even in the cynical history of contemporary international relations seems unequalled for open blackmail, the Chinese Ambassador in Delhi informed the Government of India that China disliked having to concern herself with both the United States and India, and added: 'Friends! it seems to us that you too cannot have two fronts. Is it not so? If it is, here then lies the meeting point of our two sides. Will you please think it over?'[105] In other words, China was hinting at the danger to India of Sino-Pakistani collusion.

However, Nehru held firm to his dual policy of patience with China and firmness towards Pakistan; and, for a while, there was a slight toning down in Chinese attacks on India. On the issue of Tibet, allegations ceased; 'It is', said Nehru,[106] 'a wall of silence with muffled whispers occasionally.' But it was an uneasy and short-lived calm. In Tibet itself, the remaining Indian trade agents were treated harshly, probably with a view to driving them out. The Chinese also stepped up their incursions across the border into India. In the western sector, they moved into Spanggur and arrested in July an Indian police party which was proceeding towards Khurnak fort. On the Government of India protesting, a few weeks later the Indian party was released. Then, in early August, in the eastern sector, an armed Chinese patrol intruded into Khinzemane and pushed back Indian personnel before withdrawing. About three weeks later, in the same sector a strong Chinese detachment crossed into Indian territory south of Migyitun, encircled an Indian post at Longju and overpowered it.

It was not immediately clear whether any general strategy lay behind these incidents or whether the Chinese were merely reacting to the irritant of India's sympathy for the Dalai Lama and his followers. Nehru still made sure that such sympathy did not develop into anything more tangible. Asked by a journalist if he had reconciled himself to the position that nothing could be done for the Tibetans, he replied with a touch of impatience, 'My dear sir, I

102 Nehru to R. Dayal, 5 April, 26 May and 2 July 1959.

103 Press conference at Delhi, 14 May, *National Herald*, 15 May 1959.

104 'India is a country that has gained independence after shaking off the colonial rule of British imperialism. It desires to develop its national economy in a peaceful international environment and has profound contradictions with the imperialist and colonialist forces. This is one aspect of the picture. Another aspect is that the Indian big bourgeoisie maintains innumerable links with imperialism and is, to a certain extent, dependent on foreign capital. Moreover, by its class nature, the big bourgeoisie has a certain urge for outward expression. This is why, while it opposes the imperialists' policy of intervention, it more or less reflects, consciously or unconsciously, certain influences of imperialist policy of intervention.' 'The Revolution in Tibet and Nehru's Philosophy', *People's Daily*, 16 May 1959.

105 Statement of the Chinese Ambassador to the Foreign Secretary, 16 May 1959. White Paper I (Delhi 1959), p. 72.

106 Press conference at Delhi, 10 June, *National Herald*, 11 June 1959.

have not reconciled myself to this position or a hundred or a thousand other positions. But I do not pretend to have authority or power to change the shape of the world, the face of the world. As things come up, one tries to act to the best of one's judgment.'[107] But India needed to formulate her own policy in regard to these provocations on the border. Chinese maps showed, with broad brush-strokes, large parts of Indian territory in both the western and eastern sectors within China; and the Chinese were no longer trying to explain this away as being merely a reprinting of old Kuomintang maps. The clearing of a road in Aksai Chin and the later, frequent incursions at various parts along the border now fitted logically with the Chinese decision that the time had become ripe for making the boundary issue a live one. So Nehru reiterated that in the north-east, the McMahon Line was the firm frontier – firm by treaty, by usage and by geography.[108] He also reaffirmed the responsibility of the Government of India for the protection of Sikkim and Bhutan and made clear that any aggression against these territories would be considered as aggression against India. However, he was willing to treat the Aksai Chin in the western sector on a different footing, for here the boundary had not been clearly demarcated in some stretches; so disputes about any particular area could be discussed.[109] There was no alternative to the defence of India and on this the Government would not yield; but they would not panic either and would be willing to settle differences by negotiation. Of such settlements he was still optimistic, for he could not believe that China sought armed confrontation with India. 'It seems to me so foolish for anybody, including the Chinese Government, to function in that way and I do not give them the credit, or rather the discredit, for folly.'[110] India too would take no rash step; and he rejected outright foolhardy suggestions in Parliament that the road which the Chinese had constructed across Indian territory in Aksai Chin be bombed. While borders had to be defended, it was not normal for big countries like India to behave as if they were at war and hit out all round. If the Chinese did not reply to notes and reminders about intrusions into Indian territory, India could only send further reminders.[111] Though the problem was serious, no grave crisis was imminent; so India would avoid treating it as such or taking any step that might lead to a break with China.[112]

FIVE

This refusal to precipitate matters with China was accompanied by no

[107] Press conference at Delhi, 7 July 1959. File 43 (73)/59–P.M.S.

[108] 13 August 1959. Lok Sabha Debates, Second Series, Vol. XXXII, pp. 2,243–7.

[109] 28 August 1959. Lok Sabha Debates, Second Series, Vol. XXXIII, pp. 4,793–804. See also speech of 12 September 1959. Lok Sabha Debates, Second Series, Vol. XXXIX, pp. 8,104–29.

[110] 28 August 1959. Lok Sabha Debates, Second Series, Vol. XXXIII, pp. 4,860–71.

[111] 31 August 1959. Rajya Sabha Debates, Vol. XXVI, pp. 2,281–92.

[112] Nehru to Vijayalakshmi and to H. Macmillan, 30 August 1959.

weakness in dealing with Pakistan. The resolve was strengthened by the knowledge that Pakistan had received from the United States a large number of armoured vehicles adaptable for amphibian purposes and therefore obviously meant for use to cross the river boundaries with India rather than against the Soviet Union. Nehru could not refuse to meet Ayub when the latter proposed to break journey in Delhi for a few hours on his way to Dacca on 1 September. But their talks amounted to little. Nehru was concerned with improving the atmosphere while Ayub was eager for immediate results. So Nehru stressed the importance of a no-war declaration and the creation of a background of understanding between the two countries; and Ayub sought the establishment of machinery for settling outstanding issues and a solution of the Kashmir problem.[113] Nor was Nehru swayed by the clear indication by the Pakistan Government of a desire to reach a settlement on the boundary issues between India and East Bengal. For the crucial question was Kashmir, and on this there could be no weakening of the Indian stand because of preoccupation with China.[114] The suggestions from official circles in the United States that China's aggressive attitude made a unified system of defence all the more necessary were dismissed as too facile, and the Embassy in Washington was instructed to refute the State Department's assumption that India was not serious in objecting to military assistance to Pakistan in these changing circumstances. In fact, the objection was all the stronger as India was now faced with threats from both the north and the west.[115] This stand secured justification and the whole concept of common defence was shown to be hollow when Ayub, while boasting that he would 'slaughter' the Chinese if they came into conflict with Pakistan, publicly questioned Nehru's authority in dealing with China about Ladakh, on the ground that Ladakh, being a part of Kashmir, was territory in dispute between India and Pakistan. Common defence, therefore, did not, in Ayub's view, imply support of India against Chinese aggression across the northern border.

SIX

However, Nehru's effort to freeze Sino-Indian relations till the political climate improved was made infinitely more difficult by Zhou's long letter of 8 September 1959. Rejecting the Indian position as again stated by Nehru on 22 March, that the alignment on Indian maps was based on natural features, supported by tradition and, over a large part, confirmed by treaties, Zhou claimed for China the boundary as shown on their old maps and incorporating about 40,000 square miles of Indian territory.[116] Nehru, reversing the policy

[113] Ayub Khan, *Friends not Masters*, p. 124.

[114] Nehru to Chief Ministers, 4 November 1959.

[115] Commonwealth Secretary to Embassy of India, Washington, 1 October 1959.

[116] Nehru's letter of 22 March 1959. White Paper I, pp. 55–7; Zhou's letter of 8 September 1959, White Paper II, pp. 27–33.

Low's cartoon in the *Guardian*, September 1959

he had followed for nearly five years of treating the boundary disputes as matters to be discussed by the two Governments at a confidential level, now decided to place the whole correspondence before Parliament. He had, at last, been forced to recognize that this was not a matter of minor specific disputes which could be settled by discussion, of out-of-date maps which out of inertia had not been rectified and could be corrected or even of a general misunderstanding which could be cleared up. The Chinese Government, having deliberately led the Government of India to believe that they accepted broadly the boundary as shown on Indian maps, now disclosed their true intent; and this was a basic development of which Parliament had a right to be aware. The public reaction to the Indian White Paper was naturally intense, and Nehru appealed in Parliament and to the press for restraint. While there was no question of surrender or even acceptance of unequal relations with China, it remained of importance to preserve friendship with her. When nations became excited and relied on prestige, they were often driven, step by step, in wrong directions; but there could be no 'more amazing folly' than for India and China to move into a major conflict for the possession of some border areas. A firm policy should always be linked with a door open to accommodation and settlement. He himself would be willing to discuss minor rectifications of the border and, if required, agree to mediation or arbitration by third powers on the basis of treaties, maps, usage and geography.

Such restraint seemed all the more necessary as China was now not only

4 Spinning at Rajghat (where Mahatma Gandhi was cremated) 30 January 1957

5 *Below left* At Children's Day, Delhi, 14 November 1957

6 *Below right* With Vinoba Bhave, 21 September 1957

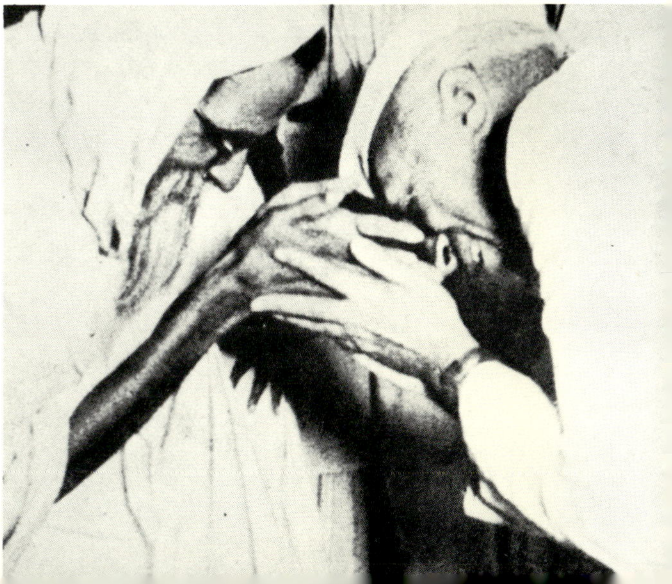

7 With Ho Chi Minh, Delhi, 7 February 1958

questioning the whole boundary alignment but hardening in her general attitude. In addition to contending that the boundary was undelimited and accusing Nehru of misunderstanding his remarks in 1956, Zhou complained that the Dalai Lama had been permitted to exceed the limits of political asylum.[117] Not comprehending the nature of the Indian political system, the Chinese authorities could not believe that the Dalai Lama's statements and activities did not have the approval of the Indian Government. That the rebellion in Tibet and the boundary problem were linked in Zhou's mind is also shown by his allegations that, immediately after the arrival in India of a large number of Tibetan refugees, Indian troops had started pressing forward across the McMahon Line, that the rebellion was being used by elements in India to create tension between the two countries and that the Government of India were trying to utilize this opportunity to compel China to accept the boundary as depicted by India.[118] The Foreign Minister, Chen Yi, went further and accused Nehru, in the matter of the Dalai Lama, of adopting not a middle course, as he claimed, but of two-faced tactics.[119] As Nehru observed, when you dig in your toes it becomes difficult to undig or pull them out. The two countries no longer seemed to be speaking the same language and China appeared not to understand Indian traditions and ways of functioning.[120] Speaking almost in a whisper and in a tone mingled with pain and sorrow,[121] he conceded that the Chinese had not been playing straight with India and obviously attached a low value to India's friendship. To give the impression that they recognized a boundary alignment and expected only some minor rectifications, to creep gradually and by stealth into the relatively inaccessible and sparsely populated territory of a friendly neighbour and then to question the validity of the whole boundary was, to say the least, a breach of faith.

> Frankly it is serious because I just do not know how the Chinese mind may think. I just do not know and I have been surprised at recent developments. So I do not know. I have great admiration for the Chinese mind, logical and reasonable and relatively calm. But sometimes I wonder if all those old qualities have not perhaps been partly overwhelmed.[122]

Dismayed and shaken by Chinese dissimulation and deviousness, yet Nehru held to his twin objectives of safeguarding the territorial integrity of India and seeking peaceful settlements so as to avoid continuing hostility

[117] Zhou's letter, 8 September, and Parthasarathi's telegram to Dutt reporting conversation with Zhou, 9 September 1959.

[118] Zhou's letter of 8 September, and his report to the standing committee of the National People's Congress, 11 September, *Peking Review*, 15 September 1959.

[119] 13 September 1959, ibid.

[120] Speech in Lok Sabha, 4 September 1959. Debates, Second Series, Vol. XXXIV, pp. 6,536–54; press conference at Delhi, 11 September, *National Herald*, 12 September 1959.

[121] Report of the correspondent in Delhi, *The Hindu*, 11 September 1959.

[122] 8 and 10 September 1959. Rajya Sabha Debates, Vol. XXVI, pp. 3,895–4,015.

between the two countries. He suggested now to the Chinese Government the maintenance of the status quo and respect for the traditional alignment, negotiations on disputed areas and the neutralization of Longju, which was claimed by both sides.[123] There was little hope of the acceptance of this formula, for the Chinese were now no longer concerned with little pockets of territory. They were disputing the whole border and claiming large pieces of territory, and they must have known full well that wide-ranging negotiations, which might conceivably have been agreed to by India in the early 1950s, were now beyond consideration. Indeed, it seemed that the Chinese really desired no negotiations for, in Nehru's words, 'it is the pride and arrogance of might that is showing in their language, in their behaviour to us and in so many things that they have done'.[124] So Nehru politely declined U Nu's offer to go to China to create a suitable political climate for discussing their problems. No Government in India was going to agree to the 'absurd' Chinese claims, and any effort by U Nu might harden the Chinese attitude by suggesting that India was frightened and anxious to find some way out.[125] But Nehru decided that India would abide unilaterally by her offer to maintain the status quo. He gave instructions that armed conflict was to be avoided and all Indian civil and military personnel should be told clearly that they should on no account open fire unless the other side fired at them. They should also keep clearly within the Indian side of the frontier and, in the event of any Chinese detachment coming across, tell them to go back and report the matter to Delhi for further orders. Checkposts in the Uttar Pradesh, Himachal Pradesh and Punjab sectors should be vigilant and, if necessary, be reinforced; and the understanding on Hoti should be respected. No armed action should be taken against the checkpost set up by the Chinese in Indian territory near Chushul, but Indian checkposts in the area should be strengthened and the airstrip at Chushul effectively guarded. Nothing need be done, for the time being, regarding the Chinese occupation of Aksai Chin and their construction of a road in that area. Officials should also be prepared for talks as regards not major changes but any minor deviations from the border as shown by India.[126]

On the larger issues of foreign policy, Nehru was not prepared to weaken non-alignment or consider military alliances. India's reputation in the world, as he had somewhat complacently assured Parliament,[127] stood high because of her foreign policy; and he had no intention of jeopardizing it because of a rebellion in Tibet and Chinese pressures. Vague ideas about searching for allies were a sign of utter weakness of character in an individual and in a nation.[128] It was possible that, hard as India might strive to avoid war, she

[123] Nehru to Zhou Enlai, 26 September 1959. White Paper II, pp. 34–46.

[124] 12 September 1959. Lok Sabha Debates, Second Series, Vol. XXXIX, pp. 8,108–29.

[125] Nehru to U Nu, 29 September 1959.

[126] Nehru's note to senior officials in Ministry of External Affairs, 13 September 1959.

[127] 17 March 1959. Lok Sabha Debates, Second Series, Vol. XXVII, pp. 6,670–93.

[128] Press conference at Delhi, 11 September, *National Herald*, 12 September 1959.

would be forced into it; but for this the best preparation was self-reliance and the building of industrial strength which could be reflected in the defence forces. Non-alignment was also indispensable because it enabled Soviet friendship, which was valuable to India both politically and in the form of economic assistance. In reply to Mountbatten's warning against the dangers of an ever-increasing dependence for such assistance on the communist bloc, Nehru pointed out that there could hardly be that danger because India's reliance on other countries was and would be far greater; but such Soviet assistance was not to be spurned.[129] Even more important was the political friendship. His commitment to non-alignment was confirmed by a statement issued on 9 September by Tass which seemed to Nehru very fair, and an unusual statement for the Soviet Government to sponsor.[130] Deploring the border incident, the Soviet Government declined to take sides between China, with whom they had 'unbreakable bonds of fraternal friendship', and India, with whom 'friendly cooperation' was developing successfully.

From statements issued much later by the Soviet Union and China, we can piece together the background of this remarkable statement. The Soviet Government advised China not to develop the dispute into a major clash of arms, while China exerted her utmost to prevent the issue of the statement, which she regarded as favouring India and condemning her.[131] The failure to dissuade the Soviet Government led to what China described as the first exposure of Sino-Soviet differences to the world.[132] Khrushchev later stated his belief that Mao himself was responsible for the trouble with India 'because of some sick fantasy' and wished to drag the Soviet Union into it. When Khrushchev went to Beijing in October, Chen Yi, on behalf of the Chinese leadership, criticized the Tass statement. 'Don't you know', Chen Yi is reported to have said, 'Nehru is nothing but an agent of American imperialism? Don't you know Nehru must be destroyed if the progressive forces in India are to prevail?' Khrushchev's reply that the Soviet Union had a different assessment of Nehru was unacceptable to the Chinese.[133] Corroboration that this was the Chinese view in 1959 has been provided by Zhou himself, who told a British journalist years later that Nehru had been intriguing with the Dalai and Panchen Lamas since 1956 with 'big-power backing' and encouraging them to rebellion.[134] This baseless allegation has at least the advantage that, to all unprejudiced observers, it ends the persistent myth that the entire problem between India and China was a limited territorial dispute inflamed by Nehru's inflexibility. All this was, of

[129] Nehru to Mountbatten, 21 March 1959.

[130] Press conference at Delhi, 11 September, *National Herald*, 12 September 1959.

[131] See statement of Soviet Government, 21 September 1963, and article in *People's Daily* (Beijing), 2 November 1963. J. Gittings, *Survey of the Sino-Soviet Dispute* (Oxford, 1968), pp. 112–15.

[132] *People's Daily*, 27 February 1963, cited in Gittings, *Survey*, p. 111.

[133] *Khrushchev Remembers – the Last Testament* (London, 1974), pp. 306–11.

[134] Interview with Neville Maxwell, *Sunday Times* (London), 19 December 1971.

course, unknown to Nehru at the time, but it justifies the importance he had attached to the Soviet position and the maintenance of non-alignment.

Moreover, Nehru did not envisage any major conflict with China in the foreseeable future. Certainly India would not provoke it. 'We cannot surrender in any sense to Chinese claims or threats. But we also remember that China is our permanent neighbour and to invite trouble from China is wisdom neither in the present nor in the future. Even in the strictest practical sense, that is the only course we can follow.'[135] Nor did he expect large-scale Chinese aggression. The long border he believed to be adequately protected; and though China might, with her enormous population and rapid industrial development, become the strongest power in the world, she was still a long way from such a position.[136]

Perhaps China was still unprepared for an open military clash with India; but she was unwilling to let the situation rest. The agreement signed on 13 September whereby the Soviet Union would double her aid to India would have confirmed, in China's eyes, the belief that the dispute with India was part of the general conflict between the two leading communist countries. It is even possible that the Chinese were thinking of the dispute more in these terms than as a substantial factor in relations with India. Ajoy Ghosh, Secretary of the Communist Party of India, found, on his visit to Beijing in early October, that the Chinese leaders were singularly ignorant of the strength of feeling in India and believed that only a few intellectuals were excited. Mao gave Ghosh to understand that, while China had no territorial ambitions, she could not as a matter of principle give up what she considered to be her rights, especially in the eastern sector.[137]

In the same month, Chinese troops came about forty miles within what India considered to be the boundary in southern Ladakh, and where all checkposts were manned not by the Indian army but by the border police. On the 21st, the Chinese opened fire on an Indian patrol near the Kongka Pass, killing five, severely wounding four, and capturing ten policemen. This incident made clear that Chinese tactics were now to move into such parts of Indian territory as they claimed in the western sector which were not occupied by Indian personnel, and for this purpose to utilize military power. Nehru had no option but to place the entire defence of the border area in the hands of the army. The full answer would have been to push troops right up to and along the whole border, but this would have raised logistic and supply problems and locked up large portions of the army in isolated areas.

These major incursions were naturally resented; 'we cannot', said Nehru,[138] 'allow China to keep a foot on our chest'. But he did not plan retaliatory military action at every point where these intrusions occurred. For even more

135 Nehru's note to Secretary-General, 14 October 1959.

136 Nehru's note to Secretary-General, 14 October, note on talks with General Shaikh of Pakistan, 15 October, and letter to Chief Ministers, 16 October 1959.

137 Nehru's note on his conversation with A. Ghosh, 5 December 1959.

138 Speech at Agra, 10 November, *The Hindu*, 11 November 1959.

important than these sporadic inroads were the larger issues raised by the Chinese action. Nehru was no longer puzzled by the deeper motives of Chinese policy. He was now of the view that the Chinese had a one-track mind, took a one-sided view of their rights and responsibilities, had a vision distorted by their semi-isolation since 1949 and were passing through one of the phases of expansionism which occurred regularly in Chinese history whenever the country was strong and united. No country in the world seemed to care less for peace.[139] But how should India react? It was galling that, at a time when the United States and the Soviet Union were seeking to improve relations and Khrushchev had visited the United States, India's relations with China were deteriorating. Just as the clouds of the cold war were lifting in the West and India could claim some success for a policy she had always urged, she herself, by 'a strange twist of destiny',[140] was drifting closer to hostilities with China. Indeed, this state of affairs was bound to weaken the efforts being made elsewhere to strengthen peace in the world. This was one of those peak moments in history when a plunge had to be taken in some direction which might have powerful and far-reaching effects not only on India but on Asia and even the world. Events were poised on the edge of history, and the issues surrounding the border dispute were so huge, vague, deep-seated, far-reaching and intertwined that one had to think and act with clarity and strength. Working to solve problems by peaceful means had to be combined with full protection to the integrity of India's borders. Despite the provocative attitude of China, in the larger interests, apart from India's own desire for peace and good relations with a powerful neighbour, everything should be done to stop the downhill slide in relations with China. 'This is not because I am enamoured of China, but because I am enamoured of India and of peace.'[141]

The situation, with its tragic paradox of Eisenhower and Khrushchev talking cordially to each other while Nehru and Zhou exchanged long letters detailing their different viewpoints, drove home the importance of India abiding by her commitment to non-alignment. Even from a narrow, selfish viewpoint, the world situation had never, since 1947, been so favourable to India. It was to Nehru ludicrous to think of military alliances in the sense of foreign troops manning Indian checkposts. Even an alliance for assistance in equipment was undesirable and betrayed a weakening mentality. It was best for India to rely on her own ability to produce whatever she required. The risk that she might be involved in a large-scale war before she had the industrial base to wage such a war was one that had to be taken. But if, in a panic, she abandoned non-alignment, which had helped to isolate China, then India was 'doomed morally, spiritually, psychologically, in every way, practically.

139 Nehru to Chief Ministers, 26 October 1959; press conference at Delhi, 5 November, *National Herald*, 6 November 1959; speeches in Lok Sabha, 25 and 27 November 1959, Debates, Second Series, Vol. XXXV, pp. 1,680–708 and 2,185-213 respectively.

140 Nehru to Chief Ministers, 4 November 1959.

141 Nehru to Chief Ministers, 26 October 1959.

Nobody will respect us in the wide world; we will become some kind of camp-follower with no energy and will of our own left.'[142]

The containment of China was a problem common to India, the Soviet Union and the United States, but each had to handle this problem in its own way. China had shown to the Soviet Union that 'socialist' countries could be rivals. In June 1959, by going back on the promise to provide China with knowledge of nuclear technology, the Soviet Union had made what has been described as the decisive break in their relations;[143] and thereafter Khrushchev had repeatedly expressed his sympathy for India.[144] But if India rushed into a military alliance with the United States, the Soviet Union would be obliged to draw closer to China, thereby increasing the chances of a world war. It was far better for India to fight back on her own and seek peaceful settlements where possible so that the Soviet Union remained friendly to her; and this was a policy which suited the United States too. Rather than ostracize China and build up Pakistan, it would have been more appropriate for the United States to have helped India economically and relieved her of the threat from Pakistan so that she could man her northern frontiers effectively without severely truncating the indispensable efforts at economic development.

Nehru, therefore, decided to adhere to his policy of conciliation while keeping his powder dry. He would, as a follower of Gandhi, not compromise on basic issues which, in this case, were the security and territorial integrity of the country; and there was no room for fear. He might, he declared, have a thousand defects, but he was not afraid; so too India might make a thousand mistakes but her hands and feet should not grow cold at the first sign of danger.[145] Fear was the worst possible companion. Rather than resort to adventurist tactics and rush troops to every point on the border, India would rely on building up communications, promoting development in the border areas and increasing industrial strength. If China did meanwhile mount a major invasion, he had been assured by the army commanders that they could meet it adequately and with success. On the border, the terrain was in China's favour but, in case of invasion, the balance of advantage would tilt progressively towards India.[146] He expected Indians, while eschewing futile gestures, not to submit on matters of principle. It was completely and absolutely wrong to think that the Government of India which he directed would be cowed or surrender through fright to China or to any other power 'or a combination of the whole damned world'.[147] The rational course was a middle one between war-mongering and panic. He would, though in no mood of appeasement, continue to seek peaceful settlements and avoid harsh

142 Talk to the Congress Parliamentary Party, 16 November 1959. Tape M–46/C, Parts I and II.

143 D. Wilson, *Mao the People's Emperor* (London, 1979), p. 355.

144 For example, speech in Beijing, 30 September, report to the Supreme Soviet, 31 October, and interview with an Indian correspondent, 7 November 1959.

145 Speeches at Ujjain and Dewas, 11 November, *The Hindu*, 12 November 1959.

146 Nehru to Chief Ministers, 4 November 1959.

147 Talk to the Congress Parliamentary Party, 16 November 1959. Tape M–46/C, Parts I and II.

language and excited behaviour. Vulgarity never strengthened any country or individual.[148]

As part of this effort to avoid injury to larger causes and the sowing of seeds of future conflict Nehru, while rejecting Zhou's proposals for the withdrawal of armed forces by both sides along the whole border since this was disadvantageous to India, suggested the demilitarization of a large area in the western sector, with India withdrawing to the line claimed by China, and Chinese forces falling back to the Indian alignment. In the eastern sector, Longju could be demilitarized.[149] Indeed, he was willing to go even further in the Ladakh area and permit the Chinese Government to utilize the area in Aksai Chin across which they had built a road. Nehru viewed this as a *de facto* concession without damage to Indian sovereignty over that area. However, because of the opposition of Pant, the Home Minister, the offer could not be made.[150]

Even as it stood, the Indian offer was a fair one. It would get Chinese forces out of Indian territory without humiliation and enable negotiations with honour to both sides. So Nehru was hopeful of a positive response from Zhou[151] – that is, of course, if China were serious about a settlement – and of a meeting, after due preparation, of the two Prime Ministers. Even stronger powers such as the Soviet Union and the United States had, in their quarrels with each other or with China, turned away from the ultimate appeal to arms and been satisfied with strongly worded notes of protest. So India would be patient, confident that her case on the traditional boundary alignment was strong, regretful at the slowing down of basic economic programmes necessitated by the need to strengthen the border defences but invigorated by the new sense of national solidarity roused by the aggressive actions of China and hopeful that it would give a new impetus to development which, in itself, especially the drive for industrialization, would lay the foundations for effective defence.[152]

Meantime, the acute tension in relations with China ensured for Eisenhower, visiting Delhi in December, a welcome of such warmth as he could not have anticipated. Even Nehru welcomed him 'at this special hour' as a great man carrying the banner of peace in the world, and large crowds turned up on their own to line the streets and cheer him. At the civic reception the audience was estimated at half a million; many more sought entry and had to be turned away for lack of room. Gazing at this vast concourse, Nehru remarked that India had presented Eisenhower with a priceless gift – a part of her heart.[153]

148 Press conference at Delhi, 5 November, *National Herald*, 7 November 1959.

149 Zhou's letter to Nehru, 7 November, and Nehru's reply, 16 November 1959. White Paper III, pp. 45–57.

150 Nehru to Pant, 15 November 1959.

151 See his talk to the press club at Delhi, 20 November, *The Hindu*, 21 November 1959.

152 Nehru to Chief Ministers, 15 December, and to Marshal Tito, 22 December 1959.

153 Speeches at the World Agriculture Fair, 11 December, and at the civic reception, 13 December 1959. P.I.B.

At their private talks, Eisenhower dissociated himself from the criticism voiced in the United States of India's policy of 'neutrality', appreciated India's desire to keep out of military alliances and said that he would not have it otherwise. He did not think such a policy need come in the way of India and the United States being close friends and expressed a wish to initiate a direct and personal correspondence with Nehru, as he had done to some advantage with Khrushchev. India's Second and Third Plans were discussed and, though economic aid was not mentioned, the necessity to go ahead fast with these Plans was accepted. Nehru suggested the possibility of cooperation in the development of atomic energy, particularly in the establishment of power stations for the production of energy for peaceful purposes. Eisenhower said he had not been aware that India had made such good progress in this field and offered to send some experts to discuss these matters.

At Eisenhower's request, Nehru gave an analysis of the border problem with China and left him with the impression that Nehru was almost bewildered by Chinese aggression and could find no logical reason for it. He showed little rancour or anger but made clear India's determination to resist. Aware that it was primarily to this issue that he owed the spectacular welcome which he had received, Eisenhower was yet tactful enough not to expatiate on it and contented himself with the expression of the hope that the problem would be settled peacefully. He spoke more fully about Pakistan. He had just visited Ayub and had been considerably impressed. Ayub had spoken with warmth about Kashmir and rejected any settlement on the basis of the cease-fire line. Reporting this, Eisenhower wondered about the feasibility of India and Pakistan acting together against Chinese aggression. Nehru ruled this out; all that India desired was that Pakistan should refrain from stabbing her in the back if she were involved in major trouble with China. Eisenhower assured him that, in case of any such misbehaviour, the United States would come down heavily against Pakistan, and added that in fact Pakistan could make no very effective use of the military assistance provided by the United States as she had not been supplied with much ammunition. Nehru remarked that the real problem about Pakistan was internal weakness. Neither the Soviet Union nor China was likely to attack Pakistan, but internal changes might well lead to a pro-communist regime and facilitate the occupation by China of bits of Pakistani territory. India could take no risks about such a possibility, and this aspect of the Kashmir problem could not be ignored. This was, for Nehru, an odd and unexpected argument, but it doubtless went down well with Eisenhower. He instructed the American Ambassador in Karachi to urge Ayub to respond to India's repeated offers of a 'no-war' declaration. Nehru had told Eisenhower that India would act unilaterally on such a commitment and would not attack Pakistan but only defend herself if attacked; and Eisenhower wished Pakistan to give a similar undertaking, either in a joint statement with India or on her own, that all problems between the two countries would be settled by negotiation and without resort to force or war.[154]

[154] Nehru's two notes on talks with Eisenhower, 17 and 18 December 1959; Nehru to H. J. Bhabha, 13 December 1959, File 17(278)/57–60–P.M.S., Vol. 1, 36A; D. D. Eisenhower, *Waging Peace* (London, 1966), pp. 501, 503–4.

5

Towards Cooperative Farming

ONE

Despite the prestige he commanded in his own country and in the world, there was, in 1958, no complacency in Nehru's thinking. The responsibilities of office for over ten years, added to all the other work which he had taken on, would have crippled any normal person. Nehru's health stood the strain surprisingly well; but his mind was, to his own knowledge, showing signs of staleness and fatigue. He had virtually given up all writing other than notes and official letters, he hardly read a book through any more and he had no time to sit back and consider large issues. 'I sometimes begin to fear that, because of my manifold activities, my own mental growth is stopping and the capacity for creative thinking gradually disappearing.'[1] With new problems emerging in a changing world, he himself seemed stuck in old grooves of thought; and this made him wonder if he was doing justice to himself or to his work.[2] Yet he would probably have slogged on uncomplainingly with the heavy routine in which he had strapped himself but for two successive emotional shocks within days of each other, caused by the deprivation of the services of two of his senior colleagues. The death of Maulana Azad, who had fought by his side in the Congress for nearly forty years, came a week after what was, in a sense, even severer, because avoidable, blow, the resignation of the Finance Minister, T.T. Krishnamachari. Feroze Gandhi, son-in-law of the Prime Minister and a backbench conscience of the Congress Party, mentioned to the Minister rumours of dubious investments made by the nationalized Life Insurance Corporation in order to assist a businessman whose record was not clean. Dismissed by Krishnamachari with scornful hauteur, Gandhi raised the matter in Parliament; and the Government agreed to a public inquiry by a judge. The report of the judge implicated the Minister and several senior officials. Nehru felt that there had been carelessness but no *malafides*, regretted the very fact of an inquiry and later even said privately that if he had been

[1] To V.N. Sharma, 14 April 1958.

[2] See Nehru to Chief Ministers, 25 March, and to Tara Singh, 26 May 1958.

present that day in Parliament he would not have allowed it.[3] This was one of the occasions when Nehru's stubborn loyalty to his friends weakened his sense of fairness. He recognized that on the basis of the report, Krishnamachari would have to accept responsibility and resign; but he felt the loss severely. Krishnamachari's acid tongue had made him many enemies and even Nehru had not always found him an easy colleague; but he had proved an imaginative Finance Minister who had introduced a wealth tax and a short-lived expenditure tax and generally geared the economy to the rigours of planning.

So it was an internally battered Nehru who announced to the Congress Party that he needed a spell as a private citizen. Never a leader who cared very much for leadership, he now felt he 'was not in tune with many things, sometimes not in tune with the party but that is a small matter, but not in tune with the country, not in tune with the organization.' This thought was making him rather querulous, irritated with problems and so not coming to grips with them. The atmosphere in the country too he had begun to find suffocating; there was a growing loss of the sense of mission which had been present in the first years of freedom and an increasing concern with jobs and elections.[4] But he left the final decision to the party.[5] He did not insist on resignation and was probably considering only a short break. Yet, although there was no sharp crisis at this time anywhere in the world and even some hope of progress towards disarmament, Nehru's absence, however temporary, was apparently unthinkable to the leaders of other countries. It must have been gratifying to Nehru that, apart from pressure of opinion in India, the Governments of both the United States and the Soviet Union seemed to regard his presence in office as indispensable. Eisenhower appealed to him not to go too far away or for too long a time. There were faint indications that the conflict between the Soviet Union and the Western countries might be sufficiently moderated to become tolerable; and it also seemed possible that some of the problems between India and Pakistan might be soluble. 'Under all these circumstances it would indeed be a misfortune perhaps for all of us if at what may prove to be a critical formative period your own influence was not actively present over any really protractive period.'[6] These sentiments were echoed unknowingly a few days later by Khrushchev. He expressed his delight at Nehru's decision not to resign, for that would have been a great blow not only to India but to all the forces fighting for peace and friendship among the peoples of the world. 'Your name is indissolubly linked with the successes which independent India, playing an ever-growing part in international affairs, has achieved on her difficult but glorious path of development.'[7]

[3] M.C. Setalvad, *My Life, Law and Other Things* (Bombay, 1971), pp. 270–1. Setalvad, as the Attorney-General, assisted the judge in the inquiry.

[4] Addresses to the Congress Parliamentary Party, 1 and 3 May 1958, Tape M-33/C, Parts I and II; press conference at Delhi, 4 June, *National Herald*, 5 June 1958.

[5] Nehru's statement at annual general meeting of Congress Party in Parliament, 29 April 1958.

[6] Eisenhower to Nehru, 1 May 1958.

[7] Khrushchev to Nehru, 8 May 1958.

Indeed, Nehru had planned a few weeks, if not months, away from office to ponder not only India's problems but international affairs. He had hoped that 'a slow pilgrimage' to a few places in India, meeting friends and thinking over issues without pressures, would help even in the wider context, in suggesting new ways of breaking up the petrification of cold war attitudes.[8] But the protests of Eisenhower and Khrushchev, which sounded more than stylized politeness, alongside the resistance of the Congress Party, led him to narrow his holiday to a few weeks in Manali, in the Himalayan foothills. From there, in order to get away from his normal work and as far as possible from human beings, he had thought of crossing the Rohtang Pass, at about 13,600 feet, into Lahaul and Spiti and spending a fortnight among the glaciers. This part of the trek had to be abandoned as he would have been out of touch with Delhi; but the Rohtang Pass he was determined to reach despite a last-minute injunction from his doctor in London, Sir Horace Evans. He went up, mostly on horseback, walked on the top of the pass for one or two miles and came down on foot. For a man aged sixty-eight, it was a considerable achievement.

TWO

The problems besetting India which Nehru wished to consider after recuperating mentally were to him fundamental. 'How do we stand in our minds and spirit, how far do we adhere to the basic principles that give strength to our people?'[9] The deterioration in public life, in the Congress as well as in other parties and groups, was matched by growing disruptive tendencies, rooted in province, religion, caste and language. People intrinsically decent were forgetting major issues and getting excited over minor matters and thereby harming the country's unity, strength and progress. There was need for new thinking, in terms not of slogans and dogmas but of a calculated idealism related to both modern conditions and human values. It was not necessary for all Indians to think alike; indeed it would be unfortunate if they did. But they should try to share some broad objectives and methods and, within that wide framework, seek to persuade each other if they differed on specific issues.[10]

However, the break in Nehru's routine was too short for any deep and detailed consideration of such vital questions; and the immediate issues were too pressing to permit of their being set aside for a while. The shortage of foreign exchange again assumed a serious aspect. The recession in the United States threatened a substantial decline in India's earnings from exports, the payments to be made against outstanding commitments increased and there

[8] Nehru to Chief Ministers, 18 May 1958.

[9] Ibid.

[10] Nehru to Chief Ministers, 25 March, and to Tara Singh, 26 May 1958.

was a delay in the receipt of assistance from the United States. An extra effort was clearly required to reduce expenditure involving foreign exchange and to increase exports. Unprecedented drought and floods in three successive years compelled the import of foodgrains. As part of the immediate programme to reduce this import, Nehru called on the people to substitute wheat for rice. Rather than depend on charity, Indians should accustom themselves to a varied diet. But this was a marginal remedy. A basically sound economy was threatened with a total breakdown and, believing that the failure to utilize available resources was due to a lack of will, Nehru considered, apart from efforts to give greater vitality to community development and to make the peasants self-reliant, the adoption of Gunnar Myrdal's suggestion of compulsory social service for young men and women.[11] This would create, especially among urban youth and graduates, both a psychology of work and a sense of community. 'I feel we have got into certain grooves and we cannot get out of them. The steps we take are right enough to meet a certain situation but we stop at the fringe of the problem. We seem to accept certain present-day conditions as being axiomatic.'[12] But real addition to production could come only from basic social changes in the population which gave them a feeling of reliance and dynamism.

Little came of these intentions to mobilize the youth and galvanize the peasantry; and no more than administrative measures were taken to deal with the food crisis. Nehru tried to shake up the food departments both at the centre and in the states and to have clear targets laid down for the *rabi* crop which was due in six months.[13] The only immediate measure of official intervention that Nehru decided upon was to make trade in foodgrains the monopoly of the state. This was linked with the promotion of village cooperatives; but till the latter became numerous and viable, the Government were obliged to appoint the existing traders as their licensed agents – an unavoidable step but self-defeating if careful supervision were lacking.

With heavy rains and floods hindering the movement of grain to the states in need, prices rose; and the result was a considerable increase in profiteering. The situation was particularly grave in Uttar Pradesh, where the opposition parties threatened to break into the warehouses and distribute the grain. To avoid such confrontation, Nehru treated the food crisis as a non-party matter and sought to work in cooperation with the opposition. He also directed Congress workers to visit food shops and ensure that exorbitant prices were not being demanded.

> More and more we become supine and expect the gods to help us or some law to come to our rescue. I am sure we could have dealt with the situation better as a rebellious Congress in the old days than we can today

[11] Cabinet minutes, 4 and 5 June, and 30 July 1958.
[12] To A.P. Jain, Food Minister, 24 July 1958.
[13] To A.P. Jain, 6 July and 6 August 1958; to Chief Ministers, 31 July 1958.

> with all the machinery of government . . . I wish I was a district magistrate or just the president of the Congress committee in a district so that I could function as I think people ought to function. Unfortunately I am prime minister which in such matters is rather a helpless position.

Rapid thinking and action would not only secure quick results but help to change the outlook of the people by showing that there was still life in the Government. Nothing was so bad for a Government or for an organization as to give the public the impression of slow action or no action at all.[14]

So, while with determined effort, aided by foreign loans and credits, there were fair prospects of India pulling through the crisis, the effort was not always forthcoming and much aid from abroad had to be spent on food imports and freight charges. 'The basic fact, of course, remains, and we shall have to live a half-life for the next year or two at least till we turn the corner. I am sure we will turn the corner but what happens in between is anybody's guess.'[15]

THREE

Despite these pressures of lack of foreign exchange and shortage of foodgrains, Nehru refused to lower the revised estimates of the Second Plan of Rs 4,500 crores. He ignored the warning that the Government were likely to fall short of this sum by Rs 200 crores because to him planning was more than a matter of figures and projects. India was rich in resources and manpower and as large an element as possible of this manpower should be yoked to resources. Much could be achieved in this matter without additional expenditure. Foreign exchange was undoubtedly an extraneous restraint but its importance should not be exaggerated. Nehru had bravely proclaimed that India would not be deflected from her policies by the need for foreign aid;[16] and he saw no great hardship in this, for internal resources could be exploited fully so as to prevent shrinkage of development. There was a minimum rate of growth in regard to which there could be no choice; and to achieve this risks, if necessary, should be taken, for to remain static was the greatest and most dangerous risk. An underdeveloped country with a rapidly growing population could not afford to slow down but had to plan continuously and well ahead if it were to break out of the cage of an arrested economy and ensure self-generating growth.

Nehru believed that by the summer of 1958 India was gradually crossing the threshold in planning. Though the Third Plan was still over two years away, the approach had even now to be clearly defined and production formulated and controlled in the right direction and at the right pace so that,

[14] Nehru to Sampurnand, Chief Minister of Uttar Pradesh, 28 August 1958.
[15] Nehru to Vijayalakshmi, 1 September 1958.
[16] Speech at the Congress session, 19 January, *The Hindu*, 20 January 1958.

by the end of the Third Plan, India would have crossed 'that dreadful barrier which separates an underdeveloped country from a developing country, developing through its own resources'.[17] One might not go very fast, but the direction should be clear and there should be no reverse process. Merely to make lists of schemes and add up the cost without formulating basic policies was not planning for socialism or even for expansive capitalism. India was a pioneer, setting out on her own path, which Nehru and his colleagues thought was best suited to the Indian situation. The economy, though said to be geared to socialism, was far less under official guidance and direction than even that of the United States and obviously very far from the Soviet system.[18] But the danger was that India, wavering between capitalism and socialism, might follow neither path with assurance. 'I do not myself see where socialism comes in the present policies that we are pursuing. It is true that we have some major industries in the public sector. That is hardly socialism.'[19]

For the leap 'across this mighty moat of poverty'[20] and the creation of a self-generating economy, equal emphasis would obviously have to be given to the expansion of heavy industries, the increase of agricultural production and rural development. The purpose of planning was controlled growth, balances in agriculture and in industry, and between production, consumption and purchasing power – all maintained in equilibrium on an ever-rising spiral.[21]

Nehru was now more aware than he had been in earlier years of a possible 'disease of gigantism'.[22] He who, at the end of 1956, surveying the large Bhakra-Nangal dam had whispered to himself, 'These are the new temples of India where I worship',[23] confessed nearly two years later that he doubted very much if the Government would have initiated such a project if it came before them at this time. Such a dam was exceedingly expensive, involved a considerable amount of foreign exchange and took a long time to be completed. All that India had gained from it was electric power and a little irrigation.[24] With China's example in mind, he now saw the advantages of small blast furnaces and of rural electrification based on little power stations driven by mountain streams. But such ventures, while yielding quicker returns than multi-purpose projects, did not deflect from the importance of heavy industry. Total industrialization would only come when millions of units of small industries were functioning in different parts of the country; but, in the first phase, priority had to be given to production of steel and power and stress placed on machine-making plants or 'parent machines' rather than on consumer goods industries. Building steel plants was much more

17 12 February 1959. Rajya Sabha Debates, Vol. 24, pp. 546–62.

18 J.K. Galbraith. 'Rival Economic Theories in India', *Foreign Affairs*, July 1958.

19 Nehru to Deputy Chairman, Planning Commission, 12 November 1958.

20 Speech at the A.I.C.C., 9 January, *The Hindu*, 10 January 1959.

21 Address to the Federation of Indian Chambers of Commerce and Industry, 7 March, *The Hindu*, 8 March 1959.

22 Speech to the Central Board of Irrigation, 17 November, *The Hindu*, 18 November 1958.

23 Report in *The Hindu*, 1 January 1957.

24 To S. Saxena, 1 September 1958.

important for socialism than anything else.[25] Even though it would take time for results in this sphere to show, there should be a sense of urgency. He was satisfied with the working of the public sector, which now seemed to him to have proved 'infinitely superior' to the private sector in efficiency and general outlook;[26] and he wanted it both to expand and to intensify rapidly. To move forward slowly meant that India would never catch up and her progress would be countered by such factors as growing numbers and heavy unemployment. A decisive stage had been reached with the production of pig iron at the steel plants at Rourkela and Bhilai, and now India should think of relying less on foreign consultants and technological assistance and speed up the training of Indian personnel to do the work at every level themselves. This might cost more and take longer, but in the long run it was sounder. It hurt Nehru that even for project reports they had to rely on foreigners, so that experts from the United States could tell him, with a measure of contempt, that it would take India over twenty years to build a big plant and at the moment, for all her industrial advance, she could not even produce a pin. For training Indians, the Soviet Union would be more helpful than the United States, whose private firms would naturally be concerned with their own interests. Hereafter, except for the occasional individual expert, India should develop greater self-reliance in industrial development. In this respect, the private sector in India could also be encouraged in preference to resort to foreign agencies.[27]

A new and encouraging development in the process of industrialization was the prospecting for oil. On receiving reports in March 1956 that the possibility of locating large supplies of oil in and around India was good, Nehru was eager to go ahead as fast as possible with exploration and exploitation.[28] The Oil and Natural Gas Commission, set up in 1956, began to train young Indian engineers with Soviet assistance; and the Soviet experts, who were employed for drilling and exploration, were invited to provide details about setting up a refinery.[29] The royalties and profits collected by the private foreign companies Nehru regarded as pure loot and wished the Cabinet to consider how this could be reduced, if not stopped.[30] The criticism in the West that India was relying too heavily on Soviet assistance in this matter did not worry Nehru. Soviet technology was highly developed and Nehru was confident that, in three or four years, India would enhance greatly her oil resources and save much in foreign exchange.[31] So he sought an integrated perspective of plans for exploration and development

25 Address (in Hindi) to the Congress Parliamentary Party, 24 February 1959. Tape M-41/C, Part I.

26 Address to the Indian Institute of Public Administration, Delhi, 25 April, *The Hindu*, 26 April 1959.

27 To Swaran Singh, Minister for Steel, 3 May, and to Lal Bahadur, Commerce Minister, 20 May 1959.

28 To K.D. Malaviya, Minister in Charge of Oil, 21 March 1956.

29 Ibid., 9 May 1956.

30 To Swaran Singh, 6 June 1957.

31 Nehru's note, 2 August 1958.

and assured the ministry concerned that, if success could be shown even at one place, there would be no difficulty about funds from the Planning Commission.[32]

The first piece of good news was the discovery in 1958 of oil in Cambay on the west coast. It was decided that further exploitation would be the responsibility of the state, with Soviet experts continuing the work, especially as training was being given to a large number of Indians, as against the private companies from the Western countries with their levy of huge royalties. On the other hand, India could not ignore the need for capital, which these companies could provide, for large-scale exploration. So Nehru assured Mountbatten, who wrote to recommend British oil companies, that private enterprise would not be debarred if the terms were satisfactory. The fact that Soviet cooperation had proved successful might lead these companies to offer India better terms; but – as Nehru told Morarji Desai but not Mountbatten – it was unlikely and, even if they did, he was not sure that it would be wise to conclude agreements with them.[33] But, a few months later, Nehru was obliged to change his mind. As oil resources had to be developed rapidly and without detriment to other parts of the programme for development, the Government were obliged, while reserving the most favourable areas for themselves, to invite foreign companies to explore other areas at their own cost and risk. This would ensure quick and widespread exploration even if it conceded large profits to foreign firms if they were successful.[34]

FOUR

Especially in comparison with achievement in industry, there was in agriculture a sense of stagnation. The yield per acre was uneven in various parts of India and, taken overall, was extremely low – almost the lowest in the world. Traditional practices of cultivation had hardly changed and very little use was made of fertilizers. The trends indicated by the fall in the annual production of foodgrains by 6·7 million tons and the rise in population by about five millions every year had clearly to be reversed. Intensive cultivation to enable not only self-sufficiency but a surplus was crucial if India were to progress and the Plan have any life in it.[35] Scientific, as well as mechanized, agriculture had to be promoted and attention given to providing better ploughs, seeds and manure rather than tractors and to extending credit and market facilities. 'If I have to say in one word what is wrong with agriculture in India, I would say it is the complete lack of anything that might be called

32 To K.D. Malaviya, 19 August 1958.
33 Nehru to Morarji Desai, 18 March, and to Mountbatten, 21 March 1959.
34 Nehru to K.D. Malaviya, 22 July 1959.
35 Nehru's speech at the fourth National Convention of Farmers, New Delhi, 15 March, *The Hindu*, 16 March 1958.

scientific agriculture.'[36] But India was primarily a land of small holdings and this stood in the way of better utilization of resources and techniques. Despite official decisions at every level, the average cultivator with a small holding seemed to have become less self-reliant than ever before. Nehru's mind reverted repeatedly to cooperative farming, with the peasant owning his small holding but working with his neighbours for purposes of production. Indeed, given that both the other alternatives, of large estates in the hands of landlords and collectivization by the state, were now ruled out by him on principle, the only solution, midway between individualism and expropriation, was cooperative farming. Small cooperatives, run by the villagers themselves, would increase production and help in securing reasonable prices for the produce, strengthen the self-reliance of the peasantry and provide the momentum for development. Nehru even suggested that, to encourage farmers to step out of the ruts of old thinking, Ministers and officials might provide evidence of their own earnestness by working in the fields for a while. 'If we have to shake up the millions of agriculturists, we have first to shake up ourselves.'[37] Nehru was obviously influenced by the Chinese example of awakening the latent powers of the people, although he did not contemplate farm labour for urban folk as a form of punishment and rejected the element of compulsion involved at this time in Chinese communes. To discipline the whole country as in a military camp could never be to him the right way for India.[38]

There were already, by 1959, 1,357 joint farming societies in various parts of the country; and their multiplication seemed the obvious and the appropriate solution in the Indian context. So the Congress, which had been committed to cooperative farming on principle for many years, resolved, at its session at Nagpur in January 1959, at Nehru's bidding, to foster, over the next three years, cooperatives for servicing agriculture in every village as a prelude to joint farming. There should be about 400,000 such cooperatives for the 550,000 villages in the country. These service cooperatives, as far as possible non-official and administered by the *panchayats*, would provide, as of old, credit to the cultivators and, in addition, assist them with seeds, fertilizers, and even, if need be, small tractors and help them to sell their produce.

The resolution sounded unambitious and businesslike, but its implementation would obviously require courage, hard work and a revolutionary mind.[39] Cooperation was at once an economic doctrine, a higher form of social organization, a democratic process and an attitude to life. There would be no uniform pattern for these cooperatives and the state should do no more than train personnel in cooperative management. Conversion of cooperatives into

[36] Speech at seminar on planning, Ootacamund, 30 May 1959. A.I.C.C. papers, Box 312, File G36 of 1959.

[37] Nehru to Chief Ministers, 6 September 1958.

[38] Speech at Bhopal, 1 November, *National Herald*, 2 November 1958.

[39] Nehru at the A.I.C.C., Nagpur, 9 January, *The Hindu*, 10 January 1959.

official organizations was a waste of time and of national resources; 'our cooperatives must be run by villagers, ignorant villagers, foolish villagers, knavish villagers, scoundrelly villagers'.[40] Membership would be voluntary in the cooperative village farms when they came into existence; and, even after joining, members would continue to retain their individual proprietary rights. Provision would also be made for them to opt out of the farms under certain circumstances if they so wished. There would be no rigid rules, and service cooperatives would decide many points for themselves; but generally they would be expected to work closely with the village *panchayats*. In the joint farms, peasants should be discouraged from selling land to outsiders and, except in the case of minors and widows, would be expected to till their own lands. Members would be paid in accordance with their share of the land and their labour.

In enhancing agricultural production and moving towards joint cooperative farming, land reforms were obviously crucial; yet little had been done to implement them. In 1954–5, less than 10 per cent of rural households owned more than half of the land; on the other hand, 25 per cent of the households owned no land and another 25 per cent had little more than 1 per cent of the total land.[41] Nehru was aware of this failure to carry out the commitment to transfer land to the tillers. 'Indeed it has become rather a joke in some foreign countries when they refer to land reforms in India. We have talked tall and done little.'[42] So the Congress called on state Governments to enact legislation on this subject by the end of 1959. Ceilings on land holdings and not on incomes should be the first step towards the ultimate objectives of the elimination of all intermediaries in land tenure and the establishment of separate ownership with joint cultivation under the supervision of the village cooperative. But Nehru gave greater importance to relieving the pressure on the land by providing industrial employment and to increasing the yield by better techniques than to distribution of land and tenancy reforms.[43]

Nehru believed that, with the enforcement of ceilings on landholdings, recognition of the disadvantages of minuscule plots and the successful working of such cooperative farms as existed, the attractions of joint farming would become increasingly manifest. Small holdings meant semi-starvation at the best of times and disaster when the harvest was poor, while cooperative farming greatly increased the yield. The attention of the cultivators should be drawn to these facts. 'I shall go from field to field and peasant to peasant begging them to agree to it. Knowing that (if) they do not agree, I cannot put it into operation.'[44]

So decentralization, diminution of bureaucratic control, lack of compulsion and voluntary collaboration would be the distinctive marks of the Indian

40 Address to the Congress Parliamentary Party, 28 August 1958. Tape M-36/C, Part I.

41 R. Sau, *India's Economic Development* (Calcutta, 1981), p. 9.

42 Nehru to H.K. Mahtab, 20 December 1958.

43 Speech at the A.I.C.C., Nagpur, 9 January 1959, A.I.R. tapes.

44 19 February 1959. Lok Sabha Debates, Second Series, Vol. 25, pp. 1,930–59.

model of socialism in the countryside. An agrarian economy of small farms organized cooperatively on a village basis seemed the ideal solution. It would change gradually the whole social fabric of the countryside, strengthen democratic tendencies, raise the yield, provide a 'glimpse of socialism', improve the quality of the individual and lift the peasantry as a whole to a higher level of life. If one of the basic problems of the modern world was to balance the inevitable tendency to centralization with the individual freedom and initiative which came from decentralization, the cooperative method offered a proper combination of the two. Closer contact, social cohesion and mutual obligation would be its essential characteristics. Obviously every country should evolve its own policies to fit in with its own conditions, as the best of theoretical approaches might not fit in with the objective situation; and the set of ideas elaborated in the Plans and the Nagpur resolutions appeared to offer the right way for India to mobilize the people for building a socialist society. One should change with the times and not be the prisoners of phrases. Socialism for India was not just an emotional commitment or an ideological preference; it was the only scientific way of solving social problems, the pragmatic means of achieving quickly higher standards of living for all.[45] A capitalist programme for progress was theoretically possible however undesirable ethically; but, apart from the inequities inseparable from capitalism, it would take very long, during which time a variety of upheavals could occur. So there was no alternative in India to the socialist approach if one were to bring about as rapidly as possible the industrial revolution, increase technological knowledge and prepare for the atomic revolution.[46] To reject it was to condemn the people and peasantry of India to perpetual poverty.[47] Such material progress could also be achieved without divorce from values if the people absorbed the right ideals and acted up to them. India had thought a great deal about these values through hundreds and thousands of years and it would be a misfortune if she forgot them in the pursuit of material well-being or if, as she grew in strength and prosperity, arrogance crept in.[48]

Nehru urged the Chief Ministers to act promptly and the Congress Party to give them full support. After the abolition of the *zamindari* system and the commitment to a socialist pattern of society, this was the third great step which the party had taken; and on its successful implementation depended the party's own future. It was a matter of life and death for the Congress because, if it failed this time, the opposition parties would get the better of it and the party would never be able to raise its head again. It might drag on for years but would not flourish nor lead the country towards progress. At least 90 to 95 per cent of the people were in favour of the approach in the Nagpur resolutions and

45 Speech at the A.I.C.C., Hyderabad, 24 October, *The Hindu*, 25 October 1958.

46 Speeches at the A.I.C.C., Nagpur, 9 January, *The Hindu*, 10 January 1959, and in the Lok Sabha, 28 March and 11 April 1959, Debates, Second Series, Vol. 28, pp. 8,394–413 and Vol. 29, pp. 11, 117–27 respectively.

47 Speech at Madurai, 15 April, *Indian Express*, 16 April 1959.

48 Nehru to B. Hollowood, editor of *Punch*, 22 May 1959.

the Congress should set out to reach that vast majority rather than wait on events. The best preparation for anything was to do it. Indians had a habit of discussing such matters at inordinate length till staleness set in and the opportunity of creating a psychological situation in favour of the programme was lost.[49] Advance to socialism under a democratic system need not necessarily be slow, for the pace of progress depended ultimately on the quality of a people and their capacity for work. But, while Nehru was eager that service cooperatives should be set up rapidly, he did not wish joint farms to be established in a hurry. These presumed a large number of trained workers; and priority should be given to the creation of these cadres and the selection of villages where conditions were favourable.[50] Also, although Nehru felt that the models of other countries could not be adopted wholesale by India, he recognized that foreign experience could be utilized profitably and, despite basic differences with Israel, he sent some experts to that country to study the working of the cooperative movement.[51]

The Prime Minister's efforts to whip up enthusiasm and effort in support of the Nagpur resolutions evoked scant response.

> We are going through a bad patch in India. It is probably not so bad as people imagine, and there are certainly many bright spots. Nevertheless, it is true that we have to face at the same time many difficulties. The worst difficulty of all is the general sense of depression among our people.[52]

But the intense public feeling generated by the border crisis in the second half of 1959 had the advantage that it could be utilized to speed up nation-building activities. Merely to recruit an additional 250,000 men to the armed services was not enough. The needs of defence in themselves stressed the importance of rapid industrialization. The prospect of long-continuing danger made the future even more crucial than the present. Military strength was only a part of defence; behind it, and as important, were the industry, the general economy and the morale in the country.[53]

Nehru wished the administrative procedures to be revised so as to expedite implementation of economic programmes. Could a gigantic economic revolution, such as India planned, be carried through by the Indian political system, with its 'almost Victorian mildness' and a British-style administration? Walter Lippmann, at this time on a visit to India, doubted it: 'For India does not have all the time in the world to solve its basic problems by education of its

49 Address (in Hindi) to the Congress Parliamentary Party, 24 February 1959, Tape M-41/C, Part I; Nehru to Chief Ministers, 21 March 1959.

50 Nehru to Chief Ministers, 2 July 1959.

51 To A.P. Jain, Food Minister, 21 May, and to S.K. Dey, Minister for Community Development, 2 July 1959. Files 31(30)/56-61-P.M.S., Vol. II, 228A and 17(263)/57–59-P.M.S., 111A respectively.

52 Nehru to Vijayalakshmi, 25 August 1959.

53 Address to the Congress Parliamentary Party, 16 November 1959. Tapes 46/C, Parts I and II.

masses and by persuasion. The essential economic problem must be solved within a few years, or it may well become insoluble.' Though Nehru believed this to be a pessimistic conclusion, he saw no reason why, while retaining the characteristics of a parliamentary democracy, methods of work should not be speeded up. He was more inclined to agree with another experienced American observer, Max Millikan, that India should try to do too much rather than too little; if a number of economic projects were taken up simultaneously the total result might very well be greater than from each individually taken by itself.[54] India was making progress in heavy and small industry, in the decentralization and mechanization of agriculture, in even the spread of education. While he would have liked to have seen more extensive programmes in child welfare and in compulsory education at the primary level, it was still encouraging to have over forty million students in schools and colleges and to observe the growing spread of technical training. But in every sphere of the economy, there was need for a greater momentum, the multiplication of small schemes rather than over-reliance on large profits, and the increasing utilization of manpower. The community development programme had also lost its original drive and become increasingly an official organization; and here too there was need for fresh initiative and impetus.

FIVE

These efforts on Nehru's part to change the face of Indian agriculture precipitated the formation of the Swatantra Party. Though Nehru and Rajagopalachari had, since 1954, been drifting apart on various issues, Rajagopalachari had declined to assume the leadership of the conservative elements in India and organize them into a party of opposition, till the resolutions of the Congress at Nagpur in January 1959 on cooperative farming, which formed, according to Rajagopalachari himself, the proverbial last straw.[55] Making no effort to conceal opposition to Nehru at a personal level, Rajagopalachari and other right-wing critics contended that the Prime Minister was in favour of compulsion and the formation of communes as in communist countries. Such a travesty of his views Nehru could only believe had been put out either by persons 'wholly and totally' lacking in intelligence or by 'deliberate falsifiers'[56] – Nehru's euphemism for liars. 'It is slightly irritating, for everybody to become a Pope without knowing what the Catholic religion is.'[57] For Nehru was not advocating collectivization and was saying nothing more than what the Congress had been commending in all its

[54] Nehru to Chief Ministers, 15 December 1959.
[55] H.L. Erdman, *The Swatantra Party and Indian Conservatism* (Cambridge, 1967), pp. 68–9 and 74.
[56] Address to the Congress Parliamentary Party, 14 March 1959. Tape 41/C, Part II.
[57] Nehru at press conference in Delhi, 7 February, *National Herald*, 8 February 1959.

election manifestos since 1945. His strong advocacy of cooperative farming was not inspired by Marxist ideology but had root in his conviction that to do nothing was to entrench backwardness.

> I agree with passion [with the Nagpur resolutions] because I agree in the progress of India with passion. I am not a politician out for a job. I am a man to do something in India, to change India within the few years left to me, to change the peasant in India . . . I may go wrong, as I do often, but even if I go wrong, it is, I hope, in my desire to reach a certain goal.

He regretted that Rajagopalachari, in his bitter and personal criticisms, was being less than charitable.[58] Rajagopalachari made no public comment but replied with a private letter replete with pious sentiments: 'I envy your restraint. I am grateful for your affection. I trust I shall always deserve it.'[59]

Nehru claimed that cooperative farming was not a party programme but as near an approach to a national effort as was possible on such a matter. But the landed elements did have some cause for alarm for, if the Nagpur resolutions on land ceilings and joint farming were seriously implemented, the rich landlords stood to lose some land and to have the remainder pooled. To this extent the way could have been opened for radical social and economic change. So the opponents of the Nagpur resolutions condemned Nehru for intending to bring red ruin and civil war to India, and then widened the campaign into a general assault on the domestic and foreign policies of the Government and on Nehru in particular. Though, faced with the facts of economic life, terms like capitalism and socialism had by now for Nehru lost their ideological edge, the conservative critics exploited them to belabour his pragmatic policies. They were as passionate in denunciation as Nehru in advocacy; but it was, Nehru said, a different kind of passion, that of a vested interest which was afraid.[60] The opposition to the Nagpur resolutions was to Nehru a form of class conflict.[61] He himself had an aversion to increasing class conflict, as he believed the Communist Party was eager to do;[62] but when there was a clash of class interests, he had no doubt as to which side the Government and the Congress should support. Indeed, the intense opposition to cooperative farming was, according to Nehru, born of the sudden realization that the Congress, so long thought to be a static, sleeping body with no ideas left and with no strength except to organize elections, was still alive and kicking.[63]

Rajagopalachari's conduct at this time seemed to bear out all of Nehru's suspicions. He charged Nehru with lack of good faith,[64] referred to him

[58] Ibid.

[59] C. Rajagopalachari to Nehru, 8 February 1959.

[60] Speech at session of the Federation of Indian Chambers of Commerce and Industry, 7 March, *The Hindu*, 8 March 1959.

[61] Address (in Hindi) to the Congress Parliamentary Party, 24 February 1959. Tape 41/C, Part I.

[62] Speech at Bombay, 3 February, *The Hindu*, 4 February 1958.

[63] Address to the Congress Parliamentary Party, 14 March 1959. Tape M-41/C, Part II.

[64] Speech at Madras, 14 April, *The Hindu*, 16 April 1959.

publicly as a 'megalomaniac'[65] and decided to form the Swatantra Party as the party of conservatism and free enterprise. Nehru, in contrast, sought to maintain a serious debate at an impersonal level. He welcomed the formation of the new party as helping to lift the fog over the mind of the Congress and likely to enliven Indian politics. He suggested that the Swatantra Party should draw up a constructive programme instead of confining itself to criticism of the Congress and decried its phantom fears. 'I fear nobody. I am not a religious man. I do not fear even God. I cannot understand this mentality of fear.'[66] Nehru also laughed at what had by now become irreconcilable differences with Rajagopalachari. 'He likes the Old Testament. I like the New Testament.'[67] When one of the leaders of the new party described Nehru as having been elected by the illiterate people of India, he retorted that to object to democracy on the ground that the electors were not wise or sensible enough to exercise their franchise correctly was the beginning of a fascist approach and an attempt to impose decisions on the people. Imposition was the word in his lexicon which he most detested. But generally he treated the Swatantra Party and its leaders with good-humoured contempt. Rajagopalachari appeared to be motivated by 'solidified anger' and none of the others had put forward any positive proposals. The Swatantra Party was to Nehru not a serious opposition but a diversion, full of noise but with no content, avoiding sustained argument and making God a senior partner, a throw-back with no future in India. Indeed, it was frightened of the future and drew inspiration from the ghosts of past ages.[68]

The intensification of Chinese activities on the border from the autumn of 1959 provided the Swatantra Party with fresh opportunities to attack the Government and the Prime Minister. Rajagopalachari was in the forefront of this campaign 'with sword and shield and lance. It is really sad that he should have descended in many ways as he has done.'[69] Piqued by the Swatantra Party's opposition to heavy industry at a time when, with the development of Chinese hostility, it was to Nehru more than ever necessary to build up a strong economy, the Prime Minister lashed out at 'the utter bankruptcy of thought' of 'an utterly worthless party'.[70] But he still could not take very seriously this atavistic phenomenon, an emergence of the dark state of mind of the past, a creature of cobwebs.[71] This was not a far-fetched description of a

65 M. Masani, *Against the Tide* (Delhi, 1981), p. 140. Masani himself, starting on the far left, 'reconsidered' socialism in the 1940s and, after a disastrous tenure as Nehru's first Ambassador in Brazil, became a pillar of the Swatantra Party. Cf. Gramsci: 'Renegades are all the same, whatever party or idea they have abandoned. They are all contemptible, because you never know whether they were more insincere yesterday, or whether they are more insincere today.'

66 Speech at Ootacamund, 1 June, *The Hindu*, 2 June 1959.

67 Press conference at Delhi, 10 June, *National Herald*, 11 June 1959.

68 Nehru to Chief Ministers, 2 July 1959; press conferences at Delhi, 7 July and 7 August 1959, *The Hindu*, 8 July 1959, and *National Herald*, 8 August 1959, respectively.

69 Nehru to Vijayalakshmi, 3 November 1959.

70 Speech at New Delhi, 22 November, *The Hindu*, 23 November 1959.

71 Speech at the annual Congress session, Bangalore, 14 January 1960. A.I.R. Tapes.

party which claimed to see in Nehru's slow efforts to move towards socialism an attempt at imposing on India a dictatorship of the party bosses.[72]

SIX

The Swatantra Party does not seem to have realized that it was not in the directives of economic and foreign policy but in weaknesses in administration that the telling criticisms of Nehru could be made. An underground economy was growing and the integrity of the bureaucracy had become very ragged at the edges. On coming out of prison in 1945, Nehru had spoken repeatedly, and in the strongest terms, of the moral degradation which corruption, profiteering and black-marketeering implied. One remark in particular became famous: 'I do not kill even a small insect, but it will give me the greatest pleasure if all these profiteers were hung by the neck till they are dead.'[73] For this rot in the administration he had held the highest executive organs in the Government responsible.[74] It could therefore be expected that, as Prime Minister, he would take the most stringent measures to root out corruption. There was, in fact, little change in his dislike of profiteers and 'black marketeers' and he suggested to Patel, the Home Minister, that they be taken into preventive detention.[75] But his detestation of corruption was now qualified by concern about the drag which a climate of suspicion and accusations applied on rapid decision-making and assumption of responsibility in official circles. When his attention was drawn to any accusation of dishonesty or impropriety, he usually asked the accused for his version of the matter; if satisfied, he closed the case by conveying the rebuttal to the complainant and, if not, he passed on the case to the police for further investigation. If the matter were only one of impropriety, a warning seemed to him sufficient. He also frequently told the persons concerned to take the initiative. People in high office tended to attract wild allegations; these could not be disregarded and the persons concerned should refute them publicly and, if necessary, take legal action.[76]

However, if neither step were taken, Nehru now presumed not that the person was guilty but that he was thick-skinned. There had, in other words, been a shift in Nehru's thinking; his bias was now in favour of the Ministers and senior officials rather than of the critics. When charges of corruption

[72] C. Rajagopalachari's article in *The Hindu*, 15 October 1959. It should be added, in fairness to Rajagopalachari, that he was one of the few Swatantra leaders to proclaim his general agreement at this time with Nehru's foreign policy. See his speech at Tirunelveli, 23 November, *The Hindu*, 28 November 1959.

[73] Interview to the press, 23 June 1945, *Selected Works of Jawaharlal Nehru*, Vol. 14 (Delhi, 1981), p. 20.

[74] To Jogendra Singh, member of the Viceroy's Executive Council, 16 October 1945. Ibid., p. 111.

[75] 20 August 1950.

[76] Nehru to Jagjivan Ram, 28 January 1959.

appeared to Nehru to be politically motivated, he tended to react with a vigorous defence of fellow-Congressmen and, in almost every case, to consider them blameless if the evidence was not cast iron. In the case of charges against those in the subordinate cadres, Nehru decided that the Government would assist the accused to defend themselves in court or, if the accusations were specific, request a judge to investigate. Not to do anything would necessarily lead to people thinking that there was some truth in the charges.[77] Yet almost always nothing was done. Convinced by this time that there was more talk than evidence of corruption, Nehru relied on the normal procedures and the remedial actions of the special police establishment set up for this purpose.

By themselves, these steps were insufficient wholly to satisfy the public and a current of opinion persisted that corruption was being allowed to corrode the administration. Perhaps there was less than was thought; but the case of M.O. Mathai, which burst into public view in February 1959, seemed to bear spectacular testimony to all that was suspected. For Mathai had been special assistant to Nehru since 1946 and exercised a vast and irregular power. After charges of corruption were made in Parliament, Mathai offered to resign. Nehru believed Mathai to be innocent and rejected suggestions of a police investigation or a judicial or even a departmental inquiry. But, not wishing to ignore persistent charges and insinuations against a person closely associated with him, he asked the Cabinet Secretary, as the most senior civil servant, informally to ascertain the facts. The Cabinet Secretary publicly exonerated Mathai in order, as he later privately said, to protect the Prime Minister's reputation; but Nehru was informed that Mathai could not account for his great wealth and without doubt had received money from the C.I.A. as well as from businessmen in India.[78] It can indeed be safely assumed that, from 1946 to 1959, the C.I.A. had access to every paper passing through Nehru's secretariat. The Prime Minister, believing, as was his wont, that the opposition was always seeking to bring down those close to him and that the vehement criticisms of Mathai were, to an extent, attacks on himself, continued to assert his confidence in his assistant; 'a more bogus agitation I have not been able to find . . . I am really and honestly amazed at the gullibility of persons'.[79] But, at the same time, he accepted Mathai's resignation and did not, after the inquiry, re-employ him.

The Mathai case had the advantage of making Nehru realize that he must treat seriously the widespread allegations of corruption. 'I think that probably the most important thing about an administration is the belief in its fairplay and integrity. Hence my anxiety to deal with this as thoroughly as possible.'[80] But he was unclear as to how this should be done. He still favoured the existing practice, although it had not proved very satisfactory, of *ad hoc*

[77] To N. Sanjiva Reddi, Chief Minister of Andhra, 29 January 1959.

[78] Record of later conversations of V. Sahay, Cabinet Secretary, with S. Radhakrishnan, 17 February and 31 October 1966. Radhakrishnan papers.

[79] Press conference at Delhi, 10 June 1959. P.I.B.

[80] To Bakshi Ghulam Mahomed, 6 March 1959.

arrangements for preliminary inquiries into all complaints and, if substance were found in them, of full investigations and judicial proceedings. It looked almost as if, while Nehru recognized the seriousness of the problem, a part of his mind would have liked to have ignored it. But this became even more difficult when Deshmukh, the former Finance Minister, drew public attention to what he regarded as the great extent of corruption, particularly among Ministers. Nehru wrote to Deshmukh asking for particulars to satisfy himself and perhaps consult a few colleagues. He was unwilling to go further and make a commitment to set up a tribunal with wide terms of reference to inquire into all such charges for this would encourage the habit, already deep-rooted in India, of making baseless accusations. An inquisitorial tribunal roaming about India to receive complaints would make all government impossible. The country would be gripped by an atmosphere of charge and counter-charge and probably no person in authority would escape. 'Really extraordinary! You might soon (have to) pack up the Five Year Plan, you can't do anything substantial. We are a gossipy people.'[81] Believing that there was less corruption in India than elsewhere, he suspected that opposition parties exaggerated the extent of corruption in order to belabour the Government and the Congress; 'this kind of underground, over-ground and middle-ground propaganda of every type and when you enquire into it, it falls to the ground.' The attitude of the critics of the Congress in Parliament was apparently to assume that Ministers were guilty of corruption unless they proved their innocence. The flinging about of charges itself set up a spiral; for the creating of an atmosphere in which corruption was thought to be widespread helped to spread it. So, while refusing to accept that India was 'a sea of corruption', he was willing to have an inquiry in any case where it seemed to him that there was at least some *prima facie* substance in the charge.[82] But Deshmukh was willing to provide information not to the Prime Minister but only to a tribunal with assurances of indemnity to those making the charges. All he gave Nehru was a list of the types of charges. To set up a tribunal to inquire into such general allegations seemed to Nehru a wrong and undemocratic step which would be harmful to the community. As a compromise, Nehru suggested, and Deshmukh agreed, that a retired Chief Justice of the Supreme Court be asked to look informally into the charges and advise the Prime Minister.[83] In the event, this procedure proved unsatisfactory. The judge found the charges unproven and his findings carried little conviction to Deshmukh or to those making the charges.

Again, a single prominent instance drew attention both to the undoubted existence of irregularities in the administration and to the ambivalence of

81 Nehru at press conference in Delhi, 8 January 1960. P.I.B.

82 Speech at the annual Congress Session, Bangalore, 14 January 1960, A.I.R. tapes; speech in the Rajya Sabha, 12 February 1960, Debates, Vol. 28, pp. 602–26; address to Congress Parliamentary Party, 14 February 1960. Tape 49/C, Part I.

83 Press conference in Delhi, 24 February, *National Herald*, 25 February 1960; Nehru's correspondence with Deshmukh, January–March 1960.

Nehru's approach to them. Partap Singh Kairon, the Chief Minister of the Punjab, combined qualities of drive and industry with a tendency to circumvent established procedures. Though he had ordered the police to deal with Hindu and Sikh agitation in his state without resort to firing, it was widely believed that the police had shot people in cold blood. When Nehru suggested an informal inquiry, Kairon was honest enough to reply that there was no need as the charges were mostly true.[84] But, on the whole, Nehru was impressed with Kairon's handling of the Punjab and asked him only to keep an eye on the methods adopted by the police.[85]

> So far as I am concerned, as you know well, I rely upon you more than on anyone else in the Punjab. This is not only because you are Chief Minister, but also for personal reasons; because I have faith in you and your great capacity for good work. I know that there is a deliberate attempt being made by many people, including some of our friends, to discredit you. I do not like this at all and, whenever an opportunity offers itself, I shall make my views clear on this subject.[86]

Once the agitation in favour of the Hindi language had been formally withdrawn in December 1957, Nehru advised Kairon to be generous to his opponents and not to hold them in prison longer than necessary.[87] But by now the dislike of Kairon within his own party was considerable. A charge-sheet, signed by many Congressmen of the Punjab, was sent to the Chief Minister; and his rejoinder was considered by the Working Committee. Its resolution, drafted by Nehru, sided with Kairon. While recognizing that high traditions of public administration and service had to be maintained, the Committee also stressed its duty to protect persons in responsible positions from harassment and unfair charges. It felt that Kairon had emerged with enhanced reputation from the long trial of strength with the communal agitators and said it had found nothing which might remotely justify any charge of corruption. It thought him to be a man of personal integrity, free of communal bias and devoted to popular causes. His very virtues, to some extent, had become his defects; constant touring had led to less time and interest being given to routine administration and eagerness to deal promptly with problems had resulted in the bypassing of normal procedures. Urban interests resented the priority he gave to rural issues. The Committee recognized that some members of Kairon's family had not behaved creditably. All these incidents, by themselves of no great significance, cumulatively produced an effect and indicated how careful anyone in high office should be. But the major fact remained that Kairon, carrying a heavy burden and working at high pressure, had done nothing, according to the Committee, which might be called

[84] Nehru to Kairon, 2 May, and to Pant, reporting conversation with Kairon, 3 May 1956.
[85] Nehru to Tara Singh, 6 December 1956, and to Kairon, 28 August 1957.
[86] Nehru to Kairon, 6 September 1957.
[87] Nehru to Kairon, 11 December 1957.

lacking in honesty and had faced many difficult situations with considerable courage.[88]

So Nehru, clear-sighted about Kairon's weaknesses, still felt that he deserved support and should continue as Chief Minister. He had worsted both the Hindu and Sikh reactionary elements and retained the confidence of the majority of Congressmen in the Punjab. Kairon 'has his failings, no doubt, as all of us have. But in this land where communalism is always raising its head in some form or other, it was a relief to have as a comrade a person who was above this failing.'[89] Nor had the charges of corruption been, in Nehru's view, substantiated; and he asserted that he had never seen anything more fantastic and frivolous.[90] But, as neither the resolution of the Working Committee nor the Prime Minister's firm backing of the Chief Minister ended faction in the Punjab Congress, Kairon was instructed to seek a vote of confidence. He secured a large affirmative majority but drawn mostly from members of the upper house. This indication that Kairon's position was weaker than was thought disappointed Nehru. 'It is extraordinary how he has succeeded, in the course of a few months, in alienating so many different types of persons. He cannot carry on effectively without winning over some of these persons.'[91] His public support of the Chief Minister remained as staunch as before, but privately he advised Kairon to treat his colleagues and officials more gently and restrain the police from interfering too much in people's private lives.[92] Kairon's reply was so worded as to appeal to Nehru: 'Knowing that you are very kind to me, the sole aim of my political rivals has all along been to prejudice against me the mind of my most esteemed and beloved leader.'[93] So Nehru's support did not waver and, after the elections of 1962, he intervened to make sure that Kairon was unanimously re-elected leader of the Congress Party in the Punjab. His attitude throughout these years was summed up by his comment to one of Kairon's critics: 'Few of us are without faults, but one has to judge of a situation in all its bearings, and in this context I have no doubt that every Congressman should have helped Sardar Partap Singh Kairon fully.'[94]

In assessing Nehru's attitude to corruption, one has to start from the fact of his own unblemished financial probity. When the wealth tax was first introduced in 1957, the Allahabad municipality assessed Nehru's home, Anand Bhawan, at a ridiculously low figure. Nehru vigorously protested to the Finance Minister and had the figure raised nearly five times.[95] In 1959, on his seventieth birthday, he received from G.D. Birla, the industrialist, a

88 Nehru's draft resolution for Congress Working Committee, 14 May 1958.
89 Nehru to Tara Singh, 26 May 1958.
90 Press conference at Delhi, 4 June, *National Herald*, 5 June 1958.
91 Nehru to C.P.N. Singh, Governor of the Punjab, 6 June 1958.
92 Nehru to P.S. Kairon, 27 June 1959.
93 P.S. Kairon to Nehru, 19 December 1959.
94 Nehru to Prabodh Chandra, 11 June 1961.
95 Nehru's letter to T.T. Krishnamachari and note, both dated 21 November 1957.

cheque for a little over seventy thousand rupees. Though Birla had suggested that the amount be used for public purposes, Nehru politely returned the cheque.[96] His own acquisitive instinct not having developed, he could not recognize the possibility of its dominance in those round him. He thought that charges of irregularity and corruption were often exaggerated. It is also possible that Nehru did not expect in others the standards which came so effortlessly to him and that he did not concern himself as much as he should have done with their lax financial morals. Honesty and integrity in his colleagues Nehru did not seem to regard as absolute values but only as important elements in a general context. A candid plaint to Sampurnanand reveals much of Nehru's way of thinking. 'One can put up perhaps with a person who is able but otherwise undesirable, or with a person of integrity who has no great ability. But what is one to do with persons who have neither integrity nor ability?'[97] In fact, he put up with even such persons if they were colleagues of long standing or with pretensions to progressive views. His justification for such unbroken loyalty was that every individual had a credit and a debit account and, when the credits were bigger, then the debits were covered.[98] One should take people as they are and situations as they are.

So Nehru's immediate reaction to charges of corruption gave ground to the belief that he did not treat them seriously enough. It is true that the critics were frequently motivated by pettiness; and Deshmukh did not build up a strong case. But Nehru's attitude also suggested casualness and a proneness to insist on offsetting factors. A belief that corruption was not endemic and an assumption that private advancement need not always be at the cost of public interest weakened Nehru's moral condemnation of official impropriety and dishonesty.

[96] Nehru to G.D. Birla, 13 November 1959.
[97] Nehru to Sampurnanand, 20 July 1958.
[98] Press conference at Delhi, 7 February, *National Herald*, 8 February 1959.

6

The Growing Rift with China 1960

ONE

Very soon after Eisenhower's departure from Delhi, Nehru received Zhou's letter of 17 December which, for all its mildness of tone, made clearer than ever the lack of any common ground on the border issue. No indication was given to suggest that the Chinese would abate their territorial demands; and stress was laid on the importance of Aksai Chin to China. The only positive note in the letter was the repetition of the advantages of a meeting of the two Prime Ministers to reach agreements of principle as a guidance to concrete discussions, which might otherwise get bogged down in endless debate.[1] Nehru was prepared to agree to such a meeting. Even though he saw no scope for negotiation except to carry out minor rectifications of an accepted alignment, India would discuss matters 'to the bitter end', for the alternative was war. However, to China's demand that the boundary along its entire length should be regarded as a subject for discussion India could not agree; she would not, as Nehru said more than once,[2] hand over the Himalayas as a gift.

So clearly the tension between the two countries would continue if not intensify; and while Nehru still optimistically refused to contemplate major hostilities, he recognized that a situation had developed which could be met only by some of the speedy methods associated with organizing for war. Apart from resisting any further encroachments by China, India would have to build up her defences and her industrial strength, even if only to negotiate with greater confidence.[3] A sense of urgency was essential. The Indian people, instead of oscillating, as was their wont, between panic and complacency, should begin to acquire the mentality associated with a fight for survival. They should not tolerate obstacles and should be prepared to take many risks.[4] At

[1] Zhou's letter to Nehru, 17 December 1959, White Paper III, pp. 52–7.

[2] For example, speeches at Bombay, 4 October, *The Hindu,* 5 October 1959, and at Delhi, 27 January, *National Herald,* 28 January 1960.

[3] Speeches in Lok Sabha, 21 and 22 December 1959, Debates, Vol. 37, pp. 6,266–77 and 6,709–27 respectively, and in Rajya Sabha, 22 December 1959, Debates, Vol. 27, pp. 3,460–71.

[4] Nehru to Chief Ministers, 1 January 1960.

the same time, he put down sternly suggestions, even within his own party, for seeking military assistance from abroad or, as it was euphemistically termed, cooperative defence. This to Nehru was softness and weakness. If Indian armies could not defend India, then freedom was lost. From every viewpoint, practical, opportunist, idealist, or whatever, non-alignment was the only policy for India. If her honour and integrity were attacked, India would fight back at any cost; but she would do so on her own. Whatever the consequences, there would be no foreign armies on India's soil.[5]

Alongside such calls to confidence and courage, Nehru warned his people against overheated rhetoric and loose talk of confrontation with China. If two large countries like India and China, both proud, strong and fairly well equipped, came into conflict, it would not be a minor matter but would last long and spread far. The disagreements on the border would not be resolved quickly and he shared to a large extent the deep and strong feelings roused by Chinese actions. But India would have to learn to live with this problem, do what she could to prevent its escalation and await a friendly, even if remote, future. It was as part of this effort not to inflame an explosive situation that he formulated in very moderate terms the reference to Chinese incursions in the President's address to Parliament. A breach of faith by China could not mean that India lost faith in the principles she regarded as basic in the relations between nations.[6]

It was, therefore, a heavily nuanced policy which Nehru had worked out – no yielding on the basic issues, a willingness to talk but an unwillingness to negotiate on the major question of the boundary as a whole, a strengthening of the Indian position in the border areas but a reluctance to take any step which might bring war nearer. 'You do not seem to realise that a mind may not be so thick as to see only in one direction. It can see in two or three directions.'[7]

TWO

In these circumstances, the fact that Krishna Menon was Minister for Defence gained more than normal significance. Menon had been dissatisfied since 1956 with being merely a Minister without Portfolio. He had wished to give up his seat in the Rajya Sabha and contest the elections to the Lok Sabha in 1957 from a major city like Bombay;[8] and he had combined this demand, as usual, with emotional blackmail. He told Nehru in December 1956 that he wished to give up office as he was out of touch with the Prime Minister and not wanted by his colleagues or the country. He was ineffective and an embarrassment to Nehru

[5] Speeches at the A.I.C.C., Bangalore, 15 and 16 January, *The Hindu*, 16 and 17 January 1960.
[6] 8 February 1960. Lok Sabha Debates, Second Series, Vol. 38, p. 18.
[7] Press conference at Delhi, 24 February, *National Herald*, 25 February 1960.
[8] Telegram to Nehru from New York, 11 December 1956.

8 *Above left* In Tibet on the road to Bhutan, September 1958

9 *Above right* At Gangtok, September 1958

10 *Right* With the Maharaja of Bhutan, September 1958

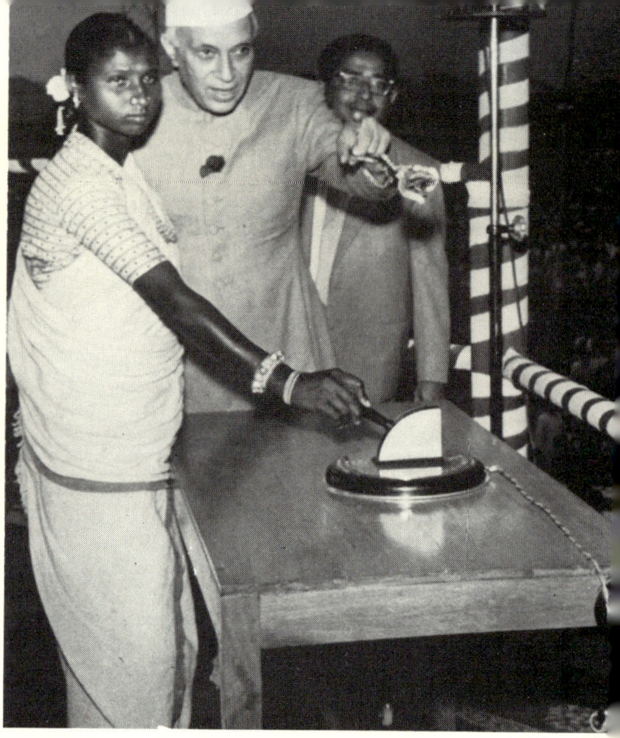

11 *Above left* With his grandsons, 1958
12 *Above right* Inviting a woman worker to inaugurate the Panchet hill dam, 6 December 1959

13 Addressing defence personnel at Srinagar, July 1960

and it was therefore not right that he should continue in office. 'You have no escape in the scheme of things and you do not seek it. I am the wrong kind and create more conflicts and difficulties – so it is best for me to "go" . . . I have realized for a long time that I was being kept on and am quite a stranger.'[9] Nehru still had a high opinion of Menon and believed that he was by 'far the ablest and the most outstanding figure in the United Nations. In carrying out India's policy, he comes into conflict with some policies of other countries and, because of his great ability, he creates an impression in the United Nations. This irritates others.'[10] So, ignoring the offer of resignation, Nehru arranged the seat in Bombay for Menon, whose general standing in India had been improved by his speeches at the Security Council on Kashmir. There was little public dissent when Nehru applauded Menon's performance at the United Nations and described him as a very clever man who had worn himself out in the service of India.[11] Even Rajagopalachari supported him.[12] Menon was easily elected, and Nehru was sufficiently impressed with his knowledge of defence matters on which he had been writing to Nehru not, he claimed, 'without responsibility or without some knowledge',[13] to entrust Menon with the defence portfolio when he reconstituted his Government after the elections in April 1957.

This proved one of Nehru's less fortunate decisions. Menon had many qualities, but they were not suited to the Defence Ministry, Nehru had hoped that Menon would bring new drive and a breath of fresh air into this Ministry. Menon's devious ways of functioning and his propensity to create coteries were known to Nehru but thought by him to be minor drawbacks, more than balanced by his energy, his commitment to national self-reliance and his experience of world affairs. To the public it appeared that Menon had reached as near the top of the pole as he ever would and his pushful ambition should be now satisfied. But, even in high office, Menon remained a whining egotist with a talent for grievance. Within two months of taking up the defence portfolio, he burst into Nehru's room and went back, after a painful interview, to write one of his characteristic letters of masochistic bitterness, bemoaning his unfriended plight and offering to resign.

> You do not need me and such of whatever I may have had has no place . . . I must therefore bring things to an end . . . I can make no impact on your mind and your collective Prime Ministerial self or function to any purpose. I have tried hard and endured much, but it is all to no purpose. I do not mind or grudge the effort or the pain, but there comes a time when one cannot live with oneself any more, deprived of purposeful

9 Krishna Menon to Nehru, 26 December 1956.

10 Nehru's note to Deputy Principal Information Officer, 9 January 1957.

11 Speech at Madras, 31 January, *The Hindu*, 1 February 1957; appeal to electors of Bombay, 6 February, *National Herald*, 7 February 1957.

12 T.J.S. George, *Krishna Menon* (London, 1964), p. 216.

13 Menon's telegram from New York to Nehru, 5 February 1957.

function . . . I have always loved you and will not stop doing so wherever I may be. But that is my own concern and feeling![14]

Nehru sent no reply to this letter, but probably assured Menon orally of his continuing confidence. Menon certainly had no cause to doubt it. With responsibility for defence and the handling of major issues in external affairs such as Kashmir, Indo-China and United Nations matters, Menon had become one of the key men in the Government, and his outburst seems the result more of temperament than of reason. He needed periodic emotional reassurances from the Prime Minister.

About a year later, in May 1958, Menon offered again to resign, but on this occasion for the substantial reason that the Cabinet was taking up once more the matter of the purchase of poor-quality jeeps during his term as High Commissioner in London. Nehru, as Menon must have expected, refused to let him go. 'You are only remotely connected with this matter . . . If it is anybody's fault, most of us are involved.'[15] But by now Menon had fallen out with some of his Cabinet colleagues. He was on particularly poor terms with Krishnamachari and, after the latter's resignation, with his successor, Morarji Desai, who blocked Menon's suggestion for an increase of senior military posts on financial grounds. But Menon also had a more general grievance, that Krishnamachari and Desai promoted the ascendancy of right-wing influence in Indian policies; and it was for this reason that, in November 1958, he once more went through what was by now the standard ritual of asking Nehru to ease him out of the Government. Nehru did not deny the existence of right-wing trends but assured Menon that, while he had to work within certain limitations, he would try to check these trends.

> You know how I have valued not only our personal relations but the advice I have had from you. But neither of us perhaps can uproot himself from his own approach to matters and, as a consequence, what should be done in a particular set of circumstances. We have to decide for ourselves. I would not like to press you to do something which you dislike, just as I am sure you would feel the same way about me. But we should certainly try to understand each other's viewpoint and try to explain one's own and thus influence the other's thinking.[16]

However, more serious problems arose from Menon's handling of the Defence Ministry. Nehru was gratified by Menon's efforts to effect economy by reallocations within the sanctioned budget and to increase production in defence factories for the needs of the armed services as well as for the ordinary market. This was in itself unobjectionable, although Menon took it to absurd lengths by ordering the production of such items as hair-clippers and

[14] Krishna Menon to Nehru, 10 June 1957.

[15] Krishna Menon to Nehru, 15 May 1958, and Nehru's reply of the same date.

[16] Krishna Menon's telegram from New York, 24 November, and Nehru's reply, 26 November 1958.

pressure-cookers and was planning, at the time of the Chinese aggression, the manufacture of mechanical toys.[17] The drive for self-reliance was, in the long run, the only correct policy; but it would take years to yield returns and Menon erred in neglecting purchases abroad till India was in a position to produce all the military equipment she required. He did not expect China to go to war. Indeed, he went further and, at a time when China had occupied a large portion of Indian territory, blandly denied it. 'I am not aware of any aggression, incursion, encroachment or intrusion by the Chinese into any part of Indian territory.'[18] With such a perverse refusal on the part of the Defence Minister to face facts which had been officially disclosed by the Government of India, it is not surprising that, when China did launch large-scale attacks, India was unprepared.

The same belief that India would never have to engage in serious fighting with any country other than Pakistan underlay Menon's irresponsible and offensive ways of conducting official business. Any improvement in morale brought about by the increase of the number of posts at the higher levels was more than offset by unpleasant bossiness and supercilious bullying. His arrogance was now even more aggressive and articulate than before and wholly without grace. His dependence on Nehru was matched only by his spite towards almost all others who were not his acolytes. His curt ridicule and lethal sarcasm were widely felt and deeply resented. In particular, Menon could not get on with Thimayya, who had become Chief of Army Staff at almost the same time as Menon took over the defence portfolio. In temperament the two men were poles apart. With little interest in politics and an outstanding record for courage and professional ability, Thimayya enjoyed unparalleled popularity among the ranks. He also, at this stage, commanded the confidence of Nehru, who had been impressed by his cool handling of the prisoners of war in Korea and by his energetic conduct of the campaign in the Naga areas. But the differences between Menon and Thimayya mounted and, on 1 September 1959, Thimayya, without concerting his action with the Chiefs of the Navy and Air Staff, who were also known to be unhappy,[19] almost casually sent in his resignation to the Prime Minister. A more studied approach by Thimayya might well have embarrassed Menon, especially as news of the resignation quickly reached the press; but, as it was, Nehru dealt easily with what sounded like a comic-opera *putsch*. He persuaded Thimayya to withdraw his resignation without giving him any specific assurances. He then dealt with the matter in Parliament in such a way as to strengthen Menon's position and shrink Thimayya's reputation. He stressed the importance of the Government's control of the armed services and hinted that Thimayya had acted irresponsibly.[20]

[17] George, *Krishna Menon*, pp. 224–5.

[18] Address at the air force station, Agra, 10 September 1961, quoted in N. Prasad, *The Fall of Towang 1962* (Delhi, 1981), p. 9.

[19] Admiral R.D. Katari, *A Sailor Remembers* (Delhi, 1982), pp. 102–4.

[20] 2 September 1959. Lok Sabha Debates, Second Series, Vol. 34, pp. 5,851–70.

Perhaps by now Menon had also placed in the Prime Minister's mind thoughts of the danger of a military *coup* – a fear that is never absent in an under-developed country where the democratic tradition has no long history. The Indian army had played no part in a national movement committed to non-violence; and one main reason for Nehru's defence, immediately after the war, of the Indian National Army had been his desire to bring the armed services into the mainstream of the national life of free India. The army, on its part, had not shown any interest in politics. But now Nehru seems to have begun to share Menon's distrust of the officer corps as a whole. This is the probable explanation for his rejection, over a year later, on Menon's advice, of Mountbatten's suggestion that the post of Chairman of Chiefs of Staff be created and Thimayya appointed to it, for he was 'one of the most outstanding generals that I have ever come across in any country'.[21]

Clearly, therefore, the bonds between Nehru and Menon were becoming closer than ever before; and such closeness enabled Menon to evince seemingly little interest in defence matters. The Prime Minister had to pull him up for remaining in New York in the winter of 1959, when the Chinese advance in Ladakh had created intense public excitement in India, and to order him to return as soon as possible. 'For the Defence Minister to be continuously away when questions of defence are coming up daily is difficult to explain . . . You can have no idea of the anger and passion in the Indian mind at present. Our first duty is to deal with the situation here. Everything else is secondary.'[22] He also rebuked Menon for suggesting in New York that the problem with China was more political than military.[23] Then Menon, swinging to the other extreme, sought the Prime Minister's permission to proceed to the Kongka Pass, where a clash with the Chinese had occurred, or, at least, to Leh; but Nehru, as Menon probably expected, vetoed any such act of bravado.[24] More important was the prosaic task of expediting the construction of roads and communications in the border areas.[25] To keep Menon at his task Nehru turned down his request to join him at the Conference of Commonwealth Prime Ministers in London in the summer.[26] But the confidence remained unshaken; and Nehru denounced those Congressmen who had dared to criticize Menon – 'perfectly scandalous from any point of view, party or truth'.[27]

21 Mountbatten to Nehru, 9 December 1960, and Nehru's reply, 18 January 1961; Mountbatten's interview with the author, 28 May 1970.

22 Nehru's telegram to Krishna Menon, 2 November 1959.

23 Krishna Menon's telegram, 3 November, and Nehru's reply, 4 November 1959.

24 Menon's telegram, 9 November, and Nehru's reply, 10 November 1959.

25 Nehru to Menon, 20 January 1960.

26 Nehru to Menon, 19 April 1960.

27 Address to Congress Parliamentary Party, 23 April 1960. Tape M-50/C, Part I.

THREE

The conciliatory strands of Nehru's policy, the stress on peaceful approaches within the ambit of general firmness and the determination not to move away from non-alignment, which was not just a fair-weather policy, were especially valuable in retaining for India the friendship of the Soviet Government. Such support was, of course, of inestimable advantage in this critical situation. The Chinese leaders strove hard to persuade Khrushchev that he was wrong to 'maintain strict neutrality' on the boundary question in a way which, far from being neutral, censured China and was in favour of India. But, rejecting this advice, the Central Committee of the Soviet Communist Party informed the Chinese that no one could possibly think seriously that India, immeasurably weaker than China militarily and economically, would launch a military attack and commit aggression against China.[28] The Soviet Government made clear that, as they understood the problem, it was not a limited territorial one precipitated by India but part of the Chinese ambition to expand, to weaken India and to embarrass the Soviet Union in its efforts to promote peaceful co-existence and reach a *détente* with the United States.

These details were not, of course, known at the time in India and, while Nehru relied on Soviet friendship, he did not expect that the Soviet Government would be able to influence China to any marked extent or, indeed, would want to do so.[29] In February 1960, when Khrushchev twice passed through India on his way to and from Indonesia, neither he nor Nehru mentioned, at the public functions, the dispute with China. But, speaking in Parliament while Khrushchev was in Delhi, Nehru declared that there was no room for negotiations with China.[30] As for Khrushchev, he took every opportunity to proclaim that India and the Soviet Union were 'good neighbours and great friends', that he approved of India's foreign policy and that there would be no slackening of Soviet economic assistance. Even in their private talks, Nehru hardly mentioned the boundary problem. But a week before Khrushchev's visit he had written to Zhou that, although there could be no negotiations on the basis of an undelimited border, it might be helpful, as Zhou had suggested, for them to meet; and he invited Zhou to Delhi.[31] Nehru also reiterated in Parliament that he would continue to strive for a peaceful settlement and for that purpose would be willing to meet with anyone despite the fact that there seemed to be no bridge between the positions of the two countries.[32]

Such acceptance of a lack of understanding secured confirmation from

[28] 6 February 1960, quoted in 'The Truth about How the Leaders of the CPSU Have Allied Themselves with India against China', *People's Daily*, 2 November 1963.

[29] See his interview with Robert S. Elegant in early February, reported in *Newsweek*, 22 February 1960.

[30] 12 February 1960. Rajya Sabha Debates, Vol. 28, pp. 602–26.

[31] Nehru to Zhou Enlai, 5 February 1960, White Paper III, pp. 83–4.

[32] 12 February 1960, Rajya Sabha Debates, Vol. 28, pp. 602–26, and 16 and 22 February 1960, Lok Sabha Debates, Second Series, Vols 38, pp. 1,166–71, and 39, pp. 2,102–42 respectively.

Chinese attempts to isolate India by reaching boundary agreements with Burma and Nepal on the basis of China's stand. This policy was in line with Zhou's maxim: 'you make friends in order to isolate your enemies'. From Burma China secured in January pieces of territory demanded by her and confirmed the stretch of the McMahon Line between China and Burma as a traditional boundary in return for Burma's acceptance that it had till now been undelimited. A joint survey committee, as desired by China, was also set up. Then, towards the end of March, amid a flood of oratory about peace in Asia and Panch Sheel, and with a combination of pressure tactics and vague promises of financial aid, a Nepalese delegation in Beijing was pushed into a position which was manifestly aimed at India. A vague procedure appeared to have been laid down for the settlement by joint commissions of discrepancies and disputes on the Tibet–Nepal border; but it was not clear whether such settlements would be based on any principles or what would happen if the joint commissions failed to reach agreement. The chief objective was obviously not to resolve Nepal's problems but to suggest that India was intransigent. But of more concern to India was the decision of Nepal and China to sign a non-aggression treaty in the near future. For, if China's treaty with Burma were any guide, Nepal would be bound down not to commit aggression against China or to take part in any military alliance directed against her; and such a treaty could only be considered as having India in mind and intended to strengthen China's diplomatic position.[33]

It was against this background of general ill-will towards India that Zhou came to Delhi in April. It was to be the last meeting of these two men, with so much in common – intelligence, finesse, sensitivity to wider issues; easily, at that time, the world's two most intellectual Prime Ministers. But Zhou had always a clearer idea than Nehru of where power and interest lay, and by now they had become paired antagonists locked together. Only the stylized courtesies were maintained in a chill atmosphere. Nehru had no high expectations. Both sides had stated their positions with considerable vigour and left no room for compromise on any major point. Willing to discuss any specific dispute, India had no intention of yielding on her general stand that the frontier was a fixed one which had been peaceful for many years. At an earlier stage Nehru had sounded uncertain about Aksai Chin; but now, aware of the varied evidence in India's favour, his attitude was set. 'I think that our case is a strong one and I see no reason why we should weaken in it at any point.'[34]

As a result, in the talks between the two Prime Ministers, there was not even a distant approach to a solution. Nehru elaborated India's position in great detail. It was incorrect for Zhou to state that the Chinese had never realized that there was any dispute in the western sector. They had had full knowledge, at least since 1954, of the alignment as recognized by India but it

[33] Nehru to B.P. Koirala, Prime Minister of Nepal, 31 March, and to B.C. Roy, 3 April 1960.
[34] To B.P. Koirala, 13 April 1960.

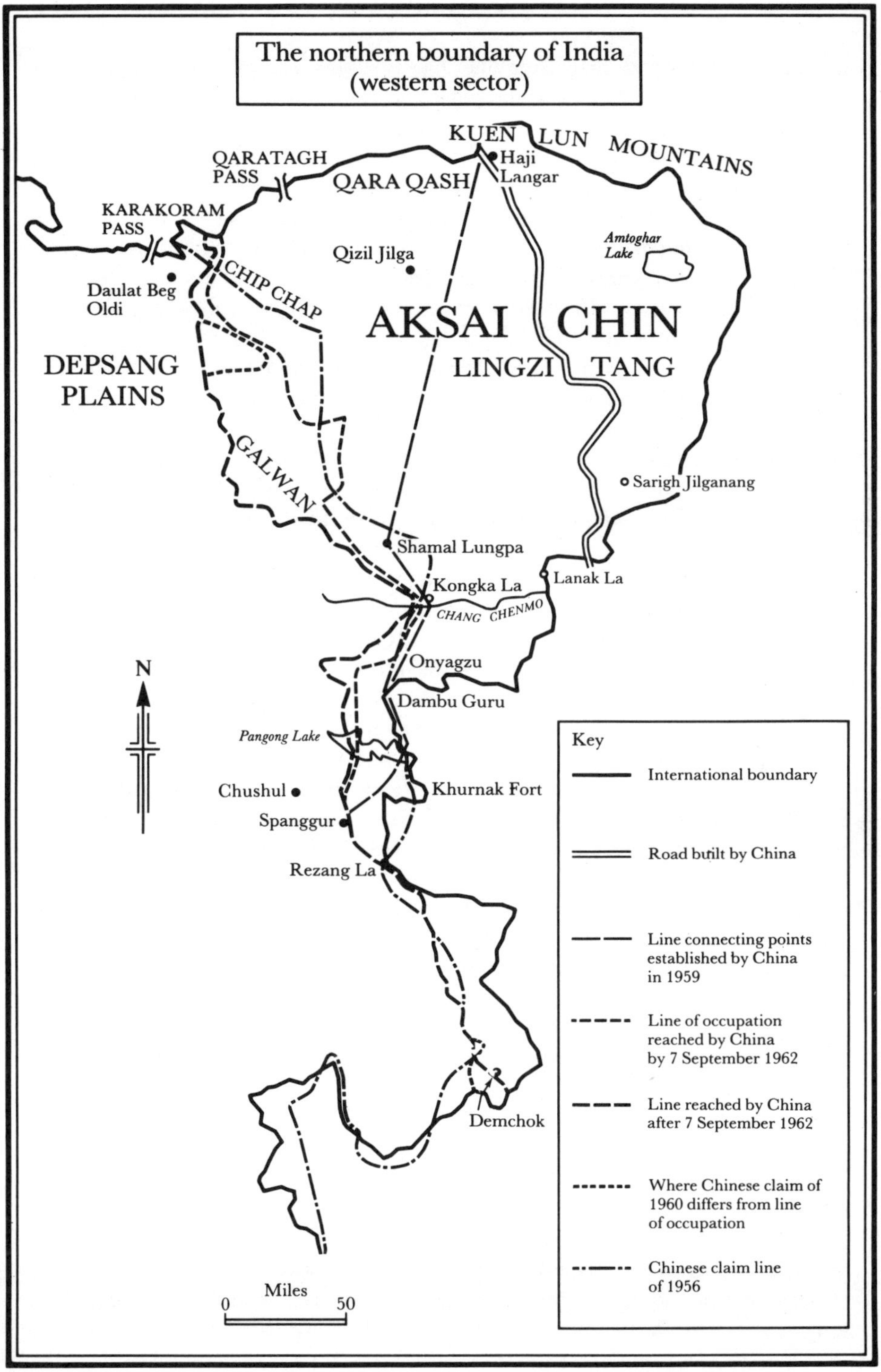

The northern boundary of India
(western sector)
KUEN LUN MOUNTAINS
QARATAGH PASS
QARA QASH
Haji Langar
KARAKORAM PASS
Qizil Jilga
Amtoghar Lake
Daulat Beg Oldi
CHIP CHAP
AKSAI CHIN
DEPSANG PLAINS
LINGZI TANG
GALWAN
Sarigh Jilganang
Shamal Lungpa
Kongka La
Lanak La
CHANG CHENMO
Onyagzu
Dambu Guru
N
Pangong Lake
Chushul
Khurnak Fort
Spanggur
Rezang La
Demchok
Miles
0
50
Key
International boundary
Road built by China
Line connecting points established by China in 1959
Line of occupation reached by China by 7 September 1962
Line reached by China after 7 September 1962
Where Chinese claim of 1960 differs from line of occupation
Chinese claim line of 1956

was only in recent months that they had questioned it in correspondence or entrenched themselves in various places on the ground. The whole problem had arisen because Chinese forces had moved on to traditionally Indian territory during the past twelve to eighteen months. This position India could not accept, for she regarded the boundary as well known and firmly delimited. As for Zhou's insistence that the whole border be negotiated, with the two sides maintaining the status quo and putting forward no territorial claims, Nehru could only express his puzzlement. To talk of the status quo was meaningless when the Chinese were incessantly pushing forward, showing varying alignments on their maps and declining to be precise about the boundary as claimed by them; and it was odd to speak of making no territorial claims even as they were demanding vast areas of territory which India had always regarded as belonging to her.

So, with each side viewing the facts differently, no meeting ground could be found. Contrary to persistent rumour then and later, at no time during these talks did Zhou offer explicitly to recognize the McMahon Line in the east in return for the secession by India of Aksai Chin in the west. His position throughout was that the boundary for its entire length should be negotiated and, pending negotiations, the status quo should be maintained. His suggestion that territorial claims should not be put forward to areas no longer under administrative control may have been intended as an implicit acceptance of the McMahon Line. Perhaps because Nehru did not respond, Zhou later explained his remark to mean that there should be no preconditions, i.e. that nothing should be taken for granted.

However, presumably to gain time, Zhou proposed the appointment of experts to ascertain the historical and material facts and, when asked to amplify, said that he had in mind joint boundary committees visiting the border areas. As this would entail groups wandering for years in the high mountains, Nehru made the more practical suggestion that officials of the two sides jointly examine the evidence available on the alignment. Zhou replied that his party had come to Delhi to discuss principles and not to go into details. So it was agreed that the officials should meet later to examine the material in their possession with regard to the facts of the boundary alignment and present a report; meantime, both sides should make every effort to avoid friction and clashes on the border.[35]

The very fact of a meeting of the two Prime Ministers, followed by a decision to examine the evidence relating to the border and to avoid clashes, could be expected to lower the tension at least for a time. It was proof that, while no solution had been found, the effort to find solutions would not be given up. Nehru hoped that Zhou and his colleagues had realized the strength of Indian feeling on this question. But it was also clear, as a result of the talks, that the major differences between the two countries would continue and be long-drawn-out. When Nehru informed Parliament that they had come up,

[35] Record of talks between the Prime Ministers of India and China, 20–25 April 1960.

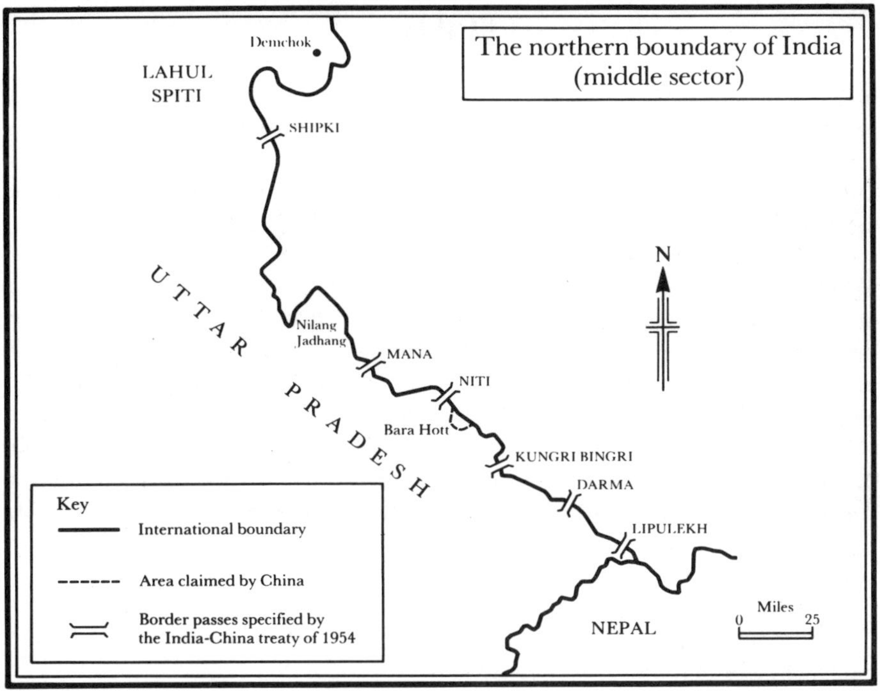

during these talks, against the rock of wholly different approaches,[36] the Chinese reacted sharply. It was alleged that the Indian government, under the influence of 'imperialist and reactionary' forces, were seeking unilateral concessions; and Zhou, in Khatmandu to sign the treaty of peace and friendship, accused Nehru of being 'not so friendly towards China'.[37] No heed was paid to Krishna Menon's warning to Zhou that China, by her hostility to the Nehru Government, was strengthening reaction in India and the forces of tension in the world;[38] for China claimed to believe that Nehru was already a prisoner of reaction. When a delegation of the Communist Party of India suggested to Zhou that he should follow Leninist precedents and settle with a 'bourgeois' government such as that of India to prevent anti-Chinese feeling and to strengthen the left movement in India, Zhou replied that the Leninist example did not apply. He saw no danger of American imperialism attacking China through these border territories; the threat was from the Nehru Government.[39]

[36] 26 April 1960. Lok Sabha Debates, Second Series, Vol. 43, pp. 13,791–804.

[37] *People's Daily*, 27 April 1960; Zhou's press conference at Khatmandu, 28 April, *China Today*, 7 May 1960.

[38] M. Brecher, *India and World Politics* (London, 1968), p. 152.

[39] K. Damodaran, 'Memories of an Indian Communist', reprinted in K. N. Pannikar (ed.), *Prospects of Left Unity* (Delhi, 1979), pp. 131–2.

FOUR

India now had to frame a policy appropriate to the circumstances. Clearly a peaceful solution was not going to be easy; and Nehru was by now driven to concede that China could become a potential threat to world peace.[40] It was known that Chinese troops and rebel elements were engaged in large-scale fighting in Tibet and that, throughout the summer of 1960, the Chinese were strengthening their military position in Tibet.[41] The incident on the Nepal–Tibet boundary, when the Chinese opened fire on a Nepalese party in violation of the provision in the treaty which had just been signed creating demilitarized zones on both sides of this border, 'does indicate that the general attitude of the Chinese in Tibet is very objectionable. They throw their weight about and do not care much for frontiers and the like.'[42] But Nehru was still of the view that China would hesitate to provoke a border war with any of her neighbours as this could well lead to major hostilities with unforeseen consequences. He also publicly asserted, presumably as a warning to China, that India was strong enough to counter any attempt at an invasion and it was childish to think of her in terms of any weakness.[43]

To prevent the situation on the ground from deteriorating further, the Government of India decided to send patrols into their border areas. Indian patrols had been moving in these areas for years and they should continue to do so. Such patrolling had become all the more necessary, particularly in the western sector, as the Chinese had provided India with no precise delineation of the boundary as claimed by them and were moving continuously well into Indian territory. But, in accordance with the agreement between the two Prime Ministers, Indian patrols were instructed to avoid clashes with Chinese posts and personnel. The sole purpose of this decision to establish checkposts and despatch patrols, wherever possible, up to the boundary and to constitute a special board to complete the building of roads in the border areas within two years was to make clear that any further Chinese advance was obvious aggression.[44] The checkposts and patrols were meant to show the flag, as it were, and provide symbols of Indian sovereignty. It has been said that this 'forward policy' – a curious phrase, for, as Krishna Menon said later, no country can follow a 'forward policy' in its own territory[45] – was provocative, and looked ultimately to a military challenge;[46] and an eminent soldier has described it as 'militarily nonsensical'.[47] These criticisms are beside the point, for the policy was no more than a limited defensive action. Provocative it was,

40 Press conference in London, 2 May, *National Herald*, 3 May 1960.
41 Nehru at press conference in Delhi, 24 June, *National Herald*, 25 June 1960.
42 Nehru's telegram to Krishna Menon in New York, 1 July 1960.
43 Speech at Pune, 3 June, *The Hindu*, 4 June 1960.
44 Nehru to Indian Ambassador in Burma, 6 July, and to G.B. Pant, Home Minister, 8 July 1960.
45 Brecher, *India and World Politics*, p. 153.
46 N. Maxwell, *India's China War* (London, 1970), pp. 176, 179.
47 Lord Carver, *War since 1945* (London, 1980), p. 217.

if by provocation is meant India's refusal to permit China to take whatever Indian territory she coveted without resistance. As the Chinese had been steadily moving southwards into Ladakh wherever they found no Indian presence, the Indian Government decided to establish posts and to send patrols into areas regarded by India as belonging to her, and where the Chinese were not as yet present, with the limited purpose of setting up a parallel Indian position. This might halt the flow of Chinese encroachment and help to create a climate where good sense would prevail and negotiations could begin. It was a no-risk action which China could hardly have viewed as a threat.[48] 'So far as we were concerned, there was no more question of forcing a military decision than there was of running in the face of aggression or attack.'[49] This contention of Menon many years later is borne out by contemporary evidence, such as the continuous reduction in the years 1959–62 of the percentage of defence expenditure in the annual budgets. India had no intention of fighting a war with China, and Nehru believed that China would not fight either, if only because such a war would not be confined to the border areas or to any one country.

As to the Indian territory already occupied by the Chinese, the Government had arrived at no clear answer as to what should be done to recover it. Resentment in India of Chinese bullying and concern at Chinese behaviour in Tibet were so deep that Nehru had difficulty in restraining these feelings. He who had guided Indian opinion on foreign affairs for many years now had to take it into account. Steering between such fevered emotion and the cold implacability of China he realized, even as he strove for moderation, that the room for compromise was limited.

> I do not myself see any kind of a settlement which we can accept, though we shall work for it. The Chinese have dug in their toes, and we are not prepared to accept this position at any cost. Indeed, no Government in India will accept this position now or in the foreseeable future.[50]

There would be no hurried action and no attempt at warlike solutions; but there would be a strengthening of the Indian presence in the Indian border areas, a commitment to defend the integrity and sovereignty of the country, a continuous building up of industrial strength and a perseverance in probing the mind of China, seeking to understand her motives and exploring all avenues for settlement. There should be no cognitive failure, a drift to disaster because of misperceptions on either side. 'Two big countries challenging each other – the moment you do that, you shut the door, and when you shut the door, what remains? Either sitting sullenly and doing nothing, just cursing like an old woman or going out sword in hand or whatever weapon you have,

[48] A.S. Whiting, *The Chinese Calculus of Deterrence* (Ann Arbor, 1975), pp. 10–11, 49.
[49] Menon in Brecher, *India and World Politics*, p. 151.
[50] Nehru to U Nu, 19 August 1960.

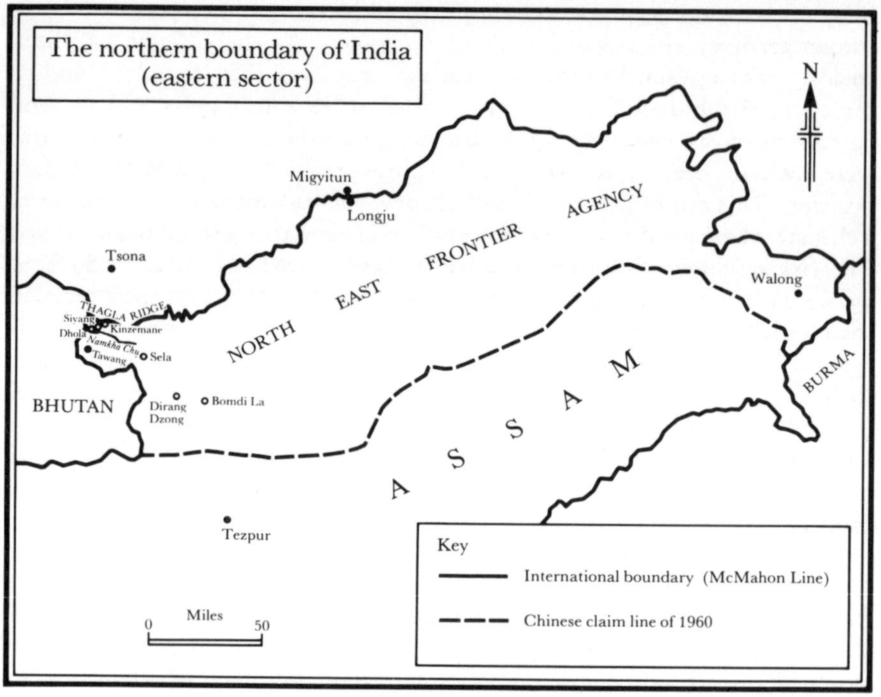

and fighting. There is nothing else left.'[51] From 1949 Nehru had adhered to a policy of friendliness combined with firmness towards the People's Republic of China, and the tension, growing over the years, brought home to him the importance of persisting with this two-pronged policy. Both India and China would benefit from friendly relations, but such relations would not be promoted by India adopting a weak attitude to a strong country. He was convinced of the correctness of India's case on the border, and reluctance to resort to military solutions and lose himself in a 'sea of hatred' did not mean that he did not feel strongly in the matter.[52]

FIVE

Nehru was also determined that there should be, in the world context, no weakening of non-alignment, which, in his view, was based not on some profit of the moment but on the essential realities of international affairs.[53] To avoid entanglement of this issue in the cold war he cautioned the Dalai Lama that

[51] 29 April 1960. Lok Sabha Debates, Second Series, Vol. 43, pp. 14,828–43.

[52] 1 September and 23 November 1960. Lok Sabha Debates, Second Series, Vols 46, pp. 6,202–17 and 47, pp. 1,934–62 respectively; speech at Bangalore, 15 September, *The Hindu*, 16 September 1960.

[53] Press conference in Delhi, 24 June, *National Herald*, 25 June 1960.

any fresh appeal to the United Nations would be unhelpful and possibly harmful[54] – advice which was not taken. But the general insistence on non-alignment and holding aloof from the cold war also gave scope for the continuous process, encouraging to India, of deterioration of Sino-Soviet relations. It was Nehru's belief that the Soviet Union and China still had need of each other, and neither would just then do anything to weaken the other. But there was a basic difference in outlook. The Soviet Union, hopeful that rapid economic growth and technical progress would by themselves establish the superiority of communism, was feeling more secure and had no wish for territorial expansion, while China was rigid, aggressive and afflicted with a pronounced sense of isolation. Western hostility might hold the two countries together; but, if tensions in the world lessened, the Soviet Union would draw away from China, whose growing strength and expansionist tendencies filled her with apprehension. For in twenty years China would be a country with about a thousand million people, highly organized and disciplined, with vast industrial and military resources and doubtless possessing nuclear weapons.[55]

Immediate developments supported this reading of the situation. At the Congress of the Rumanian Workers' Party in Bucharest in June 1960, Khrushchev told the Chinese delegation that, as Indians were killed in the border affrays, this meant that China had attacked India. The dispute had nothing to do with capitalism and socialism and was a purely nationalist one which had done untold harm to the socialist cause.[56] In fact, the year 1960 marked a qualitatively new stage in the confrontation between the Soviet Union and China as all the issues – political, strategic, ideological and economic – came to a head. The Soviet Government recalled all their experts from China and, at the conference of Communist and Workers' Parties in Moscow in November, the Chinese party insisted on its right to 'fractionalism'. Mao later declared, 'We spent the whole of 1960 fighting Khrushchev.'[57] This growing dissension in itself gave India immeasurable advantage, which it would have been folly to throw away.

While in earlier years Nehru's efforts had been devoted to leading China away from the Soviet Union, his preoccupation now was to deprive China of Soviet friendship. One area in which progress in improving relations between the Soviet Union and the Western Powers seemed possible was disarmament. Nehru urged that the new Soviet proposals, centring on the elimination of carriers of weapons of mass destruction and the termination of foreign bases, demanded careful consideration, for they appeared to be more than debating points. But the obstacle to any serious discussion was the fear of both parties that the other might gain an advantage. For this reason, the Western Powers

[54] Nehru to the Dalai Lama, 7 August 1960.

[55] Nehru's remarks at the Conference of Commonwealth Prime Ministers, 3 May 1960. Nehru's forecast of developments in China has been proved substantially correct.

[56] *People's Daily*, 2 November 1963; D. Wilson, *Mao the People's Emperor* (London, 1979), p. 357.

[57] J. Gittings, *The World and China 1922–72* (London, 1974), p. 255; J. Gittings, *Survey of the Sino-Soviet Dispute* (Oxford, 1968), pp. 24, 145; Wilson, *Mao the People's Emperor*, p. 357.

were reluctant to liquidate their foreign bases in the early stages of any programme of disarmament and Nehru, while disapproving of foreign bases on principle, recognized that the fear of the Western bloc could not be ignored. So he suggested to the Soviet Government that their proposals be treated as a basis for discussion rather than a rigid offer. At the same time, he requested the Western Powers not to reject out of hand the Soviet proposals, which seemed to him constructive.[58]

In fact, hopes of progress on disarmament or any other issue were destroyed that summer by the bringing down of the U-2 plane in the Soviet Union and the consequent collapse of the summit conference amid a torrent of invective. Nehru, then in Cairo, issued with Nasser a statement refraining from denunciation of either side and stressing the need to continue efforts for lessening tension. The non-aligned countries did not wish to remain silent spectators of the approaching catastrophe, although it was unclear how they could help in avoiding it. But significant and alarming was the reaction of the Chinese Government. They expressed their pleasure at the breakdown of the summit conference and used the occasion to run down India in an obvious effort to poison her relations with the Soviet Union.

SIX

The pause in relations with China in the second half of 1960, while the officials of the two sides were in session, enabled Nehru to turn his attention to relations with Pakistan. The cordiality evinced during Eisenhower's visit to Delhi in December 1959 seems to have, judging from his speeches, angered Ayub; but he could not afford to break away from the United States. With that power adopting a relatively low posture in world affairs after the collapse of the summit conference, the *coup* in Turkey and the demonstrations against Eisenhower in Tokyo, there was hope that the rulers of Pakistan would also tone down their hostility to India. To any such development, Nehru was willing to respond. The obvious step was a 'no-war declaration' such as Eisenhower had urged Pakistan to announce; but, if she were not prepared to go that far, Nehru offered to consider a practical arrangement not to use force and to reduce the strength of the forces on both sides of the borders between India and Pakistan. He was also less outspoken than in 1959 about the idea of joint defence and presumed that Ayub had made his offer in a 'friendly spirit',[59] even though there was no change in his view that India could not accept a proposal which meant

[58] Nehru's instructions to Secretary-General and Foreign Secretary on replies to be sent, 19 June 1960; press conference in Delhi, 24 June, *National Herald*, 25 June 1960.

[59] Press conference in London, 2 May, *National Herald*, 3 May 1960.

uprooting herself from the basic foundations of her policy.[60] But, even without joint defence, formal or informal agreements on bilateral matters and defence could be considered.

Nehru also expected, as part of a policy of lessening border tensions, that the authorities in Pakistan would cease to encourage incidents of sabotage within Kashmir. But he could see no prospect of any progress towards a settlement on Kashmir.

> The fact is that it is quite beyond any possibility for the Government of India to agree to hand over any part of our territory to the Pakistan Government or to agree to any process which might lead to this. I do not want to shout this out, but that is a basic fact and the leaders of Pakistan should remember this.

So the only course open was not to try to reopen this question in a basic way, but to help to create conditions which would gradually lead to its settlement. This might take time, but there was no other way.[61]

One hopeful sign in relations between the two countries was the agreement on the Indus canal waters, reached at this time with the help of the World Bank. The three western rivers, the Indus, the Jhelum and the Chenab, were allotted to Pakistan, except for minor use in Kashmir, and the three eastern rivers, the Ravi, the Beas and the Sutlej, were reserved for India; and the period of transition would be ten years which could be extended by another three years if desired by Pakistan. India would also pay Rs 83 crores to Pakistan as compensation. Nehru went to Karachi in September to sign the agreement and was received with warmth. Quoting an Urdu couplet which claimed that success comes to those who approach problems with open hearts, Nehru told his audiences in Pakistan that the signing of the canal waters agreement could prove a symbol of cooperation with psychological and emotional benefits to both countries.[62] In such an atmosphere, more relaxed than usual, Ayub raised the issue of Kashmir. He desired a speedy settlement because delay might worsen the situation and, if it were not achieved between Nehru and him, it might become much more difficult and even impossible later on. No doubt mistakes had been made on both sides, but he was not concerned with past history. Nehru replied that the only practicable and feasible course was to allow matters to rest more or less where they were. Once the basic position was accepted, minor adjustments of the cease-fire line could be made; but any marked change would have a greatly upsetting effect not only in Kashmir but throughout India. The Muslims in India would be affected injuriously and their total integration in the Indian community would be prevented. Also, for any major transfer of territory, the Kashmir

60 31 August 1960. Lok Sabha Debates, Second Series, Vol. 46, pp. 5,926–40.

61 Note to Commonwealth Secretary, 20 June 1960.

62 Speeches at Karachi, 19 September, and Lahore, 22 September, *The Hindu*, 20 and 23 September 1960.

Assembly would have to be consulted and then the Constitution amended; and both steps would involve prolonged discussion with consequent unsettling results. The turmoil over the suggested transfer of part of the small enclave of Berubari on the Bengal border indicated the kind of upheaval which would be caused by any major redivision of Kashmir. Ayub would not accept this and argued that the cease-fire line only indicated the position of the armies of the two countries; but, when pressed by Nehru, he declined to give any indication as to the settlement he had in mind. He only stated repeatedly that Nehru should give full thought to this question and try to find some solution satisfactory to all the three parties, India, Pakistan and the people of Kashmir. The objective should first be determined and then a machinery could be established to work out the method of attaining this objective.[63]

So these talks marked no progress. On his return to India, Nehru tried to enact legislation transferring half of the enclave of Berubari to East Bengal. This had been agreed to years before as a rectification of the boundary award of 1947, but now there was opposition from the Government and people of West Bengal. An informal approach by Nehru to Ayub suggesting postponement evoking an almost offensive reply, Nehru sought to go ahead with the transfer. Taken with the canal waters agreement, such efforts, even if abortive, should have promoted goodwill; but, in fact, relations between the two countries remained, at the end of 1960, relatively cool.

[63] Nehru's note on talk with Ayub at Murree, 21 September 1960: M. Ayub Khan, *Friends not Masters* (Oxford, 1967), pp. 125–6.

7

Crusade in the Congo

Just when, in 1960, national interests were intensifying a major problem in foreign policy, a demand was made on the altruistic side of India's commitments. The tensions in the world in the summer of that year spread into a fresh arena with the attainment of independence by the Belgian Congo on 30 June. A vast area, the size of Western Europe, rich in minerals but with a population of less than thirteen million, the Congo was weakened, from the first days of its freedom, by the determination of the Belgians to retain their authority. They had done nothing over many years to promote the advancement of the Congolese people and now their intention was to render independence a sham. A large number of them lived in the southern province of Katanga, whose economy contributed a considerable portion of the Congo's production, revenue and foreign trade, and was controlled by foreign companies. On 11 July they encouraged Moise Tshombe to proclaim the 'independence' of Katanga, or virtual reversion to the status of a Belgian colony, while the Belgian Government sent troops to Leopoldville, the capital of the Congo, ostensibly to protect Belgian nationals. Within two weeks, therefore, the Belgians had succeeded in transforming the freedom of the Congo into a fantasy. To counter this, the Prime Minister of the Congo, Patrice Lumumba, appealed for military assistance to both the United States and the Soviet Union, sought the help of the United Nations in maintaining law and order and, till that organization was in a position to act, requested help from Ghana.

That Lumumba should have appealed simultaneously to the United States, the Soviet Union and the United Nations and not just to one of them made clear his hopes of keeping the Congo out of the cold war. The United States under Eisenhower was not likely to take action against the Belgians; and the Soviet Union made no immediate response to Lumumba's invitation. But Hammarskjöld promptly secured the Security Council's sanction for intervention by the United Nations. The Secretary-General was authorized to provide such military and technical assistance as was required till the Congolese security forces were able to function adequately on their own. Nehru welcomed this decision and spoke appreciatively of the vision and wisdom which Hammarskjöld had shown. To an extent support of the United Nations was to Nehru a personal act of faith; even Krishna Menon was lukewarm.[1] Recognizing that it would be a long and arduous journey before the Congo, though independent, could look after its own affairs properly, Nehru was hopeful that the United Nations could bring a measure of balance into the situation and prevent to some extent the ambitions of outside powers to take advantage of the local crisis.[2] As a token of support, non-combatant troops were sent as requested for distribution of supplies, for signalling duties and for running a hospital.

While, in his efforts to control the situation in the Congo, the Secretary-General could rely on the support of the Asian and African countries, he found the United States and the Soviet Union striving to push him in different directions. At first the Eisenhower Government were prepared to work with Lumumba and were friendly to him when he visited Washington;[3] but it was not long before the Congo was dragged into the rivalries of the great powers. Anti-communism was thought to require the support of Tshombe's secessionist move in Katanga, for Lumumba was expected to encourage Soviet influence.[4] So the United States encouraged Tshombe; but the Soviet Government pressed Hammarskjöld to utilize United Nations forces to restore the authority of the central Congolese authorities in Katanga. As a compromise, Hammarskjöld established a United Nations presence in Katanga and secured the withdrawal of Belgian personnel without interfering on the issue of secession, which he regarded as a matter of domestic politics. This did not satisfy Lumumba and the Congo problem developed an added complication in the form of an antipathy between Lumumba and Hammarskjöld. Lumumba was a patriot[5] but too volatile and voluble for Hammarskjöld, who spoke of him in private as a 'monkey on hot bricks' and guilty of 'inverted racism'.[6]

The Secretary-General now appointed a senior Indian diplomat, Rajeshwar Dayal, as his special representative in the Congo. Dayal reached Leopoldville on 5 September and walked straight into a crisis. Lumumba had by now secured Soviet military assistance on a bilateral basis, and the President, Kasavubu, on the advice and with the support of the United States and believing that he was acting with Hammarskjöld's unspoken approval,

[1] M. Brecher, *India and World Politics* (London, 1968), p. 98.

[2] Nehru to Chief Ministers, 30 July 1960; press conference at Delhi, 11 August, *National Herald*, 12 August 1960; speeches in Rajya Sabha, 17 August 1960, Debates. Vol. 30, pp. 1,128–36 and in Lok Sabha, 31 August 1960, Debates, Second Series, Vol. 46, pp. 5,926–40.

[3] S.R. Weissman, *American Foreign Policy in the Congo, 1960–1964* (Cornell University Press, 1974), p. 66.

[4] Cf. Sir Roy Welensky's advice to London: 'The fact is that Tshombe is pro-Western and Lumumba is not . . . if the young paranoiac Lumumba wins control of the whole of the Congo, there will be a strong Communist influence right in the middle of Africa.' Quoted in I. Colvin, *The Rise and Fall of Moise Tshombe* (London, 1968), p. 14.

[5] Even Major General H.T. Alexander, the British commander of Ghana's troops in the Congo, although not prejudiced in Lumumba's favour, concedes that his attitude was non-tribal and patriotic. *African Tightrope* (London, 1965), pp. 45, 47.

[6] R. Dayal to the author.

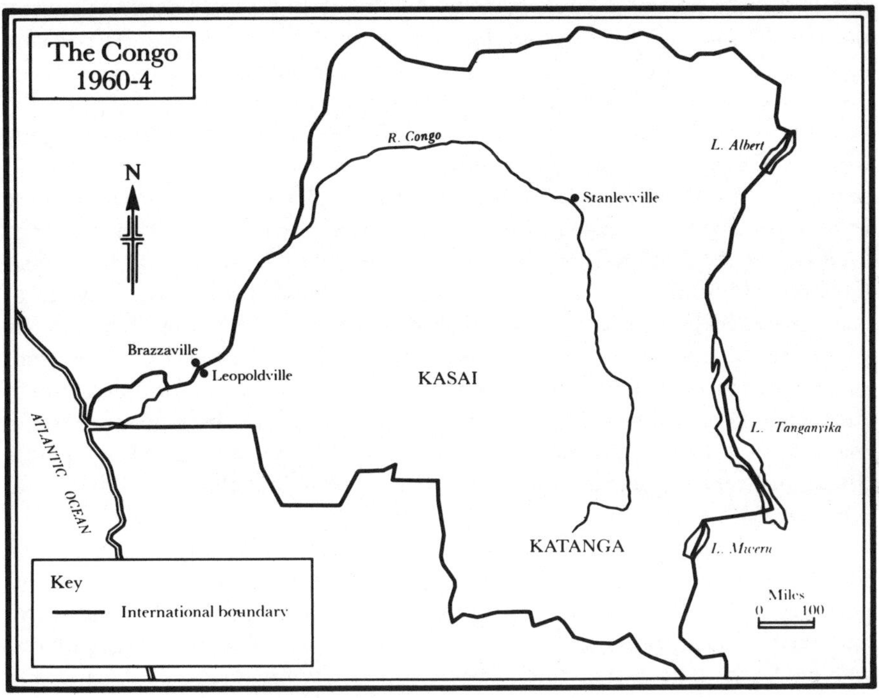

announced the dismissal of Lumumba. In turn, Lumumba charged the President with high treason. At this stage Andrew Cordier, the senior United Nations official in interim charge till Dayal formally took over, ordered the closure of the airports – a step clearly intended to hamper Lumumba if he planned to fly in troops and aircraft to the capital in order to oust the President.[7] Egypt, Ghana and Guinea, as well as the Soviet Union, were highly critical of Cordier's partisan action and were embarrassed at having to choose between Hammarskjöld and Lumumba; but Nehru willingly gave the United Nations the benefit of the doubt and was prepared to believe that the airfields might have been closed to restrict military movements by foreign powers.

However, Cordier next closed down the broadcasting station. This was a step even more blatantly biased against Lumumba than the closure of the airports, for Kasavubu had full use of the radio station across the river at Brazzaville. Although Hammarskjöld doubted the legality and necessity of these actions of Cordier,[8] he did not publicly criticize them, but they weakened considerably the position of the United Nations in the Congo.

Neither Lumumba nor Kasavubu was able to prevail over the other; and the army commander, Mobutu, stepped in, as he said, to neutralize both. In fact,

[7] C. Hoskyns, *The Congo since Independence* (Oxford, 1965), p. 208.

[8] R. Dayal, *Mission for Hammarskjöld* (Delhi, 1976), p. 46.

it was foreign powers who mattered.[9] As a reply to Nehru's query as to how the United Nations force could allow constitutional processes to be so easily subverted, Hammarskjöld sent him a copy of Dayal's report;[10] and the circumstance that both Hammarskjöld's special representative and his military adviser were Indians doubtless strengthened Nehru's instinctive support for the United Nations and made him less critical of Hammarskjöld's manifest support of Kasavubu than were other Afro-Asian and non-aligned countries. The idea, favoured by Nkrumah of Ghana and Sékou Touré of Guinea, of sending military assistance directly to Lumumba did not find favour with him, especially as Hammarskjöld had made this a matter of confidence. So he instructed the Indian delegation at the United Nations not to intervene on any major issue and to propose, if necessity arose, that important matters should await the arrival of full delegations for the session of the General Assembly. India should avoid finding herself in opposition to the majority of African and Arab states but, if pressed, would have to vote against direct military assistance, for abstention was not possible on such a vital issue.[11]

Two days later began the session of the General Assembly which Nehru, like many other Heads of Government, attended. His intention was to support the United Nations, which he thought had shown itself to be an 'active and virile' institution, and he set the tone by announcing, on his arrival in New York, that he had much admiration for Hammarskjöld.[12] The Congo was but one of the issues drowned at this session in the bitterness of the cold war. The conflict between the two blocs was deep and they engaged in bullying and threats rather than in efforts to draw closer. The atmosphere seemed to Nehru thick with hatred and suspicion; one could almost feel the breath of violence and, despite the desire for peace among the peoples of the world and the full realization by all of the potential of nuclear weapons, war did not seem very far off. It was a depressing experience; but he kept his footing and sought to help in finding ways out of this intermesh of problems. Non-alignment, as he had defined it a few weeks earlier, was not an acrobatic feat of sitting on a spiked fence and balancing between the two sides; it had to be an effort to uproot the fence and throw it away.[13] On the Congo, as the United Nations was generally doing well and functioning with integrity, he broadly supported the attempts to secure a meeting of Parliament, to control the army and Tshombe and to reduce the influence of the Belgians who had come back to Katanga. But otherwise he was '*strictly neutral*'[14] and tried to

[9] T. Kanza, *Conflict in the Congo* (London, 1972), p. 303. Kanza was a member of Lumumba's Cabinet.

[10] Dayal, *Mission for Hammarskjöld*, pp. 76–7.

[11] Telegram to Krishna Menon at New York, 18 September 1960.

[12] Statements to journalists at Delhi airport on eve of departure to New York, 24 September, and at New York, 25 September, *National Herald*, 25 and 27 September 1960 respectively.

[13] 31 August 1960. Lok Sabha Debates, Second Series, Vol. 46, pp. 5,926–40.

[14] H. Macmillan's diary entry, 5 October 1960, *Pointing the Way* (London, 1972), p. 281. Emphasis in original.

leave the field to Hammarskjöld and not to involve India further in Congo affairs.

Despite Hammarskjöld's courage in initiative and desire to be impartial and Dayal's presence at Leopoldville, the policy of the United Nations was weakened, in Nehru's view, by the continuance of Cordier as Hammarskjöld's principal adviser and by the fact that the latter's whole background and thinking were in line with the West. It was not that Hammarskjöld was deliberately partial; he just could not help himself. 'All we can do', Nehru said,[15] and this was the nearest he came to public criticism of Hammarskjöld, 'is deliberately to try to be impartial. But our own thinking colours our actions. While we may be men of high integrity, we cannot get rid of our own minds in our approach to a question.' There was some truth in this implied criticism. Moreover, one of Hammarskjöld's failings, serious in an United Nations official, was his inability to communicate with the Soviet side.[16] On his part Hammarskjöld, though grateful for Nehru's refusal to give the lead to Asian and African countries in support of Khrushchev's direct attack on the Secretary-General, was disappointed that Nehru seemed to be unqualifiedly in favour of Lumumba.[17] But it was also clear that Nehru's firm loyalty to the United Nations, well-established commitment to support whichever policy seemed best suited to the Congolese people and lack of self-interest in the matter had vested him with crucial importance. Though he modestly described himself later as 'a humble pilgrim' at the United Nations 'who walked on foot in the midst of mighty charioteers',[18] the facts were very different. 'The Afro-Asian front', reported Hammarskjöld to Dayal,[19] 'holds when there is no gallery. The role of Nehru will now be decisive. If he sways, the public Afro-Asian front may break with very far-reaching consequences for the Organisation and, as subordinated matter, for my attitude.'

Probably to retain Nehru's sympathy and no doubt influenced by Dayal, who stressed the unconstitutional nature of the Mobutu regime and the return of Belgian advisers to the Congolese ministries,[20] Hammarskjöld fell in line at this time with the efforts to bring Tshombe to heel and to 'fully circumscribe the Belgian factor and eliminate it'.[21] It was now the turn of the Western Powers, led by the United States and Belgium, to try to thwart the efforts of the United Nations. Mobutu was strengthened in the Congo and Kasavubu was flown to New York and seated in the United Nations, despite the efforts of

[15] Press conference in New York, 4 October 1960, P.I.B.; see also Nehru to Vijayalakshmi, 21 October 1960.

[16] Dayal, *Mission for Hammarskjöld*, pp. 308–9.

[17] Telegram to Dayal, quoted in ibid., pp. 98–9.

[18] Speech at the A.I.C.C., Raipur, 29 October 1960. A.I.C.C. papers, Box 17. File G-23A/1960. N.M.M.L.

[19] Dayal, *Mission for Hammarskjöld*, p. 100.

[20] Dayal's report, 2 November 1960. R. Higgins, *United Nations Peace-Keeping*, Vol. III, *Africa* (Oxford, 1980), pp. 153–5.

[21] The phrase is Hammarskjöld's, quoted in Weissman, *American Foreign Policy in the Congo, 1960–1964*, p. 103.

India and other countries to prevent the acceptance of Kasavubu's credentials. But Nehru did not react to this failure by adopting extreme positions and continued to insist that the convening of the Congolese Parliament was the essential step. Even the United Nations should not impose any solution by the use of force.[22] Though anxious that India should not be entangled further or committed to send more troops or even technicians to the Congo,[23] he rejected Khrushchev's suggestion for the creation of an African army in the Congo, separate from the United Nations force.[24] He also took care not to back Nkrumah without reservation, for he believed that Nkrumah was over-playing his hand in his support of Lumumba and was developing ambitions in the Congo. The fact that the African countries were not agreed on policy in the Congo strengthened this caution.[25]

Nehru's critical assessment of Hammarskjöld's policy in the Congo during the earlier stages of the session of the General Assembly reinforced his general sympathy for Khrushchev's demand for a recasting of the structure and machinery of the United Nations. While pointedly dissociating himself from the personal attacks on the Secretary-General, he suspected a pronounced bias in favour of the West in the higher counsels of the United Nations;[26] and the additional responsibilities which Hammarskjöld had justifiably assumed exposed the inadequacies of the Secretariat. There was an obvious need for the machinery of the organization to reflect the fact that the number of Asian and African member-countries was rapidly increasing. So Nehru was keen that, without impairing the Secretary-General's authority and capacity for taking quick action by creating 'a kind of three-headed god'[27] as suggested by Khrushchev, it should be made manifest that the Secretary-General was regularly securing the advice of all major groups of world opinion. For this purpose, Nehru was thinking broadly in terms of diffusing the powers of the Secretary-General by the appointment of deputies or the creation of an advisory council, which could be set up without any basic change in the functions of the Secretary-General or any amendment of the United Nations Charter. Organizational rather than structural changes might be sufficient for the time being, and the Secretary-General himself might consider ways of broadening the base of his office.[28]

Hammarskjöld, who was relying heavily on the support of Asian and

22 Press conference at Delhi, 21 October 1960. P.I.B.

23 Nehru's note to Commonwealth Secretary after return to India, 17 October 1960.

24 Khrushchev to Nehru, 9 November, and Nehru's reply, 13 November 1960.

25 Nehru's telegram to Krishna Menon, 5 November 1960.

26 The facts bear out Nehru's suspicion. An American scholar acknowledges: 'In the Secretariat a high percentage of the staff was at least basically Western in outlook. Americans, British and Frenchmen held 49 of the 102 senior positions. Hammarskjöld's closest advisers were all Americans who had survived a McCarthyite purge of the Secretariat in the 1950s.' Weissman, *American Foreign Policy in the Congo, 1960–1964*, p. 60.

27 Press conference, 21 October 1960, ibid.

28 Statement in General Assembly, 4 October 1960, *Speeches*, Vol. 4, pp. 314–24; press conference in New York, 4 October 1960, P.I.B.; television interview, 8 October, *The Hindu*, 9 October 1960; statement on departure from New York, 10 October, *The Hindu*, 11 October 1960.

African countries and, in particular, of India in his defence against Khrushchev, could not conceal his disappointment at Nehru's seemingly half-hearted attitude. But he was able, with the assistance of the delegations of Ireland, New Zealand and Egypt, to ensure that Nehru did not formally present his compromise proposal of a consultative council.[29] Perhaps Nehru did not require much persuasion to leave unchanged the existing situation, with all its drawbacks, as he recognized the general desire of the member-countries not to push the issue to the extent of endangering the existence of the organization itself. He was also put off by both sides in this tussle. Khrushchev spoiled a good case with rough behaviour, bellicose language and personal criticism of Hammarskjöld; but the Western Powers, while more decorous in debate, were in fact rigid and unyielding. 'Thus, in this age of terror, nations try to protect themselves by exhibiting their strength of muscle, breadth of jaw and stiffness of the upper lip. Or is it that this exhibition of concentrated power is a reaction to the fear and suspicion within their minds and hearts?'[30]

The most worrying aspect of this cold war at the General Assembly was the freezing of the negotiations for disarmament. There was much to be said for the Soviet approach and its opposition to German rearmament; but, as in other matters, the means adopted to influence others had often the opposite effect. Nehru was at this time for phased disarmament, achieved in such a way as to maintain broadly the balance of armed power.[31] India, along with Egypt, Ghana, Indonesia and Yugoslavia, moved a resolution recommending renewal of contacts between the United States and the Soviet Union. It was intended as no more than a 'holding' resolution, to prevent further deterioration of relations till the presidential elections in the United States were over. It embodied, said Nehru, no more than a hope that the glacier which was surrounding the nations might be pushed or made to melt a little so that discussions could take place at some suitable time in the future. But the Western Powers moved amendments and pressed for votes which virtually nullified the intention of the non-aligned countries. Even a 'casual' gesture in response was not forthcoming,[32] and a moral issue was reduced to meaningless jargon. So Nehru withdrew, with some bitterness, the original resolution.[33] As he later privately admitted, he 'went for Mr Menzies', the Prime Minister of Australia who took the lead in moving the amendments, because he had heard that their purpose was 'to cut Nehru to size'.[34] It seemed to him that Khrushchev, with all his faults, at least knew how to deal with the countries of the Third World, while the United States was making a grave mistake by showing its contempt for the non-aligned and insisting that to be friends with

[29] B. Urquhart, *Hammarskjöld* (London, 1972), p. 462.
[30] Nehru to Chief Ministers, 24 October 1960.
[31] Speech at the General Assembly, 4 October 1960.
[32] Television interview at New York, 8 October, *The Hindu*, 9 October 1960.
[33] Two speeches at the General Assembly, 5 October 1960, *Speeches*, Vol. 4, pp. 327–35.
[34] Address to the Congress Parliamentary Party, 18 October 1960. Tapes M-52/C, Parts I and II.

the United States one had to join in the cold war.[35] But the resolution, even though withdrawn, had served its purpose, of drawing forceful attention to the need for some contacts between the two powers.[36]

So the world crisis, far from becoming less acute, appeared as if, at any moment, it might grow worse. The Congo and the 'troika' proposals together ensured that disarmament, or any further effort at steps leading to a summit meeting, was not seriously considered at this session of the General Assembly. 'If the Great Powers are bent on self-destruction and, in the process, destroying the rest of the world also, they will no doubt do so.'[37] In his private conversations with Nehru in New York, Khrushchev urged a special session of the General Assembly early the next year, preferably at Geneva, solely to discuss disarmament. Nehru, while approving of the idea of a meeting at Geneva, preferred a session of the disarmament conference rather than of the General Assembly, where other issues than disarmament were bound to be raised; but Khrushchev insisted on a session of the General Assembly as having higher status, attracting more attention and inducing Heads of State and Government to attend.[38]

Meantime, in December, after the session of the General Assembly had ended, the situation in the Congo boiled over again. The Kasavubu regime in Leopoldville was defied by Gizenga, who owed allegiance to Lumumba, in Stanleyville, while the provinces of Katanga and South Kasai claimed to be independent. Lumumba's escape on 27 November from the protective custody of the United Nations and his arrest by Kasavubu's troops five days later added to the tension. The representatives of the Western countries impeded the efforts of the United Nations to secure a meeting of the Congolese Parliament and to reduce the interventions of foreign powers in the internal affairs of the Congo. Their general attitude was summed up by Mobutu: 'These Indians who run the United Nations here are doing everything they can to bring Lumumba back into power and turn the Congo into a Soviet State.'[39] Tito blamed the United Nations for allowing itself to be pushed into a negative position and withdrew the Yugoslav diplomatic mission as well as all the personnel sent at the request of the United Nations.[40] Nasser was known to be as upset while the Soviet Government were planning counter-measures. Nkrumah favoured an African high command.

Nehru's first reaction was also to pull out of the Congo. Anti-Indian slogans and the harassment of Indian army and civilian personnel had caused considerable resentment in India. But refusing to be provoked by the 'fantastic and Gilbertian' situation, where 'a so-called army' had turned into a

35 Nehru's interview in *L' Express* (Paris), 17 October 1960.

36 Nehru in the Lok Sabha, 23 November 1960. Debates, Second Series, Vol. 47, pp. 1,934–62; answer in the Rajya Sabha, 28 November 1960, Debates, Vol. 31, pp. 23–5.

37 Nehru's telegram to Krishna Menon from Delhi after his return from New York, 22 October 1960.

38 Nehru to K.P.S. Menon, Ambassador in Moscow, 24 October 1960.

39 *New York Herald Tribune*, 9 November 1960, quoted in Hoskyns, *The Congo since Independence*, p. 254.

40 Tito to Nehru, 7 December 1960.

mob,[41] Nehru decided to retain the Indian presence in the Congo provided it was subjected to no further indignities, in the hope that this would help to halt the drift of the United Nations into helplessness. Tito's proposal, that in certain circumstances the troops in the Congo should not accept orders from the United Nations but should report to their own national commands, did not seem to Nehru wise or practical for it would mean the virtual disintegration of the United Nations force and encouragement to foreign armies to join the feuding Congolese groups. He also did not favour direct support for Lumumba as this might mean a break with the United Nations, the weakening of the forces working for the independence of the Congo and the creation of a vacuum into which foreign powers could move. If the Congo were not to go to pieces, there was no alternative to the strengthening of the mandate and authority of the United Nations. It was the responsibility of Hammarskjöld and his officials to abandon discriminating attitudes and to ensure the release of prisoners by all sides and the convening of the Congolese Parliament. Nehru also sent for the American Ambassador and warned him that India would be no party to the rebuilding of the Belgian empire in a new garb, for it was to this that the policies of the Western Powers were leading. The result could well be the biggest disaster the world may have seen.[42]

> I do not know if there is any realization in England about the anger that is spreading, not only in India but in many countries, over the handling of the Congo issue by the United States, the United Kingdom and France. These countries and, of course, Belgium have behaved in a scandalous manner which has no justification in principle, in constitutional theory or even in any practical results. It is largely due to their attitude and policies that the situation has deteriorated very rapidly.[43]

To demonstrate that he might be obliged to revise his policy if the performance of the United Nations did not improve or if the Western Powers continued to behave as before, Nehru held up further commitments of Indian personnel to the United Nations in the Congo and hinted that the withdrawal of even those already there might have to be considered.[44]

So the crisis of the Congo, 'most depressing and sometimes rather exasperating',[45] seemed to be moving beyond control. To give Hammarskjöld a

[41] Nehru in the Lok Sabha, 24 November and 5 December 1960, Debates, Second Series, Vols 47, pp. 2,085–98 and 48, pp. 3,770–3 respectively.

[42] Nehru's letters to Tito and to Nasser, 8 December, and telegrams to Krishna Menon, 8 and 11 December 1960; statements in the Lok Sabha, 9 and 12 December 1960, Debates, Second Series, Vols 48, pp. 4,814–16 and 49, pp. 5,043–58 respectively; press conference at Delhi, 15 December, *National Herald*, 16 December 1960.

[43] Nehru to Vijayalakshmi, 7 December 1960.

[44] Speeches in the Rajya Sabha, 20 and 21 December 1960; Debates, Vol. 31, pp. 2,689–711 and pp. 2,945–74 respectively; Nehru's note to Secretary-General, Ministry of External Affairs, 21 December 1960.

[45] Nehru at the Congress session, Bhavnagar, 6 January, *The Hindu*, 7 January 1961.

further opportunity to tone up his policy, Nehru declined to participate in the conference convened by the King of Morocco and attended by all other Asian and African states involved in the Congo operation. India was, therefore, not a party to the ultimatum served on the United Nations that these countries would consider themselves free to act on their own if Mobutu's troops were not disarmed, foreign advisers expelled and the Congolese Parliament summoned. But Nehru advised Hammarskjöld to seek an agreement between the Western and the Eastern blocs on a minimum policy. If the West could be persuaded to withdraw all Belgian personnel and to direct Kasavubu to summon Parliament and if Mobutu's troops were disarmed, the Soviet Union and the more important African countries might agree to keep the Congo out of cold war alignments, thereby making it easier for the United Nations to play a more effective role. The refusal to accede to Kasavubu's formal request to withdraw Dayal had been more than offset by the failure to control Mobutu and to secure the release of Lumumba and other political prisoners. This had damaged the prestige of the United Nations and created a widespread impression that the organization was the victim of pressures from various countries. If, because of this, African troops were withdrawn from the United Nations Command, India could not be expected to replace them.[46] Nehru sent a message in similar terms to Macmillan[47] and expected the new administration in Washington to reformulate American policy. There was certainly a shift in the policy of the United States after Kennedy became President, transforming 'the whole political ecology'[48] in the United Nations. But as Macmillan's reply gave no indication of any change in British thinking, Nehru got in touch with him again, requesting him to reconsider the entire situation before it became too late to have any policy at all.[49] He also, on receiving reports that Lumumba had been killed, conveyed to Hammarskjöld India's concern and asked him to take every possible step to find out the truth.[50]

These messages had hardly been despatched when, on 13 February, official news of Lumumba's death was received, although this had occurred almost a month before. The failure to save Lumumba's life damaged considerably the authority of the United Nations and cast a permanent shadow on Hammarskjöld's reputation. For the murder was the culmination of a long process beginning with Cordier's biased actions, the legitimacy extended to Kasavubu by Hammarskjöld primarily because of his personal dislike of Lumumba and the proneness of the United Nations representatives to assume legalist attitudes. Nehru had no doubt as to what had happened. 'Murder has been committed and murder probably by people who occupy high places.'[51]

[46] Nehru's two letters to Hammarskjöld, 25 January 1961.

[47] Nehru's telegram to Macmillan, 1 February 1961.

[48] C.C. O'Brien, 'The Congo, the United Nations and Chatham House', *New Left Review*, May–June 1965.

[49] Nehru's telegram to Macmillan, 12 February 1961.

[50] Nehru's instructions to Secretary-General, Ministry of External Affairs, 11 February 1961.

[51] Nehru to journalists in Delhi, 13 February, *National Herald*, 14 February 1961.

Reacting strongly to this 'international crime of the first magnitude', he warned Hammarskjöld that if the United Nations did not meet this challenge and take immediate and strong measures against the guilty, India would have to reconsider her policy.[52] He also urged the Kennedy administration, whose policy was much nearer India's position than that of the Eisenhower regime, to stand up against those states which were weakening the United Nations in the Congo and to ensure the withdrawal of Belgian and other such foreign elements.[53]

However, with the Soviet Government concentrating their criticism on Hammarskjöld, there was little chance of a concerted policy among the great powers; and Nehru now placed his hopes in the countries of Asia and Africa holding together and framing an approach which would not be rejected by the United States and the Soviet Union. Unilateral action, such as withdrawal of recognition of Hammarskjöld as Secretary-General advocated by Moscow, recognition of the Gizenga regime as granted by Egypt and Guinea or withdrawal of troops from the United Nations force as suggested by Sékou Touré, was rejected by him as leaving the field open to conflict between the great powers. He preferred to continue to rely on the United Nations in the hope that it would abandon its posture of passivity and stop the civil war, control the rebellious factions and secure the withdrawal of all foreign personnel except those under its own command. He even hinted that, if the Security Council gave a sufficiently strong mandate to the Secretary-General along these lines, India would be willing to despatch combat troops. Once these immediate objectives had been achieved, the reconvening of Parliament and the formation of a new Government could be considered.[54] The crisis had to be firmly handled, for it was having wide repercussions. It cast a huge shadow over the whole continent of Africa and raised basic doubts about the future of the United Nations; and 'behind it all perhaps the big guns of the big countries are also showing their ugly noses'. It looked almost as if a new type of empire was being sought, established on the ruins of the old. The murder of Lumumba could be a turning-point in history, with Lumumba dead infinitely more important than alive.[55] For Lumumba had become the symbol of African nationalism and, as Fanon observed later, it was less the truth of what Lumumba said than the truth of his person which was important.[56] The United Nations, with all its inadequacies and mistakes, was the Congo's only hope.[57]

[52] Nehru's telegram to Hammarskjöld, 13 February 1961.

[53] Address to the Congress Parliamentary Party, 13 February 1961, Tape M-54/C, Part I; Nehru's instructions by telegram to M.C. Chagla, Indian Ambassador in Washington, 13 February 1961.

[54] Nehru's telegram to S. Touré, 14 February 1961; statement in Lok Sabha, 15 February 1961; Debates, Second Series, Vol. 50, pp. 132–40; telegrams to Chagla, 16 February, and to K.P.S. Menon in Moscow and to Macmillan, 17 February 1961.

[55] Nehru's speech at the seminar on the problems of emergent Africa, 17 February, *The Hindu*, 18 February 1961.

[56] F. Fanon, *Towards the African Revolution* (New York, 1967), p. 193.

[57] Speech in the Rajya Sabha, 20 February 1961. Debates, Vol. 32, pp. 473–97.

The Security Council's resolution of 21 February seemed to meet Nehru's demands. In fact, it had been drafted in consultation with India by those countries of Asia and Africa which were members of the Council. It insisted on the immediate withdrawal of Belgian and other foreign personnel of certain specified categories and authorized the Secretary-General to take positive measures so as to enable the Congolese leaders to initiate the political steps which would restore the equilibrium of the country. Nehru, therefore, rejected Khrushchev's request to him to support the Soviet attitude on the Congo by recognizing the Gizenga Government as the legitimate successor to that of Lumumba and demanding the withdrawal of United Nations forces from the Congo, so that matters could be decided by the African countries concerned. He also asked Khrushchev not to mix up this issue with that of the reorganization of the United Nations and of the office of the Secretary-General. If Khrushchev agreed to this, it was possible that Kennedy could be persuaded to eliminate Belgian influence from the Congo and even to agree to keep that country free from all foreign intervention except as authorized by the United Nations. The Congo could then become a parallel with Suez, when Soviet-American agreement had been facilitated by the non-aligned countries. Kennedy's hand would be strengthened by the Soviet suspension of recognition, however justified, of the Gizenga Government. It was an occasion for world statesmanship and the joint initiative of the great powers rather than for support of one or the other side.[58]

In the Congo itself, Kasavubu and his supporters reacted violently to the Security Council's resolution and in particular blamed India in the persons of Nehru and Dayal. It was rumoured that Nehru and Lumumba had reached a secret agreement permitting the immigration of two million Indians into the Congo in return for India's support.[59] But Nehru continued to favour the United Nations operation and to back up Hammarskjöld. He rejected Nkrumah's suggestion of an African contingent under an Indian commander.[60] Meantime, Hammarskjöld, acting on Nehru's encouraging hint in his speech in Parliament, requested India for the services of a brigade of about 4,700 troops. As success in the Congo now seemed as important to the United Nations Organization as to the Congo itself, Nehru agreed; and if troops were to be sent at all, it was better to send a brigade which could function as a unit, rather than odd battalions which would be attached to other groups. But he insisted that these troops should not be scattered or used for the suppression of popular movements or in support of any parties or factions that were challenging the United Nations. While critical of the Secretary-General's actions in many respects, Nehru believed that he represented an organization which demanded allegiance and hoped that, with this accession of fresh

[58] Khrushchev to Nehru, 18, 22 and 25 February, and Nehru's reply, 26 February 1961.

[59] Dayal, *Mission for Hammarskjöld,* p. 221.

[60] Telegram to Nehru from Indian mission at U.N., 6 March, and Nehru's reply from London (where he was attending the Commonwealth Prime Ministers' Conference), 7 March 1961.

strength, Hammarskjöld would utilize the United Nations force in a more purposeful manner. In the context of Soviet denunciations of Hammarskjöld as an organizer of crime, African attempts to shake off responsibility for United Nations activities, a discouraging and panicky situation in the Congo itself, opposition in his own Cabinet (led by Krishna Menon) to support of Hammarskjöld and the growing military menace on India's borders, it required considerable moral courage for Nehru to take this decision, symbolic of his trust and belief in the international organization. For the Congo the alternative to the United Nations was civil war backed by the great powers. To the world, it was important that the United Nations, having decided to play a positive role in the Congo, should succeed, and succeed in the right way; and India could not shirk active participation when it was sought by the Secretary-General. At a critical time the despatch of an Indian brigade to the Congo strengthened Hammarskjöld, who gratefully described it as a great act of faith which would go down in history as a most remarkable and in many ways decisive event.[61]

The first contingent of Indian troops, flown out to the Congo by American military aircraft, landed in Leopoldville on 15 March 1961, to be greeted by Kasavubu's Prime Minister with the threat that blood would flow. Tshombe added, for good measure, that India's action was tantamount to a declaration of war. Nehru complained at the encouragement which the British and American Ambassadors seemed to be providing for such vilification;[62] but it was not as if these envoys were acting in defiance of their superiors at home. For, whatever the lip-service in London and Washington to the resolution of the Security Council, in fact efforts were directed to defeating it. Nehru contended that the United Nations and the Western Powers could not hope to follow two contradictory policies at the same time; they would have to choose between implementation of the resolution of the Security Council and support of Kasavubu. Double-dealing could only lead to the failure of the United Nations in the Congo and a consequent weaking of its structure and a strengthening of Soviet policy. The crux of the situation was the withdrawal of the Belgians and letting the Congolese run their own affairs with such help as they needed coming from the United Nations. If evasion and fumbling persisted on these issues, and the Western Powers continued, as he later described it, 'thinking in two directions',[63] supporting the United Nations but demanding that it should do nothing, then India would have to decide on her own attitude. To live under the threats of Mobutu or Tshombe or Kasavubu and be rendered helpless by them was an impossible situation for India as well as the United Nations.[64]

[61] Telegram to Nehru from Indian mission at U.N., 12 March 1961.

[62] Nehru's telegram to Chagla in Washington, 11 March 1961, and later verbal protest in London to Macmillan.

[63] 11 December 1961. Rajya Sabha Debates, Vol. 36, pp. 1,850–76.

[64] Telegrams to Indian mission at New York, 23, 25 and 30 March; letter to Nasser, 1 April, reporting conversations with A. Harriman and D. Rusk in Delhi; interview in *U.S. News and World Report*, 10 April

This disillusion with the attitudes of the Western countries, which seemed not to have rid themselves of their imperial past, coloured Nehru's attitude in these years to the Commonwealth. He had stated bluntly in 1960 that membership was worthwhile, from India's point of view, for the friendliness and warmth regardless of the problems, the common democratic form of organization and the lack of racial discrimination.[65] The Congo was showing the first benefit to be wearing thin, the second had been weakened by military rule in Pakistan and the third threatened by the tolerance of apartheid in South Africa. Not surprisingly his position hardened on the last issue,[66] which he thought 'might well shake the very foundations of the Commonwealth'. If the Commonwealth Prime Ministers did nothing about it, the association might well become so vague and cloudy as to have no shape or form at all.[67] So he insisted that, despite the convention barring discussion of matters of domestic concern, the racial policies of South Africa could not be ignored. The Prime Ministers had to consider how best to deal with it, for otherwise some of them would be placed in an extremely embarrassing position in their own countries. He himself favoured informal discussions in small groups rather than casual talks between some of them and the South African representative. So the subject was discussed in polite and moderate phrases behind which, as everyone realized, lay hidden volcanos. Reference was also made, at Nehru's insistence, to the subject in the final communiqué, for absence of all mention would have been, in his view, a serious indictment of all of them.[68]

Such a clear rejection of apartheid, however satisfactory, obviously was not the end of the problem; and Nehru emphasized that the future of the Commonwealth depended on the way in which it was finally settled.[69] Irritated by British policy in the Congo, Nehru was losing interest in the Commonwealth association and was seriously considering secession if South Africa were permitted to remain after becoming a republic.[70] The matter came up again at the Conference of Prime Ministers in March 1961. Despite Krishna Menon's worry that Nehru's presence would be exploited as support for the Western positions on disarmament and other issues, the Prime Minister decided to attend. This in itself was a concession to the British Government, who had pleaded that without him the conference would be meaningless.[71] At the meeting, Macmillan and Menzies strove for a com-

1961; telegrams to missions in New York and London reporting conversations with American Ambassador J.K. Galbraith, 12 April, and letter to Kennedy, 16 April 1961.

[65] Press conference in London, 2 May 1960. P.I.B.

[66] H. Macmillan's diary entry, May 1960, *Pointing the Way*, p. 172.

[67] Speech at London, 6 May, *The Hindu*, 7 May 1960.

[68] Nehru's remarks at Conference of Commonwealth Prime Ministers, 3 and 12 May 1960; Nehru to Chief Ministers, 8 June 1960.

[69] Speeches in the Rajya Sabha, 17 and 18 August 1960. Debates, Vol. 30, pp. 1,128–36 and 1,334–54 respectively.

[70] Nehru to Vijayalakshmi, 7 December 1960.

[71] Nehru's telegram to Krishna Menon in New York, 31 October, Menon's replies, 31 October and 7 November, and Nehru's telegram, 10 November 1960.

promise; but the members from Asia and Africa, under Nehru's guidance and with the support of Canada, were not prepared to temporize. Nehru did not threaten to take India out of the Commonwealth but warned of the dangers of the association disintegrating if apartheid were tolerated. South Africa, realizing that its application would be rejected, begged leave to withdraw it.[72]

This diplomatic victory enabled the Commonwealth as conceived by Nehru to survive; but it marked no improvement in relations between Britain and India. Criticism of Dayal in Western Europe as 'rabidly anti-Belgian'[73] rose to a new pitch. Nehru asserted his unqualified opposition to the withdrawal of Dayal and hinted that, if Dayal were replaced, India might have to consider pulling out her troops.[74] Yet the criticism of Dayal was so continuously shrill that Hammarskjöld had to yield and in May 1961 agreed, with Nehru's prior knowledge, to remove Dayal.

However, Indian troops were active and gradually gained control of northern Katanga without firing a shot.[75] Many foreign advisers also had to leave Katanga. But thereafter the situation worsened. The United Nations was obstructed by the Western countries in its efforts to remove foreign mercenaries from Katanga province and Nehru denounced such unabashed support of Tshombe. 'I think the whole thing is perfectly amazing and scandalous in the extreme.'[76] It demonstrated to him how deep were the roots of colonialism and how pervasive its influence even when it had no hope of a future. Then, on a flight to Katanga, Hammarskjöld died in an air crash. The feeling against Britain in India was intense. Even Nehru believed that, though Hammarskjöld had not been murdered by the British, his death was certainly a consequence of British policy in the Congo.[77] But he did not permit this event to push Indian policy off course and, at the United Nations, declined to support the Soviet proposal for not electing a successor to Hammarskjöld or dividing the world into three zones for United Nations purposes.[78] He also, at the request of the United States, instructed Menon not to sponsor any arrangement for a compromise which might preclude direct negotiations between the United States and the Soviet Union.[79]

After Adoula had formed the central Government in the Congo in August 1961, Nehru promised him full assistance in securing unity and maintaining independence.[80] There was no halfway house; unless the foreign elements were

[72] Nehru at a press conference in London, 17 March, *The Hindu*, 18 March 1961; R. Menzies, *Afternoon Light* (London, 1967), p. 214; Macmillan, *Pointing the Way*, p. 298; J.D.B. Miller, *Survey of Commonwealth Affairs, Problems of Expansion and Attrition 1953–1969* (Oxford, 1974), pp. 154–5.

[73] I. Scott, *Tumbled House* (Oxford, 1969), p. 74. Scott was British Ambassador in the Congo at this time.

[74] Speech in Lok Sabha, 3 April 1961. Debates, Second Series, Vol. 53, pp. 8,897–927.

[75] B. Chakravarty, *The Congo Operation 1960–63* (Ministry of Defence, Delhi, 1976), p. 56.

[76] Press conference at Delhi, 17 September, *National Herald*, 18 September 1961.

[77] Nehru to Padmaja Naidu, 19 September 1961.

[78] Telegram to Krishna Menon, 22 September 1961.

[79] Telegrams to Krishna Menon, 28 and 30 September 1961.

[80] Nehru to C. Adoula, 31 October 1961.

removed, the Congo would split up and the United Nations would suffer a serious setback. For the Congo was still to him the symbol and the touchstone of the success of the United Nations.[81] It was 'monstrous' to encourage the break-up of the United Nations by supporting Katanga while accusing India of defying the United Nations by her action in Goa. 'All this piles up in our minds, makes us angry and very angry. I am not talking about my mind. I am talking about the generic mind of Asia and Africa.' Perhaps the most distressing aspect of issues like Congo and Goa were that they divided world opinion 'to put it crudely, between white and black'. Values and standards clearly differed and the alarms raised about the 'danger' to the United Nations obviously emanated from fears of the growing weight of Asian and African opinion.[82]

So, after the Goa operation, Nehru was even more determined than before to support the United Nations in the Congo. India provided more troops than any other state for the operation to end the secession of Katanga and, throughout the year 1962, they were actively engaged in this area. Though, with the increasing Chinese pressure on her own borders, India could ill spare a brigade, Nehru contemplated withdrawal only if it were not properly employed.[83] Even after the massive Chinese aggression in the autumn, he informed the United Nations that India would like the troops back as soon as convenient but set no date because even urgent requirements at home should not upset the plans of the United Nations or come in the way of India's international commitments.[84] In the event, Indian troops completed the task of bringing the whole country under the control of the central Government before returning home in March 1963.

The crisis in the Congo impinged on two deep moral commitments of Nehru, to the people of Africa and to the values of the United Nations. He believed that newly independent countries should be given all possible aid to enable them to function in full freedom and thereby help others less fortunate than themselves to reach the same goal. This was particularly so in Africa, for imperialism had probably been seen at its worst in that continent and her people had suffered the most. 'In India, an incident took place which has come to be known as the "black hole of Calcutta" . . . But for the African people, their entire life till now has been spent in a black hole.'[85] But 'an astounding revolution' had begun on that continent with large parts of it shedding their colonial status with amazing rapidity;[86] and any assistance required in this process could not be denied. He regarded it, therefore, as India's duty to help

[81] Address to the United Nations General Assembly, 10 November 1961.

[82] Press conference at Delhi, 28 December, *National Herald*, 29 December 1961.

[83] D.N. Chatterji's account of interview with Nehru, 12 October 1962. *Storm over the Congo* (Delhi, 1980), p. 3. Chatterji had served as Indian Ambassador in the Congo from 1960 to 1962.

[84] Nehru's answers to questions in the Lok Sabha, 8 November 1962. Debates, Third Series, Vol. 9, pp. 26–30.

[85] Speech at Delhi, 31 January, *National Herald*, 1 February 1960.

[86] Speech in the Rajya Sabha, 12 February 1960. Debates, Vol. 28, pp. 602–26.

14 With Khrushchev, Delhi, 11 February 1961

15 *Above left* With Aneurin Bevan, Asheridge farm, 2 May 1960
16 *Above right* At the United Nations General Assembly, September 1960

17 With Paul Robeson, London, 5 May 1960

the Congo to stand on its own feet as a united and independent country. This became even more important when the United Nations was involved; for failure to achieve what the organization had set out to do would greatly weaken it as a force working for a world order. Nehru had not always been happy with Hammarskjöld's ways of functioning; but he approved of the Secretary-General's determination to provide the United Nations with a positive role in world affairs. So, despite his reservations on specific matters, he gave Hammarskjöld full support on crucial occasions and time and again turned away from alternatives suggested by the Soviet, Yugoslav or African Governments, even if this involved the risk of India isolating herself on matters of more direct concern to her. One can well understand Hammarskjöld's remark, 'Thank God for India!'[87] Later, the Congo ceased to be the scene of acute tension and problems nearer home demanded Nehru's prime attention. But the Congo crisis was throughout to Nehru a matter of principles and all his actions and interventions in the nature of a crusade for Africa and for the United Nations.[88]

[87] Nehru's speech at Patna, 6 January, *The Hindu*, 7 January 1962.

[88] cf. 'In a real sense India and the United States were the two countries the United Nations operation most depended upon, both for political support in New York and for military support in the Congo. Despite some differences in interpreting the mandate, the United States–India partnership remained solid throughout the Congo drama. The Congo operation would probably have collapsed if either New Delhi or Washington had withdrawn its support before the integration of Katanga in January 1963.' E.W. Lefever, *Crisis in the Congo* (Washington, 1965), p. 62.

8

Strengthening National Feeling

ONE

As the pressures of foreign policy multiplied, the wider aspects of planning assumed greater prominence. Increase in production and promotion of self-reliance were parts of the programme for strengthening India; but they were also important in the campaign against social backwardness and for the strengthening of Indian unity. Nehru still adhered to his view of planning as a scientific technique rather than an ideological procedure and to the premiss that industrialization was the first priority. An intelligent and logical approach was required for laying down objectives and indicating the way to attain them. Science and technology were governed by no ideology, and planners, be they from the United States or the Soviet Union, relied on organized thinking. The methods of production employed in both countries were much the same; they both worshipped science and the machine. The fog of the cold war could not conceal the fact that the real differences in the world were between, not the United States and the Soviet Union, but the developed and the undeveloped countries. As in so much else, Nehru was among the first to discern the outlines of what is today known as the North–South problem.

Whether the economy was said to be capitalist or socialist it was only, in Nehru's view, hard work on scientific lines that produced results. A few discrepancies were bound to arise because some individuals worked harder than others; but this did not mean that the economy should be based on private enterprise. As a system, a poor country like India had no alternative to socialism, for capitalism was a luxury she could not afford. In a poorly developed country, the capitalist method offered no chance. Socialism was the inevitable consequence of a civilization based on science and inspired by human values. It was a 'technologically mature' society, with the emphasis on greater production and equitable distribution, rather than a society of private profit and mass consumption.[1] The quest for socialism was rightly a matter of

[1] J. Nehru, *India Today and Tomorrow* (Delhi, 1959); press conference at Delhi, 8 January, *National Herald*, 9 January 1960; speeches at annual Congress session, Bangalore, 14 and 16 January 1960, A.I.R. tapes; address to the National Development Council, 19 March 1960. P.I.B.

sentiment, the desire to better the conditions of the poor; but to say that socialism was bad was tantamount also to saying that logic and reason were bad. Realistic socialism was the best way to solve India's problems; it was also the ethical and the moral way, for an acquisitive society was an immoral society. Only someone completely out of touch with modern conditions could be opposed to socialism. Nothing else was suited to 'the innate spirituality of the human being'.[2]

More than ever Nehru was averse to doctrinaire and rigid thinking and placed emphasis on primary necessities and fundamental values such as fair opportunity. To go further and seek to define socialism would be futile and even harmful, for no two persons had the same understanding of the details of socialism; and definitions would also vary, depending on whether they were formulated a hundred years or fifty years or twenty-five years before or in the present day. There could be no rigid general principles of universal application; each country had to develop its own approach to economics, keeping in view its own problems. Marx had written over a hundred years ago and, the world having changed considerably since then, it was unreal to expect from Marx answers to present-day problems. The spread of democracy, the development of technology, the changes in the nature of the capitalist system and the advances in armaments which made violence unthinkable – these were all factors which made Marx's forecasts out of date. Yet the stress Marx had laid on certain objectives was still valid. 'You can learn from Marx. You can respect him. But to accept everything blindly that Marx said or wrote would be wrong. To oppose it, I consider to be more wrong.'[3]

In the drive to a socialist society, heavy industry remained for Nehru the main avenue; there could be no socialism without technological growth. In addition, with the growing menace on the borders, heavy industry had become vital for defence. From both the economic and the military viewpoints, there could be no independence or freedom for India except through heavy industry.[4] Steel, oil, power, transport, machine-building and some chemical industries – these had to be developed and retained in the public sector. Nehru relied increasingly on this sector for he now felt that the private sector had neither the capacity nor the mental approach to undertake the industrialization of India. As the capitalist mind lacked vision and was interested primarily in quick dividends, the country could go ahead rapidly only through the expansion of major public enterprises.[5] He was particularly keen on the establishment of one more steel plant in the immediate future. There could not be an over-production of steel and, if India could not, for years

[2] Address to the annual session of the Federation of Indian Chambers of Commerce and Industry, 27 March 1960, P.I.B.; speech in the Rajya Sabha, 6 September 1960, Debates, Vol. 30, pp. 3,630–56; address to Congress Parliamentary Party, 16 December 1960. Tape M-54/C, Part II.

[3] Speech at the A.I.C.C., 30 October, *The Hindu*, 1 November 1960.

[4] Address to the Congress Parliamentary Party, 16 November 1959. Tape M-46/C, Part II.

[5] Speech at the A.I.C.C., 30 October, *The Hindu*, 1 November 1960; address to the National Development Council, 13 January 1961. P.I.B.

to come, utilize all the steel manufactured, it could be exported.[6] Because of Chinese hostility and the goodwill generated by Eisenhower's visit to Delhi, Nehru was now friendly to the United States and, in the same spirit in which he asked his officials to reconsider the ban on the establishment in India of American Libraries,[7] he was willing to turn to the United States for a new plant at Bokaro.

The Third Five Year Plan, which would commence in 1961, was designed by Nehru to reflect a new dimension in his thinking, of planning and industrialization paving the way for socialism in which the content of social philosophy would be more prominent than before. Increased production was indispensable but as a means to more important objectives. 'When we talk about socialism or a socialist pattern of society, we mean social justice which is so lacking today, in spite of our efforts and declarations.'[8] One was constantly brought back to the fact that the entire structure of Indian society as it existed was capitalistic. While socialistic leanings or ideas pulled in one direction, the whole base was different. Merely to put up public undertakings was not socialism but a relatively small step in a direction which might gradually lead to socialism. But it was still very far from socialism.[9] Economic growth was needed not only for itself but as the remedy for the real ill of social backwardness, whose amelioration could not wait indefinitely. It was an age of social revolution and India's problems were the result of a conflict between traditional society and a new temper. The basic requirement was to bring about the necessary economic and social changes while avoiding and opposing disruptive tendencies. 'We stand on the frontiers of a new land, provided we escape these tremendous dangers due to our social backwardness.'[10] The Third Plan would be an attempt to visualize the march of vast numbers of people towards desired goals, 'to think of the future that we are aiming at and to think it with the present'. It presumed a clarity of vision about the objectives of human equality and opportunity and of a society based on the principle of cooperative endeavour; and it demanded a mood of not only optimism and urgency but 'ferocity' in seeking these objectives.

Advantage should be taken of science and technology without forgetting the human, moral and spiritual values which make life worthwhile. The historic importance of this work should make participation in it an exhilarating experience. India was living simultaneously in all the centuries of the past and the present with a foot in the future; and her struggle to move out of the past into the present was an exciting moment in her history. India was progressing not merely materially but in some inner sense, crossing the centuries fairly fast. The facts of yesterday were being replaced by the facts of today and more so by the facts of tomorrow. It was a changing India, bursting

[6] To Swaran Singh, Minister for Steel, 5 February 1960.
[7] Note to Foreign Secretary, 14 January 1960.
[8] Nehru to Chief Ministers, 7 June 1961.
[9] Nehru at the National Development Council, 1 June, *The Hindu*, 2 June 1961.
[10] To Chief Ministers, 27 June 1961.

at the seams; and the basic vitality which Nehru believed to exist in all sections of the people made him confident that India would, given the opportunity, make good.[11]

So the signing of the Third Plan gave the Prime Minister a sense of thrill at a great work accomplished and a great journey well begun.[12] Industrialization was forging ahead; and the 'hump of agriculture' seemed to Nehru to have been crossed.[13] The foundations of a self-sustaining economy having been laid, these could now be strengthened and widened and a super-structure constructed so that, after about ten years, the pattern of a socialist society would begin to take shape. There was an intensification of economic trends in the Second Plan; 'every plan should stretch us to our utmost'.[14] The emphasis remained on heavy industry and the public sector. The most significant development of the five years of the Plan was expected to be the rapid growth of machine-building and engineering industries. For the new steel plant at Bokaro, Nehru was still confident that the United States would, under pressure, accept whatever proposals India might make.[15] Of the total investment of Rs 10,400 crores, Rs 6,100 crores would be in the public sector, which would have to find Rs 7,500 crores in all. But it is difficult to see in the Third Plan the lineaments of social change which Nehru envisaged. On the increasing importance of social change which Nehru spoke about, there was little more than tepid rhetoric in the Third Plan. Growth continued to be given priority over equity and the creation of a self-sustaining economy was seen to be more crucial than the reform of society and the weakening of caste. So production continued to receive primary emphasis and, for this reason, to maintain incentives, Nehru refused to consider ceilings on incomes. Even in the rural areas, there was to be a limit on holdings and not on earnings.[16] The need to enhance agricultural production was stressed but the paragraphs on land tenures did no more than make mild exhortations to the state Governments.[17]

So the results of planning in the social sphere continued on the old lines. It was estimated in 1960–1 on the basis of a poverty line of Rs 20 per capita per month that, despite the process of growth, 'half of the people

[11] Nehru's speech in Rajya Sabha, 6 September 1960, Debates, Vol. 30, pp. 3,630–56; address to the National Development Council, 13 January 1961, P.I.B.; inaugural address at session of World Health Organization, Delhi, 7 February 1961, P.I.B.; inaugural speech at Conference of Asian Economic Planners, Delhi, 26 September 1961, P.I.B.; address to the general meeting of the Associated Chambers of Commerce of India, Calcutta, 2 December 1961, P.I.B.; speech in the Lok Sabha, 2 May 1962, Debates, Third Series, Vol. 2, pp. 2,058–82.

[12] Nehru to Chief Ministers, 5 August 1961.

[13] Interview for Moscow radio, *National Herald*, 28 January 1961.

[14] Address to the Congress Parliamentary Party, 6 August 1961. Tape 58, Part I.

[15] Nehru to Swaran Singh, 16 December 1961.

[16] Press conference at Delhi, 3 January, *National Herald*, 4 January 1959; speech in the Lok Sabha, 22 August 1960. Debates, Second Series, Vol. 45, pp. 3,974–4,000.

[17] A.H. Hanson, *The Process of Planning* (Oxford, 1966), pp. 217–19; F.R. Frankel, *India's Political Economy 1947–77* (Delhi, 1978), pp.183–5.

lived in abject poverty'.[18] An expert assessment in 1962 was that the dominance of the rich and the influential in all projects and programmes was a marked feature of the Indian situation. The private sector was expanding with the help of the state, which made no effort to control it. Production before distribution was a plausible thesis, but it was very doubtful if this could later be reversed to secure distributive justice. A group of leading capitalists had virtually taken over the economy, politics and society. The 'ugly business-man' was the major character on the Indian scene, making large profits, promoting corruption, securing the support of officials and manipulating the administrative machinery.[19] Nehru had sadly to accept that there was considerable truth in this account.[20] A capitalist economy and society were developing; and the influence of the private sector in politics was also increasing. Socialism was certainly more than a doctrine of levelling and equal sharing out of poverty; but the creation of wealth which could later be fairly distributed had already tended to make the second phase a distant vision.

TWO

This awareness of the large gap between his hopes on the one hand and the language of the Third Plan and the achievements so far on the other led Nehru, not to resigned disillusion, but to emphasis on rigorous implementation of narrow commitments rather than large promises which might well remain airy theorizing. There was too much of a 'theoretician's complex' in India, of believing that to put down projects on paper was in itself an achievement.[21] So, in most cases, the trend in the Plan was sought to be transformed from the general to the particular. But charts and schedules would have very little meaning unless behind them was 'a passion, the passion with a tinge of anger at delays, anger at anybody not doing his part, anger at not achieving where achievement is possible'.[22] Nehru had not tired of repeating that this was the test for every Congressman for, if they failed now, the party would be gradually wound up. So those who did not approve of the policy embodied in the Nagpur resolutions and the Third Plan should leave the party and let others carry on with the work. If the will were alive, there was now enough scope for a positive advance. But such will was not manifest in the action taken on the Nagpur resolutions. None of the camps planned for training personnel to manage the service cooperatives were held and state

[18] Report of the perspective planning division of the planning commission, quoted in S.D. Tendulkar, 'Economic Inequality in an Indian Perspective', in A. Beteille (ed.), *Equality and Inequality* (Delhi, 1983), p. 106.

[19] D.R. Gadgil's convocation address at Nagpur university, 20 January 1962.

[20] Nehru to Chief Ministers, 17 May 1962.

[21] Address to State Ministers of Community Development, 3 August 1962.

[22] Speech to the National Development Council, 31 May 1961. P.I.B.

trading in foodgrains was soon discarded in favour of wheat imports from the United States.[23]

A new spirit was expected to be evoked by the decentralization emphasized by the Third Plan in both industry and agriculture. More small-scale plants were coming up and Nehru had asked for greater attention to be given to the production of raw material for them.[24] Development in the rural areas was even more fundamental. In a country like India, far behind in all sectors of the economy, first place had no meaning for advance was required on many fronts;[25] but agriculture was clearly of primary importance. Here Nehru wished to limit the role of the state to securing the active participation of the farmers and inducing them to employ better implements and to adopt more scientific methods. The root of the problem was to Nehru still the promotion of new ways of thinking and the removal of administrative curbs and delays. Mechanization could wait till industrial progress was sufficient to provide employment for those who could no longer find work in the fields; and till then the manpower so largely available should be utilized for improved cultivation. Nehru refused to believe that the mind of the Indian peasant was locked up even though he was often trapped in antiquated customs. The community development programme and the spread of village cooperatives had not succeeded in destroying, or even considerably weakening, these barriers. Community development had by now lost its original drive and become increasingly an official organization. Rather than promoting a spirit of self-help among the people, the community development units tended to rely on help from the Government. A committee set up in 1957 to assess the working of the programme reported that one of its least successful aspects was the failure to evoke popular initiative.[26] In line with the committee's recommendations, Nehru decided to reactivate the *panchayat* system. The adults of a village would elect the members of a *panchayat*, with added representation given to women and scheduled castes and tribes as these groups were unlikely to secure it through elections; beyond the village *panchayats* would be the *panchayat samitis*, each covering about forty to fifty villages, consisting largely of indirectly elected members and with jurisdiction coextensive with the development block; and the *zila parishad*, comprising mostly the chairmen of the *samitis*, would deal normally with an administrative district.[27]

These three bodies, fully elected and non-official, could give the farmers a sense of responsibility and help to unleash the latent energies in the rural areas; and Nehru, now that the community development programme had lost its

[23] Frankel, *India's Political Economy 1947–77*, pp. 170–4.

[24] Nehru to Minister for Industry, 4 April, and to Deputy Chairman, Planning Commission, 5 April 1960.

[25] Speech at Ernakulam, 18 January 1960. A.I.R. tapes.

[26] Report of the team for the study of community projects and national extension service 1957 (Balwantray Mehta committee report).

[27] H. Maddick, *Panchayati Raj* (London, 1970), pp. 3–4, 54–5.

flavour, glamour and colour and become a pale replica of officialdom, looked to the cooperatives and the *panchayats* for accelerated rural development and fresh springs of rural life. The *panchayat* bodies, rather than the bureaucratic administration, should form the effective district organization, distributing foodgrains, providing irrigation, arranging double cropping and supplying seeds and fertilizers. 'I believe that the real foundations of freedom and a democratic structure are being firmly laid by these movements. This is the real *swaraj* of the people. Even as we put our faith in our people, so will they respond and help in building up this great country of ours.'[28] He believed that these *panchayats* had enabled India to turn the corner in agriculture by stepping up production;[29] and he expected them to do even more and help to create better men and women. 'What I mean is that changes don't come about by some sudden type of thunder. Changes creep in in a society.'[30] It was the building up of the right type of men and women which underlay all planning and made possible industrial and agricultural progress; and *panchayat raj*, to Nehru now 'the most important thing in India',[31] should, above all else, improve the quality of the human being. The *panchayats* should provide the peasants with opportunities for exercising responsibility, giving them the confidence to function in a modern world. A passive revolution, in Gramsci's phrase, which the state seeks to effect, would be replaced by an active, democratic revolution carried out by the masses themselves.[32] *Panchayat raj* was the most revolutionary development in India because behind it were hidden all the forces which, when released, would change the structure of the country.[33] That sometimes the *panchayat* institutions might fail to function adequately and in the right spirit was no reason for not encouraging them. 'They could either go to God or to the devil. But unless they had the freedom to go to the devil they could not go to God either.'[34]

The state Governments were given freedom in implementing the general principle of a three-tier structure of *panchayats* with adequate resources to exercise power and responsibility. Some states were enthusiastic. Andhra and Rajasthan were the first to take action with encouraging results. But, on the whole, the response to Nehru was lethargic. The Madhya Pradesh Government, for example, even brought forward a Bill providing for the nomination of the presidents and members of all the *panchayat* committees. Yet Nehru did not slacken in resolve. Recognizing that these local self-governing bodies, even if given encouragement by the official authorities, could only hope to succeed if villagers were equipped to run them, he demanded a renewed stress

28 Nehru's message on the first anniversary of the inauguration of *panchayat raj* in Andhra, 20 October 1960.

29 Speech in the Lok Sabha, 23 February 1961. Debates, Second Series, Vol. 50, pp. 1,682–706.

30 Press conference at Delhi, 14 August 1962. P.I.B.

31 Speech at Ernakulam, 18 January 1960. A.I.R. Tapes.

32 C. Mouffe (ed.), *Gramsci and Marxist Theory* (London, 1979), p. 13.

33 Address to State Ministers for Community Development, 9 December, *The Hindu*, 10 December 1960.

34 Nehru's message to the Major Industries of India Annual, 26 July 1960.

on the spread of primary and secondary education. Mass education was, of course, important for industrialization, which was not a matter merely of putting up steel plants at odd places but of building up from below a nation used to thinking in terms of technical change and advance. Though the Government had not been able to fulfil the directives in the Constitution that by 1961 every child up to the age of fourteen should have free and compulsory education, it set out to do so by 1966 and to reduce the age to eleven. The Third Plan aimed to have in school about twenty million children comprising 60 per cent of those aged six to fourteen years. But it was also proposed to provide in nearly 30 per cent of schools the type of education which was suited to the developmental activities of the local community. The object was the schooling of the Indian peasant, the promotion of his ability to adapt himself to the changing environment, teaching him to modernize without losing his roots in the cultural past. Some people seemed to believe that one of the fundamental human rights was that to be stupid. 'Are we to encourage stupidity in this country? Is it a fundamental right to stand on one leg in the river Yamuna when the eclipse is taking place?'[35] Education was the foundation of social and economic progress and a major step towards the equalizing of opportunity; and Nehru was prepared, despite his keenness on industrialization, to reduce expenditure on engineering projects rather than education. 'I have come to feel that it is the basis of all and, on no account unless actually our heads are cut off and we cannot function, must we allow education to suffer.'[36] In the final analysis, a modern nation was not the product of heavy industry and scientific agriculture but of educated and trained human beings. Nehru also revived his old idea of a year's compulsory training for students in social work. The numbers in urban schools and colleges were increasing fast and many were attaining proficiency in engineering and technology; but they had little knowledge of rural conditions. A stretch of work outside the towns would provide a rounded view as well as strengthen the sense of discipline.[37] It was Nehru's adaptation, in the context of free India, of Gandhi's constructive programme of the 1930s, intended to draw together the cities and the countryside.

Nehru also had the imaginative idea of setting up *panchayats* in the schools. He wanted the pupils of each village school to elect a small body for dealing with such matters as discipline, recreation and sanitation and even to run a cooperative.[38] But the Prime Minister was really looking too far ahead; and his images of maintaining and coordinating the rhythms of life between the individual and society and the past and the present and getting the Indian peasant in line with the rhythm of the modern world, all by means of the cooperatives, the *panchayats* and the schools, were well beyond the under-

[35] Address to the Congress Parliamentary Party, 14 April 1961. Tape M-56/C.
[36] Speech at the National Development Council, 31 May 1961. P.I.B.
[37] Nehru to K.L. Shrimali, Minister for Education, 24 January 1960.
[38] Nehru to K.L. Shrimali, 4 June 1961.

standing, let alone the reach, of his officials and party men. Adapting a phrase of Lenin, and bringing together his two favourite concepts of village democracy and industrialization, Nehru asserted that *panchayat raj* plus electric power would change India. 'Power is the key to changing the countryside and to the growth of industry and to everything.' It would not only increase production but would bring about a change in physical and mental habits,[39] just as the working of *panchayats* was expected to do.

Ultimately, it was a question of having faith in the people; and Nehru had full faith. 'That is enough religion for me.'[40] But, while the political consciousness of the villager intensified to the extent that a new dimension has been said to have been added by *panchayat raj* to the political culture of India,[41] the *panchayats* were haunted by officials and politicians and did not result in the psychological mobilization which Nehru had expected. They failed to release huge resources of popular energy and direct them towards reconstruction. So Nehru looked to education in itself, rather than as a prelude to the proper working of *panchayats*, for giving confidence to the peasants. Education took, in his view, the place which first community development, and then *panchayat raj*, had occupied as the most revolutionary factor which would change the face of the country.[42] Apart from enabling the institutions at the local level to be operated with healthy vigour, the spread of education would give adult suffrage proper scope. Nehru always optimistically saw continuous improvement in the conditions of the Indian people; but the decisive factor in such development kept changing in his mind. Realist enough to note the decline of each of his hopes, he was also buoyant enough to find a new lever when the old ones failed him. But education, by its very nature, could not be expected to yield quick results.

THREE

Despite all the inadequacies in implementation and the reinforcement of existing social biases, on the whole, planning, the results which the first two Plans had achieved and the prospects opened out by the Third Plan, strengthened Nehru's belief that the country was getting a grip on the future. A threatened general strike, which would have arrested for a while the machinery of development, petered out; and Nehru roundly condemned those

[39] Address to the National Development Council, 13 January 1961, P.I.B.; speeches in the Lok Sabha, 23 February 1961, Debates, Second Series, Vol. 50, pp. 1,682–706, and in the Rajya Sabha, 15 March and 3 May 1962, Debates, Vols 37, pp. 368–91 and 38, pp. 1,727–50 respectively.

[40] Speech at the annual session of the Federation of Indian Chambers of Commerce and Industry, 27 March, *National Herald*, 28 March 1960.

[41] A.H. Hanson and J. Douglas, *India's Democracy* (London, 1972), p. 195.

[42] Address to the tenth session of the General Assembly of the World Confederation of Organizations of the Teaching Profession, Delhi, 2 August 1961. P.I.B.

leaders of the opposition who had promoted it. They sought to ride a tiger when they could not ride a donkey and, what was worse, did not recognize their mistake. The test of a person to him was not that he did not err — only angels in heaven or saints, if they existed, were perfect — but that he tried to correct his error.[43] But there were other trends which were alarming. Divisions based on religion and language threatened to loosen whatever integrative strength was provided by economic development.

> In India we always have two aspects: one is heartening and enlivening, the growth of a great country struggling under adverse circumstances and making good; the other is this lowering of spirit, the absence of idealism and living confined to one's petty self and the growth of all manner of narrowminded, petty jealousies.[44]

While talking in terms of the *Gita* and the *Upanisads*, Indians led a social life which was extremely backward compared with that in any other part of the world. 'We are backward, let us admit it.' Life in India was full of barriers, all the more formidable because the people, having been brought up in that atmosphere, were unaware of it. 'And no country in the wide world has such great differences as India, leave out money, that of course, caste system, social strata . . . we are the country most sunk, most undeveloped, most backward in this, because of caste chiefly plus poverty.' Caste, even if disappearing, as Nehru liked to believe, in its original form, was putting on a political garb, which was to him even worse. But the worst aspect of this backwardness was the communal mindedness of the Hindu majority for, when passions were aroused, they were as communal as anyone else. Minorities could be dealt with in a hundred ways but a majority in a democratic system could become dangerous if it functioned as a religious majority.[45] Secularism, or the acceptance that a citizen's religion was a private matter, had been explicitly formulated in the Constitution, but had not been generally accepted; and communal rioting was still more than a memory. It broke out in Bihar and Madhya Pradesh in April 1959 and, soon after, in Uttar Pradesh. If premeditated, such riots were obviously bad; but, if sudden, they were to Nehru in a sense worse for they indicated the popular temper and clearly suggested that some Indians, both Hindu and Muslim, had not quite come out of the barbarian stage.[46] He confessed that, for this reason, he felt a sense of darkness creeping over him.[47] That such deep hostility should come to the surface at the slightest provocation was a serious matter. Constant vigilance was required

[43] Speech in the Lok Sabha, 9 August 1960. Debates, Vol. 44, pp. 1,665–82.

[44] Nehru to Chief Ministers on return from New York, 23 October 1960.

[45] Letter to Congressmen, 5 December 1954, A.I.C.C. Papers File RC39, N.M.M.L.; message to All-India Adult Education Conference, 12 December 1958; addresses to the Congress Parliamentary Party, 14 April and 10 May 1961 and 21 June 1962. Tapes M-56/C, M-57/C, Part II and 63(1) respectively.

[46] Nehru to Chief Minister of Bihar, 21 April, and to Chief Minister of Madhya Pradesh, 25 April 1959.

[47] Speech at Patna, 30 April, *The Hindu*, 2 May 1959.

apart from continuous propaganda; but ultimately the wide spread of education alone could strengthen foundations which were clearly weak. Nothing was more dangerous for India than the communal approach; for communalism and nationalism were wholly opposed to each other, even though some forms of communalism adopted the garb of nationalism. These communal disturbances revived old fears in the minds of many Muslims about their future in India and undid the quiet, constructive work which had been carried out since 1947. The effect on Muslims all over the country had been very deep and upsetting.

Conditions in India were such and the Muslims relatively so few in number that they would not normally be aggressive for fear of the reaction; so in Nehru's view the responsibility for communal peace rested primarily on the Hindus. Like Sartre, to whom the Jewish question was a gentile one, to Nehru the Muslim question was a Hindu one. The test of social solidarity was the feeling of confidence given to the minorities. Whenever there was a communal disturbance, Nehru presumed the failure of the district authorities and the activity of Hindu communal elements. If Muslims did on occasions behave aggressively, Nehru regarded such conduct as the reaction of an inferiority complex and fear of the future, to be handled by a friendly approach along with firmness.[48]

To win the confidence of Muslims in India, Nehru passed on to the Chief Ministers the suggestion of his colleague in the Cabinet, Hafiz Ibrahim, that the administration of Muslim *wakfs* or charitable foundations should be the responsibility of any Muslim member in the state Cabinet.[49] He also, in defiance of logic, refused to consider alterations in Muslim personal law on matters of monogamy and inheritance so as to place all Indian women on a par. There should be no impression of the Hindu majority forcing anything, however justified, on the Muslim minority and changes would only be enacted when the Muslims wanted them.

Such concessions, however, were of no major consequence so long as communal rioting had not been eliminated. In February 1961 there was communal trouble again in Madhya Pradesh, indicating that there was still something wrong with the mental health of the people. It was disgusting and abhorrent to Nehru that even a single Indian could forget India, 'forget everything', cease to be a thinking human being and behave like a passionate animal.[50] It disgraced and shamed India before the world. But trouble-makers could function with such effect only because the atmosphere was conducive and public sympathy was in their favour. Nehru thought the state and district authorities had been too weak and passive in handling these disturbances and,

[48] Nehru to Indira Gandhi from Patna, 1 May, to Chief Ministers 18 May, and to Sampurnanand, 31 July 1959.

[49] 4 January 1960.

[50] Address (in Hindi) to the Congress Parliamentary Party, 13 February 1961. M-54/C, Part I. Speech in the Rajya Sabha, 20 February 1961. Debates, Vol. 32, pp. 473–97. Speech at All-India Newspapers Editors' Conference, Delhi, 25 February, *The Hindu*, 26 February 1961.

on the eve of the *Holi* (spring) festival, instructed all state Governments to deal promptly and firmly with trouble-makers.[51] In Jabalpur, after riots which Nehru was convinced had been carefully organized,[52] Muslims were said to be in a state of terror because of the attitude of the police, in whose ranks communal feeling was strong; and this in itself was to the Prime Minister testimony of the immaturity of the popular mind and of the increasing strength of religious revivalism. The bitter, bigoted, communal approach was the greatest of all the dangers facing India from time to time, for it brutalized the people. The progeny of evil was evil; an evil act would lead to evil reactions. He considered the banning of communal parties but found this to be impractical, if only because communal parties deny being communal.[53]

> What then are we to do? We cannot take refuge in a negative despair. We have to face whatever happens with courage and endurance. The memory of what I saw in Delhi and in the Punjab soon after partition is before me. It was terrible and broke one's heart, and yet one faced it and to a large extent overcame it then. But the roots of this trouble lie deep and we shall have to be vigilant all the time.[54]

As a remedial measure he ordered the Chief Minister of Madhya Pradesh to have recourse, if necessary, to the Preventive Detention Act to deal with communalists;[55] the test of efficiency was to take action before violence erupted and not after. But even such drastic action obviously would not extinguish a problem which went to the root of national life. The only answer was raising the broad level of the community and discarding the relics of tribalism; for social changes could not be brought about by compulsion.

FOUR

The differences created by linguistic rivalries were less deep than the disruption caused by communal rancour; but they too weakened the cohesion of the Indian people. States quarreled with each other over border districts and set up 'action committees' on such matters as the sharing of river waters. 'It seems to me that we are gradually losing all sense of a united country and, at the slightest provocation, function as if we were independent states.'[56] Even the problem of linguistic provinces had not been finally solved. The decision to maintain Bombay as a bilingual province had clearly not been to the liking

51 Telegram to Chief Ministers, 26 February 1961.
52 Address to the Congress Parliamentary Party, 27 February 1961. Tape M-54/C, Part II.
53 Nehru's note to Law Minister, 31 March 1961. File No. 2 (397)/61–70 P.M.S., Vol. 1, Serial 7A.
54 To J.P. Jyotishi, 2 April 1961.
55 25 April 1961.
56 To T. Visvanatham, 3 July 1961.

of the electorate in 1957 in either Maharashtra or Gujarat; and this had been followed by riots and police firing in Ahmedabad. Nehru had no intention of reversing the decision on Bombay, but he sensed the public feeling of a lack of sympathy and human touch in the provincial Government and was anxious to set this right before the popular anger and bitterness sank deep and became even more difficult to deal with later. So he advised the new Chief Minister, Y.B. Chavan, to be generally friendly to the members of the opposition and to acknowledge, when occasion arose, that the Government were very unhappy about the incidents involving firing. The approach should be sympathetic and there should be no hesitation in expressing regret. But, though an inquiry into any instance of firing was the norm, to have one now after a long interval would be most unwise and would only sustain bitterness.[57]

With time, the atmosphere in Bombay city and Gujarat improved; but Maharashtra continued to be sullen. In Vidharba and Nagpur it seemed to Nehru that there was still a feeling that the interests of these areas had been somewhat neglected and, if there were to be a change, these areas should be constituted into a separate state.[58] But in August 1958 violent riots occurred in Ahmedabad and other places in Gujarat, with reactive disturbances in Maharashtra. The President suggested that, now that the people of Gujarat had reconciled themselves to the loss of Bombay city, there was no justification for persisting with the composite province. Nehru agreed that sheer obstinacy was no policy; but he was not convinced that the bilingual state had been an error.[59] Meantime, he directed the Chief Minister to hold an inquiry into the agitation in Gujarat to ascertain its extent and who was behind it.[60]

Then, on a visit to Maharashtra, Nehru argued vigorously that the formation of a composite Bombay state had been a correct decision. It was like a joint family; and India would not survive if people speaking different languages were opposed to living together. 'I am a Maharashtrian while in Maharashtra and a Tamilian while in Tamil Nad. I belong to all states.' But he added that if, by peaceful methods, Parliament were persuaded to revise its decision, he would not stand in the way.[61] He would adhere to the democratic approach, whatever the consequences, and accept any settlement agreed upon by all sides, even if it be illogical, for life was more important than logic. The matter was not one of theoretical principle but of balancing various factors and looking at the good of the country as a whole. But there should be no bullying; and he reacted strongly to the methods of violence adopted by the supporters of the demands for separate Maharashtra and Gujarat.[62]

57 To Sri Prakasa, Governor of Maharashtra, reporting conversation with Y.B. Chavan, Chief Minister, 25 March 1957.

58 Nehru to Y.B. Chavan, 5 July 1958.

59 Rajendra Prasad to Nehru, 13 August, and Nehru's reply, 15 August 1958.

60 Nehru to Y.B. Chavan, 15 August, and reminder, 4 September 1958.

61 Speech at Aurangabad, 23 August, *The Hindu*, 24 August 1958.

62 Speech at the A.I.C.C. Hyderabad, 26 October 1958, A.I.C.C. papers File G 14 of 1958, N.M.M.L.; to B.S. Hiray, 21 October, and to D.K. Kunte, 14 December 1958.

By 1959 Nehru was under pressure, from within the Congress, to agree to bifurcation;[63] and in September he convened a private meeting with Pant, Desai, and Chavan to consider the matter in all its aspects.[64] Later the Working Committee appointed a group consisting of representatives from the various areas to examine the question. But, despite Nehru's wish to have the matter explored fully before decisions were taken so that no one might feel ignored, the current of events was pushing him along. Though still in favour of the composite state, he did not feel strongly on the issue and, recognizing that some revision would have to be made, was willing to abide by the recommendations of Sri Prakasa, the Governor, and Chavan, the Chief Minister.[65] So, in 1960, Bombay was again split up. Nehru accepted the compromise with no great enthusiasm so as to prevent narrow sentiments gaining strength from frustration. 'In a long perspective these internal changes are not likely to make too much difference. There are other and greater forces at work moving in the right direction.'[66] If it disposed of a problem and assuaged feelings in Maharashtra and Gujarat, he would willingly go along.

FIVE

Problems centred on language also developed in other parts of the country. Nehru supported Kairon, the Chief Minister, in firmly resisting the demand of a section of the Sikh community for a division of the Punjab. The increasing influence of regionalism in Tamil Nad he treated with disdain and wondered 'if the Dravida Kazhagam in Madras is not more primitive than any primitive tribe in India'.[67] He also made it clear, in the face of loose talk about secession, that he was prepared even for war to put down any effort at separation. But the agitation in Assam was more serious. Mob violence broke out in that state in the early days of July 1960 in support of the Assamese language and Assam for the Assamese. To Nehru these riots appeared in some ways 'the most ghastly and deplorable' events in India since 1947, for they revealed a new type of emotional fission of which every true Indian would be ashamed. Nationalism seemed to be but a superficial layer cracking open at the slightest irritation. Democracy and nationalism should go together, for the essence of democracy was not merely to think of oneself or of one's group but to work for the larger group or community which was the nation. But most Indians did not seem to

[63] Y.D. Phadke, *Politics and Language* (Bombay, 1979), pp. 221–3.

[64] To Sri Prakasa, 3 September 1959.

[65] Nehru to Morarji Desai and to Sri Prakasa, 30 September 1959; statements at press conference in Delhi, 8 October, *National Herald*, 9 October 1959.

[66] To J.S. Akanta, 6 April 1960.

[67] Speech at Tiruchirapalli, 9 December, *The Hindu*, 10 December 1957. The Dravida Kazhagam was the anti-Brahmin, regional party.

have a common idea of nationalism but each one a particular brand; and events in Assam had brought this skeleton out of the mental cupboard. 'It is not merely a question of Bengali or Assamese; each one of us is affected and affected in many ways.'[68]

The attacks in Assam were chiefly against Bengalis settled in the state and such narrow intolerance Nehru denounced as certain to set back the progress of Assam as a whole. In central projects like the oil refinery Indians from every part of the country, and even foreigners, would be employed and, if the Assamese objected to this, then the central Government would have to reconsider their plans for locating industries in Assam. The disturbances had also raised the whole question of the association of the hill areas with Assam and complicated the problems peculiar to a broader state. 'I have always liked Assam and the Assamese people and have looked forward to their rapid growth. But how can they grow if they continue to be infantile in their thinking? One cannot compromise with this kind of folly.'[69]

Nehru went to Assam and found the atmosphere thick with excitement and recrimination. It also came home to him that admonishing the Assamese and ordering them to atone for their misdeeds was in itself inadequate; they felt they had a legitimate grievance and this had to be tackled. In a province with large Bengali and Bihari elements and with growing unemployment among the uneducated, the development of narrow loyalties was understandable. So he rejected Bidhan Roy's advice that President's rule be introduced at once in Assam as well as the suggestion that the army be brought in, and tried instead to strengthen the authority of the Assam Government, never very strong, in their efforts to maintain law and order and lead the Assamese majority back to calmness.[70] But the exodus of over 50,000 Bengalis from Assam had roused considerable excitement in Bengal, and Nehru advised Chaliha, the Chief Minister of Assam, to invite back the Bengali refugees and offer them a measure of compensation. Financial assistance from the central Government would be available for this purpose, for it was not merely a matter for the states concerned. The movement of evacuees from one state to another within India would end ultimately in civil war. One could not move around large sections of the population or leave them to fight it out. Only a sense of goodwill could form the basis for a national community in India.[71]

The central Government were not helped in their efforts to bring the situation in Assam under control by the emotional reaction of Padmaja Naidu, the Governor, and the Roy ministry in Bengal. Their decision to treat

[68] Speeches in the Lok Sabha, 1 August, and 1 and 3 September 1960; Debates, Vols 44, pp. 126–32 and 46, pp. 6,217–51, 6,713–40 respectively; press conference in Delhi, 11 August, *National Herald*, 12 August 1960.

[69] To B.P. Chaliha, 12 July 1960.

[70] Nehru to B.C. Roy, 13 July, and statement at press conference in Delhi, 11 August 1960, *National Herald*, 12 August 1960.

[71] Nehru to B.P. Chaliha, 14 July, and to F.A. Ahmed, Minister in the Assam Government, 17 August 1960; speech in the Lok Sabha, 1 September 1960. Debates, Vol. 46, pp. 6,217–51.

15 August almost as a day of mourning was sharply criticized by Nehru as wallowing in morbidity. 'Perhaps if we cut off the heads of some of the Assam ministers and presented them, that might have some soothing effect!'[72] To forget that India was bigger than Assam or Bengal was to serve neither. But he did suggest to the Assam Government that they consider the levy of a punitive fine in areas where the disturbances had been the most violent and looting had occurred. If rehabilitation and relief were also prompt and rapid with the army being called in to assist, the Bengali state of mind might be calmed and the Bengalis encouraged to return.[73] But the Assam Government, ignoring the advice of the central authorities, pushed through legislation making Assamese the official language – a step which was resented by the Bengalis still in the state, while those who had left were determined not to return. The people in the hill areas also, dissatisfied with the state Government and encouraged by developments in the Naga areas, clamoured for a state of their own.

The statute about the Assamese language was more on paper than in observance. Bengali and English continued to be used in the secretariat in addition to Assamese, and Bengali remained the official language in Cachar district. But the police opened fire on a mob at Silchar and, though this seems to have been done without official instructions, Bengali feelings, both in Assam and elsewhere, were roused to passionate resentment. The decision of the Assam Government to hold a judicial inquiry did not help much. So 'this terrible wound'[74] did not heal and continued to concern the Prime Minister not only in itself but as a warning of a deep-seated and spreading force of disunity in India. 'That indicates how skin-deep is our nationalism and how we lose our anchorage over relatively small matters.'[75]

Such tense feelings obviously had an unhealthy influence in the neighbouring Naga areas. When Nehru was there in January 1960, he had found the situation much better than it had been for a long time, largely because of a change which seemed to have taken place in the mind of the Naga people.[76] But sporadic violence continued; and subduing it was made difficult by differences of approach between the military and the civil authorities. The soldiers favoured strong measures to crush hostile activity and blamed the civilians for following a policy of appeasement; but the Commissioner was convinced of the growing success of his policy of winning over the Nagas. The army, exasperated by guerrilla harassments, fell back on burning and destroying villages; and the natural result was greater support for the hostiles. As a compromise, Nehru ordered the raising of a battalion of Assam Rifles from the local population.[77]

Before this experiment could be tried, the Naga People's Convention,

[72] To S. Radhakrishnan, 10 August 1960.
[73] To F.A. Ahmed, 17 and 18 August 1960.
[74] Nehru in the Lok Sabha, 1 August 1960. Debates, Vol. 44, pp. 126-32.
[75] Nehru to Chief Ministers, 27 June 1961.
[76] Nehru in the Lok Sabha, 22 February 1960. Debates, Vol. 39, pp. 2,102–42.
[77] Nehru's note to Foreign Secretary, 12 January 1960.

which had been encouraged to consider all steps short of independence, sought the establishment of Nagaland as a separate province within the Indian Union. Nehru, prepared for the maximum devolution so long as it did not enable the hostiles to extend their activities, had ordered the local authorities to work out proposals for autonomy, with the Governor retaining only general financial supervision and ultimate responsibility for law and order.[78] But the creation of a Naga province would go very much further. For an area the size of a standard Indian district, with a population of little more than 400,000 and with a revenue of only about half a million rupees, to be converted into a state, seemed at first sight 'to be completely unreal and verging on the fantastic'.[79] General Srinagesh, who had been appointed Governor of Assam after the death of Fazl Ali, was instructed not to enter into detailed discussions with the delegates of the Naga Convention and to inform them that their first duty, as that of the Government, was to end the hostile activity which still persisted. As for the demand for a state of their own, the Government of India would have to consider the possible reaction in the other hill districts to a total severance of the Naga area from Assam; but there was also a more general issue. A sustained effort was being made, even in existing states much larger in size and population than the Naga area, to render the administration less elaborate and top-heavy and to provide funds mainly for development. Autonomy meant decentralization and not the duplication of the official apparatus. It would, therefore, be more appropriate for the Nagas to seek, within existing resources, a recasting of the administration in the newly created unit in accordance with local customs.[80]

A settlement of the Naga problem was not, however, just a matter of logic and administrative reform. In pressing its demand, the Naga People's Convention was strengthened by the knowledge that the Government of India could not afford to see the Convention weakened in face of the activity of the hostiles and the intense propaganda being carried on abroad against India's policy, and even presence, in the Naga area. Phizo had arrived in Britain with a forged passport purchased under a false name in the black market. The Government of India did not ask for his extradition because they did not wish either to provide him with the publicity he sought or to embarrass the British; but it was pointed out to them that he was a fugitive from justice on a charge of murder and should not be permitted to indulge in anti-Indian activities.[81] However, Phizo succeeded in gaining the ear of various groups and persons in Britain. He was particularly fortunate in winning the sympathy of Michael Scott, who commanded considerable goodwill in India because of his work in the cause of the Hereros in Africa. When Scott asked for an interview, Nehru replied that, while always glad to see Scott, he could not receive him as a

78 Nehru to Fazl Ali, Governor of Assam, 3 March 1959.

79 Nehru's note to Foreign Secretary, 5 March 1960.

80 Nehru to General Srinagesh, 2 April 1960.

81 Nehru's note to Foreign Secretary, 16 June, and telegram to Vijayalakshmi in London, 18 June 1960.

representative of Phizo or to hear charges against the Indian army; for such purposes he should deal officially with the High Commission in London.[82] In fact, Nehru made no effort to conceal his mild annoyance:

> This whole story, ever since Michael Scott appeared on the scene and produced Phizo, has been quite extraordinary. It almost sounds like some detective fiction. Why Michael Scott or David Astor should have proceeded in this particular way is beyond me. They could have functioned quite normally, told us what the matter was and taken our reply without getting too excited about it. If after that they wanted to do something, they could have done it. But they have surrounded this with mystery and secrecy, and tried to create an impression of terrible things happening in the Naga territory which apparently we are hiding . . . When the famous day comes when these charges are made public, we shall look into them and deal with them . . . Astor and Scott can go ahead and do just what they like.[83]

Phizo then sought safe conduct to accompany Scott to Delhi and meet Nehru to discuss a cease-fire, an inquiry into allegations of atrocities and the constitutional future of Nagaland, without prejudice to the basic positions of the two sides. Nehru declined to meet him on these terms, especially as Phizo had repeated charges against the Indian army which the Government of India regarded as baseless; but he too was told that he could meet an official of the Indian High Commission in London.[84]

These developments obviously made it all the more important for the Government of India to reach an agreement with the Naga Convention. Failure to do so would force resort once more to military measures and strengthen the charge that India was playing a colonial role in this area. 'In any event, we shall have failed in our basic aim of making the Nagas a real part of India.'[85] So, although still not convinced of the merits of the proposal, Nehru decided to concede the creation of a state of Nagaland, stipulating only that there would be a common Governor for Assam and the new state and that the jurisdiction of the Assam High Court would continue. The Governor would also retain responsibility for law and order as long as hostile activity persisted and for ensuring proper expenditure of funds provided by the central Government.[86] Such links were regarded as insufficient by the Assam Government but Nehru was prepared to go no further. 'When a limb has become gangrenous, for God's sake cut it off at once before the whole body is infected. Can't you see you will be doing yourself more harm than good by trying to cling on to the Nagas?'[87]

[82] Nehru's telegram to Michael Scott, 15 July 1960.

[83] Nehru to Vijayalakshmi, 16 July 1960.

[84] Nehru in the Lok Sabha, 4 August 1960. Debates, Second Series, Vol. 44, pp. 899–914.

[85] Nehru to B.P. Chaliha, 25 June 1960.

[86] Nehru's statement in Lok Sabha, 1 August 1960. Debates, Second Series, Vol. 44, pp. 146–57.

[87] Nehru's remark to the Assam Ministers is quoted in N. Rustomji, *Imperilled Frontiers* (Delhi, 1983), p. 55.

With this agreement Nehru felt once again, with irrepressible optimism, that the tide had been turned and the process of return to normality would move steadily, if slowly, forward. 'My conscience is at ease now.'[88] But the activity of the hostiles did not diminish and they even succeeded in bringing down an aircraft of the Indian Air Force and capturing the crew. The decision to create a new state had not alleviated the situation and Nehru had to express his great dissatisfaction as much with the seeming inertia of the army as with the incompetence of the civil authorities.[89] A party of foreign correspondents which visited the area in December 1960 returned with the impression that the desire for independence was widespread.[90]

The creation of the state of Nagaland formed, therefore, a settlement only of the political aspect of the Naga problem; the military aspect, of subduing the rebels, would clearly have to continue.[91] But, faced with growing resentment, Nehru was prepared to be more accommodating. Though it was by now well known that the Naga rebels were being assisted in various ways by the authorities in what was then East Pakistan, the Prime Minister permitted informal, non-official contacts with Phizo in London and authorized a visit by Scott to Nagaland. Having no desire to be vindictive, he was willing to consider, if a peaceful atmosphere were restored in Nagaland, a new approach to the hostiles. The situation did show some signs of improvement and the new Naga council began to function fairly well. But then the leader of the moderate Nagas was assassinated and Nehru ordered the army to resume active campaigning.[92] On learning from Krishna Menon, who was passing through London, that the British Government were considering the grant of citizenship to Phizo on the assumption that he was not an Indian citizen, Nehru instructed that the British High Commissioner be informed of the Indian Government's objection to any such step implying that Nagaland was not a part of India. The British Goverment were also told that, at a later stage, India might seek the extradition of Phizo. Although not in favour of such a step, Nehru wished to keep it in reserve.[93]

SIX

Both Assam and the Naga areas, therefore, continued to be worrying and indicative, along with the more serious communal riots, of the general need

88 Nehru to Chief Ministers, 30 July 1960.

89 Nehru to Srinagesh, 17 October 1960.

90 See N. Maxwell's memorandum to the editor of his paper, *The Times*, 1 January 1961, reprinted in Maxwell, *India and the Nagas* (London, 1973), pp. 25–7.

91 Answer in the Lok Sabha, 24 April 1961. Debates, Second Series, Vol. 55, pp. 13,348–9.

92 Nehru's note to Foreign Secretary, 15 September 1961.

93 Krishna Menon's telegram to Nehru, 1 October, and Nehru's notes to Secretary-General, Ministry of External Affairs, 4 and 11 October 1961.

for positive action for drawing the Indian people closer together. National cohesion was not disintegrating; but measures to buttress it were clearly required.[94] The Congress as a unifying element was useful but insufficient; and merely to rely on the long-term consequences of industrialization and modernization was not enough. No one in India was free from blame. 'The devil which had been pushed away into some corner of our minds displays itself again and it becomes evident that we are still far from having developed a broad-minded, tolerant and all-India nationalism.'[95] Nationalism in the modern sense was in India less than a hundred years old and easily corroded by atavistic feelings of caste, language, religion and region. 'In spite of all our growth, a certain tribalism clings to us.'[96] In the past, Indians had been rather weak and compromising; but it had now become clear that any compromise with an evil tendency, whatever temporary good it might apparently bring, did great harm later.

The Congress, therefore, at its Bhavnagar session in January 1961, set up a national integration committee; then the Prime Minister called a meeting of Chief Ministers for this purpose; and finally a National Integration Conference, representative of all parties, was convened in September 1961. It made wide-ranging suggestions, including a mass campaign for a pledge of non-violence to be taken by every adult citizen, reorientation of education, more extensive teaching of English and Hindi, facilities for instruction in minority languages, a code of conduct for political parties and regional balance in economic development. Nehru ordered the Chief Ministers to report on the actions taken on all such recommendations and reminded them that many acts, not wrong in themselves, might have pernicious results in the existing context. In particular, he wished the proportion of minority representation in the services, especially the police and the defence services, to be maintained at a high level.[97] Education also was of importance in this regard. Text-books for schools should be prepared with national unity in mind and English should be retained as the medium of instruction in higher education, for regional languages in universities would strengthen separatism and discourage collaboration in research and the building of a corporate intellectual life in India.[98] The Prime Minister also appealed to officials of the central Government to bear in mind in all their activities the necessity of reinforcing the emotional integration of the country; and he instructed the Chief Ministers to issue similar directives to the civil servants working in the states.[99]

Yet, despite all the problems besetting India in the early 1960s, Nehru's natural optimism asserted itself:

94 Address to the Congress Parliamentary Party, 13 November 1960. Tape M-52, Part II.

95 Nehru to Chief Ministers, 3 June 1961.

96 Address to the tenth session of the General Assembly of the World Confederation of Organizations of the Teaching Profession, Delhi, 2 August 1961. P.I.B.

97 Nehru to Chief Ministers, 3, 4 and 27 June 1961.

98 Nehru to Chief Ministers, 3 July 1961.

99 5 July 1961.

> all depends on how one looks at things. One can be distressed at many developments in India and one can also, taking a broader viewpoint, feel exhilarated at what is happening . . . the basic fact is that India is moving forward in a big way and this produces a sensation of success and triumph over difficulties.[100]

The mere fact that a consciousness of the need to strengthen national feeling had been created and people's minds turned in a particular direction should have in itself a healthy impact.

It was in this context of Chinese aggression and increasing domestic pressures that the country moved into the general elections in the spring of 1962. The campaigning of the parties accentuated the forces working against emotional convergence. As Nehru observed, though democracy was patently a higher form of civilization, at times of elections the devil seemed to be particularly obvious and present everywhere and to take hold of people.[101] But elections were a good occasion for placing ideals and programmes before the public and not only convincing vast numbers but carrying them along.

> In India we have to raise hundreds of millions of people and get them out of the rut of traditional thinking and living. Even an authoritarian state cannot do this by fiat, much less a democratic state. We do not live in the upper stratosphere but in an imperfect world which we are trying to improve and change.[102]

In 1962 the lines were drawn clearly, not so much in Bombay, where Krishna Menon contested with the unproclaimed support of left-wing parties, as elsewhere in the country – between the Congress in the middle, the Communist Party on the left and the Jan Sangh and the Swatantra on the right. The continuous Chinese aggression on the borders had placed the Communist Party in a quandary. If it supported China directly or indirectly it condemned itself in the eyes of the Indian public; but if it moved towards criticism of China it weakened to some extent its ideological commitments. Nehru had no intention of resolving this dilemma of the communists by banning the party. He sanctioned the arrest of individuals who defied the law and the exercise of stricter control of processions; but otherwise he wished the communists to be left to solve their own problem.[103] He accused the communists of not only wobbling at a moment of national danger but wobbling the wrong way and of functioning in a manner completely divorced from truth and patriotism.[104] Their way of thinking was 'absolutely anti-

[100] To Vijayalakshmi, 6 June 1961.

[101] Speech in the Lok Sabha, 19 March 1962. Debates, Second Series, Vol. 61, pp. 1,003–31.

[102] To K.K. Sinha, 18 June 1961.

[103] Nehru to B.C. Roy, 2 December 1959.

[104] Speeches at the A.I.C.C., Bangalore, 15 January 1960, A.I.R. tapes, and in the Rajya Sabha, 17 August 1960, Debates, Vol. 30, pp. 1,128–36.

nationalist'; they leaned more towards China than towards India and did not seem to mind if major chunks of the country were taken over by a communist state. He even accused them of seeking to exploit trends working against national unity for their own narrow advantage.[105]

Wide as were Nehru's differences with the approaches of the Communist Party, he felt even more alienated from the Jan Sangh and the Swatantra Parties. The communists had at least objectives which he could accept although he disapproved of their rigidity, methods and seeming submissiveness to directives from other countries. But the Jan Sangh was to him a dangerous organization of Hindu communalism weakening the whole fabric of Indian society, while the Swatantra he regarded as a collection of superannuated minds, exhibiting the 'bullock-cart mentality' in an atomic age.[106] He could only express his astonishment that there were still such backward-thinking intellectuals left in India.[107] Yet, because the Swatantra Party was in opposition, he had been all the more inclined to ensure that it was not treated unfairly. When Rajagopalachari sent Nehru a copy of his letter to the election commission seeking a separate symbol for the Swatantra Party in the elections, Nehru, without interfering with the commission's right to decide, instructed the Law Minister to support the request and expressed his Government's regret when the election commission turned it down.[108] But in the election campaign itself he struck back hard at a 'continually angry' Rajagopalachari[109] and at a party which 'represents an attitude which is so thoroughly and absolutely bad that I find it difficult to imagine that any person with intelligence can accept it'.[110] They were reacting to cooperative farming 'like some wild animals'.[111] But the Swatantra Party was to him more than stupidly reactionary; it represented a tendency towards fascism. It also astounded him that even the successful operation in Goa which, to most Indians, formed a bright spot of national achievement, was denounced by the Swatantra Party as a partisan act of Government intended to help the Congress Party in the elections. So he declined donations from industrialists who intended to contribute to the funds of both the Congress and the Swatantra Parties.[112] Even Nehru could not prevent collections being made by the party on the eve of elections; but his way of keeping this practice within limits and under control was to authorize a few selected persons to collect and to insist that these funds be not used for private purposes and no favours be shown in return. Collections should not be a form of 'gentle bribery',[113] and

[105] Speeches at Bhuvaneshwar, 25 May, *The Hindu*, 26 May 1961, and at the A.I.C.C., Durgapur, 28 May 1961. A.I.C.C. papers, Box 19, File G-22/1961. N.M.M.L.

[106] Speech at Bombay, 1 January, *The Hindu*, 2 January 1961.

[107] Address to the Congress Parliamentary Party, 21 April 1961. Tape 57/C, Part I.

[108] Nehru to Law Minister, 3 and 21 June 1961, and to Rajagopalachari, 7 June 1961.

[109] Speech at Madras, 8 October, *The Hindu*, 9 October 1961.

[110] Address to the Congress Parliamentary Party, 27 November 1961. Tape 61, Parts I and II.

[111] Speech to State Ministers for Cooperation 30 October, *The Hindu*, 31 October 1961.

[112] Nehru to J.R.D. Tata, 18 August 1961.

[113] Address to the Congress Parliamentary Party, 27 November 1961. Tape 61, Parts I and II.

this led him to decline funds from those who so obviously had no commitment to the Congress cause.

It seemed, then, that the political cleavages in the elections of 1962 ran so deep as to form one more element in the slackening of the integration of the Indian people. But, ironically, the solution to this particular domestic problem was provided not by the exhortations of the National Integration Committee, Conference and Council or by the efforts of the Prime Minister but by external aggression. The massive reinforcement of Indian unity came from China.

9

Round the World – to Goa

ONE

In the second half of 1961, the Congo and the Berlin crises were portents which had made Nehru feel uneasy. 'I am glad that you will be here in India soon. Let us be together before the world tries to blow up.'[1] From the practice of occasional brinkmanship the world had moved to living continuously at the very edge of the precipice, and the feeling of some dreadful fate descending upon humanity had become its constant companion. Both the blocs had taken rigid attitudes and Nehru feared that the period of grace might not last beyond the end of the year. It seemed doubtful if India or the non-aligned could do anything to avert this approaching conflict of Titans.[2]

However, Tito and Nasser were keen that a conference of non-aligned countries be held in the near future. India had not been enthusiastic about such a conference. Krishna Menon felt that the conference, whose purpose was to create a bloc or at least a platform, would damage non-alignment, the essence of which was the retention of freedom from pre-commitment.[3] While agreeing with this assessment, Nehru realized that, if a conference were held, India could not refuse to participate. But he instructed his representative at the preparatory meeting not to commit himself to any particular line of action or to the creation of a third, non-aligned bloc. Non-alignment did not mean standing aloof only from the Soviet Union or the Western Powers; it meant non-alignment with other countries also. To be tied up with a group of countries except in terms of broad policies was to limit one's freedom of decision and action. The invitation should also be as broadly based as possible.[4] Egypt and Yugoslavia agreed to this; but Nehru's reluctance was still perceptible. Hearing that some invitees were meeting earlier to concert their policies, Nehru wrote to the sponsors that if small groups began to get

1 To Vijayalakshmi, 2 August 1961.
2 To Chief Ministers, 5 August 1961.
3 Telegram from Geneva, 4 June 1961. File 30(245)/61-P.M.S.
4 Telegram to R.K. Nehru at Cairo, 6 June 1961.

aligned with each other, the conference would face difficulties and he would be hesitant to attend.[5]

The day before the conference assembled at Belgrade on 1 September, the Soviet Union resumed nuclear testing, and it was partly with Nehru's earlier censures of testing in mind that Kennedy did not take similar action in reprisal.[6] However much it might be resented by some, it was clear from the start that it was Nehru's presence that gave force and vitality to the assembly of the non-aligned;[7] and Nehru utilized the occasion to readjust the priorities of the member states in the new context of growing rivalry in nuclear armament. At first he had the majority of the countries against him. Sukarno of Indonesia placed the emphasis on colonialism while Tito generally supported Soviet policies. But Nehru asserted that the era of classical colonialism was essentially over and the immediate and predominant danger was that of a world war. First things should come first and nothing was more important than this crisis. He wrested the conference out of the old ruts of ritual opposition to colonialism, imperialism and racism and forced it to face the danger of nuclear warfare. The final resolution, adopted at his instance, stressed that never had war been a greater threat to mankind but recognized that imperialism was weakening. The participants also decided to appeal to Kennedy and Khrushchev to resume direct negotiations.[8] As for the question of Berlin, stress was laid on the need for negotiations between the great powers rather than on the merits of the issue. The Belgrade conference was Nehru's last triumph in world affairs.

From Belgrade, Nehru went on to Moscow in response to a previous invitation; and he also agreed to present, along with Nkrumah, the conclusions of the non-aligned conference to the Soviet Government. There was not, on this occasion, the exuberance which had been shown on Nehru's previous visit. He spoke warmly of Soviet friendship, which India valued more than any gift or assistance;[9] and Khrushchev in return used, for the first time, the word 'unbreakable' to describe that friendship.[10] But it was clearly a meeting of old friends who did not see eye to eye on some important issues. Unconvinced by Khrushchev's long explanations for resuming nuclear testing, Nehru contended that this action was not only bad in itself but had worsened an already bad situation. Khrushchev emphasized the need for an agreement on disarmament and blamed Adenauer and de Gaulle for the general world crisis. Nehru's impression was that the basic factor influencing Soviet policy was the growing fear of the German Federal Republic. Khrush-

[5] To Tito, to Nasser and to Sukarno, 23 June 1961.

[6] A.M. Schlesinger Jr, *A Thousand Days* (Boston, 1965), p. 449.

[7] See Andrew Boyd, 'Belgrade Notebook', *Encounter*, November 1961.

[8] Nehru's speech, 2 September, two Declarations of Heads of State or Government, and letter to Kennedy and Khrushchev, *Proceedings of Conference of Heads of State or Government of Non-Aligned Countries* (Belgrade, 1961).

[9] Speech at the banquet in the Kremlin, 6 September, *National Herald*, 8 September 1961.

[10] Speech at the public meeting in Moscow, 8 September, *The Hindu*, 10 September 1961.

chev would welcome negotiations but would insist on the recognition of East Germany — and this did not seem to Nehru an insuperable obstacle. From the Soviet side, Nehru's visit perhaps did some good. Outwardly there was no change, but Nehru felt that there was a toning down which might prove of use in the future.[11] There is other evidence to substantiate Nehru's assessment. Before seeing Nehru, Khrushchev had spoken to a visiting American editor of testing a powerful megaton bomb and thought there was no use in meeting Kennedy again; a day later, after his talks with Nehru, he revised the record of the interview to suggest testing only of the detonator and not of the bomb itself and said he would always be glad to meet Kennedy.[12]

TWO

Nehru followed up his visit to Moscow with a journey to Washington. He had first met Kennedy many years before, in 1951, when John and Robert Kennedy had had dinner with him in Delhi; but, on that occasion, Nehru had hardly spoken except to their sister.[13] Later, Nehru had been impressed by the efforts of John Kennedy, as a young Senator, to convince his people that it was in the interests of the United States to grant massive economic aid to India. His election as President had therefore been welcome to Nehru, and Kennedy, in turn, had gone out of his way to speak appreciatively, in his inaugural address, of Nehru's 'soaring idealism'. Intelligence, style, humanity, wit — these qualities Kennedy and Nehru shared and sought to build upon. Kennedy sent a warm letter introducing the new Ambassador, Professor Galbraith, and Nehru replied in similar terms. Though unhappy at the Bay of Pigs adventure and the failure to check the anti-Indian activities of the American Ambassador in the Congo, Nehru recognized the affinity of the two Governments on the last issue; and he had, at Kennedy's request, intervened at Hanoi and Moscow to secure a cease-fire in Laos.[14] Kennedy was duly thankful. 'I want you to know how much I appreciate your continuing efforts to create a peaceful world community. We have been particularly grateful for the strong support you gave to the opening session of the reconvened International Control Commission for Laos and the stress you laid on the necessity for a prompt cease-fire.' Kennedy also committed himself to assistance for India's economic development; and Nehru was not far behind in expressions of cordiality. 'Our task, great as it is, has been made light by the goodwill and generous assistance that has come to us from the United States. To the people of the United States and more especially to you, Mr. President,

11 Nehru to U Nu, 26 September 1961.

12 C.L. Sulzberger, *The Last of the Giants* (London, 1971), p. 802.

13 A.M. Schlesinger Jr, *Robert Kennedy and His Times* (London, 1978), p. 91.

14 Kennedy to Nehru 26 April, Commonwealth Secretary's telegram to Indian mission at Hanoi 27 April, and Nehru's telegram to Indian Embassy in Moscow, 27 April 1961.

we feel deeply grateful.'[15] He also stated publicly that despite its grant of military assistance to Pakistan, the Kennedy administration was more friendly to India than its predecessor.[16]

However, goodwill and economic assistance did not constitute the sum of relations between the two countries. Kennedy would have liked India to assume the leadership in South and South-East Asia against China and if, for this purpose, the countries of this area should be non-aligned, Kennedy was willing to guarantee this.[17] But this proposal Nehru could not be expected to favour for it amounted virtually to a military alliance. Moreover, while India had her own difficulties with China, Nehru had no wish to line up with President Diem of South Vietnam. So it was with no great enthusiasm that Nehru accepted Kennedy's invitation to visit Washington after the Belgrade conference and his trip to Moscow.[18] His reluctance to undertake the long journey was not only because of problems in India. 'It is something deeper than that, this politics of summits and conferences attracts me less and less.'[19]

Everyone is agreed that the visit was not a success. Kennedy spoke of it later 'as the worst head-of-state visit I have had'. Talking to Nehru was like trying to grab something, only to have it turn out to be just fog.[20] The fact that Nehru was severely critical of Soviet resumption of nuclear testing did not in itself help to improve the atmosphere. The American assessment was that Nehru had aged and was a tired old man who had stayed around too long. Harriman, who had met him a few months earlier in Delhi, did not think there was a real Nehru policy and believed that the contest for succession in India had already begun.[21] Nehru's hosts in the United States did not realize that, if he seemed remote and withdrawn, he and his officials had their own dilemmas. Kennedy had won the election by a very narrow majority and appeared insecure in his handling of power. They were concerned by the Bay of Pigs fiasco and could not accept the untroubled certainty of judgments at the White House, particularly as they knew of the differences of opinion between Kennedy's advisers and the State Department, and were faced with repeated requests in Washington to strengthen the influence of those Americans who were advocating liberal policies.

At the start, Kennedy talked almost entirely of Laos and Vietnam. On Laos Nehru had already done what he could to secure its neutrality and independence; but when Kennedy asked Nehru to suggest ways of securing a mid-way position between American military intervention in Vietnam and a loss of the country to the communists, the Indian side could only urge that Diem be

[15] Kennedy to Nehru, 8 May, and Nehru's reply, 24 May 1961.

[16] 23 August 1961. Rajya Sabha Debates, Vol. 35, pp. 1,374–97.

[17] Kennedy's interview with M.C. Chagla, retiring Indian Ambassador. M.C. Chagla, *Roses in December* (Bombay, 1973), pp. 270–1.

[18] Nehru's note to Secretary-General, Ministry of External Affairs, after interview with J.K. Galbraith, 22 June 1961.

[19] Nehru to Dorothy Norman, 25 June 1961.

[20] Schlesinger, *A Thousand Days*, p. 526.

[21] Sulzberger, *The Last of the Giants*, p. 751.

directed to reform his administration. They refused to consider either an approach to Ho Chi Minh or a United Nations observer corps or, more vaguely, Indian leadership in establishing a neutral belt across South-East Asia.[22] They did not think that any Indian initiative was possible in Vietnam apart from the proper working of the International Commission under the Geneva agreements, although they are said to have promised to 'look the other way' when evidence of military activity by the United States appeared and to press vigorously charges against the Viet Cong.[23] Such reluctance to come forward with any more positive move was justified by what we now know, that the Kennedy administration was already engaged in deepening its military involvement in South Vietnam and that, even while Nehru was in Washington, the President had decided to expand the military advisory mission and vest American troops with combat-support roles.[24]

Kennedy also raised the Kashmir issue. Nehru explained the Indian case but sought no support from the United States for, when Ayub visited Washington a few months earlier, the joint communiqué had made no reference to the anti-communist basis of their alliance and had spoken only of Pakistan utilizing military assistance from the United States to maintain her security; and it was known that Kennedy had promised Ayub a squadron of the latest military aircraft. Kennedy somewhat apologetically told Nehru that it was easier to secure allocations from Congress for military than for economic aid and, when Nehru made no comment, added that he would have to consider this matter and confine assistance to Pakistan to economic aid. They then discussed in general terms India's dispute with China, Sino-Soviet relations and the Berlin crisis. Goa only came up incidentally, when Nehru observed that, in the context of world problems, Goa was a minor matter, yet to Indian opinion that was a major issue which coloured its views on most aspects of international affairs.[25]

On this visit, Nehru got through, as usual, to sensitive men and women outside politics and the administration. Christopher Isherwood, for example, was swept off his feet. 'When I first met Nehru I was overwhelmed by his greatness. He was like a tremendous nanny, talking of Khrushchev and Kennedy as if they were naughty nephews, hoping they wouldn't get into a war.'[26] But there had clearly been a failure in communication between Nehru and Kennedy. To some extent it was the result of the gap between the generations. To Nehru, Kennedy, though 'top class',[27] appeared brash, aggressive and inexperienced while Kennedy found Nehru passive and

[22] J.K. Galbraith, *A Life in Our Times* (London, 1981), p. 470.

[23] S.S. Harrison, *The Widening Gulf* (New York, 1978), pp. 176–7.

[24] *The Pentagon Papers* (New York, 1971), p. 85.

[25] Notes of M.J. Desai, Foreign Secretary, on Nehru's talks with President Kennedy and officials of the State Department, dated 9 and 20 November 1961.

[26] Janet Watts, 'Mr Isherwood Changes Sides', *Observer*, 13 July 1980.

[27] Address (in Hindi) to the Congress Parliamentary Party on his return from the United States, 27 November 1962. Tapes M-61, Parts I and II.

inward-looking. He did not seem interested in issues and places not immediately relevant to India's borders and had suggestions to make only on Pakistan or Kashmir.[28] He carried little conviction with his repeated emphasis on the geographical conditioning of the mind and on the emotional involvement of peoples with their own problems even while they accepted intellectually the importance of issues of universal significance. Perhaps his own exceptional recognition of the need to give primacy to the prevention of nuclear warfare led those who now listened to him in the United States to criticize him for devoting undue attention to India's specific problems in foreign affairs. To Eleanor Roosevelt he gave the impression of being 'a calm centre' amid raging controversies – a great and a strong, but also a sensitive and gentle, person.[29] But to the men in power in Washington Nehru appeared remote from the realities of the world. His claim that to India peace was a passion and his admonition that a strong country did not lose its strength by a gentle approach seemed to Kennedy and his assistants empty words with little bearing on the practical demands of international problems.

Of the American Presidents of his time, it was, curiously, Eisenhower with whom Nehru got on best. Truman's cocky vulgarity had grated on him; and so did the affluence and glitter with which Kennedy was surrounded. Lyndon Johnson he hardly knew. But Eisenhower's sincerity and goodwill, especially in contrast to the blinkered preachiness of Dulles, struck a chord.

THREE

For a brief while after his return from the United States, world issues, even the danger of nuclear war, took second place in Nehru's mind to the decisions which could no longer be avoided on the issue of Portuguese rule in Goa. Nehru's policy on Goa had always three strands: no solution short of merger with India was acceptable, the use of force for this purpose was not ruled out, but he would avoid it as long as he could in the interests of larger policy and India's general approach to world issues. However, it was generally thought that his commitment to peaceful methods was so intense that it virtually nullified the theoretical willingness to abandon them in the last resort; and it must be said that, in rebutting his critics who urged him over the years to occupy Goa, he often used language which suggested that he would in no circumstances resort to arms in this matter. Nehru himself made it easy for observers to forget that he was not a pacifist but a pacificist and that events might take such a turn that even his patience would be exhausted. As he had urged the world for years to get out of the rut of thinking that there was

[28] J.K. Galbraith, *Ambassador's Journal* (London, 1969), p. 265.

[29] See speech of the Chairman of the Overseas Press Club, New York, welcoming Nehru, 10 November 1961.

normally no other way of solving a problem than by hitting an adversary with a club, the world tended to forget that he had never denied that sometimes there might be no other way. His work for peace over the years blurred the fact that he had not totally rejected war as an instrument of policy.[30]

By the end of 1956, the Government of India had reached an impasse on Goa. Nehru had been determined that India, though very angry, should act with responsibility and wisdom; but what such action should be was not clear, and the whole policy had obviously to be reconsidered after the elections in the spring of 1957 and Kashmir and other international issues were, at least temporarily, out of the way.[31] But such reconsideration only made clearer the dilemma about method. Ellsworth Bunker, the American Ambassador, suggested that Goa might be purchased from Portugal in the manner in which the United States had bought Louisiana from France.[32] But this ingenious proposal presumed what was far from being the case, Portugal's willingness to part with Goa. Nehru had to decide whether, and for how long, he was prepared to wait, if force would at any stage be used, and, if so, when. At a meeting with Members of Parliament belonging to various parties, he once again ruled out any form of military action;[33] but significantly, writing to Vinoba Bhave, the most distinguished of the surviving disciples of Gandhi, he cited Goa as an argument against creating a peace brigade and reducing the size of the army. Refusal to use force was in keeping with India's general outlook and policy and the important and immediate question was how to deal with Goa without resort to arms; but not to do anything effective was obviously bad.[34] That hundreds of Goans were being treated harshly in Portuguese prisons and, what was worse, losing heart was a source of continuing sorrow and anxiety. Their incarceration was linked with the larger question of the future of Goa and he had to give constant attention to the question as to what action should be taken.[35]

However, Nehru could find no obvious answer and continued to worry over the various aspects of the problem and to take refuge in postponing a decision. He publicly announced that, while the Government were not contemplating any kind of military action in Goa, any other type of action that might be feasible would be taken.[36] Though it was depressing to rule out quick action, India could not allow herself to lose her bearings and act in the excitement of the moment in a manner which would have harmful results. The problem of Goa, like many other problems in the world, should therefore wait for a solution.[37]

[30] For an elaboration of this distinction between pacifism and pacificism, see A.J.P. Taylor in the *London Review of Books*, 2–16 October 1980.

[31] Nehru to Peter Alvares, 27 August 1956, and letter to S. Nijalingappa and note, both 21 January 1957.

[32] Nehru's note recording conversation with E. Bunker, 8 May 1957.

[33] Nehru's note on discussions with some Members of Parliament, 27 May 1957.

[34] Note for Vinoba Bhave and letter to U.N. Dhebar, 4 May 1957.

[35] Nehru to Sindhu Deshpande, 15 August 1957.

[36] Answer to question 5 September 1957. Lok Sabha Debates, Second Series, Vol. 6, pp. 12,000–3.

[37] Nehru to Chief Ministers, 23–4 January 1958.

Yet he could not ignore India's singular record of failure in this matter, and thought it necessary to be clear in mind and know exactly what India could and could not do.[38] The trade embargoes had achieved little and there was scant prospect of progress along these lines. It would seem that Nehru saw hardly any hope of effective peaceful action by India and was relying on Britain and the United States to apply pressure on Portugal. There was no logical reason why the British, who had compelled the Sultan of Muscat to transfer Gwadar to Pakistan, should not take similar action about Goa.[39] Chagla, appointed Ambassador to Washington, was instructed to discuss the matter regularly with both the Department of State and Cardinal Spellman. They should be told that India could never agree to the indefinite continuance of a foreign foothold on what was obviously Indian territory with a predominantly Indian population. Roman Catholics in India had full religious freedom and the Government of India were committed to treating Goa as a separate entity. The Ambassador should not suggest a plebiscite which, with a reactionary Portuguese Government supervising it, would be absurd, or an independent administration in Goa; it was for the United States to consider what should be done. 'The ultimate solution', Nehru added,[40] 'can only be close association with India, with possibly internal autonomy' – a choice of words which may have been casual but which implied that Nehru, in October 1958, in deference to world and particularly American opinion, was willing to consider, in defiance of Indian public opinion and in contravention of his own preference and commitments, at least an interim settlement short of merger of Goa with India. What he had in mind was possibly some arrangement on the lines of the *de facto* transfer of French possessions in India. He also specially asked Chagla, whenever occasion arose, to draw attention to India's rejection of the military way of dealing with any problem. Force was out of date, solved nothing and only added to difficulties; nor did it fit in with India's general outlook and the special conditioning her leaders had received during the national movement and the Gandhi era.[41] Hopeful of the United States securing some response from Portugal, such as at least the release of political prisoners, he requested the presiding officers of the two Houses of Parliament in November 1958 not to allow questions or motions on Goa for about two weeks.[42]

Yet, throughout 1959, there was hardly any advance. Nehru confidently asserted that Goa was a part of India and bound to come to India; but it was not still clear how this was to be achieved and all that the Prime Minister could do was counsel patience and point out the unwisdom of any resort to force.[43] The

[38] Note to Foreign Secretary, 2 July 1958.

[39] Note of Secretary-General, Ministry of External Affairs, and Nehru's comment, 7 September 1958.

[40] Nehru's instructions to M.C. Chagla, Ambassador in Washington, 21 October 1958.

[41] Further instructions to M.C. Chagla, 20 November 1958.

[42] Nehru to the Speaker of the Lok Sabha, 16 November, and to the Chairman of the Rajya Sabha, 20 November 1958.

[43] Speeches at the Congress session, Nagpur, 10 and 11 January, *The Hindu*, 11 and 12 January 1959.

18 Receiving the Queen at his residence in Delhi, January 1961

19 At the Congress session at Madurai, 4 October 1961

20 *Above left* A word to an official, Delhi airport, 24 September 1960
21 *Above right* With Tom Mboya, Bhavnagar, 5 January 1961

22 With Krishna Menon, 1962

inhabitants of the Portuguese enclaves of Dadra and Nagar Haveli declared the accession of their territories to India, and Portugal sought from the International Court confirmation of rights of passage to these areas across Indian territory. But as regards Goa itself, India's efforts to isolate it economically rebounded in that Goa ceased to be dependent on her. The boycott resulted in widespread smuggling, and the cessation of direct traffic weakened national sentiment in Goa. Nor was there a noticeable increase of international pressure on Portugal. So, all in all, the situation was deteriorating from India's point of view. To pull policy out of a rut, Nehru ordered the more effective suppression of smuggling and the restoration of facilities for communication.[44] As for the basic problem, Nehru was driven gradually and reluctantly to the conclusion that his approach had failed. He thought it obvious to everyone, including the Government of Portugal, that Goa should become a part of India; but no one was willing to act on the obvious fact and India's insistence on adhering to ways of peace gained her no more than commendation. The decision of the Hague Court in India's favour in the matter of rights of passage to Dadra and Nagar Haveli strengthened her moral position but opened no way to a practical solution of the main issue of Goa. Yet Nehru could not bring himself to revise his policy and clung to inaction as a means of attaining his objective. 'We really have no policy at present aimed at achieving success in the near future. We can only prepare the ground for it and wait for other events to happen. As a matter of fact, these other events in the world are slowly working against the present Portuguese regime.'[45] But it was not obvious what these events were and Nehru would have found it difficult to specify them.

So, for another year, there was no development within Goa or outside; nor was the Government of India particularly active. Nothing was done beyond repeatedly proclaiming that Goa was bound to come to India and that the Government had the courage to adhere to peaceful methods. Nehru thought that the real work for Goa should take place in Goa itself, though people outside Goa could help; but there was little sign of such work. However, the situation in the world seemed to improve. Whereas earlier Nehru had been aggrieved that such questions as Goa were not considered on merits but by cold war attitudes,[46] he now felt that, for a variety of reasons, sympathy was much more with India than it used to be and, because of events in Angola, Portugal was being criticized bitterly almost everywhere. The situation was a developing one and India should be prepared to meet it.[47] He assured his people that Goa would join India, but he would not make a promise or set a date as to when that would be. Though the Indian army could push the Portuguese forces out of Goa within twenty-four hours, the Government would wait; for, if they started a war, it would not remain confined to Goa.[48]

[44] Nehru's notes to Foreign Secretary, 6 March, and to Commonwealth Secretary, 12 March 1960.

[45] Nehru's note to Commonwealth Secretary, 20 June 1960.

[46] Answers to questions in the Lok Sabha, 25 November 1960. Debates, Vol. 47, pp. 2,256–60.

[47] To Y.B. Chavan, Chief Minister of Maharashtra, 28 June 1961.

[48] Speech at Srinagar, 19 July, *National Herald*, 21 July 1961.

Consideration of this matter could not be isolated from other problems in the world and for India to initiate a war, however minor, was to take a step fundamentally opposed to her general policy. Even a little spark was dangerous and it was not for India to light it. So he could say no more than that the question was not a closed one.[49] He welcomed the Portuguese threat to reach Dadra and Nagar Haveli by land, across Indian territory, or by sea, because this would then give India a free hand to deal with Goa;[50] but the Portuguese were too prudent to act on their threat. As to whether India should act on her own without any such provocation, Nehru was still in two minds. When the time came to deal with the Goa issue by means of arms, India would do so; but India's stock had gone up in the world because she stuck to certain basic policies and did not function just in anger or in an adventurous way. He gave Parliament an assurance that whether these policies should be varied would be regularly considered.[51] But clearly, in his view, the time for this had not yet come; and all the arguments he used for not immediately resorting to armed action were later to be turned by his critics against him.

Although it was, to Nehru's way of thinking, absurd to tie up the problem of Goa with events in Africa,[52] the growing crisis in Angola impinged increasingly on Indian policy. Goa and Angola had become parts of a single problem – that of Portuguese colonialism. At the conference of non-aligned countries in Belgrade, Nehru had placed the prime emphasis on the imminent danger of a world war and the urgent necessity of disarmament; but he had also spoken of 'the horror of Angola',[53] and this intolerable anomaly of Portuguese imperialism had been denounced in the final communiqué. While the blood being continuously shed in the Portuguese colonies in Africa helped to build international opinion against the Salazar regime, it also focused public attention, particularly in Africa, on Nehru's inaction on the Goa issue. The significance of this should not be exaggerated; the Chinese image has not been tarnished by their acceptance of Portuguese rule in Macao. But, in a sense, the price Nehru had to pay for his success at the Belgrade conference in giving disarmament priority over anti-colonialism was a deeper commitment to decisive action against the Portuguese presence in India. The possibility, which he had never ruled out, of circumstances arising which might compel armed intervention in Goa, was now emerging more clearly. Addressing a seminar in New Delhi on Portuguese colonies but having mainly an African audience in mind, Nehru, disclaiming that he had not become completely 'a highly-bred Prime Minister', pointedly stressed that non-violent methods had been adopted in the national movement because of the special circumstances of

[49] 16 August 1961. Rajya Sabha Debates, Vol. 35, pp. 379–86.

[50] Nehru's note to Krishna Menon, 18 August 1961.

[51] Speeches in the Lok Sabha, 16 and 17 August 1961. Debates, Second Series, Vol. 56, pp. 2,405–31 and 2,766–86 respectively.

[52] Speech in the Lok Sabha, 14 August 1961. Debates, Second Series, Vol. 56, pp. 2,285–9.

[53] Speech at Belgrade, 2 September 1961, *Proceedings of Conference of Heads of State or Government of Non-Aligned Countries*.

India. If the Government had so far desisted from forceful methods on the Goa issue it was not solely for moral reasons and, while their effort would always be to settle the problem by pressures and action other than war, at no time had they in their minds or in action renounced recourse to a military solution.[54] A few days later he moved even closer to the possible use of force by confessing that the Portuguese were pushing the Government of India into thinking afresh and adopting other than peaceful methods to solve the problem. 'When and how I cannot say now. But I have no doubt that we will do it . . .'[55]

Meantime, both within and outside Goa, matters were coming to a head. The Portuguese started firing at Indians across the border as well as on Indian ships on the high seas – probably in the hope that India would retaliate by occupying one of the offshore islands, enabling Portugal to refer the matter to the Security Council, where it would be bogged down for years. But international pressures were also building up on India. In 1960 the General Assembly of the United Nations had passed resolutions denouncing colonialism in general and Portuguese colonialism in particular; and the next year, in November 1961, Portugal was again condemned for non-compliance with its obligations under the Charter and creating an increasingly dangerous situation in many parts of the world. These resolutions gave added legitimacy to the almost unanimous feeling in India that the use of force in Goa would not constitute international aggression but complete the process of national liberation. Ethnically, culturally, economically – in fact, every way but politically, Goa was an obvious part of India and its merger would be the final chapter of the Indian risorgimento, part of the 'logic of the historic process'.[56] In the Congress Party itself the Finance Minister, Morarji Desai, was one of the few against the use of force; but, while he claims to have voiced his objection when the defence committee of the Cabinet was asked to fix a date for marching into Goa,[57] he did not think it a matter of sufficient importance to require his resignation. Desai was always prone to brandish his self-righteousness; but there was clearly as much elasticity as exhibitionism in his commitment to principle.

The intensification of world opinion against European, and particularly Portuguese, imperialism, generally regarded as the worst of its kind, by resolutions at the United Nations and at the conference of non-aligned countries and by the testimony of events in the Congo and Angola, both strengthened and forced Nehru's hands on Goa. He was now much better prepared in mind, if it came to the worst, to use force to drive out the Portuguese; but he was not yet sure that it had come to this. He confessed that Goa, for years an irritant and a humiliation, was now, because of reports of

[54] Inaugural address at the seminar on Portuguese colonies, New Delhi, 20 October, *National Herald*, 21 October 1961.

[55] Speech at Bombay, 23 October 1961, quoted in A.N. Rubinoff, *India's Use of Force in Goa* (Bombay, 1971), p. 83.

[56] Sir J.M. Richards, *Goa*, Indian edn (1982), p. 76.

[57] M. Desai, *The Story of My Life*, Vol. 2 (Delhi, 1974), p. 175.

increased Portuguese repression, causing him acute mental agony; and he appears to have been contemplating phased action leading ultimately, step by step, to the liberation of the territory.[58] But his advisers warned him that drawn-out action would play into Portuguese hands and enable them to convert it into an international issue; if action were taken at all, it should be swift and decisive. So Indian forces round Goa were increased; but still Nehru wavered. It was a strain to mass forces and await events; as Nehru said later, it was difficult to remain on tip-toe all the time.[59] On the other hand, all his conditioning and previous policy made Nehru reluctant to act. Nehru had boxed himself in by his earlier attitudes and speeches in such a way that action, which would have been easy for any other Head of Government, became peculiarly difficult for him. His long delay in expelling the Portuguese and his argued defence, on numerous occasions, of inaction reinforced the criticism of him when finally he was driven to exercise the last option which he had never foreclosed. But he was still hoping for internal revolt or international intervention to relieve him of the need to make a decision; and on 11 December he told the Rajya Sabha that he still wished to avoid the use of force and it was for the Government of India and others to consider what steps should be taken for the future.[60] It was perhaps this anxiety to involve others in settling the issue that led the American Ambassador, Galbraith, to conclude that, although the Indian authorities were building up public opinion on this question, they would decide in the end against the use of force.[61]

However, meeting Nehru that same afternoon, Galbraith was obliged to change his view and return with the impression that Indian action was likelier than he had thought. So he urged Nehru not to blot his, and India's, record for not using force and still India's voice and influence in the world by moving armies even in circumstances conducive to grave annoyance, but to seek the support of the United Nations. Nehru replied that the cup was full and beginning to spill over. 'Step by step, we were drawn into this whirlpool, much against our will.' Unless the Portuguese underwent a complete change of outlook and woke up to the fact that they were living in the middle of the twentieth century, there was no way of leaving matters as they were. No Government in India could do so or would want to do so. Matters had reached a stage when there could be no half-way approach to this problem, and the Portuguese should agree to quit Goa.[62] The tone of this letter suggested that Nehru had decided to press forward with military action; but, in fact, there was as yet no firm decision and, indeed, Nehru was struggling to avoid one and clutching at every hope, however faint, of a settlement. He first looked to Brazil and some other Latin American countries for mediation and pushed off

[58] See his two speeches in the Lok Sabha, 7 December 1961. Debates, Second Series, Vol. 60, pp. 3,848–68 and 3,975–98 respectively.

[59] Press conference at Delhi, 28 December, *The Hindu*, 29 December 1961.

[60] Two speeches, Rajya Sabha Debates, Vol. 36, pp. 1,765–78 and 1,850–76 respectively.

[61] *Ambassador's Journal*, p. 276.

[62] J.K. Galbraith's letter to Nehru, and Nehru's reply, 12 December 1961.

suggestions from Krishna Menon for fixing a date for intervention. But this vague approach came to nothing, for Portugal proposed no more than an invitation to independent observers to ascertain the attitudes of the confronting forces on the Goa border.[63] The British too, while assuring India that, despite the Anglo-Portuguese alliance invoked by Salazar, they would not assist the Portuguese against a Commonwealth Government, searched in vain for a midway position between the forcible expulsion of the Portuguese and immediate Portuguese withdrawal; and Nehru declined to promise Macmillan that he would not in any circumstances resort to the use of force.[64]

However, he still hesitated to take a positive decision. By this time Krishna Menon and the Defence Ministry had fixed a date for the entry of Indian troops into Goa; but again Nehru, on the urging of Galbraith, ordered postponement by two days. He was encouraged by Galbraith to believe that the United States, being opposed to colonialism, would compel the Portuguese Government to agree to leave Goa on the understanding that India would take a generous view of the economic and cultural interests of Portugal in Goa – a commitment which Nehru had no difficulty in giving.[65] But Galbraith was over-estimating his influence in policy-making in the United States, for the State Department had already extended support to the Salazar regime. Dean Rusk and the Foreign Minister of Portugal discussed how best to bypass the United Nations, with its anti-colonial postures, and to bring pressure on India to desist from action. Not even a hint was given to Portugal that President Kennedy believed that India had a legitimate case on Goa and that the United States Government were opposed to colonialism.[66] So, whatever the good intentions of Galbraith, the United States was of little use in helping Nehru to avoid force. On the other hand, sympathy declared by the State Department strengthened the Salazar regime in its adamant attitude and, when U Thant suggested negotiations, the Portuguese Government were willing to discuss the issue only on the basis of the coexistence of India and Portuguese Goa and not on that of the United Nations resolutions.

On 16 December, Nehru received a message from Kennedy expressing again his general concern at the use of force in Goa and his particular concern that, with Indian troops playing a prominent role in the Congo, a simultaneous use of force in Goa would give rise to an undesirable image of Indian belligerency.[67] To link Goa with the malicious insinuations evoked by India's support of the United Nations operation in the Congo was not an argument likely to carry weight with Nehru. Then Galbraith suggested that India sponsor a resolution on Goa in the General Assembly and request the Security

[63] Note of the Government of Brazil, 13 December 1961.

[64] Nehru's note on conversation with British High Commissioner, 14 December 1961; H. Macmillan to Nehru, 14 December, and Nehru's reply, 15 December 1961.

[65] Note of M.J. Desai, Foreign Secretary, recording interview with Galbraith, 14 December 1961.

[66] Galbraith, *Ambassador's Journal*, pp. 182–3; Schlesinger, *A Thousand Days*, p. 526.

[67] B.K. Nehru's telegram communicating Kennedy's telephone message, 15 December, received 16 December 1961.

Council to implement it with the despatch of a United Nations force to evict the Portuguese. He could not have been surprised by the reply that, with the examples of Kashmir and the Congo before them, the Government of India were not enamoured of intervention by the United Nations.[68] Later the same day the United States Government came up with a fresh proposal that India should postpone action for six months to enable the Governments of the United States and, perhaps, other countries to help to solve this problem. But the officials of the State Department were themselves not hopeful and felt that the Portuguese Government, anachronistic and unaware of the climate of change, would prefer an Indian occupation of Goa to a voluntary surrender. When Galbraith saw Nehru on the evening of 17 December to press this proposal, the Prime Minister, clutching at straws, was inclined to agree to further postponement; but Krishna Menon informed him that it was too late, as the advance parties of the Indian army had already begun to move.[69] Mountbatten doubtless had this primarily in mind when he blamed Nehru for letting Krishna Menon 'bounce' him into military action in Goa. He thought that Menon had put Nehru in a position when he would either have to sanction the entry into Goa or it would be known that it was Nehru who had stopped it.[70] Later Mountbatten elaborated this to say that Menon did 'the most frightful thing' to Nehru by forcing him to bless the Goa operation, thereby destroying him: 'not only his credibility, his prestige, his reputation, but he destroyed his faith in himself, for he felt that he had been betrayed'.[71] This is, to say the least, gross over-statement. Nehru's hands had been forced on the timing but with no effects on his self-confidence. Certainly hindsight does not provide cause for regret on the particular point that the last American proposal was not given a chance. For, although Nehru did not know it, the offer of the United States Government was an empty one, the State Department having no desire to coerce the Portuguese Government to offer any compromise solution, let alone to quit Goa.

So, on the night of 17 December, Indian troops moved into Goa; and the whole operation was over in twenty-six hours. The Portuguese authorities had been threatening to fight to the end and asserting that the Goans would stand by their imperial rulers and die after each of them had killed, at least, ten Indians. But the Governor-General of Goa, in defiance of orders from Lisbon, surrendered without a fight.[72] Indian casualties amounted to eight, of which four deaths were the result of a Portuguese party opening fire after showing the white flag.

[68] Note of M.J. Desai recording conversation with Galbraith, 16 December 1961.

[69] B.K. Nehru's telegram reporting conversation with Ball and McGhee of the State Department, 16 December 1961; Galbraith, *Ambassador's Journal*, pp. 284–5; Brecher, *India and World Politics*, pp. 130–2.

[70] Mountbatten's interview with the author, 28 May 1970.

[71] Mountbatten's remarks in 1971 or later, reported in L. Collins and D. Lapierre, *Mountbatten and the Partition of India* (Delhi, 1982), pp. 31–2.

[72] See interview with M.A. Vassalo e Silva, the last Portuguese Governor-General of Goa, *India Today* (New Delhi), 1–15 July 1980.

Nehru claimed that this virtually peaceful take-over was the most striking justification of the military action. It proved clearly the goodwill of the vast majority of the people of Goa and had prevented much violence and looting. It established the hollowness of Portuguese rule and seemed to bear out the Indian argument that repression was a cloak for imminent chaos and, if India had not intervened, the administration in Goa would have quickly dissolved into anarchy. Moreover, the large number of Goans and Indians who had collected on the borders of Goa would have marched in on their own, forcing the Indian authorities either to shoot them down or to watch them being shot by Portuguese guards. But there were even more substantial arguments in favour of Indian action. The declaration that Goa was a province of Portugal could not conceal the blatant fact of colonialism and the withdrawal of the British and the French from India made all the more glaring the absurdity of the Portuguese presence. The reactionary authoritarianism of the Salazar Government at home and in the colonies in Africa and Asia underlined the outmodedness of Portuguese imperialism; and the refusal over the years to discuss even ways of reaching a settlement finally left India with no option but unilateral action. It seeemed to Nehru that nothing that had happened since 1947 had so excited and thrilled the Indian people as the liberation of Goa. It was as if some great burden had been removed, some corroding evil had been eliminated. There was certainly no widespread criticism of the action within the country. Rajagopalachari and some of his followers in the Swatantra Party were alone in denouncing it; but Nehru attached little importance to this. Rajagopalachari 'stands on a mountain peak by himself. Nobody understands him, nor does he understand anybody. We need not consider him in this connection. All his policies in regard to India, if I may say so, are bad — bad economics, bad sense and bad temper.'[73] Desai had claimed that, in the Cabinet, he expressed his strong disapproval of the action;[74] but he was still not prepared to resign and clung firmly to his place.

Yet, despite these basic merits of India's position and the wide support it commanded among the people, the action of the Government of India was severely criticized not only in Britain and France, whose outlook was as yet not wholly free of colonial overtones, but even in the United States. Adlai Stevenson told Krishna Menon that it would take 'a long, long time' for opinion in the United States to get over this episode; and he spoke bitterly and with extravagance in the Security Council, contending that India's resort to force was the beginning of the end of the United Nations. He ignored the resolutions on colonialism, indeed he ignored the issue of colonialism altogether and denounced India in terms which Portugal could not have bettered. Stevenson and the State Department were not perhaps representative of American opinion. At least in the highest quarters, it was recognized that

[73] Press conference in Delhi, 28 December, *National Herald*, 29 December, 1961.

[74] Report of later interview with Desai in J. Bandhopadhyaya, *The Making of India's Foreign Policy* (Calcutta, 1971), p. 143.

India in December 1961
CHINA
TIBET
Lhasa
LADAKH
KASHMIR
Leh
Srinagar
HIMACHAL
Manali
PRADESH
Bhakra
Nangal
PUNJAB
PAKISTAN
DELHI
NEPAL
UTTAR PRADESH
RAJASTHAN
Yatung
SIKKIM
Gangtok
Darjeeling
BHUTAN
Paro
Kalimpong
NEFA
Tuensang
NAGALAND
Kohima
ASSAM
Silchar
CACHAR
MANIPUR
MIZORAM
TRIPURA
EAST
BENGAL
BURMA
BIHAR
Bokaro
WEST
BENGAL
Jamshedpur
Calcutta
Rourkela
ORISSA
Jabalpur
MADHYA PRADESH
Bhilai
Ahmedabad
GUJARAT
Bhavnagar
Nagpur
VIDARBHA
DADRA
NAGAR
HAVELI
MAHARASHTRA
Bombay
BAY OF BENGAL
ANDHRA
PRADESH
GOA
KARNATAKA
Madras
Andaman
Islands
MADRAS
Cochin
KERALA
Trivandrum
CEYLON
Miles
0 100 200 300
INDIAN OCEAN
N

India's case was legitimate and that Portugal had no right to Indian territory. President Kennedy throughout acknowledged India's right to Goa and sought to dissociate the United States from Portuguese imperialism. What had happened now, Kennedy told the Indian Ambassador, should have happened fifteen years ago.[75] But he questioned the method and the timing of India's action and on these points was sore and sarcastic; 'all countries including, of course, the United States, have a great capacity for convincing themselves of the full righteousness of their particular cause. No country ever uses force for reasons it considers unjust.' India's action would have a chain effect and make it harder to hold the line for peace in other parts of the world. It would also influence American opinion against the grant of aid to the developing countries. 'You are justified in asking that American action be considerate of the problems of Indian democracy. Similarly I think it is reasonable that American public opinion should be a subject of concern to you.'[76]

Kennedy was particularly upset that Nehru had not warned him, while in Washington in November, that India might have to resort to military action and that, even till a few days before the advance of the Indian army, Galbraith had been led to believe that India would adhere to the ways of peace. The answer to this, of course, was that Nehru had had no intention in November of ordering the occupation of Goa although he had not ruled out the possibility in principle; and he could not inform Kennedy of a decision which he had not taken. But he had told Kennedy, and stated also in his interview on television at New York,[77] that Goa excited the Indian people far more than the bigger questions and problems that afflicted the world. To say more than this was not in his nature. 'I must confess that I am rather hesitant – or I have too much of conceit – to appeal to people. I put across an idea. It is up to them to accept it or not. I do not go on my knees to anybody, whoever he may be.'[78] Nor had Galbraith been later deliberately misled, for Nehru had been genuinely wavering till the last.

Nehru's action was also criticized not in itself but because it was feared that it might be a prelude to military action by others in different circumstances elsewhere. Just as the action was welcomed throughout Africa as marking the beginning of the disintegration of the Portuguese empire, in Britain and Australia it was thought that Sukarno might exploit it as a precedent for the occupation of Western Irian (New Guinea). It was also alleged that a crisis had been created and Goa occupied to improve the image of Congress and of Khrishna Menon in particular (even the critics did not claim that Nehru's image required any improvement) in the coming general elections, at a time

[75] B.K. Nehru's telegram to Foreign Secretary, reporting conversation with Kennedy, 18 January 1962. File 30 (115)/57-62-P.M.S.

[76] Kennedy to Nehru, 18 January 1962.

[77] 'Meet the Press' programme, 6 November, *National Herald*, 7 November 1961.

[78] 14 March 1962. Lok Sabha Debates, Second Series, Vol. 61, p. 303–10.

when Chinese aggression had damaged the prestige of the government.[79] Of all the charges, this hurt Nehru the most for, in fact, the prospect of elections had tended to hold India back. 'Really I am shocked that we should be thought so utterly irresponsible as to take action of this kind for a wretched election. I am prepared to lose a hundred elections but not the good name of India.'[80] But Nehru himself conceded that India's restraint in face of Chinese aggression had served to push her into action on Goa. Failure to react to Portuguese provocation, he told Galbraith, 'would, I feel sure, be disastrous both for the people of Goa, who would have to suffer terribly, and our own people round about the border, and the position of India generally in regard to other problems that we face, including other borders'.[81]

More far-fetched was the apprehension, strengthened by the presence of President Brezhnev in India at this time and his public approval of the liberation of Goa, that Nehru had secured this support in return for agreement to the Soviet occupation of Berlin.[82] But, basically, the general failure in Western Europe and the United States to recognize the occupation of Goa as no more than the erasing of a small outpost of antiquated colonialism was largely attributable to India herself. If Nehru was now castigated for a seeming act of cheap jingoism, for hypocritically divorcing Indian rhetoric from Indian behaviour, it was because he had so persistently denounced the use of force anywhere and refused till now to resort to it in the case of Goa because of the wider repercussions. Even as late as 7 December, he had condemned adventurist action, especially by persons in responsible positions in Government.[83] Thereafter, to speak of large-scale violence in Goa and of the grave threat to stability in India seemed very much like the generation of self-justifying zeal. The movement of large masses of troops to the border of Goa and the appeal to 'the immutable principles of humanity and the irreversible processes of history'[84] weakened the moral standing of Nehru and India, built up since 1947 by policy, approach and thinking. Extravagant charges, exaggerated action and booming clichés, so unlike the normal style of the Government of India in Nehru's time, suggested the cant of hypocrisy. So it could be said that it was the friends and not the enemies of India who had felt the greatest shock.[85] It would have been more convincing if Nehru had adhered to the argument that Goa was a part of India and there was no ethical stigma attached to its occupation – 'you cannot invade yourself'.[86] If the occupation of Goa were an act of aggression, then logically the securing of the transfer of power in

79 For example, 'Fallen Idols', *The Economist*, 23 December 1961, and profile of Nehru in *Observer*, 24 December 1961.

80 Press conference at Delhi, 28 December, *National Herald*, 29 December 1961.

81 Nehru to J.K. Galbraith, 12 December 1961.

82 B.K. Nehru's telegram to Foreign Secretary, reporting conversation with Dean Rusk, 18 December 1961.

83 Speech in Lok Sabha, 7 December 1961. Debates, Second Series, Vol. 60, pp. 3,975–98.

84 Note of the Ministry of External Affairs to the Brazilian Embassy, 15 December 1961.

85 Francis Williams in *New Statesman*, 24 December 1961.

86 Woodrow Wyatt in *Observer*, 31 December 1961.

1947 could be regarded as a major act of aggression by the Indian people. Yet India had desisted for fourteen years from action in Goa because of other possible consequences till the situation came to a head almost by its own impetus and the Government, committed not to non-violent, but, as far as possible, to peaceful methods, were forced to act. It was a compromise with evil in order to serve the good.[87] 'We chose what to our thinking was the lesser evil.'[88] Nehru had always been conscious of this dilemma, which confronts those who are called to rule. The way of the prophet, wedded to basic principles whatever happens, cannot always be the way of the leader of men, who has to consider all the time how far he can take with him those whom he leads. It is the lot of the prophet to be stoned; but a leader has to strike a compromise between truth and men's receptivity to truth. The leader always has a problem as to how far he should compromise with his principles. If he compromises too much he loses his principles; if he does not compromise enough he loses his leadership. To compromise is to embark on a slippery slope, yet refusal to compromise can sometimes mean isolation and betrayal of those who have given their trust. Striking a balance was not easy, especially in democratic communities.[89] The action on Goa was such a compromise which had been forced on him. In sacrificing the ways of peace for the ideal of anti-colonialism Nehru, despite all his spirited contentions and the knowledge that there was finally no other option, realized that he had lost much; and his conduct, in the weeks immediately after the Goa operation, revealed to discerning observers his personal unhappiness.[90]

[87] John Grigg, 'Nehru was Right', *Guardian*, 21 December 1961.

[88] Nehru to J.F. Kennedy, 29 December 1961.

[89] Nehru's quotation from Liddell Hart on this subject, *The Discovery of India* (Calcutta, 1946), p. 448; speech at the Unesco seminar on the Gandhian outlook, Delhi, 5 January 1953, Press Information Bureau; speech at a luncheon in New York, 21 December 1956. A.I.R. tapes.

[90] W.R. Crocker, *Nehru* (London, 1966), p. 124; Lord Gore-Booth, *With Great Truth and Respect* (London, 1974), p. 283. In 1961 Crocker was the Australian High Commissioner and Gore-Booth the British High Commissioner in Delhi.

10

China Goes to War

ONE

In the latter half of 1960, while the officials of the two sides studied the border question, the relations between India and China, if they did not improve, at least did not worsen. To maintain this position, Nehru refrained from acting on the suggestion of Roy, the Chief Minister of Bengal, that the Chinese trade agency at Kalimpong be closed down. There being virtually no trade, the agency served no purpose; but Nehru recognized that a closure would have to be seen in a larger context and therefore held his hand.[1] However, though direct confrontation was suspended, there was little change in the outlook of China. That to her it was not a limited border problem, to be settled on the basis of evidence, again became clear when Zhou accused India of seeking to turn Tibet into a buffer state and of fomenting provocation along the border to secure foreign aid in order to attack 'progressive forces' within India. Nehru repudiated this sharply and insisted that the problem was that of Chinese occupation of Indian territory; he was even surer now than before of the correctness of India's position.[2] But the clearance of aggression was a serious matter and whatever steps were contemplated should be taken with all effort and earnestness and without shouting or merely expressing helplessness.[3] Such caution coupled with firmness was not just a product of reluctance to contemplate long-drawn enmity between India and China or of a dislike of resorting to methods of force. The Chiefs of Staff warned in January 1961 that if the policy to resist to the full and evict any further Chinese aggression led to more than a limited war, it would be beyond the capacity of the Indian army for more than a short period.

So India's policy had to be one of delicate balancing, of building up her military and industrial strength even while seeking peaceful solutions, of

[1] Nehru's note to Foreign Secretary, 8 January 1961.

[2] Zhou's interview with Edgar Snow, later published in *Look*, 31 January 1961; Nehru's remarks at press conference at Delhi, 18 January, *National Herald*, 19 January 1961.

[3] Speech at the Congress session, Bhavnagar, 6 January, *The Hindu*, January 1961.

preparing if need be for war while striving to avoid it. But these were long-term problems. With the border temporarily dormant, the immediate concern was the possibility that China might manoeuvre for position in the Himalayan countries. When King Mahendra of Nepal dismissed and arrested his Ministers and proclaimed a dictatorship, Nehru made no secret of the fact that all his political instincts had been outraged and decided that his Government, while respecting the sovereignty of Nepal, would only carry on with the existing projects of assistance in that country and undertake no new ones.[4] The King, in reaction, encouraged an obedient press to conduct a virulent campaign against India. He then wrote to Nehru justifying his action in seizing power, and Nehru's didactic reply did not help matters. He declared that his long political experience and reflection had made him a firm believer in democracy and in what might broadly be called a socialist structure of society with as much equality as possible. All feudal privileges and the amassing of huge wealth by individuals seemed to him unsocial and rather vulgar; these would have to be eliminated but by peaceful methods and democratic procedures. So he had hoped for a fully independent Nepal developing into a democratic society and maintaining close and friendly contacts with India. As the only two major stabilizing factors in Nepal seemed to him to be the King and the Nepali Congress, which was the only organized political party with popular support, he had repeatedly advised King Mahendra that these two elements should work in full cooperation. His distress, therefore, at the dismissal of the Cabinet and the dissolution of Parliament was natural and generally shared in India. There was no way out of this tangle except to revert as soon as possible to a democratic structure. Without a stable and progressive Government Nepal might well be rent by civil war and even economic development, on which the King was said to be keen, would be arrested; and there was the danger of an aggressive China on the northern frontier. However, because of her desire to isolate India, China might make friendly overtures. 'It is for your Majesty to consider whether ultimately this would be in Nepal's own interest since there is little in common between China and Nepal. We feel that friendly relations with India would itself prevent any possible Chinese aggression.'[5]

Relations with Bhutan were friendlier and less complicated, but Nehru wrote also to the Maharaja of Bhutan, setting the bilateral nexus in the wider context of the world situation. There had till now been no difficulty in abiding by the terms of the treaty whereby Bhutan enjoyed full freedom in internal affairs but was guided by India's advice in external policy; but the new developments on the frontier flowing from Chinese claims and aggression now gave the treaty a special importance. It was India's responsibility to protect Bhutan from any aggressor and, indeed, because of geographical considerations, she was the only country who could do so. It was China's objective to

[4] Nehru's note to Foreign Secretary, 5 January 1961.
[5] Nehru to King Mahendra, 23 January 1961.

create barriers between India and Bhutan as part of the general policy to isolate India from her neighbours so that China could more easily deal with each of these countries separately. For this reason, although India, at the request of the national assembly of Bhutan, had raised the question with China of Bhutan's northern frontier, the Chinese Government had consistently avoided discussing the matter. So it would be desirable for the Maharaja to state publicly, on some appropriate occasion, that his Government had asked the Government of India to deal with this question; for it was important that China should realize that she had to deal with India in regard to Bhutan and could not isolate that country. Meantime, India would help Bhutan in both internal development and training of her personnel to assume responsibility for foreign affairs. When the time came for this, the existing treaty would not be allowed to stand in the way.[6]

The report of the officials on the boundary question, which was in fact two separate reports bound together, was presented to the two Governments in February 1961 and published by India but not by China. The officials could obviously reach no conclusions; they could only present evidence on which the Governments could act if they wished. But the report was of considerable revelatory significance. It established that China declined to recognize India's legal authority in Kashmir or her special relations with Bhutan and Sikkim. While the Indian side produced a large amount of material to establish their claim to the traditional boundary shown on Indian maps, the Chinese submitted scanty evidence and relied on assertions. Indeed the Chinese seemed to have little precise knowledge of the boundary areas and were unwilling even to provide a detailed description of the alignment claimed by them. Perhaps this was due to a reluctance to commit themselves, for even on the small-scale map provided by them the alignment in the western sector was different to that which Zhou had earlier claimed to be the correct delineation, and took in another two thousand square miles of Indian territory.

Nehru believed that the report, by establishing the superiority of India's case, would strengthen India's efforts to continue her middle course between firmness and anger, between a defeatist mentality and adventurist action. While there could be no solution short of Chinese withdrawal from Indian territory, a war with China was unthinkable. So India would not create 'unbridgeable chasms' but would rely on her growing strength and a certain momentum of feeling and of knowledge in the eyes of the world. The right policy was to remain firm on basic attitudes, to prepare for every contingency, to build up strength and to await developments. Now that the Indian case had been shown by documentation to be 'almost foolproof', Nehru even thought it possible that the pressure of facts and of India's attitude might lead the Chinese to recognize their mistake and withdraw voluntarily.[7] It was further

[6] Nehru to the Maharaja of Bhutan, 11 February 1961.

[7] Speech in the Rajya Sabha, 20 February 1961, Debates, Vol. 32, pp.473–97; speeches in the Lok Sabha, 1 and 3 April 1961, Debates, Second Series, Vol. 53, pp. 8,572–81 and 8,897–927 respectively;

testimony to the basic innocence as well as the underlying goodwill of his whole approach to China. But he was right to the extent that the Chinese, even if they had no intention of withdrawing from Indian territory, had not yet come round to committing themselves to a full-scale war with India.[8]

A few months later, R.K. Nehru, a former Ambassador in China and now Secretary-General in the Ministry of External Affairs, visited Beijing on his way back from Mongolia. Zhou told him that he would examine the reports of the officials, which should be followed up through diplomatic channels. The Prime Minister's impression was that there had been no marked change in the Chinese position, though they had perhaps weakened a little.[9] At this time Nehru was more concerned with menacing speeches in Pakistan than with Chinese activity,[10] and was prepared for further negotiations on the border. 'We have to talk, always talk, till we give up talking and fight; there is no middle course left in it.'[11] But any hope of a more temperate attitude on China's part was dispelled in the formal diplomatic exchanges, where the language of the two sides remained as sharp as before.[12] The situation on the ground also deteriorated. Chinese incursions continued in every sector; a strong post was set up about seventeen miles south-east of Daulat Beg Oldi and, when an Indian patrol went to reconnoitre, an effort was made to encircle and capture it. By the summer of 1961 Chinese forces had advanced nearly seventy miles south-west of their positions in 1958; and thereafter they established checkposts in the upper Chip Chap valley and Nyagzu and Dambuguru, and built roads connecting these posts with their bases in the rear. The Chinese Government and press denounced Nehru's role at the Belgrade conference, Indian policy in the Congo and the Prime Minister's visit to Washington. Clearly the Chinese Government were determined to ignore the reports of the officials and regarded their preparation as, at best, a time-gaining device.

To Nehru, with his honesty and open-mindedness, this did not make sense. He could not conceive of the Chinese authorities having read the reports of the officials and not having felt that their position was a weak one.[13] This faith in non-chauvinistic reason, added to his belief that any major Chinese aggression would spark off a world war which would not be fought on India's frontiers,[14] led him to envisage no more than limited hostilities. But these seemed likely

address to the Congress Parliamentary Party, 10 May 1961, tape M-57/C (ii). For a detailed analysis of India's case on the border, see Appendix.

8 A Chinese army bulletin of 25 April 1961, for example, while denouncing Kennedy and the Prime Minister of Japan, only censured Nehru for his 'policy of non-violence acting as an escort for American imperialism'. A.S. Whiting, *The Chinese Calculus of Deterrence* (Ann Arbor, 1975), p. 37.

9 Nehru's note to R.K. Nehru, Secretary-General, 29 July 1961.

10 Address to the Congress Parliamentary Party, 6 August 1961. Tape 58(i).

11 Speech in the Lok Sabha, 17 August 1961. Debates, Second Series, Vol. 56, pp.2,766–86.

12 See note of the Chinese Ministry of Foreign Affairs, 6 August and reply of the Indian Ministry of External Affairs, 19 September 1961. White Paper V, pp. 34–7.

13 22 August 1961. Rajya Sabha Debates, Vol. 35, pp. 1,137–51.

14 Interview in the *Guardian* (London), 23 October 1961.

to continue, for there was no diminution of China's 'aggressive intention'.[15] So, after consulting the Defence Minister and senior military and civilian officials, Nehru issued fresh and detailed instructions on 2 November 1961 for border policy. These instructions were based on a note from the Intelligence Bureau that the Chinese would move into areas claimed by them when there was no Indian presence, but would keep away if Indian personnel had established themselves; the Chinese, it was thought, were unlikely to use force against any Indian post even if in a position to do so. No one questioned either the credentials of the Intelligence Bureau to provide advice rather than information, or the unjustified jump in the logic of its argument, that Chinese reluctance to engage in confrontation in the past necessarily guaranteed such inactivity in the future; and the warning of the General Staff, that the army was in no position for such operations along the whole border, was ignored by Krishna Menon.[16]

So Nehru, who was probably unaware of this warning, ordered that, in the western sector, patrols should proceed as far forward as possible towards the international border to prevent the Chinese from advancing further and from dominating from any posts already established; but this should be done without involvement in any clash with the Chinese unless this became necessary in self-defence. In the middle and eastern sectors, efforts should be made to establish effective occupation of the whole frontiers and any gaps should be covered by patrolling or by posts. But, bearing in mind the numerous administrative and operational difficulties that such a policy of patrols and posts would involve, Nehru insisted that major concentrations of forces should be established in convenient places behind the border for maintenance of the forward posts. From Nehru's speeches at this time, it is clear that he attached great importance to the establishment of these rear and 'intermediate' bases and regarded it as the only sound and thorough way of strengthening India's position.[17] It was a cautious, well-thought-out policy, envisaging action from secure bases, 'because we must have a base whatever step we take'.[18] The directive was shown again in draft to Army Headquarters and issued only with its approval. But in the orders issued by Army Headquarters in furtherance of Nehru's decision, the stipulation about strong bases in the rear was omitted. No explanation for this lapse is available, though the later justification of General Thapar, the then Chief of Staff, that it would have taken years to build these bases, particularly in the eastern sector, by which time the Chinese would have occupied considerable areas of Indian territory, suggests that the omission was deliberate.[19] But, whatever the

[15] Address to the Congress Parliamentary Party, 27 November 1961. Tape 61(ii).

[16] See General D.K. Palit, at this time Director of Military Operations, 'Intelligence: Crucial Mistakes', *Hindustan Times*, 11 April 1971.

[17] For example, speeches in the Rajya Sabha and Lok Sabha, 28 November 1961, Rajya Sabha Debates, Vol. 36, pp. 358–65, and Lok Sabha Debates, Second Series, Vol. 59, pp. 1,846–61, respectively.

[18] Rajya Sabha Debates, Vol. 36, pp. 358–65.

[19] See General Thapar's article, 'The Chinese Invasion', *The Statesman*, 9 January 1971.

reason, the decision to push ahead with patrols and posts without supporting bases clearly was a departure from Nehru's policy and apparently not known to him.[20]

No appreciable action was possible on this directive during the winter, and the army's attention was centred on the operation in Goa. But Nehru was confident that, although the aggressive intent of China was still manifest, progressively the situation in the areas occupied by China had been changing in India's favour from military and other points of view; and he gave an assurance that this strengthening of India's position would continue till she was ultimately in a position to take effective action to recover lost territory.[21] 'We have to throw them out but we should do so only when the right time comes.'[22] It does not seem that he had worked this out clearly, but what he had in mind would appear to be the increase of posts and patrols supported by strong and secure bases, the improvement of communications and the building of industrial sinew so that India could deal with China on equal terms in this area and, by applying various forms of pressure and utilizing the 'developing world situation', secure a settlement honourable to both sides. There was no question of acquiescing in loss of territory or of 'any kind of peace' on the frontier so long as Chinese occupation continued. But war with China, though in theory not ruled out, was unimaginable, for it would develop into a world war, an indefinite war and a nuclear war.[23] For the same reason, he did not believe that China would use force on any large scale; 'one must not go by all the brave words that are said in these communications to us by the Chinese Government. But other factors work also.'[24]

TWO

The Chinese reaction, however, was one of unconcealed hostility. She sought to explain India's attitude to the boundary problem by 'the needs of the domestic and foreign policies of India's ruling circles'.[25] The early months of 1962 saw a continued exchange of diplomatic notes, with China protesting at the patrolling and the establishment of border posts by India. U Nu, who came to India after visiting Beijing, believed that the Chinese Government would now be more reasonable if India took the initiative and suggested that Nehru should go to China for this purpose. Nehru replied that any such move

20 Even Mr Neville Maxwell, whom no one would accuse of a bias in Nehru's favour, concedes this: 'It seems certain, then, that the change in the forward policy directive was not made at Nehru's behest, and likely that it was made without his knowledge.' *India's China War* (London, 1970), p. 224.

21 Speech in the Lok Sabha, 28 November 1961. Debates, Second Series, Vol. 59, pp. 1,846–61.

22 Address (in Hindi) to the Congress Parliamentary Party, 27 November 1961. Tape 61, Part II.

23 Speech in the Rajya Sabha, 6 December 1961. Debates, Vol. 37, pp. 1,339–52.

24 Speech in the Lok Sabha, 5 December 1961. Debates, Second Series, Vol. 60, pp.3,237–66.

25 'The Truth about the Nehru-Instigated Anti-Chinese Campaign in India', *People's Daily*, 7 December 1961.

by him, in the context of fierce anti-Indian propaganda by China and overtures to Pakistan, would be resented greatly by the Indian public. It was for China to open the way to negotiations by at least an indication of willingness to withdraw from Indian territory and agreement to consider the reports of the officials. India would not insist on a physical withdrawal but there should be some suggestion of a helpful approach on the part of the Chinese authorities. Nehru authorized U Nu to convey this message to Beijing;[26] but there was no response. So Nehru allowed the agreement of 1954 on Tibet to lapse, and both sides withdrew their trade agencies. China's suggestion, that the renewal of the agreement be considered independently of the boundary problem, was clearly out of the question, for it was absurd to renew an agreement embodying the Panch Sheela when China had made such inroads, in fact and in claim, into India's territorial integrity.

In such circumstances, it was vital to keep the armed services in psychological trim; and Nehru was satisfied that Menon was taking care of this. He attached no importance to the atmosphere of personal tension in which Menon's personality thrived and was clearly not informed of the Defence Minister's cavalier treatment of his senior professional advisers. On one occasion, for example, in the summer of 1961, addressing a large number of junior officers, Menon vilified the Chiefs of Staff in their absence. 'Seventy five per cent of our difficulties come from Chiefs of Staff. I am not saying they have not made up their minds, because they haven't got minds to make up.'[27] This was after he had selected P.N. Thapar, from whom he expected little trouble, as successor to Thimayya as Chief of Army Staff. Then, knowing Nehru's liking for B.M. Kaul, Menon appointed him Chief of the General Staff. Kaul was ambitious and courageous but was endowed with no sharp intelligence and was essentially a military bureaucrat, inexperienced in battle. Nehru unhesitatingly assumed responsibility for both selections.[28] Indeed, as Menon became the chief figure in the demonology of Indian politics and many at home and abroad saw him as Nehru's chief adviser in such matters as Goa, the Prime Minister's defence of him became correspondingly more vigorous and unqualified. He thought Menon was a substitute target for himself and saw in criticism of Menon a general assault on the policies of the Congress. In the general elections of 1962, Menon was opposed for the seat in Bombay by a candidate with the support of all right-wing parties and even a considerable section of the Congress Party. Nehru's retort was, 'Go to hell.'[29] He accused Menon's critics of McCarthyism and claimed that Menon had brought about a 'complete reawakening' in the army by giving it new life and spirit and equipping it with modern weapons.[30] Menon won by a large majority and Nehru rightly saw in this result a reaffirmation of public confidence in himself;

[26] Nehru's note on discussions with U Nu at Varanasi, 13 January 1962.
[27] General J.N. Chaudhuri, Chief of Army Staff, to Y.B. Chavan, Defence Minister, 1 July 1963.
[28] 12 April 1961. Lok Sabha Debates, Second Series, Vol. 54, pp. 10,819–35.
[29] Speech at Bombay, 15 January, *National Herald*, 16 January 1962.
[30] Speech at Delhi, 20 February, *The Hindu*, 21 February 1962.

'all the tin gods and tin newspapers put together could not make any difference'.[31] But to the officer corps of the armed services this meant added strength to Menon's vicious grip.

In March and April 1962 some posts were established by India on the Depsang plains and one post twelve miles north-east of Daulat Beg Oldi. These posts were intended to affirm Indian sovereignty over these border areas rather than to withstand Chinese attacks, it being well known that Chinese presence and strength in these areas were far greater; but it was not expected that China would resort to aggressive tactics. Indian patrols reported intense Chinese activity in the western sector, especially in the Chip Chap, Chang Chenmo and Pangong regions, but after May protests were only lodged by India when there was confrontation or firing. Both Governments also reached informal agreement to avoid excessive publicity and delayed publication of their notes of protest till they had been received by the other side. As for the stray attempts at fraternization by Chinese troops when they came across Indian personnel, the instructions of the Government of India were to 'just smile and ignore'. But all this suggested no likelihood of major hostilities and encouraged Nehru to abide by the policy of firmness linked to a willingness to seek a settlement. There should be no rushing into steps which closed the door and barred any approach to peaceful solutions. The support of world opinion and the preparedness for war themselves helped to create conditions which made a peaceful settlement possible.[32] Without yielding to bullying tactics India would be prepared to talk to the Chinese if they at least showed some inclination to withdraw from Indian territory even though they did not in fact do so.[33]

Such hopes, moderate as they were, received no encouragement from the Chinese resumption of forward patrolling between the Karakoram Pass and Kongka La and announcement that they would extend it to the rest of the border if Indian patrolling in Ladakh did not cease.[34] The General Staff in Delhi, understanding this to mean that the Chinese would be increasingly aggressive, proposed reinforcement of Indian posts and offensive air action in case these posts were overrun. The Government gave no orders on these suggestions; but Indian posts in the Chip Chap and the Galwan valleys were not withdrawn despite Chinese advance and encirclement. Nehru informed the army that this was necessary to study the 'behaviour pattern' of the Chinese; and the fact that the Chinese refrained from attack confirmed him in the belief that they had no plans of large-scale aggression. So in May India again proposed that, in the western sector, each side should withdraw to the line claimed by the other and added that, till the boundary question was settled, India would permit Chinese civilian traffic to use the Aksai Chin road.

[31] Address to the Congress Parliamentary Party, 21 April 1962. Tape 62(ii).

[32] Speech in the Lok Sabha, 19 March 1962. Debates, Second Series, Vol. 61, pp. 1,003–31.

[33] Nehru to R.B. Singh, 26 April 1962.

[34] Note of the Chinese Government, 30 April 1962, White Paper VI, pp. 37–9.

It seemed to Nehru a fair proposal, for, though China would have to withdraw from much more territory than India, it was territory which she had recently occupied and, by moving so far within the Indian boundary alignment, converted the problem into a much wider one than a matter of correction of boundaries. But China rejected the proposal.[35]

At about this time, the authorities in China, 'cold-blooded practitioners of power politics',[36] appear to have decided to secure a military solution of the border problem. A political issue would be settled by war – a classic demonstration of Clausewitz. The message that Han Suyin, a writer sympathetic to China, claims to have received at about this time from the Chinese authorities was, 'We know there will have to be a show of force, sometime or other, do not worry . . . Sometimes it is necessary to do a *little fighting* to unblock people's minds.'[37] They were worried by the economic crisis at home which, as has been recently acknowledged, resulted, in the three years from 1959 to 1962, in twenty million deaths from starvation or related diseases.[38] A corollary of this was a large exodus to Hong Kong in the east and from Sinkiang to the Soviet Union in the west. This crisis was deepened by the continuously simmering rebellion in Tibet kept alive by the C.I.A. and the increasing threat of attack from Taiwan; and the adversary attitude of Nehru's Government, supported by both the United States and the Soviet Union, fitted into what seemed, in Chinese eyes, a general context of hostility.[39]

All the advantages, in case of large-scale aggression, seemed to lie with China. India stood alone, unbuttressed by any alliance, with an army smaller and less well-equipped and with border communications 'getting better and better'[40] but still not wholly satisfactory; and military victory against a country of considerable size and numbers, and with independent aspirations in foreign and domestic policies, would consolidate Chinese occupation of territory and divert attention from her economic failures. The Chinese warned, in a note to India on the little village of Longju, which was a point of dispute on the eastern sector, that they 'will not stand idly by'[41] – a phrase which had been used in 1950 before the intervention in Tibet but which, on this occasion, was ommitted in reports of this note in the Chinese press. In June, the Chinese Consulate in Calcutta was known to be informing sympathizers in India that military action had become essential.[42] The reduction of tension in the Taiwan straits by the end of June, followed by the developing sense of crisis over Berlin and Germany and the increasing involvement of the Soviet Union in Cuba, gave China a freer hand in the Himalayas; and it has been suggested that the

[35] Indian Note of 14 May and Chinese reply, 2 June 1962. White Paper VI, pp. 41–3, 56–8; Nehru's press conference at Delhi, 13 June, *The Hindu*, 14 June 1962.

[36] H. Kissinger, *The White House Years* (London, 1979), p. 747.

[37] *My House Has Two Doors* (London, 1980), pp. 267–8. Italics in original.

[38] P. Short, *The Dragon and the Bear* (London, 1982), p. 265.

[39] Whiting, *The Chinese Calculus of Deterrence*, p. 199.

[40] Nehru in the Lok Sabha, 20 June 1962. Debates, Third Series, Vol. 5, pp. 11,934–6.

[41] 19 May 1962, White Paper VI, p. 46.

[42] B.N. Mullik, *My Years with Nehru: The Chinese Betrayal* (New Delhi, 1971), pp. 329–30.

final decision to pass from political pressures to extensive military action against India was taken in Beijing in the first half of July.[43] Rapidly building up her military strength in Tibet, China awaited an opportune moment for launching a full-scale offensive against India. The facts belie all later allegations, born of the mesmerism evoked by Chinese success or of the blindness created by ideological affinity,[44] that it was India which precipitated a major conflict.

Yet, till events overtook him, Nehru believed that China desired a settlement and would not bring large numbers of troops into the border areas while, on his own part, he had no wish to see India entangled in a war anywhere, least of all in the high mountains.[45] Chinese notes were truculent and menacing, and an official Chinese spokesman declared on 13 July that the situation in the Galwan valley had developed to a point where an explosion might be touched off at any moment. It was difficult to decide whether such wordy warfare indicated military action in the coming months,[46] for Chinese notes had a 'characteristic ambivalence',[47] breathing fire and advocating negotiations; but Nehru thought that there would be no major clash.[48] The Chinese Foreign Minister, Chen Yi, when he met Krishna Menon at Geneva, spoke of negotiations, and only a failure in communication with Delhi prevented the issue of a joint communiqué proposing further talks.[49] So, though on 21 July Chinese troops fired on an Indian patrol for the first time since 1959, on 26 July India gave a soft answer restating her willingness to enter into further discussions on the basis of the reports of the officials as soon as current tensions were eased and the appropriate climate created.[50] It proposed discussions without even a token Chinese withdrawal and spoke in terms of the alignment claimed by China in 1960 and not of the earlier one of 1956. Expecting a positive response, Nehru was confident enough to repeat that, while an armed conflict might break out 'suddenly, by some chance', a major crisis was unlikely in the near future for China was also hesitant to fight in Ladakh, and that he was still hopeful of a peaceful settlement.[51] When Chen Yi asserted in a broadcast that China was not prepared to assist in creating a

[43] H.C. Hinton, *Communist China in World Politics* (London, 1966), p. 297.

[44] There is a third category, of British journalists supporting the Chinese for no obvious reason. They bring to mind George Orwell's comment: 'Circus dogs jump when the trainer cracks his whip, but the really well-trained dog is the one that turns his somersault when there is no whip. And that is the state we have reached in this country . . .', *Collected Essays*, Vol. 3 (London, 1968), p. 181.

[45] Nehru's statements at press conference at Delhi, 13 June, *The Hindu*, 14 June 1962; address to Congress Parliamentary Party, 21 June 1962, Tape 63(i).

[46] Nehru's note to Foreign Secretary, 10 July 1962.

[47] Statement in the Lok Sabha, 6 August 1962. Debates, Third Series, Vol. 6, pp. 120–4.

[48] Nehru's statement to the press, Delhi, 14 July, *National Herald*, 15 July 1962.

[49] 'The Afterthoughts of Premier Chou', *Sunday Times* (London) 19 December 1971; A. Lall, *The Emergence of Modern India* (New York, 1981), pp. 155–7.

[50] White Paper VII, pp. 3–4.

[51] Letter to three members of the opposition in Parliament, 26 July, and speech at Allahabad, 27 July, *National Herald*, 27 and 28 July 1962, respectively, speech at Lucknow, 28 July, *National Herald* and *The Hindu*, 29 July 1962.

climate for talks by any withdrawal from Indian territory but desired immediate discussions on the boundary problem,[52] Nehru went even further than in the note of 26 July and offered to discuss what steps should be taken to remove the tensions and create the proper atmosphere for discussions on the boundary.[53] India was obviously going as far as she could, even at the risk of inviting accusations of weakness in the face of threats and aggression, in order to improve relations with the adversary. What India had in mind was talks leading to, at least, a measure of Chinese withdrawal from territory which she knew was claimed by India and which she had begun to occupy only since 1957 and particularly since 1959, in order to enable India to seek a boundary settlement with honour. Nehru repeated that, while India could not submit to bullying tactics, continuing hostility with China was not desirable. Reduction to dust and ashes would be preferable to dishonour, but he would continue to strive for a peaceful settlement; for war between India and China would be bad for India, for China and for the world.[54] The drift towards war had to be halted, and it was for China to take a step in this matter, as it was China which had created the situation by encroaching steadily on Indian territory and pushing forward the alignment on her maps.

THREE

The growing crisis in relations with China had the expected impact on India's relations with Pakistan. At the Conference of Commonwealth Prime Ministers in March 1961, Ayub said that Kashmir was a burden on the armies of both countries and, if that were settled, relations would be very friendly with no problems remaining. He proposed that Kashmir be made into a separate unit like Switzerland. Nehru made no comment beyond a general remark that he was anxious to settle problems.[55] He also publicly emphasized that the 'family quarrel' with Pakistan could not be compared with India's deteriorating relations with China.[56] But thereafter Pakistan's attitude became markedly aggressive. Ayub was reported to have told a private meeting of editors that Pakistan would take advantage of India's difficulties with China and that, in any dispute between India and China, Pakistan would be on China's side.[57] Though Nehru could not believe that Pakistan would indulge in big adventures on the frontier, he remained wary.[58] At a time when Goa was

[52] 3 August 1962.

[53] Statement in the Lok Sabha, 13 August 1962. Debates, Third Series, Vol. 6, pp. 1,477–81.

[54] Speeches in the Lok Sabha, 14 August, Debates, Third Series, Vol. 6, pp. 1,750–77, and in the Rajya Sabha, 22 August 1962, Debates, Vol. 40, pp. 2,876–82 and 2,981–3,002.

[55] Nehru's note on talk with Ayub, 16 March 1961.

[56] Press conference in London, 18 March, *The Hindu*, 19 March 1961.

[57] Acting High Commissioner for India in Karachi to Ministry of External Affairs, 28 April 1961.

[58] Nehru to Chief Ministers, 27 June 1961.

becoming a live issue, Pakistan advertised her friendly feelings for Portugal and Ayub, on a tour abroad, used bitter language, especially in the United States, against India even on formal occasions. Nehru, speaking in Kashmir, replied with some frankness, for clarity seemed necessary to preclude errors about India's feelings and intentions. Frustration at her own lack of progress in comparison with India appeared to fan Pakistan's enmity, and Kashmir seemed but a pretext for venting this anger. Nehru deemed it a mockery for a country which had no free elections of its own to commit aggression and then demand a plebiscite. Pakistan and the world should understand that India would not tolerate any kind of attack under any name on Kashmir.[59]

With the gradual darkening of the northern horizon, towards the end of 1961 Nehru repeated that he was always prepared for talks with Pakistan if the atmosphere improved and for consideration of adjustments on the basis of 'acceptance of things as they are' in Kashmir.[60] But he assured Krishna Menon that these remarks did not imply any softness or any pressure from a foreign country.[61] In case this were the general impression, he declared publicly that there was no question of surrendering Kashmir or gifting it to Pakistan under any circumstances.[62] But the Kennedy administration was interested in a settlement on Kashmir. Galbraith suggested an indirect approach; rather than seek to formalize a boundary between the state and that part of it occupied by Pakistan, India might consider converting the cease-fire line into a 'soft' boundary by granting facilities to Pakistan in Kashmir such as easier entry or a share in trade and commerce. This vague proposal Nehru brushed off on the ground that such concessions could only follow Pakistan's acceptance of Kashmir as a part of India; till then there was always the danger of saboteurs coming across the cease-fire line in large numbers.[63] Then Kennedy followed this up by offering the services of a mediator and said that Eugene Black, the President of the World Bank who had helped in the conclusion of the Indus waters treaty, would be glad to assist the two countries in 'patient and continuing' discussions for reaching an 'accommodation' – meaning, presumably, a compromise.[64] Nehru rejected such informal mediation as unacceptable in principle, but sought to reduce tension in relations with Pakistan. The latter's support of Portugal and conduct of large-scale manoeuvres near the Indian border at the time of the Goa operation had obliged the Government of India to send up reinforcements to the Punjab. The attitude of perpetual hostility adopted by the rulers of Pakistan was tiresome, and became a matter of concern when exploited to secure greater aid from the United States. But he reiterated that India would never attack Pakistan, though, if Pakistan were to start a war, India would

59 Speech at Srinagar, 19 July, *National Herald*, 20 July 1961.

60 Press conference at Delhi, 28 December, *National Herald*, 29 December 1961.

61 Note to Defence Minister, 1 January 1962.

62 Speech at Patna, 6 January, *The Hindu*, 7 January 1962.

63 Nehru's note to Foreign Secretary on discussions with Galbraith, 9 January 1962.

64 Kennedy's letters to Nehru and Ayub, undated but delivered on 16 January 1962.

meet it fully.[65] He also assured the United States once again that India would not use force to alter the status quo in Kashmir and, when Pakistan complained to the Security Council that an Indian attack was imminent, directed the Indian delegation, while denying the charge, to seek an adjournment of the debate till March,[66] that is, till after the general elections in India were over and the atmosphere more relaxed.

Later, as part of the same effort to give no cause for inflamed feelings despite a virulent campaign against India in Pakistan, Nehru discouraged strong reactions in India to communal rioting in East Bengal and frowned on suggestions for an exchange of minorities.[67] Granted that the whole base of Pakistan was communal, it was also true that many in India, especially when passions were aroused, were as communal as anyone else.[68] War with Pakistan would be a tragedy not only for the Governments but for the peoples of these two countries who were so closely allied to each other.[69] But the troubles in East Bengal, Ayub's repeated statements that he would use American arms against India if need be, the Pakistani Government's decision to negotiate with China on the boundary between Sinkiang and 'Azad Kashmir' and the exchanges in the Security Council precluded the possibility of immediate negotiations with Pakistan.[70]

Soon after, Ayub charged Nehru with ill-will towards Pakistan and designs to destroy her. The charge was presumably provoked by Nehru's frequent expression of his poor opinion of Pakistan's ruling class. Ayub preferred to ignore the distinction which Nehru always carefully made between the Governments of Pakistan, which he regarded as feudal and reactionary, and her people, for whom Nehru repeatedly proclaimed India's goodwill as they were 'once our part and parcel'.[71] But he was prepared to consider no other solution of the Kashmir problem than a broad confirmation of the status quo. 'Any acceptance of the two-nation theory in regard to Kashmir will have the most disastrous consequences in the whole of India. Not only will our secularism end, but India will tend to break up.'[72] In London in September, at the Conference of Commonwealth Prime Ministers, Ayub thanked Nehru for easing the situation in the east by forbidding large-scale expulsion of illegal migrants from Assam and Tripura and urged a speedy settlement of the river

[65] Speeches at Ferozepur, 24 January, and Amritsar, 31 January, *The Hindu*, 25 January and 1 February 1962 respectively; at Lucknow, 2 February, and at Visakhapatnam, 3 February, *National Herald*, 3 and 5 February 1962 respectively.

[66] Telegram drafted by Nehru to Indian delegation in New York, 30 January 1962; Nehru's telegram to B.K. Nehru, Ambassador in Washington, 31 January 1962.

[67] To A.K. Sen, 23 May 1962; statement in the Lok Sabha, 4 June 1962, Debates, Third Series, Vol. 4, pp. 8,569–75; to Rajendra Prasad, retired President, 9 June 1962 and to B.P. Chaliha, Chief Minister of Assam, 30 June 1962.

[68] Speech to the Congress Parliamentary Party, 21 June 1962. Tape 63(i).

[69] To Chief Ministers, 10 July 1962.

[70] To K. Nkrumah, 25 July 1962.

[71] Speech at Delhi, 12 August, *National Herald*, 13 August 1962.

[72] To M.C. Chagla, High Commissioner in London, 2 August 1962.

waters problem between the two Bengals.[73] The two conversations did not add up together to more than five minutes.[74] Nothing was said about Kashmir.

Perhaps the best testimony to Nehru's determination, in the face of all the evidence, to refuse to conceive of a major war with China is his viewing, in the summer of 1962, of all questions of Indian armament in the context of Pakistan rather than of China. With that country receiving Sabre jet planes from the United States, the Indian Air Force was anxious to secure up-to-date aircraft; and the Government wished to link any such purchase with manufacture in India. The Soviet MiG planes were attractive from both viewpoints; and in addition the price was about one-fourth of that of similar machines produced in the United States. The American Government were willing to give aircraft free but this was unacceptable on principle to Nehru, who was determined that India should pay for whatever was required.[75] He asked Krishna Menon to reach a quick decision,[76] for delay was leading to rumours and pressures. Mountbatten beseeched Nehru not to turn to the Soviet Union for arms or aircraft, as India could not get along without aid from the United States.[77] But Nehru made publicly clear that the Government would decide the matter on its merits.[78]

The Defence Committee of the Cabinet considered all the proposals and concluded that the Soviet offer was the only acceptable one. It did not worry Nehru that this might affect economic assistance from the Western countries and, indeed, he insisted that the decision should not be delayed till the meeting of the 'Aid India Consortium' countries. India should conduct herself in a straightforward manner on this issue for goodwill was more important than aid.

> I would dislike greatly to lose the goodwill of Russia or of the United States; apart from any question of aid or help, to lose this appears to me to be a lack of something on our part. The whole essence of non-alignment is watered down if we lose goodwill. Immediately we are driven into an aligned position.[79]

In the same spirit, Nehru wrote to Kennedy thanking him for all the sympathy and friendship he had shown to India, more particularly in regard to aid for development. The United States had not only given India generous assistance but had taken the trouble to induce other countries also to do so. However, it was the friendly and sympathetic attitude, even more than the aid, for which India was grateful. 'My colleagues here and I are particularly

[73] Nehru's notes to Commonwealth Secretary on talks with Ayub, 12 and 19 September 1962.
[74] Nehru's reply to question in Lok Sabha, 12 November 1962. Debates, Third Series, Vol. 9, p. 895.
[75] Nehru's note to Foreign Secretary, 4 May 1962.
[76] 11 May 1962.
[77] To Nehru, 14 June 1962.
[78] 23 June 1962. Rajya Sabha Debates, Vol. 39, pp. 1,765–88.
[79] Nehru to Krishna Menon, 18 July 1962.

anxious to have the friendship of the United States in the great tasks that confront us. I believe that this friendship is good not only for our two countries, but also for the world.' This had little to do with aid and, even if circumstances arose which might make it difficult for the United States to help India in her development, the Indian Government would still value the friendship of the United States and work for close relations between the two countries. Differences of viewpoint should not affect this friendship. 'I can assure you, therefore, that, whatever might happen, our attitude will continue to be to encourage friendly relations between our two countries.'[80]

FOUR

However, Chinese penetration into Indian territory in the western sector continued throughout the summer. At least thirty-three new posts were set up, and a road constructed along the Qara Qash valley. Worried by its weakness in men, materials and logistics, Western Command warned Delhi in August that political direction was not being based on military means. But Nehru still did not expect a major Chinese offensive and, before departing for the Conference of Commonwealth Prime Ministers in London in the first week of September, left explicit instructions that on no account, apart from winter conditions demanding it, should there be any Indian withdrawal from the posts in Ladakh. The policy of maintaining these posts and the lines of communication to them should be continued, fire being opened if necessary in self-defence. Indeed, if possible, extra posts might be set up.[81] But he expected no trouble on the north-eastern border. Here the traditional boundary between India and Tibet lay along the watershed ridges. The McMahon Line agreement of 1914 formalized this principle but, the treaty map being a small-scale one with the boundary delineated thickly on the basis of preliminary surveys, there were a few discrepancies between the line on the map and the actual boundary on the ground. At the extreme west, from the trijunction of India, Bhutan and Tibet, the watershed was the Thagla ridge, and this was made precisely clear to the Chinese both in a note of September 1959 and at the meetings of the officials in 1960. So the Chinese were fully aware that an area of about twenty-five square miles south of Thagla ridge fell within India even though it was not shown as such on the McMahon Line map, just as, in certain other sectors, areas shown on the map within India were recognized as belonging to Tibet because they lay north of the watershed ridges. In 1962, one of the posts set up by India in the eastern sector was at Dhola, south of the Thagla ridge. On 8 September Chinese troops came down the ridge and menaced the Indian post. As Nehru was not in Delhi, Krishna

[80] Nehru to Kennedy, 5 August 1962.
[81] Nehru's note to Foreign Secretary, 5 September 1962.

Menon, at a meeting on 10 September attended by the Chief of the Army Staff and senior civilian and military officials, directed that the Chinese should not be allowed to cross the border in the eastern sector and, if they did not peacefully withdraw, firing might be resorted to; the air force might assist in transport and reconnaissance but not take any supporting offensive action without previous reference to the Government. The Army Commander was called to Delhi and told to take action as soon as possible to dislodge the Chinese; and Nehru was informed in London.[82]

On 20 September occurred the first exchange of fire and, though it was now known that the Chinese were in considerable strength south of the Thagla ridge, the orders to evict them as soon as the Indian army was ready to do so were reaffirmed. But no large-scale fighting seems to have been expected and Krishna Menon also left India for the United Nations. Speaking to journalists abroad, Nehru said the Chinese had 'no business to be' south of the Thagla ridge but seemed not greatly concerned by the petty conflicts which had resulted. Floods rather than Chinese aggression dominated his mind.[83] But that the Chinese were prepared for the skirmishes to develop into major battles is clear from Mao's statement to the Central Committee of the Chinese Party in September that China wished 'to unite with so many people. But they do not include the reactionary national bourgeoisie like Nehru.'[84]

By the beginning of October, both Nehru and Menon were back and, as an indication of firm action, Kaul was recalled from leave and appointed Corps Commander in the eastern sector. But Nehru still continued to assert that he was always prepared for talks provided the other party behaved decently and the self-respect of India was not endangered.[85] When, according to Kaul, he saw Nehru on 3 October, the Prime Minister remarked that India had tolerated Chinese incursions into her territory for far too long and a stage had come when she should take – or appear to take – a strong stand irrespective of consequences. India should contest, by whatever means at her disposal, the claim which the Chinese were making in the eastern sector by intruding into Dhola. Nehru hoped the Chinese would see reason and withdraw but, if they did not, India would have no option but to expel them '*or at least try to do so to the best of our ability*'. If the Government failed to take such action, they would forfeit public confidence completely.[86]

This account makes clear that Nehru was not envisaging large-scale hostilities; but even the limited action which he seems to have had in mind was hedged around by the suggestion that it would be enough if India gave the

[82] Mr Maxwell states that Nehru from London rejected a Chinese proposal for discussions between Indian and Chinese civilian representatives about the limits of each side's control in the Thagla area, *India's China War*, pp. 299 and 308. I can find no evidence for this. The decision not to get embroiled in any such talks was taken at Delhi, in Nehru's absence.

[83] Statements at Paris, 22 September, and Cairo, 30 September 1962, *National Herald*, 24 September 1962, and record of press conference available in Press Information Bureau, New Delhi, respectively.

[84] D. Wilson, *Mao the People's Emperor* (London, 1979), p. 366.

[85] Remark to press correspondents on return to Delhi, 1 October, *The Hindu*, 2 October 1962.

[86] B.M. Kaul, *The Untold Story* (Delhi, 1967), p. 368. Italics in original.

appearance of taking strong action. He also recognized the difficulties of military action in this terrain and only asked of the army that it should make the best effort possible. As always, the Prime Minister was not goading the army into any specific action although he had laid down or approved the general policy. As for Krishna Menon, he was busy considering what he knew to be fabricated reports about heavy troop movements in Pakistan.[87]

However, the army commanders were unable to take the right decisions within the ambit of the broad policy laid down by the Prime Minister and to utilize properly the discretion which he had vested in them. There was considerable personal distrust among themselves; and the officers in local command produced a scheme for evicting the Chinese which, incredible as it sounds, was apparently a make-believe plan which was not intended to be taken seriously but on which Kaul seized as the appropriate tactics. On 9 October he ordered 'preliminary operations' to occupy Siyang, north of the Namkha Chu river but south of Thagla ridge. The Chinese reacted sharply and, when Kaul saw on the ground the strength of the Chinese and the way an infantry battalion, with heavy mortars and medium machine-guns, pushed back Indian troops, he suggested an air offensive although it had already been ruled out by the Government of India.[88] Kaul flew back to Delhi to report and Nehru again left it to the Generals to decide future action; and it was on the advice of Thapar, the Chief of Staff, L.P. Sen, the Commander in the eastern sector, and Kaul, the Corps Commander, that it was decided on 11 October that Indian troops should neither launch an offensive against the Chinese nor withdraw but remain where they were and hold a strong defensive line on the Namkha Chu river.

Having virtually allowed the senior army commanders to take this decision, Nehru left the next day for Colombo and, at Delhi airport, informed the press: 'Our instructions are to free our territory . . . I cannot fix the date, that is entirely for the Army.'[89] This statement has since elicited wide comment and formed the basis of charges against Nehru of war-mongering. But, in fact, it was a wholly unobjectionable statement. The policy of, at some time or other, evicting the Chinese from Indian territory was not a new one. As Nehru repeated in Colombo, 'I do not think they have the slightest claim, historically, politically, or anything.'[90] But Nehru made it clear that no pressure was being put on the army to rush matters. Indeed, he had, even while reiterating the old policy, elaborated that in the Thagla area winter had already set in and the Chinese were well ensconced with logistic advantages. The implication was that no early action could be expected.

[87] Y.D. Gundevia, '*Outside the Archives*' (unpublished manuscript). Gundevia, at this time Commonwealth Secretary, gives an account of a high-level meeting of officials summoned by Menon to consider these reports. I am grateful to Gundevia for allowing me to see this manuscript.

[88] J.P. Dalvi, *Himalayan Blunder* (Bombay, 1969), pp. 255–303; Kaul, *The Untold Story*, pp. 370–85; N. Prasad, *The Fall of Towang 1962* (Delhi, 1981), pp. 47–71.

[89] *Statesman* 13 October 1962.

[90] 15 October, *National Herald*, 16 October 1962.

However, there was no complacency in Nehru's approach. He saw that the situation in the eastern sector was deteriorating fast and, at long last, realized that trouble on a big scale was in the offing.[91] India now proposed a Chinese withdrawal to the positions prior to 8 September 1962 before talks on ways to ease tension;[92] but Nehru had little hope of any such gesture, even though it would leave China in possession of about 12,000 square miles of Indian territory. These fears of continued aggression came true on 20 October, when the Chinese moved down in large numbers at many places along the border in both the western and eastern sectors with heavy mortars and mountain artillery and, in one place, even tanks, and drove back Indian forces.

> There can, of course, be no surrender to this kind of thing. But we must be prepared for losses from time to time . . . We have a very difficult task, but we shall face it with a stout heart. We must realise, however, that this is going to be a long-drawn-out affair. I see no near end of it.[93]

No self-respecting nation could tolerate such 'outrageous aggression' and, if India bowed down to it, she would be dragged down to unknown depths. However long it might take, India would fight with all her strength.

> China is a great and powerful country with enormous resources. But India is no weak country to be frightened by threats and military might. We shall build up our strength, both military and economic, to win this battle of Indian freedom. We shall always be willing to negotiate a peace but that can only be on condition that aggression is vacated. We can never submit or surrender to aggression. That has not been our way, and that will not be our way in the future.[94]

FIVE

The Chinese had chosen their moment well. Khrushchev, plunged in crisis over Cuba, had no wish to be embroiled in the Himalayas; and the Soviet Union, for the first time in years, assumed a pro-Chinese stance. It has been claimed that Khrushchev had assured the Chinese on 13 and 14 October that a neutral attitude on the Sino-Indian boundary question was impossible.[95] Certainly, a week later, Nehru was rebuked for failing to display a 'due urge

91 Nehru to Morarji Desai, 11 October, and to Chief Ministers, 12 October 1962.
92 Note to the Chinese Government, 16 October 1962, White Paper VII, pp. 117–20.
93 To B.P. Chaliha, 20 October 1962.
94 Nehru to Chief Ministers, 21 October 1962.
95 Article in *People's Daily*, 2 November 1963. J. Gittings, *Survey of the Sino-Soviet Dispute*, (Oxford, 1968), p. 178.

for reconciliation' and advised to agree to the Chinese proposals for negotiations without pre-conditions and a withdrawal of twenty kilometres by both sides from their actual positions along the whole boundary.[96] Pointing out to Khrushchev the futility of preaching moderation to the victim of aggression,[97] Nehru gave his full attention to the effort of defence in a crisis where there was manifestly no scope for immediate international intervention or pressure. Nehru had not asked the army to give battle on the mountain heights rather than await the Chinese nearer the plains; but possibly Krishna Menon did. Kaul has alleged that, at Tezpur on 17 October, Menon insisted on the political importance of not withdrawing from the Namkha Chu river and rejected Kaul's protest that such a task was impossible without reinforcements in men and material.[98] Menon himself stated later that public opinion was so inflamed that it was not possible to let the Chinese come into India in depth before giving them a fight;[99] but Nehru certainly was prepared for this. As the Chinese troops rolled southwards, Nehru, in a broadcast to the nation, warned his people to be prepared for further reverses,[100] and, on 23 October, at a meeting with the senior officers at Army Headquarters, Nehru unhesitatingly left the decision as to whether Tawang should be held or abandoned to the Chief of Staff, General Thapar. 'It is a matter now for the military to decide – when and how they would fight. I have no doubt in my mind that what we lose, we shall eventually win back for us. I cannot lay down conditions about Tawang or any other place on grounds other than military.'[101]

Even as their troops pushed into India in both sectors up to thirty to fifty miles from their previous positions, the Chinese, with imperturbable double-speak, accused India of continuously changing the status quo by force and finally launching a massive general offensive, forcing the Chinese 'frontier guards' to strike back in self-defence. They posed, in Nehru's words, as meek lambs set upon by tigers – and therefore devouring Indian territory.[102] Once more the old, seemingly reasonable proposals, of negotiations, withdrawal by twenty kilometres of both sides and a meeting of the two Prime Ministers, were restated.[103] It was pointed out by India that it was senseless to speak of a 'line of actual control' when Chinese troops had been moving forward incessantly in the western sector and claiming at every stage that wherever they happened to be was the traditional boundary; but such reasoning gained

[96] Khrushchev to Nehru, 20 October 1962.

[97] Nehru to Khrushchev, 22 October 1962.

[98] B.M. Kaul, 'Facts and Fancies about Border War', *Indian Express*, 20 January 1971.

[99] 'Look Back without Anger', Krishna Menon's interview to Inder Malhotra, *The Statesman*, 20 November 1967.

[100] 22 October, *National Herald*, 23 October 1962.

[101] Quoted in General Palit, 'A Summary of Events and Policies *vis-à-vis* the Chinese Attack 1961–62', written on 9 May 1963. I am grateful to General Palit for letting me see this paper.

[102] Speech to the conference of information ministers of the states, 25 October, *National Herald*, 26 October 1962.

[103] Zhou Enlai's letter to Nehru, 24 October 1962, White Paper VIII, p. 1.

little purchase in the fog of words enveloping the Chinese advance. Once again the Soviet Union commended the Chinese proposals and warned 'progressively minded people' (presumably Nehru and Krishna Menon as well as the Indian communists) against succumbing to nationalism and becoming jingoists.[104] Two days later, when Nehru reiterated the demand that the Chinese should first withdraw to the positions of 8 September 1962 before any other step could be considered and appealed to all Governments for support in India's struggle both to preserve her honour and integrity and to maintain ethical standards of international contact,[105] China's rejoinder was to launch a personal attack on Nehru and to call on Khrushchev to repudiate Nehru as a reactionary nationalist.[106] Though unwilling to go so far, Khrushchev continued to urge Nehru in private to show courage and rise above the heat of passion and hurt feelings by accepting an immediate cease-fire.[107]

With the Cuban crisis shattering all assumptions that a serious confrontation with China could not remain a bilateral matter but would broaden into a world crisis and with the Soviet Government withdrawing from their posture of friendship, the Government of India found themselves perilously close to non-alignment deteriorating into isolation. Even the other non-aligned leaders, with the honourable exceptions of Nasser and Tito, were guarded in their responses to India's case. These developments drove Nehru to question himself and his policies, to wonder whether he had placed too much faith in the goodwill of nations and in the intrinsic superiority of the ways of peace. He now conceded, in words which have been often quoted by his critics, that 'we were getting out of touch with reality in the modern world and we were living in an artificial atmosphere of our own creation. We have been shocked out of it, all of us, whether it is the government or the people; some might have felt it less and some more.' With independence, there was a general feeling that India had reached harbour and, safely anchored, could devote herself to peaceful development; but the world was cruel and had forced India to revise her approaches. China, and the world, had betrayed India and forced her, much against her will, to take to war. Her efforts at peace and following the paths of peace had been knocked on the head.[108]

The position was daily rendered increasingly grave by a succession of military reverses. The strategy of dissuasion, which Thimayya had favoured, of highly equipped and fast-moving infantry harassing the advancing Chinese troops but not giving battle till they debouched on to the plains, had already been abandoned. Instead of waging defensive combat, for which the terrain

[104] 'In Interests of Peoples for Sake of Peace', editorial in *Pravda*, 25 October 1962.

[105] Nehru to Zhou Enlai, 27 October, and to all Heads of Government, 26–7 October 1962.

[106] 'More on Nehru's Philosophy in the Light of the Sino-Indian Boundary Question', *People's Daily*, 27 October 1962.

[107] Khrushchev to Nehru, 31 October 1962.

[108] Speech to the conference of information ministers of the states, 25 October, *National Herald*, 26 October 1962. Nehru clarified this statement on two later occasions in the Rajya Sabha, 25 February 1963, Debates, Vol. 42, pp. 915–42 and 3 September 1963, Debates Vol. 44, pp. 2,001–29.

was suited, a whole brigade had been dispersed forward, uncovering Tawang. Thapar and Sen now went to Tawang and decided to make a stand south of it at Se La and not, as Sen had earlier wished, sixty miles even further south at Bomdila. Se La had been strongly fortified and was stocked with sufficient supplies for a week; the road from the base at Tezpur to Se La was fit for three-ton trucks and there was a road for jeeps from Se La to Tawang. The latter place fell on 25 October; but General Harbaksh Singh, the commander deputizing for Kaul away ill in Delhi, also favoured a stand at Se La. A division less a brigade was posted at Se La and a brigade at Bomdila; and further reinforcements were expected. Each of these points was to be a self-contained, well-stocked stronghold, supplied by air, with the road between them discarded. This would have been a replay of Slim's tactics in saving Imphal and Chittagong in the war against the Japanese. But Kaul resumed duty on 29 October and allowed the commander of the division to move his headquarters to Dirang Dzong, the lowest point on the road between Se La and Bomdila – a fatal decision which negated the whole concept of 'fortress defence'.[109]

The immediate requirement, if the tide of defeat were to be arrested, was equipment. Nehru acknowledged past failure in this respect. 'I do not know how I shall explain to Parliament why we have been found lacking in equipment. It is not much good shifting about blame. The fact remains that we have been found lacking and there is an impression that we have approached these things in a somewhat amateurish way.'[110] He also publicly acknowledged that to the 'legitimate question' as to why India had not been prepared for a border war he did not know of any adequate answer.[111] India was now prepared to obtain arms from any source. Even with Israel there were talks, which had soon to be ended because of Nasser's opposition.[112] France, Belgium and Britain were approached for equipment and were prompt in supply. The United States too had offered practical and immediate support, and Kennedy's message to Nehru sounded higher notes than mere sympathy.

> You have displayed an impressive degree of forbearance and patience in dealing with the Chinese. You have put into practice what all great religious teachers have urged and so few of their followers have been able to do. Alas, this teaching seems to be effective only when it is shared by both sides in a dispute.[113]

But there was delay on Menon's part in informing the United States as to what equipment was needed. Nehru must have noted too that Menon's nerve was cracking. Entangled in his own temperament, he informed journalists that the

[109] Harbaksh Singh, 'Nefa 1962: How a Foolproof Defence Plan Collapsed', *Indian Express*, 25 April 1979.

[110] To Krishna Menon, 28 October 1962.

[111] Speech at Delhi, 29 October, *National Herald*, 30 October 1962.

[112] M.H. Heikal, *The Cairo Documents* (New York, 1973), p. 297.

[113] 27 October 1962.

23 *Above* With Kennedy at the White House, November 1961

24 *Right* Greeting Mrs Kennedy in Delhi, 21 March 1962

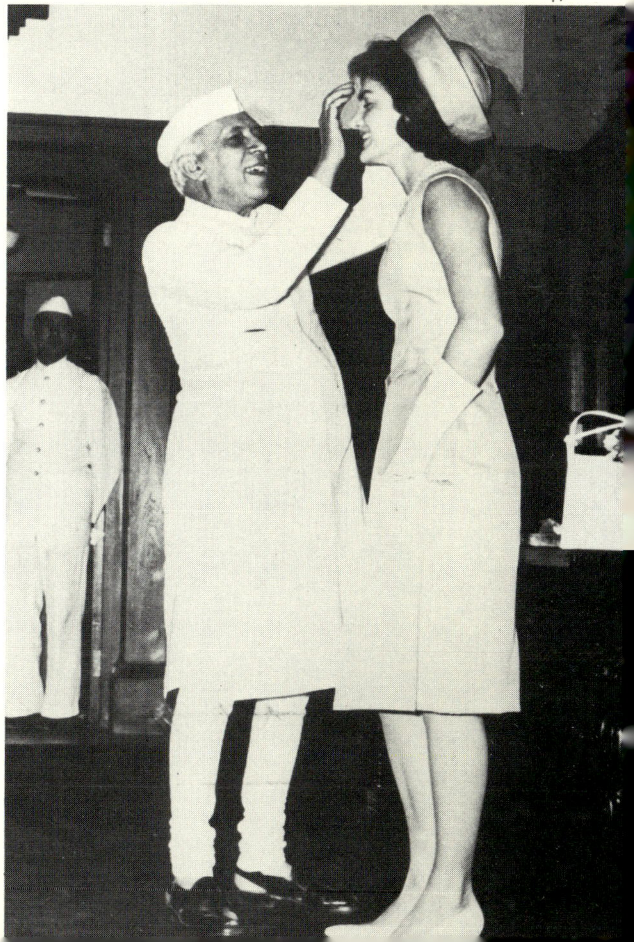

25 With Radhakrishnan and Lal Bahadur, 19 July 1963

Chinese could reach Calcutta if they wished.[114] It was now clear even to Nehru, with all his personal affection for Menon, that he would have to assume direct charge of the management of the crisis. So, on 31 October, he took over the defence portfolio with Menon continuing as a member of the Cabinet in charge of defence production.

Far from being overwhelmed by the crisis, Nehru kept his nerve. As he had said some years before, 'The first thing and the second thing and the third thing about defence is not to get panicky, to keep your nerve whatever happens.'[115] He now assured his commanders of his full confidence. On 3 November he drew the attention of the Chiefs and the principal staff officers of the three services to the 'wonderful response' to the Chinese aggression from all over the country. This 'amazing' morale testified to the fundamental soundness of the Indian people. The first priority now was determination to defeat the Chinese. The war might develop into a large-scale invasion, and they would have to proceed on the basis of the worst that could happen. It was for the soldiers to decide how best to do this. While broad strategy had to be governed by political factors, detailed strategy, and tactics especially, would have to be judged by military considerations. The only proviso Nehru laid down was that the Chinese should not be given an excuse to move through Bhutan. Otherwise it was the task of the soldiers to fight and he would leave them to do it, sustained by the morale and effort of the people behind them. He did not know how far the Chinese would advance but, as they came deeper into Indian territory, their logistical problems would increase; and recent setbacks had not diminished his confidence in the Indian army. 'Our troops are good, and better than any in the world . . . You must realize the clear and firm directive of the Government – to drive the Chinese out of our territory. We will drive them out.'[116]

On the international scene, too, in the sure confidence that time was on his side, Nehru played his hand with assurance. He refused to declare war on China or even break off diplomatic relations, abstained from taking the matter of Chinese aggression to the United Nations although the support of a majority of member states was certain, and did not rush into any military alliance – all measures intended not only to hold the crisis with precision to the immediate matter and prevent it from compromising India's commitment to world peace but to leave open the road for the Soviet Government to revert, when the Cuba crisis was over, to their earlier attitude of partiality to India. Meantime, there would be no weakening of resistance to China. Zhou refused to agree to withdrawal to the positions as on 8 September 1962 but defined the 'line of actual control' as that on 7 November 1959,[117] meaning that China

[114] Cf. Galbraith's diary entry on 25 October 1962: 'When Ronning (the Canadian High Commissioner) saw Menon last Friday, the latter talked about a ten-year war and implied that the Chinese might head for Madras.' *Ambassador's Journal* (London, 1969), p. 435.

[115] 5 December 1958. Lok Sabha Debates, Second Series, Vol. 23, pp. 3,516–33.

[116] Palit, 'A Summary of Events'.

[117] Zhou to Nehru, 4 November 1962, White Paper VIII, pp. 7–10.

would retain the areas occupied by her till that date in the west but India should withdraw all the posts she had set up in the past three years, even though none of these were on the Aksai Chin plateau. 'Shorn of its wrappings, therefore, this is in effect a demand for surrender.'[118] Nehru's tactics were justified when the Soviet Government, while continuing to urge a cease-fire and negotiations, spoke of the high value they placed on their friendly relations with India.[119] Khrushchev also assured the Indian Ambassador that India had no greater and more sincere friend than the Soviet Union. While the Soviet Government would provide arms to neither side, existing contracts with India for such items as transport planes and for spare parts and training of crew for these planes would be fulfilled.[120]

It was, therefore, in a slightly less grim situation that the two Houses of Parliament, on the Prime Minister's initiative, unanimously recorded their appreciation of the 'wonderful and spontaneous' response of the Indian people and affirmed their resolve 'to drive out the aggressor from the sacred soil of India, however long and hard the struggle may be'.[121] China's behaviour was, in Nehru's view, that of not a communist but an imperialist nation, powerful and irresponsible and with a belief in war as a means of settling problems. So India would have to be prepared for a prolonged contest which would require not only a tremendous mobilization of resources but a mental adaptation, the strengthening of the national will. Surrender to aggression would be neither peace nor freedom and much worse than armed conflict. But India, while getting her second breath and resigning herself to the context of a long war, should do her utmost to avoid a brutalization of spirit; for that would be a deeper tragedy than war.[122]

The British Prime Minister, Harold Macmillan, had, on hearing of the massive Chinese attacks, assured Nehru that the British Government would do everything in their power to help in all ways,[123] but in his private diary he gave full play to the *schadenfreude* widespread at this time in the West and gibed that Nehru had been transformed 'from an imitation of George Lansbury into a parody of Churchill'.[124] It is, of course, true that Nehru, even while speaking of a fight till the war was won and raising echoes of Dunkirk, disliked the role of a War Minister; his whole nature and training rebelled against it. There was to him no question of surrender, come what may. Once during these anxious days he was seen storming out of his room, followed by two Cabinet colleagues, his face red with anger. 'I will fight them with a stick!' he shouted again and again, brandishing the swagger-stick which he

[118] Nehru to Khrushchev, 5 November 1962.

[119] 'Negotiations in the Road to Settling the Conflict', editorial in *Pravda*, 5 November 1962.

[120] T.N. Kaul's telegram to Prime Minister, 9 November 1962.

[121] 8 November 1962.

[122] Address to the Congress Parliamentary Party, 7 November 1962, Tape M-64/C (ii); speeches in the Lok Sabha, 8 November, Debates, Third Series, Vol. 9, pp. 106–33, and in Rajya Sabha, 9 November 1962, Debates, Vol. 41, pp. 402–26.

[123] Message to Nehru, 23 October 1962.

[124] 23 October 1962. *At the End of the Day* (London, 1973), p. 228.

always carried.[125] Forced to lead his people in resistance to aggression, he did his best but without enthusiasm and seeking always to secure India from the corruption of battle. At this time his was the misfortune, said to be one class of tragedy in Shakespeare, of incompatibility between character and role,[126] of a man of peace driven by the 'logic of dire event' to wear the mantle of belligerence. But the irony of Nehru's destiny was also symbolic of India's civilized spirit roused to action by unexpected invasion. Never was Walter Lippmann's comment truer, that Nehru, like Theodore Roosevelt and de Gaulle, incarnated part of his country. 'It's as if the country is inside of them, and not they as someone operating within the country.'[127]

Yet there was no escape from this dilemma. 'So far as we are concerned, this war is pushing us into a modern world, making us realise the hard realities and the situation for which free nations must keep ready.' The world was a cruel place for the weak, be it of mind or in arms.[128] With firmness, even if without relish, Nehru set himself to lead his people in war. To remove an element of discord in official and party circles, and because the volume of criticism impeded Menon's proper functioning,[129] Nehru, on 7 November, decided to accept Menon's resignation from the Cabinet. His shattered career recalls the comment of another tragic political figure: 'What brings men to the front is much more opportunity than character.'[130] But the uncomplaining dignity with which Menon departed from office balanced to an extent his tarnished performance while in power; and his eclipse as a politician enabled him, at long last, to be respected as a personality. To Nehru, who believed that Menon was guiltless of responsibility for the débâcle, the resignation was a blow which he accepted in the national cause and not because his own position was threatened. For even a crisis of this dimension did not endanger Nehru's hold on the people.

Orders were placed with the United States for equipment for manufacturing arms and agreement was secured from the Soviet Union for the despatch of MiG-21 jet fighters and for the construction of a factory for building them. These facts were disclosed,[131] presumably to convince the Chinese of India's determination not to yield and of the all-round support on which she could rely. Then, in a formal reply to China, the spirit of the resolution of Parliament was embodied, making clear that India would not compromise with the enemy at her throat. To Nehru the invasion meant that China had taken a deliberate and calculated decision to enforce her territorial claims by force; and India could not agree to this. 'To do otherwise would mean mere

[125] Gundevia, 'Outside the Archives'.

[126] John Bayley, *Shakespeare and Tragedy* (London, 1981), pp. 64–73, 187.

[127] R. Steel, *Walter Lippmann and the American Century* (New York, 1980), p. 400.

[128] Address at Delhi, 11 November, *National Herald*, 12 November 1962.

[129] Address to the Congress Parliamentary Party, 7 November 1962. Tape M 64/C (ii).

[130] Lord Randolph Churchill in 1889, quoted in R.F. Foster, *Lord Randolph Churchill* (Oxford, 1981), p. 381.

[131] Nehru's statement to American journalists, 12 November, *National Herald*, 13 November 1962.

existence at the mercy of an aggressive, arrogant and expansionist neighbour.'[132]

In face of such firmness, Zhou wrote to Heads of Government pleading innocence;[133] Chinese propaganda, which, as Nehru observed, would have put even Goebbels to shame,[134] continued to denounce Indian 'offensives' and to claim that all territory into which Chinese armies moved belonged traditionally to China; the Chinese Communist Party railed against 'reactionary nationalism'[135] and the Chinese armies resumed their advance. Nehru had prepared the country for further withdrawals; Indian armies would fight at points of their choice and not foolishly where the terrain was advantageous to the enemy.[136] But even Nehru was not prepared for a rout. On 17 November Kaul sent a message from the eastern front that the threat from the Chinese was now so great and their overall strength so superior that foreign troops should be asked to come to India's aid. Later that night, the local commander withdrew from Se La without a fight and precipitated a disorderly retreat; and on the next day, 19 November, Bomdila fell.

It was clear that the Indian army command was in desperate confusion. Grip, insight and poise were wholly lacking. It is not known to this day who, if any one, gave the order for the withdrawal from Se La, or whether the commander withdrew on his own. A spirit of panic was abroad. Lal Bahadur, the Home Minister, is reported to have told a colleague that NEFA, Assam and northern Bengal would all be occupied, and that he was preparing to have the oil wells in Assam blown up.[137] As for the Prime Minister, despite his public assertions that he had no doubt of India's final victory against 'naked, shameless and crude' invasion,[138] he could not close his eyes to the immediate helplessness of the Indian armies to withstand the Chinese. In the west, with the shelling of the air field at Chushul, an advance to Leh seemed likely; and in the east, the loss of Assam, Tripura, Manipur and Nagaland appeared imminent. Chinese troops were also poised for moving across the border in the middle sector into the Punjab, Himachal Pradesh and Uttar Pradesh. Nehru, apparently without consulting any of his Cabinet colleagues[139] or officials, apart from the Foreign Secretary, M.J. Desai, wrote two letters to Kennedy describing the situation as 'really desperate' and requesting the immediate despatch of a minimum of twelve squadrons of supersonic all-weather fighters

[132] Nehru to Zhou, 14 November 1962, White Paper VIII, pp. 10–13.

[133] 15 November 1962.

[134] Address on Territorial Army Day, 18 November, *National Herald*, 19 November 1962.

[135] 'Carry Forward the Revolutionary Spirit of the Moscow Declaration and the Moscow Statement', editorial in *People's Daily*, 15 November 1962.

[136] Address at Delhi, 11 November, *National Herald*, 12 November 1962.

[137] S.K. Dey, *Power to the People?* (Delhi, 1969), pp. 232–3.

[138] Address on Territorial Army Day, 18 November, *National Herald*, 19 November 1962.

[139] When S.K. Patil, the Minister for Food and Agriculture, complained that the Cabinet was not being kept fully informed of developments, Nehru's explanation was that the crisis had come very suddenly and adaptation to it was taking time. He added, 'No policy decisions have been taken, so far as I can remember, without reference to the Cabinet as a whole.' S.K. Patil to Nehru, 23 November 1962, and Nehru's reply on the same day, S.K. Patil papers, N.M.M.L. Clearly Nehru's memory was not at this time at its best.

and the setting up of radar communications. American personnel would have to man these fighters and installations and protect Indian cities from air attacks by the Chinese till Indian personnel had been trained. If possible, the United States should also send planes flown by American personnel to assist the Indian Air Force in any battles with the Chinese in Indian air space; but aerial action by India elsewhere would be the responsibility of the Indian Air Force. Nehru also asked for two B-47 bomber squadrons to enable India to strike at Chinese bases and air fields; but to learn to fly these planes Indian pilots and technicians would be sent immediately for training in the United States. All such assistance and equipment would be utilized solely against the Chinese.[140] As an immediate response, Galbraith asked that units of the Seventh Fleet should move into the Bay of Bengal.[141]

Was non-alignment, then, a forgotten dream? Certainly, if India was to be defended by massive American aid, non-alignment, if it survived, would require a fresh definition; and perhaps not many in India, apart from Nehru, believed any longer in its reality.[142] Even Nehru had accepted that receipt of military assistance from the United States introduced an element of confusion into India's policy of non-alignment, although he contended that the essence of that policy was the refusal to join any military bloc, and this India had not done.[143] His later remark, that there was no non-alignment *vis-à-vis* China,[144] implied that the policy did not preclude resistance to aggression and all the steps which that required. War has its own momentum and non-alignment cannot be at the cost of national survival. Was this quibbling? The discussion would have gone on endlessly if, in fact, it had become necessary for the United States to act on Kennedy's assurance 'to be as responsive as possible' to India's needs in association with Britain and the Commonwealth.[145] But the question as to the extent to which non-alignment could survive a large-scale, long-term war with China fought with American assistance in the context of an invasion of India remained hypothetical.[146]

For the Chinese realized that the situation was changing to their disadvantage. The lifting of the naval blockade of Cuba on 20 November implied that the United States could now give full attention to Chinese aggression. Nehru was in no mood to compromise and symbolized the popular mood when he committed himself not to yield or surrender till the invader went out or was pushed out. 'I want to take a pledge . . . now and here that we shall see this

140 Nehru's two letters to Kennedy, 19 November 1962.

141 J.K. Galbraith, *A Life in our Times* (London, 1981), p. 439.

142 Cf. A.M. Rosenthal's comment that Nehru 'follows a policy which his country no longer really trusts, but which it allows him, as sons allow an aged parent the privilege of leafing through an old souvenir album.' *New York Times Magazine*, 19 November 1962.

143 Television interview released in New York, 8 November 1962.

144 Television interview released in New York, 4 December 1962.

145 Kennedy to Nehru, 21 November 1962; A.M. Schlesinger, *A Thousand Days* (Boston, 1965), p. 531.

146 For a discussion of these points, see M. Brecher, 'Non-Alignment under Stress; the West and the India-China Border War', *Pacific Affairs*, Winter 1979–80, pp. 612–30.

matter to the end and the end will have to be victory for India.'[147] For this purpose he was willing to seek Western aid but ensured that this did not lose him the sympathy of the Soviet Union. The creation of such a set of circumstances was Nehru's special achievement. He was not always helped by his colleagues. The state Governments eagerly locked up a large number of communists including senior leaders like Namboodiripad at a time when the Communist Party was struggling to assert its patriotic instincts; and Nehru, informed after the event, had to protest and urge their speedy release.[148] Y.B. Chavan, the young Chief Minister of Maharashtra of whom Nehru expected much and whom he selected as Krishna Menon's successor, told the people to expect nothing from the Soviet Union, which believed in spreading communism by force and would ultimately side with China.[149] Yet Nehru prevented a shift in foreign policy and safeguarded its independence. He had misread China's short-term objectives but his judgment on Sino-Soviet relations and the Soviet Union's attitude to India was throughout sure-footed.

The Chinese reacted promptly to this new turn of events. They had humiliated India and proved, to their own satisfaction, that China was 'one head taller than India imagined herself to be'. Their leaders, particularly Liu Xiaoqi, boasted that one chief purpose of their military campaign had been to demolish India's 'arrogance' and 'illusions of grandeur'; they 'had taught India a lesson and, if necessary, they would teach her a lesson again and again'.[150] The Chinese had, too, discomfited Khrushchev and enhanced their own prestige, they had occupied all the territory they sought in the western sector and they had ensured that India's economic efforts would be crippled by the necessity of greatly increased expenditure on defence. But China's deceit and use of force over the years had only served to strengthen India's will to resist and there was now a new spirit of unity in the country with all parties, including the communists, ranged against the Chinese. In a sense, said Nehru, the Chinese should be thanked for having suddenly lifted a veil from India's face and shown it to be strong and serene.[151] For China to continue the war against such an India and with growing problems of supplies and logistics and against an army recovering from the initial blows would secure little advantage, especially as the Soviet Union was moving away from neutrality, the United States was ready to provide full support to India and world opinion in general was critical of China. Agreed as the Chinese leaders were in their personal animosity towards Nehru,[152] and much as they might abuse him as a minion of capitalism, they could not have wished to see India wholly dependent on the West for military assistance. So it was not just a matter of

147 Broadcast to the nation, 19 November, *National Herald*, 20 November 1962.

148 Nehru to Lal Bahadur, Home Minister, 22 November 1962.

149 See Nehru to Y.B. Chavan, 16 November 1962.

150 Mr Felix Bandaranaike's report at Delhi, 12 January 1962, of conversations with Chinese leaders in Beijing. Mr Bandaranaike confirmed this to the author at Delhi on 28 August 1981.

151 Speech in the Lok Sabha, 16 November 1962. Debates, Third Series, Vol. 9, pp. 1,644–71.

152 Mr Felix Bandaranaike reported that Mao, Liu, Zhou and Chen Yi were all united on this.

Chinese ethics, of 'being a good winner',[153] of not crowing over victory, that led the Chinese Government to call off the war; it was an obvious case of diminishing returns. On 19 November, therefore, Zhou informed the Indian chargé d'affaires that the need of the hour was to settle the dispute in an objective and friendly manner;[154] and two days later the Chinese announced an unilateral cease-fire to be followed ten days later by withdrawal north of the McMahon Line in the east and the 'line of actual control' in the other sectors, with police posts in the withdrawn areas.

[153] On this concept see D. Bonavia, *The Chinese* (London, 1981), p. 57.

[154] Telegram of Indian chargé d'affaires to Foreign Secretary after interview with Zhou Enlai, 19 November 1962.

11

Light and Shadows

ONE

No one who lived in India through the winter months of 1962 can forget the deep humiliation felt by all Indians, irrespective of party. Now, however, the explanation of those events is clear and can be seen in perspective. The Chinese had been preparing for aggression over a long period of time. Battle-hardened troops, trained in mountain and guerrilla warfare and acclimatized to high altitudes, were massed on the high Tibetan plateau, roads were built so that their soldiers could move down quickly to the Indian border, and large stores were accumulated.[1] India, on the other hand, believing that China would not go beyond 'some nibbling away in the dark',[2] was physically and mentally unprepared for massive aggression. 'We did not think that a major invasion like this would take place so soon.'[3] Indeed they had thought that 'a shameless invasion of this kind' was not possible in modern times.[4] Taken by surprise by the sudden onslaughts, India had hastily to put together troops based in diverse places and rush them to the freezing Himalayan ranges. These men were neither trained nor equipped for this type of fighting and were sent into battle, short of weapons, warm clothing and boots to face an enemy far superior in numbers and in fire-power. Having worked for years on the principle that a second- or even third-rate weapon manufactured at home was better than an imported first-rate weapon,[5] India was now caught in a war before industrialization and the modernization of defence had got well under way; and the Indian army had to go into action with rifles and mortars much inferior to those of the Chinese. Obviously Nehru's Government could not have spent a large part of the public revenues over a long period of years on the military

[1] 'Neither the massive striking force nor the perfection of military planning . . . displayed by the Chinese could have been hastily improvised.' 'A Fool's Game', editorial in *Monthly Review* (New York), January 1963. The editorial is generally sympathetic to China.

[2] Television interview released in New York, 4 December 1962.

[3] Speech in the Rajya Sabha, 25 February 1963. Debates, Vol. 42, pp. 915–42.

[4] Speech at Delhi, 30 July, *National Herald*, 31 July 1963.

[5] Nehru's address to the conference on defence production, 31 August 1959. A.I.R. Tapes.

defence of the Himalayas at the expense of economic development; nor could they have chosen the other alternative of mortgaging the country's freedom to another power by signing an alliance and entrusting the defence of India to foreigners. But where the Government had failed was in not importing the minimum of equipment till manufacture in India reached the 'take-off' point. On at least six occasions in the first six months of 1962, Army Headquarters brought to the notice of the Government the low levels of stocks of ammunition and all types of necessary equipment; but, on the assumption that there would be no major campaign in the near future, the Government persisted in the political decision not to purchase large quantities of military requirements abroad.

To add to this, the maintenance of tanks and other vehicles was poor, a network of border roads had not been laid down though its need had been accepted at least since 1951, and adequate stores had not been collected. The forward troops were denied air support lest the Chinese retaliate by bombing Indian cities; the air force was used only for dropping supplies but considerable quantities were lost in these heavily forested areas. There had been no planning for a war of this kind, no detailed staff work done. When fighting broke out, therefore, *ad hoc* decisions were hurriedly taken and commanders appointed who were new to each other, to the men under them and to the terrain. Against all normal canons of military leadership, Kaul was permitted to double as Chief of the General Staff as well as Corps Commander on the battle-front when he had no obvious qualifications for either post; and Kaul greatly worsened the situation by his outrageous methods of command. He conducted a battle on the north-eastern frontier from his sick bed in Delhi; and, when he did reach the area, he hopped around the forward lines instead of remaining at his headquarters and issuing directives on the basis of an overall view of the whole front.

The situation, therefore, was as bad as it could be in every way. Had it not been true, it would be difficult to imagine. Yet the Indian army lived up to its distinguished traditions. Only in the Se La sector the troops of one division broke; and even there, before the retreat, they fought bravely. At one place north of the pass a heavily outnumbered company of the Garhwal Rifles beat back five Chinese attacks in the course of one morning. Elsewhere too there was no lack of fighting spirit, among both officers and men; and they only gave ground after inflicting heavy losses on the enemy. In some places they fought to the last man and the last round without retreating. At Rezang La near Chushul, for instance, in the western sector, out of a company of a Kumaon battalion only three wounded soldiers got back to headquarters and five were taken prisoner by the Chinese; the rest of the company were found in their positions three months later, frozen as they died, with their weapons in their hands. The Chinese had removed their dead, of whom there had clearly been many.

So in this short campaign, in which the major portion of the Indian army had not been involved, an aggressive power had taken advantage of years of planning to launch a swift and surprise attack and pushed back Indian troops from forward areas which they should not have sought to defend. India had many lessons to learn from these events, but they do not rank as a national disgrace.

TWO

The Indian armies abided by the cease-fire and did not impede the Chinese withdrawal in the eastern sector, although this meant that the Chinese would remain in possession of about 2,500 square miles recently occupied in the western sector. While the Chinese asserted that they would withdraw to the 'line of actual control' as on 7 November 1959, they also let slip that, in fact, to do so would mean withdrawal from about 6,000 square miles of territory which they had occupied since then.[6] Nehru had little hope that this cease-fire would prove more than a temporary truce, and continued to exhort the people to prepare mentally and spiritually for a struggle which would last years.[7] Even after the Chinese withdrawal on 1 December, he was unwilling, in the wake of 'one of the grossest acts of imperialist aggression', to consider negotiations which were not backed by strength.[8] China had betrayed the trust reposed in her by India; her word could not be relied upon and India would not allow herself to be deceived again.[9] She therefore had to build up an army which could defend the northern frontiers and deter any repetition of aggression.

The cease-fire and withdrawal of Chinese forces were not followed immediately by a peace settlement. Mrs Bandaranaike, the Prime Minister of Sri Lanka, in December 1962 invited the Governments of five other non-aligned countries, Burma, Cambodia, Ghana, Indonesia and the United Arab Republic, to discuss the situation created by the Chinese aggression. Their 'Colombo proposals' presented to the Governments of India and China, without terming China an aggressor, in effect called on her to give up the territory occupied by her after 8 September 1962. It was suggested that, without prejudice to the final alignment or the claims of the two sides, in the western sector the Chinese should withdraw twenty kilometres and Indian forces not move forward and, in the resulting demilitarized zone, civilian posts be established on both sides; in the middle sector the minor points of dispute should be solved peacefully; and in the eastern sector, India could move up to the line of actual control, that is the McMahon Line, except in the Thagla and Longju areas. India accepted

[6] Text of the Chinese cease-fire proposals, 21 November 1962.

[7] Speeches at Delhi, 22 and 27 November, *National Herald*, 23 and 28 November 1962 respectively.

[8] Television interview released in New York, 4 December 1962.

[9] Speech in Lok Sabha 10 December 1962, Debates, Third Series, Vol. 11, pp. 5,083–94; broadcast to the troops, 10 December, *National Herald*, 11 December 1962.

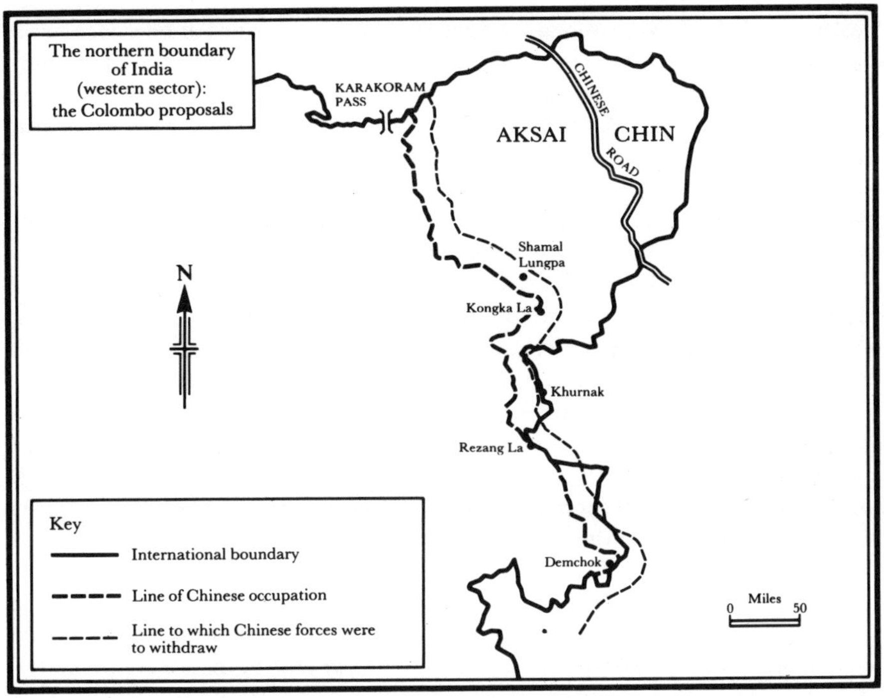

these proposals, which would virtually restore her position in the east and require China to pull back from about 2,700 square miles in the western sector. Moreover, in place of the earlier interlocking of military posts, with China in a position to wipe out the Indian posts whenever she chose, the Colombo proposals provided the better alternative of parity of civilian posts. But China rejected the proposals, as she wanted withdrawal of both sides, and not of Chinese troops alone, by twenty kilometres, and along the whole boundary and not only in the western sector.

The Colombo proposals and India's acceptance of them strengthened India's diplomatic position for she was seen not to be making suggestions of her own but, in contrast to China, consenting to a formula proposed by six non-aligned nations. Nehru followed this up by offering to commence talks once the Colombo proposals had been implemented on the ground and, if the talks failed, to refer the dispute to the Hague Court or to international arbitration.[10] China, on the other hand, was in the paradoxical position of being placed on the diplomatic defensive after spectacular military successes. She criticized the Colombo powers, quibbled that she had accepted the proposals in principle and should not be asked to accept the clarifications given by the sponsors of the proposals, set up six checkposts in what would have been the demilitarized zone without agreeing to India doing the same, blamed Nehru for insisting on

[10] Note of the Ministry of External Affairs to the Government of China, 3 April 1963, White Paper IX, pp. 34–5.

full acceptance of the proposals and rejected the suggestions of reference to the World Court or arbitration.[11] In other words, China had secured all the land which she had wanted in Ladakh and Aksai Chin – about 14,500 square miles – and was satisfied with freezing the cease-fire line. But in achieving territorial gains she had not only turned India from a friend into a foe but also shown herself to the world to be in no mood for an amicable settlement. Nehru had these developments in mind when he claimed that in a sense the invasion had done more harm to China than to India.[12]

Realizing that China had no wish at this time for any talks or negotiations with India, Nehru improved his diplomatic advantage by offering to the emissaries of Bertrand Russell who, in July 1963, shuttled as mediators between Delhi and Beijing, that he would accept no posts of both sides in place of parity of posts in the demilitarized zone. Mrs Bandaranaike gave her support to this proposal.[13] But China turned down this suggestion as well[14] and continued to build up her strength along the Indian border. There were more Chinese troops in these areas in 1964 than at the time of the campaign in 1962; and more airfields, gun emplacements, storage dumps and barracks were constructed.[15]

So continuous tension along the border became the norm. Both countries adjusted themselves to years of wintry hostility. China accused the Nehru Government of repressing their own people at home with increasing brutality, of becoming more and more obsequious to United States imperialism and of acting as its accomplice in many important international issues in the hope of more aid. 'The Nehru government's persistent opposition to China is the precise outcome of its domestic and foreign policies, which have become more and more reactionary.' So the Chinese Government claimed to have been absolutely right in waging a necessary struggle against this reactionary policy.[16] 'It's no fun', said Mao early in 1964,[17] 'being a running dog. Nehru is in bad shape, imperialism and revisionism have robbed him blind.'

India, on her part, could not easily get over the very deep sense of

[11] See Zhou's letters to Mrs Bandaranaike, 21 February 1963, and to Nehru, 20 April 1963.

[12] Speech at Amritsar, 3 March, *National Herald*, 4 March 1963.

[13] See 'The Russell Memorandum' dictated by Russell before his death and published in the *New Statesman*, 11 September 1970.

[14] Mr Neville Maxwell, reporting the next year from Delhi when this proposal of 'zero parity' by India was disclosed, was clear as to where the responsibility lay: 'Peking's failure to respond to Mr. Nehru's concession (and it is one for which he will be fiercely attacked when the opposition wakes up to what is involved) suggests that it is China that does not want negotiations. Certainly no one can now say that India is showing an over-punctilious insistence on the letter of proposals that were meant to bring the two enemies back to negotiations.' *The Times*, 14 April 1964. In his book on the subject published some years later Mr Maxwell, for reasons best known to himself, does not make this point.

[15] See Defence Minister's statements in the Rajya Sabha, 16 August 1963, Debates, Vol. 44, pp. 431–8 and in the Lok Sabha, 6 April 1964, Debates, Third Series, Vol. 29, pp. 9,362–9.

[16] 'Workers of All Countries, Unite, Oppose our Common Enemy!', editorial in *People's Daily*, 15 December 1962; speech of the head of the Chinese delegation at the Sixth Congress of the Socialist Unity Party of Germany, 18 January 1963; 'Whence the Differences? A Reply to Thorez and Other Comrades', editorial in *People's Daily*, 27 February 1963.

[17] 13 February 1964. S. Schram (ed.), *Mao Tse-tung Unrehearsed* (Penguin edn, 1974), p. 198.

resentment at the thought that China had played false with her. As Nehru once described it, the large-scale Chinese aggression was 'a permanent piece of education'.[18] The personal betrayal Nehru naturally felt intensely. 'How I worked for friendship between India and China, fought for China's legitimate interests in the world – and aggression was my reward!'[19] But such duplicity was in itself no cause for a permanent embittering of relations between countries. There was, of course, the basic issue of evicting the aggressor. 'When a bandit enters your house, you are not left with any choice but to face him and drive him out. That is our attitude towards the Chinese.'[20] No settlement could be forced by China down India's throat.[21] But India did not intend any immediate military effort to recover the land lost in Ladakh, even though she did not write it off.

However, the desire for territory, now satisfied, was to Nehru but a small part of China's confrontation with India. Nor was it just a matter of the clashes that could be expected when two large 'land powers' confronted each other across a long frontier. China had sought to humble and humiliate India primarily because India did not fit in with her world view. Her anti-Indian attitude appeared to flow from her general analysis of the international situation and reflected the aims and assumptions underlying her foreign policy as a whole. An 'unabashed chauvinism' went along with an inclination to boss other countries, a rejection, alone among the major countries of the world, of the concept of peaceful coexistence and a reversion to the traditional belief that China was 'the centre of things'.[22] While he did not wish to leave India a legacy of hostility with China and was determined to continue to seek an understanding,[23] so long as China insisted on India accepting a subordinate status, renouncing non-alignment and generally moulding her foreign and domestic policies to suit China's view of herself and of the world, the Chinese menace would have to be regarded as a long-term one. 'I don't see any real compromise. What they have in mind is different from our thinking. There is no bridge between us. We should be prepared for four or five years of war.'[24] India was not going to be one of the 'small fish' which 'this huge crocodile in the pond of Asia' was seeking to devour.[25] The people of India should be

[18] Press conference at Delhi, 9 October, *National Herald*, 10 October 1963.

[19] To Mohan Kumaramangalam sometime in June 1963. See M. Kumaramangalam, 'Some Memories of Nehru', *Mainstream* (Delhi), 21 November 1964.

[20] Speech at Rihand, 7 January, *National Herald*, 8 January 1963.

[21] Speech at Bombay, 20 March, *National Herald*, 21 March 1963.

[22] Nehru in the Lok Sabha, 10 December 1962, Debates, Third Series, Vol. 11, pp. 5,083–94; address to the Congress Parliamentary Party, 12 December 1962, Tape 66(1); interview with the political correspondent of the *Washington Post*, 4 March 1963; J. Nehru, 'Changing India', *Foreign Affairs* (New York), April 1963; speech at Ahmedabad, 10 May, *The Hindu*, 12 May 1963; interview with Italo Pietra in *Il Giorno* (Milan), 20 June 1963; speech in the Rajya Sabha, 2 September 1963, Debates, Vol. 44, pp. 2,351–62.

[23] Interview with H. Bradsher of the Associated Press, 9 September, *The Hindu*, 26 September 1963.

[24] Nehru to Robert Sherrod sometime in late November 1962, *Saturday Evening Post* (New York), 19 January 1963.

[25] Speech at Delhi, 2 January, *The Hindu*, 4 January 1963.

prepared to fight, if need be, with sticks, even with their nails, rather than accept foreign domination. The one thing for which India was not ready and would never be ready was to bow her head before the aggressor.[26]

In face of China's attitude that 'either one is for them or against them',[27] a self-respecting nation like India could hope for no lasting friendship with her. China regarded India as an ideological obstacle and sought a dominating position in Asia in a way which was humiliating to India and an insult to the conscience of the world. She had thrown all standards of international behaviour to the winds and was trying to establish the cult of brute force.[28]

> We do not want communism to come here and yet the essential conflict is more political and geographical than that of communism, although communism is an important factor in the background. Communism too is gradually developing two facets, one represented by the Soviet Union and the other by China. It is possible to live peacefully with the Soviet Union. But it does not appear to be possible to do that with China. Hence the essential conflict.[29]

It was, to quote an ugly word Nehru once employed, 'Chinese-ism'[30] that was to him the main danger not only to India but to the world.

> A country of an ever growing population of 700 million, controlled by a monolithic political structure, with its tradition of expansionism and its conceit and faith in its mission of world domination by force and revolution and a land army of several millions, poses a serious threat to the peace not only of South East Asia but of the world. The extent to which this new aggressive and expansionist power is held in check will decide the future.[31]

Did Nehru over-react? Had the sharp pain of defeat weakened his intellectual balance? Mao's theoretical analyses of formidable power, especially those written in his early years, and his leadership of the peasants in China have earned him a unique place in world history. But basically he was an outstanding Chinese figure, rooted in indigenous tradition. A hard-headed nationalist, he was determined to regain for his country not only equality among the nations but a prime position in Asia. He combined throughout his life the roles of both a revolutionary and a nationalist and, at the start, each strengthened the other. But his contribution to the resurgence of Chinese nationalism has been more enduring. In his last years, concerned that the tide

[26] Speeches at Delhi, 17 and 30 January, *National Herald*, 18 and 31 January 1963 respectively.
[27] Nehru to Ali Sabry, record of the meeting held on 27 April 1963.
[28] Speech at Rohtak, 9 March, *The Hindu*, 11 March 1963.
[29] Nehru to Chief Ministers, 2 February 1963.
[30] Interview with R. Sherrod, *Saturday Evening Post*, 19 January 1963.
[31] Nehru to Col. Nasser, 14 April 1963.

of revolution was ebbing, he sought, desperately and ferociously, to whip it up. He could not, however, ensure that the tide would keep rolling even after his death, and his successors have gone back on much which he cherished. So the permanent legacy of Mao to his country has been not continuous social and economic upheaval but a powerful state and army. China has become, under Mao's inspiration, an ambitious nation and a skilled practitioner of *realpolitik*. The People's Republic is today determined to be a strong and rich country attaching little importance to ideology. In this, as in most other issues of world affairs demanding a long perspective, Nehru was among the clear-sighted statesmen of his time:

THREE

It is a common view that, after 1962, Nehru's purpose and authority shrivelled and, like Ramsay MacDonald, he reigned in increasing decrepitude because he could not bring himself to retire and others were too good-mannered to insist on his departure. Certainly Nehru was by now tired and sick, and the enthusiasm and expansiveness of the earlier years of public activity had been diminished. But there was no despair or absence of resolve to lead the country in its fight and resistance; and among the vast majority of the people there was no visible desire for a change of leadership. The Swatantra Party gave its support to the splenetic efforts of a few members of the opposition in Parliament to denigrate the Prime Minister; but, apart from this, it was generally accepted that Nehru was the right person to organize a firm response to the challenge of China.

India, to Nehru's satisfaction, faced this challenge with 'new anger, new determination and new gratitude' – anger at Chinese perfidy, determination to accept no dishonourable settlement and gratitude to those countries which had rallied to her aid.[32] In the months which followed, there was much to provide ground for optimism and renewed faith in India's future, even while there were areas where the shadows did not lift and even deepened. The reaction to Chinese behaviour was far from defeatist and led Nehru to speak of the war repeatedly as a blessing in disguise.[33] No country which had come through the kind of upheaval which India had had could ever be suppressed or defeated. Petty domestic disputes had been swept aside by foreign invasion. So much patriotic sacrifice from an infant nation unaccustomed to war could only be explained as due perhaps to the sense of belonging and the consciousness of sovereignty imbued in the people by socialist policies and unaligned independence. India, experiencing a crisis of the spirit, had found herself, and this

[32] Interview with W.B. Friendenburg, 14 January, *Washington Daily News*, 15 January 1963.

[33] Speeches at Lucknow, 5 January, and at Soraon, 6 January, *National Herald*, 6 and 7 January 1963 respectively and at Abusa, 25 April, *The Hindu*, 27 April 1963.

new mood should be utilized to achieve both industrial advance and military readiness.[34] Defence and development were parts of the same process; and planning, socialism and non-alignment were all ways of preparing the nation to face renewed Chinese aggression.[35] Real strength came not from the purchase of arms but from the building of an industrial base which could be converted, when the need arose, into a war machine, the development of power and transport, increased productivity in agriculture, even the improvement of public health and the spread of primary and technical education. The country should, therefore, while ensuring the basic minimum of armed defence to withstand a renewal of Chinese aggression, give full attention to all aspects of the Third Five Year Plan. 'We should do this till it hurts.'[36] Even the proper utilization of foreign assistance presumed appropriate levels of economic development; and one could not rely on hopes of continuous and indefinite streams of aid from abroad.

The war crisis reinforced Nehru's views on the crucial importance of production and of the achievement of socialism of a kind suited to India. These were required even to strengthen India in the confrontation with China, which was like a marathon race in which India needed steady breath, if she were to win.[37] But one needed also a larger vision of the future. 'A country which has a wrong vision inevitably goes down, but a country which has no vision gradually loses its vital energy and perishes ultimately.'[38] That vision which he, more than anyone else, had given the Indian people was, in its basic features, unchanged; and he was optimistic that it was a vision which would be realized.

For the first time in human history, science and technology had in theory and practice provided a solution to the problem of abolishing poverty. They had made possible a colossal apparatus of production which had nothing to do with capitalism or communism, and advantage should be taken of it to build a prosperous society. General starvation and a uniform lack of opportunity constituted an absurd kind of socialism. The goals, of equal chances and decent living for all, were undisputed; and one should move towards them by the best possible ways rather than according to some theoretical commitments. India should not get lost in words or become a prisoner of phrases, for slogans limited thought. Nationalization was not a mandatory part of socialism. A private sector would have to continue if only because the Government lacked the capacity to take it over and any such move would result immediately in a huge loss of production. A mixed economy would

[34] Addresses to the Congress Parliamentary Party, 20 and 27 January 1963. Tapes 67C(1) and 68(1); speech in the Lok Sabha, 27 February 1963, Debates, Third Series, Vol. 13, pp. 1,307–42; interview sometime early in 1963, R.K. Karanjia, *The Philosophy of Mr. Nehru* (London, 1966), p. 120.

[35] Speech at the A.I.C.C., New Delhi, 6 April, *National Herald*, 7 April 1963.

[36] Address to the standing committee of the National Development Council, 18 January, *The Hindu*, 20 January 1963.

[37] Speech at Amritsar, 3 March, *National Herald*, 4 March 1963.

[38] 22 August 1963. Lok Sabha Debates, Third Series, Vol. 19, pp. 2,191–221.

clearly last in India for a long time to come and, while the private sector remained, it was sensible, while keeping it under control and within the ambit of official policy, to allow it to function effectively and goad the public sector into better performance. While profiting from Marx and other socialist thinkers of the past, the world should be seen as it was and socialism related to the actual needs and situation in the country. It was not so much a matter of definition as the acceptance of certain basic approaches:

> to produce the opportunities for every human being in India to rise materially, culturally and spiritually, and to create a sense of cooperative endeavour and cooperative living. We call this socialism as that, I think, is the nearest term which can embrace our objectives. Of course, socialism has a particular economic significance, but we use it in a larger sense even.[39]

To augment the supply of goods and keep an eye on their distribution so that there were no heavy accumulations on one side and shortages on the other formed for Nehru the most appropriate empirical way towards the evolution of a socialist society. Democracy and science had together made such a society logical; for democracy compelled socialism and science made socialism possible. A scientific way of utilizing national resources and the wide recourse to technology to secure an enormous increase of production would together enable the plenty which could be justly distributed; but if India did not accept science, she would once more be part of 'the dung-heaps of history'.[40]

Such a sustained effort at creating a socialist society would, of course, only be possible if the Indian people displayed the requisite character and nerve. A country's advance depended ultimately on the human qualities of its inhabitants, on their ability and capacity for hard work. 'All the rules in the world will not make you a sprint runner unless you have it in you.'[41] This was the ultimate justification of socialist objectives. The pursuit of them should give rise to a spirit of dynamism which was more than a mere urge to greater production. Industrialization did not mean merely the machine but the mind changing with the machine and fitting into the modern age. If science and industrialization forgot the wider aspects of social justice, the only ultimate aims of a civilized society, then planning and economic policy as a whole would have failed, for India, while transformed, would not be in tune with the spirit of the age and of her own people. The real test was the bettering of the lot of the masses struggling for a bare pittance; and to think only of improved living conditions and greater profits for a few would be to forget the real problem and lose all perspective.

In contrast, however, to the prime emphasis given by him in earlier years to

[39] Nehru to Chief Ministers, 21 May 1963.

[40] Speech at Lucknow, 12 May, *National Herald*, 13 May 1963.

[41] See full text of speech at the session of the All India Manufacturers' Organization, Delhi, 30 March 1963, P.I.B., Delhi.

industrialization, Nehru now accepted that agricultural production came first. 'I am all for industry, I am all for steel plants and this and that, but I do say agriculture is far more important than any industry.'[42] For Nehru this was tantamount to a confession of error. With development of agriculture alone the nation could not go forward; but he now realized that it would have to take priority over industrialization. The new strategy of economic development was 'first and essentially' agriculture, with foundations of an industrial structure being laid at the same time.[43]

Nehru urged the states to seek to grow more per acre rather than cultivate additional land;[44] but, for increased agricultural productivity in the long term, cooperative farming still seemed the answer. In addition Nehru thought of a volunteer corps to serve the nation as well as the village and for dealing with the 'very basic problem' in India, of drawing the rural population out of antiquated habits and ways of thought. It was ultimately a problem of changing the general outlook of the Indian people. Nehru still, with an optimism that seemed unconnected with reality, relied on community development and *panchayat raj*. He continued to regard them as among the most hopeful developments in the country, together constituting a revolutionary movement which, even if it had only yielded a fourth of the expected results, yet had proved 'an amazing success', strengthening India at the very roots and preparing millions of men and women to shoulder responsibility and to be self-reliant.[45] 'I have full confidence in its success, because I have full confidence in the Indian people.'[46] The threat to such success being excessive intervention by officials, he repeatedly urged them to exercise their leadership not to suppress others but to encourage them to develop powers of initiative in their own spheres. 'We must give power to the people, even though it leads us to hell. We will certainly come out of the hell if we get there'.[47] If self-government at the village level were fostered, democratic institutions of the upper structure would function better more easily.

In this effort to change the mental outlook of the masses, the spread of education was obviously important. Primary education was vital for this purpose just as technical education was crucial for economic growth and accelerated industrialization. So, whatever else might suffer for lack of resources because of the needs of defence, Nehru was anxious that education at all levels should not. The objectives should be both quantity and quality. Education was training not merely for employment but for the kind of civilized life for which they were

42 Address to the two houses of legislature of Andhra Pradesh, Hyderabad, 27 July 1963. A.I.R. Tapes.

43 22 August 1963. Lok Sabha Debates, Third Series, Vol. 19, pp. 2,191–221.

44 Nehru to Chief Ministers, 14 April 1963.

45 To Mohanlal Saxena, 5 February 1963, File 17(530)/62–66-P.M.S., No. 25A; speech in Lok Sabha, 27 February 1963, Debates, Third Series, Vol. 13, pp. 13,009–42; message to *Panchayat*, a journal published in Hyderabad, 16 March 1963.

46 Nehru's message to officials dealing with community development and *panchayat raj*, 22 June 1963.

47 Speech to the conference of Ministers of Community Development, Delhi, 1 August, *National Herald*, 2 August 1963.

planning.[48] 'In spite of my strong desire for the growth of our industry, I am convinced that it is better to do without some industrial growth than to do without adequate education at the base.'[49] Though it was a subject which, under the Constitution, fell within the purview of the states, Nehru instructed the Finance Minister to assist such of them as had fallen behind in implementing programmes of primary education,[50] for these were as important as any other aspect of defence or development and any attempt to reduce expenditure on education would ultimately weaken the country. Such slowing down had, in fact, taken place in some states because of the war crisis. 'That, I think, is a tragedy, nothing short of a tragedy. I do not wish to use milder terms because the whole progress of India depends on the educational apparatus working from the bottom to the top.'[51] It was as important as even soldiering, for nobody wanted an illiterate soldier.[52]

Besides the inclination to lower the priority for education, there was also, as Nehru was aware, a tendency to allow equitable distribution to be overshadowed by the drive towards greater production. Development appeared to be benefiting primarily those who already possessed the resources to take advantage of the new opportunities; and this resulted, to some extent, in making the rich richer while the poor continued to be as poor as before. Nehru believed that this was in a measure inevitable and, while every effort should be made to remove economic disparities, no step should be taken which might impede progress.[53] But obviously the drift to greater inequality would have to be checked. One could not take advantage of the willingness of the poor to wait for better days. 'I like big plants, I like the feel of machinery. I like the look of it. I feel it is essential for the planned development of the country. But we cannot ignore the fact that there are in India today areas where people do not get even clean drinking water.'[54] Indeed, the masses would not wait indefinitely and might, if little were done to improve their condition, turn away in ten or fifteen years from methods of peaceful change.

It was in the same mood of not allowing social justice to be forgotten in the effort to attain economic objectives that Nehru turned his mind again to the urgency of implementing land reforms. Wolf Ladejinsky of the Ford Foundation pressed him to take some steps immediately to stop or, at least, reduce to a trickle, the increase in the number of landless agricultural labourers by granting tenants ownership or security of tenure, insisting on reasonable rents and amending land legislation in the states to ensure that they benefited those for whom they were intended. Such steps were clearly imperative not only for

[48] Nehru to S.D. Sharma, 5 April 1963. File 17(447)61–70-P.M.S., No. 39A.

[49] Nehru to Chief Ministers, 14 April 1963.

[50] To Morarji Desai, 18 May 1963. File 40(143)/58–63-P.M.S. No. 46A.

[51] Address to the National Development Council, 8 November 1963. P.I.B., Delhi.

[52] Address to conference of Education Ministers, 10 November 1963. P.I.B., Delhi.

[53] Interventions at the seminar of Congress for Socialist Action, 4 and 5 April 1963, *Congress Forum*, Vol. 1, No. 4, May–June 1963; speech at the A.I.C.C., Jaipur, 4 November, *National Herald*, 5 November 1963.

[54] Speech at Delhi, 22 September, *National Herald*, 23 September 1963.

ethical reasons but to increase productivity.[55] Nehru was sufficiently impressed to call on his party men once again to implement the existing laws in the right spirit and work towards the principle that the land belonged to the tiller.[56] In contrast to Japan, where even small holdings produced high yields, in India 'the fact of the matter is that we, all of us who talk so much, have not quite got out of the old *zamindari* mentality. We think in terms of large acres, large areas . . .'[57] But Nehru's words were lost in the air, the Prime Minister being too busy and too tired to follow them through.

FOUR

Also as part of the policy of revitalizing the country in the wake of Chinese aggression, Nehru sought to correct the drift both in the party and in the administration. It was his belief that in the past the Congress had held India together despite many disruptive tendencies and that this was a task which it still had to shoulder. The Congress was, therefore, in his view, more than an organization for winning elections; it had to be an aggressive party fighting for its basic ideals in the most difficult circumstances. As some of the opposition parties were exploiting the national crisis of Chinese aggression for winning votes, the Congress should fight back against this 'perfectly disgusting' behaviour. But the minds of Congressmen were not clear and the leadership at the state and district levels had passed into the hands of those who had neither experience nor enthusiasm and were interested solely in self-aggrandisement. These defects and weaknesses appeared to Nehru more dangerous than even the Chinese aggression; for to him the Congress was vital to India's welfare. He strove to impress on his party men that it was for the Congress to keep India strong, united and on the right path; then no one could defeat her. Emphasis should be laid on the principles for which the party stood rather than on individuals, for even the most outstanding of them had grown with the Congress and if the party lost its stature their own stature would be reduced.[58]

Despite these exhortations, the ineffectiveness of the party machinery was revealed by the loss of three by-elections to severe critics of the Prime Minister. To Nehru this suggested a 'wind of stagnation' in the country, and he came round to the view that the Congress needed treatment if it were to flourish.[59] Defeat, complained one of the victorious candidates,[60] appeared to have gone to Nehru's head; for he was now more active than ever. Denouncing

[55] To Nehru, 11 July 1963. File 31(108)/60-63-P.M.S.

[56] Speech at the A.I.C.C., 4 November 1963. A.I.C.C. papers, Box 18. File OD II A. (1963).

[57] Address to the National Development Council, 8 November 1963. P.I.B., Delhi.

[58] Addresses to the Congress Parliamentary Party, 17 February and 8 May 1963, Tapes M-68/C (ii) (in Hindi), and M-70/C(i) respectively; speech at Kanpur, 12 May, *National Herald*, 13 May 1963.

[59] Press conference at Delhi, 15 June, *National Herald*, 16 June 1963.

[60] M.R. Masani in Ahmedabad, 15 June, *The Hindu*, 16 June 1963.

the opposition parties as inept, irresponsible – 'lately becoming positively indecent' – and reviving memories of fascism and Nazism,[61] Nehru thought it vital to reinvigorate the Congress, which was running out of steam. It was in this context that Kamaraj, the Chief Minister of Madras, proposed that he and some other Chief Ministers might resign and devote themselves to party work. Thereafter the scheme appears to have expanded under its own momentum to require the withdrawal from office of leading members of the central and state ministries; 'it was an idea', as Nehru described it, 'taking hold of the mind and growing by itself'.[62] It is unclear whether this was Kamaraj's own idea or he was acting as the instrument of others.[63] The Prime Minister frequently denied that he had inspired the Kamaraj Plan; he was not, he said,[64] a trickster. There is no reason to disbelieve him. But the scheme certainly suited Nehru at many levels. That the head of the most competent of the state Governments should have taken the lead and offered to resign gave the proposal credibility.[65] Not surprisingly, but uncharacteristically, Nehru was effusive in his appreciation of Kamaraj. 'His name has got engraved in the history of India.'[66] As if in reward, he secured Kamaraj's election as President of the Congress.

The Working Committee and the A.I.C.C. accepted Kamaraj's scheme with one proviso, exempting Nehru from its application. Thus the Prime Minister now had the resignations of all Ministers in his hands, and it was for him to select which should be accepted. He used the opportunity to send out many of those either reputed to be inefficient or rumoured to be corrupt or known to disagree with him on basic policies. Among the departing Ministers at the centre was Lal Bahadur Shastri, known for his personal loyalty to Nehru, industriousness and capacity to get on well with everybody; but he was, in a sense, a decoy elephant, leading out those whom Nehru wished to exclude without seeming to be animated by personal reasons. The Finance Minister, Morarji Desai, in particular, Nehru wished to see out of office. At this time there was no strong reason to believe that the succession to Nehru was imminent. 'This prime minister', Nehru told a press conference,[67] 'happens to be very much alive at the present moment.' But, as it happened, the Kamaraj Plan helped considerably to bar Desai from the Prime Ministership a few months later. So Nehru had, perhaps not too consciously, taken a hand in determining the course of Desai's destiny; and who, having seen Desai in the office of Prime Minister many years later, can say that Nehru was wrong?

Apart from the personal angle, the Kamaraj Plan, according to Nehru, had other advantages. Doing a rather odd thing in a dramatic way would not, as

[61] Speech at the A.I.C.C., 10 August, *The Hindu*, 12 August 1963.

[62] Address (in Hindi) to the Congress Parliamentary Party, 29 August 1963. Tape M-71/C(i).

[63] B. Patnaik, then Chief Minister of Orissa, has claimed the credit for the idea. M. Brecher, *Succession in India* (London, 1966), p. 16.

[64] Speech at Lucknow, 30 September, *National Herald*, 1 October 1963.

[65] Address to the Congress Parliamentary Party (in Hindi), 12 August 1963. Tape M-70/C(ii).

[66] Speech at the A.I.C.C., Jaipur, 3 November 1963. A.I.C.C. Papers, Box 18, No. OD-11(A)/1963.

[67] At Delhi, 9 October, *National Herald*, 10 October 1963.

Nehru acknowledged, change the whole surface of the world or reverse major trends in India; but it would wake people out of their slumber, make them think, get them out of ruts and generally help to create an atmosphere in which the right impulses were encouraged.[68] It checked the spreading obsession for office and patronage and strengthened the organization of the Congress Party. It was a step in the Gandhian tradition, a call to Congressmen not only to give up their jobs but to move away from wrong-doing. The removal of so much experienced talent from administration was, Nehru said politely, a severe loss, 'like losing one's right arm';[69] but the long-term benefits would offset this. The Plan was intended to restore the balance between the party and the Government, the organization and the administration, to the advantage of both.

It would seem, however, that only Krishna Menon took this aspect of the Kamaraj Plan seriously and offered to speak and work for the Congress. 'It is the first time in forty-five years or more that I am near unwanted and rendered functionless.'[70] But otherwise everybody else regarded it as no more than a move in the game of jockeying for power. Desai, sore at losing office, retaliated by bringing down the Congress ministry in Gujarat; and Nehru's retort was to appoint the displaced Chief Minister as High Commissioner in London. To Nehru it was all to the good that suppressed feelings had come out on the surface, hidden things had emerged in the open, and the curtain had been raised.[71] In the short term it was an effective act of political spring-cleaning; but in the long run it weakened the basis of Nehru's way of running the Congress Party. In place of the authority of the Prime Minister and his Cabinet colleagues in the party both at the centre and in the states, it gave influence to men prominent in the organization of the party, brought them from the states to Delhi and weakened the central Government.[72] This was to give rise to much trouble and confusion in the years after Nehru.

FIVE

In the administration, the major problem was prevalence of corruption. It had come increasingly to the fore at every level. There could obviously be no two opinions about the need to combat and root out corruption; but Nehru continued to think that the opposition exaggerated the extent of its prevalence. If he made such assertions as 'broadly speaking, our administration is

[68] Speech on the Kamaraj Plan at the A.I.C.C., 10 August, *A.I.C.C. Economic Review*, 1 September 1963; address to the Congress Parliamentary Party, 12 August 1963. Tape M-70/C(ii).

[69] Address (in Hindi) to the Congress Parliamentary Party, 29 August 1963. Tape M-71/C(i).

[70] To Nehru, 12 August 1963. Krishna Menon Papers, N.M.M.L.

[71] Speech at Lucknow, 29 September, *National Herald*, 30 September 1963.

[72] R. Kothari, 'Political Consensus in India', *Economic and Political Weekly*, 11 October 1969.

one of the least corrupt of the administrations of the world',[73] it was because he feared that, in the effort to trace out and check corrupt activities, character assassination, to which Indians were prone, might be encouraged. 'Our politics are gradually sinking into the mire with most people charging each other with corruption and other offences. This indicates a mind which is not at all admirable.'[74] But the balance between suppression of corruption and discouragement of calumny was not easy to strike in practice. Nehru repeatedly affirmed that, while vague charges were not helpful and difficult to investigate, he was always prepared to have specific cases of corruption and abuse of power examined.[75] How this was to be done in the case of Ministers and politicians was a 'tremendous headache to all of us'.[76] The Swedish institution of an 'ombudsman' he found attractive but feared that in a large country like India it might develop in a parallel bureaucracy.[77] So he persisted with the method of referring any complaint to the person accused and, if the reply suggested that there was a case for a *prima facie* inquiry, to start private inquiries and, on the basis of the reports of such inquiries, to decide whether any further investigation was required. This was obviously a clumsy way of handling charges and many who were guilty must have easily slipped through the net. Nehru knew this and recognized the need for a regular process of inquiry to make corruption less easy and widespread; but, in his time, no machinery was set up. This failure to proceed to the root of the problem suggests that Nehru, with no interest in money himself, did not attach sufficient importance to the tracking down and punishment of corruption among politicians. Efficiency in work or radicalism in outlook more than offset to him a tendency on a Minister's part to be lax in financial matters or to enable friends to profit by his official connections.

Two prominent instances in the course of 1963 make clear Nehru's inner difficulties in dealing with colleagues for whom he had high regard but whose image was clearly tarnished. Keshav Dev Malaviya had done much, as a Minister in the central Government, to develop oil prospecting in India without allowing foreign companies to dominate the field. Now it became known that he had requested a private firm to assist a Congress candidate in the elections. The sum involved was relatively small and Nehru believed that the firm had derived no kind of benefit, direct or indirect, in return for such assistance.[78] But the issue could not be shirked. Nehru asked a judge of the Supreme Court to conduct a private inquiry and, when the *prima facie* opinion was unfavourable to Malaviya on two out of six counts, reluctantly accepted Malaviya's resignation. So, Nehru, acting solely on his own, took the right

[73] 2 May 1962. Lok Sabha Debates, Third Series, Vol. 2, pp. 2,058–82.

[74] Nehru to A.M. Tariq, 30 June 1963.

[75] For example, Nehru to H.C. Mathur, 5 May 1962.

[76] Speech in the Lok Sabha, 22 August 1963. Debates, Third Series, Vol. 19, pp. 2,191–221.

[77] To M.C. Chagla, 31 July 1959; speech at the A.I.C.C., 3 November 1963. A.I.C.C. papers, Box 18. OD-11(A)/1963.

[78] To K.S. Ramanujan, 9 April 1963.

step; but he was unhappy about it for he was convinced of Malaviya's honesty and probity.[79] The procedure followed also was not such as to inspire confidence in either the complainants or the accused. The judge conducted the inquiry in camera, did not call many of the witnesses or allow any lawyers to be present; nor was his report published. Malaviya could well have argued that he had not had a fair and full hearing and it was a case of the Prime Minister asserting his personal authority to satisfy public opinion even though he was not convinced that the Minister was tainted. But Malaviya was too loyal to protest.

Even more awkward to Nehru was the renewal of the much more serious and extensive charges of corruption against the Chief Minister of the Punjab, Pratap Singh Kairon. Nehru did not tire of expressing his regard for Kairon, 'whose chief qualities, if I may emphasize them, are his fearlessness and his close contacts with the people of the Punjab. He appears to have grown out of the masses of the Punjab, and he is in tune with them; hence his popularity with them . . . '[80] Administrative success, in other words, meant more to Nehru than suspected corruption. The nearest Nehru came to taking notice of Kairon's connivance at shady activities was to warn him privately that there did appear to be a belief, held even by many of his staunch supporters, that his son exploited his position and sometimes used undesirable methods.[81] But in public Nehru maintained his stance of supporting the Chief Minister.

When a deputation of some members of the opposition presented a detailed memorandum of charges against Kairon to the President and a majority on a bench of the Supreme Court indicted Kairon for harassing an official, Nehru made clear his disinclination to take action for reasons wholly disconnected with the issues: 'the Punjab Government is the topmost in India, the Punjab State is the topmost in India'.[82] Evading the censure of the Supreme Court with the quibbles that Kairon had not been made a party to the case and the reference to him was not basic to the judgment, asserting that the charges of corruption had often as much 'relation to the Punjab as they had to the moon', and contending that a son's misdeeds, if any, should not be held against the father's administration, Nehru, after consulting Krishna Menon, decided that he would not advise Kairon to resign. The Punjab was a border province which was quiet and progressing remarkably and the state should not be unsettled at a time of national emergency. Kairon had shown great qualities of leadership and was popular with the armed services, which had a predominant Punjabi element. But Nehru did reluctantly agree to a judicial inquiry into all the charges – not, as in the case of Malaviya, an informal one, but a regular commission which would

[79] Nehru to H.N. Mukherji, 16 August 1963.
[80] Message for the Kairon Abhinandan Granth (Birthday Book), 25 June 1963.
[81] Nehru to P.S. Kairon, 18 August 1963.
[82] 6 September 1963. Rajya Sabha Debates, Vol. 44, pp. 3,149–58.

present a report; and, pending its receipt, Kairon was allowed to continue in office.[83] The report was not received before Nehru's death.

SIX

Defence and development, party reform and concern at corruption in the administration, all important in themselves, were yet but aspects of the wider problem of the emotional integration of the Indian people, towards the achievement of which the Chinese action had given such a fillip. If advantage were not taken of this, then indeed the country would have cause to regard the events of 1962 as a permanent setback. 'What is even success on the battle-front worth if we fail inwardly? We have too many weaknesses and disruptive forces at work.'[84] 20 October 1963, the anniversary of the massive Chinese attacks a year earlier, was designated National Solidarity Day, 'to draw lessons', as Nehru said, 'from India's failures' and convert weaknesses into strength. India had stood basically united in the crisis of 1962 but, when the Chinese danger seemed to recede, her people had gone back to their petty conflicts. Solidarity of mind and heart was required every day to meet not only possible threats from outside but 'the real menace' of poverty. Indians, while retaining the rich variety of their culture, should also function like a large family.[85]

In this connection, NEFA, the scene of Chinese incursions, was obviously of urgent concern. On the whole, the local inhabitants had refused to collaborate with the enemy and remained loyal to India; and Nehru saw in this proof of the success of India's efforts at integration.[86] But unrest in Nagaland continued. To their credit, the hostiles had remained quiet during the crisis of the Chinese invasion, when the armed forces had to be withdrawn; but the early months of 1963 saw a recrudescence of rebel activity. Bertrand Russell conveyed to Nehru a message from Phizo that he was willing to meet the Prime Minister in Delhi to discuss methods of conciliation;[87] and then Michael Scott brought Phizo's proposal for a cease-fire. This was rejected as an attempt to legitimize Phizo's position; and the Naga Government discouraged Scott's mediation or a visit by him to Nagaland. Nor was the Prime Minister willing to consider a meeting with Phizo till law and order had been restored in

[83] Nehru to the President, 1 September 1963; address (in Hindi) to the Congress Parliamentary Party, 29 September 1963, Tapes M-71/C (i) and (ii); press conference at Delhi, 9 October, *National Herald*, 10 October 1963; Nehru to Krishna Menon, 12 October 1963, Krishna Menon Papers, File 2 (official); note of the Prime Minister to the President, 25 October, published in *The Hindu*, 30 October 1963.

[84] Nehru to Chief Ministers, 21 May 1963.

[85] Broadcast, 19 October, *National Herald*, 20 October 1963; speech at Delhi, 20 October 1963. P.I.B., Delhi.

[86] 29 March 1963. Lok Sabha Debates, Third Series, Vol. 16, pp. 7,065–79.

[87] B. Russell to Nehru, 12 February 1963.

Nagaland.[88] This was later pruned down to Phizo having talks with the Government of Nagaland if he instructed his followers to abjure force.[89]

A restoration of law and order, however, was not found easy to achieve. The hostiles secured arms from East Bengal and carried out sporadic ambushes mainly to disorganize the elections scheduled to be held in the spring of 1964.[90] Despite these disruptive efforts, the elections were conducted; and thereafter a parliamentary secretary to the Prime Minister met Phizo in London and the Government of India, at the request of the Naga authorities, offered a safe-conduct to Phizo if he wished to come to India to talk with the Naga Government about the restoration of peace within the existing constitutional arrangements. Considering that Phizo was wanted for murder, this offer constituted a major concession; but Phizo was not prepared to take advantage of it and appealed to Pakistan for support. Then, in another effort to restore peace to the area, Nehru approved of a mission consisting of Jayaprakash Narayan, B.P. Chaliha, the Chief Minister of Assam, and Michael Scott. They went to Nagaland and signed a preliminary agreement a few days before Nehru's death in May 1964. Part of Nehru's general effort to leave as few problems as possible for his successor, the despatch of the mission and its initial success served to improve the atmosphere in Nagaland and make permanent solutions on the basis of firm principle easier.

In other parts of India, the question of language again came to prominence as a major barrier to national solidarity. Though the Constitution had laid down that, by a phased programme over fifteen years, Hindi should be established as the official language of the Union, in 1959 Nehru had promised that there would be no imposition and English would remain an associate, additional language for an indefinite period. The final decision for the replacement of Hindi would rest with those sections of the people who did not know Hindi.[91] In accordance with this assurance, permissive legislation was enacted in 1963. The Official Languages Act provided that English 'may' continue to be used after 1965, in addition to Hindi, for the official purposes of the Union and in Parliament. The critics of Hindi were not satisfied and would have preferred a mandatory recognition of the continued use of English. Rajagopalachari also desired a statutory stipulation that the use of English should only be given up if unanimously sought by the legislatures of the non-Hindi states.[92] He publicly criticized the Prime Minister for allowing his sense of fairness to be weakened by politics and

[88] Nehru in the Lok Sabha, 11 April 1963, Debates, Third Series, Vol. 16, pp. 9,180–8, and in the Rajya Sabha, 30 April 1963, Debates, Vol. 43, pp. 1,324–7: M. Scott's statement in Delhi, 12 April 1963.

[89] Nehru's answers in the Rajya Sabha, 10 December 1963, Debates, Vol. 45, pp. 2,736–9.

[90] Nehru's answers in the Lok Sabha, 17 December 1963, Debates, Third Series, Vol. 24, pp. 5,284–93.

[91] Nehru in the Lok Sabha, 7 August 1959, Debates, Second Series, Vol. 32, pp. 1,287–305; S.K. Agrawala, 'Jawaharlal Nehru and the Language Problem', *Journal of the Indian Law Institute*, 1977, pp. 44–67.

[92] Rajagopalachari to Nehru, 18 April 1953.

charged the Act with imposing Hindi in an 'insidious, slow and gradual' manner.[93]

To Nehru an explicit commitment to continue English seemed unnecessary and even constitutionally improper; but no Government worthy of their salt were going to budge an inch from the assurance for which the Act had cleared the way. Indeed, apart from the assurance, the imposition of Hindi seemed to Nehru impossible, because it would raise such problems and difficulties that no Government could conceivably want to secure the spread of Hindi by force. The promotion of Hindi was part of the effort of building the nation, and the life of a nation was much longer than one or two generations. So Hindi could afford to wait. Its use was spreading but any attempt at enforcement would only lead to resistance. On the other hand, to make English the official language 'more or less for ever' was harmful psychologically for it perpetuated a barrier between the English-knowing elite and the masses. It was only through the Indian languages, which had deep roots in the minds and hearts of the people, that there could be a national awakening. So Nehru favoured the functional compromise incorporated in the Act. It was as liberal an arrangement as possible, suppressing no language and enabling English to continue as a link with the outside world and as a vitalizer of the Indian languages till such time as they were ready to take over.[94] To do more, and lay down that English would be permanently the official and national language, was 'abominable and intolerable'.[95] But the problem of language was not settled by Nehru's compromise and was to plague Nehru's successor.

SEVEN

In preparing for a long phase of Chinese hostility, the domestic situation and the military requirements had to be placed in a world context. On the face of it there was no change in India's foreign policy, which Nehru claimed had proved, by and large, 'a right one, a good one and a successful one'.[96] This had also been helped by China increasingly isolating herself. But the experience of large-scale Chinese aggression and the consequent dependence on military assistance from the United States made Nehru more willing than at any time before to fit India into the pattern of American policy. After the cease-fire, his Government suggested an agreement whereby, if the Chinese came back, India would send her tactical aircraft into combat and the United States would

[93] Speech at Madurai, 12 May, *The Hindu*, 14 May 1963.

[94] Addresses to the Congress Parliamentary Party, 17 February and 19 April 1963, tapes M-68/C(ii) and M-70/C; Nehru to C. Rajagopalachari, 21 April 1963; speeches in the Lok Sabha, 24 April 1963, Debates, Third Series, Vol. 17, pp. 11,631–58, and in the Rajya Sabha, 4 May 1963, Debates, Vol. 42, pp. 2,088–102.

[95] Speech at Madras, 12 June, *National Herald*, 13 June 1963.

[96] 3 September 1963. Rajya Sabha Debates, Vol. 44, pp. 2,601–29.

undertake the defence of Indian cities; airstrips and radar facilities for this purpose would have been prepared by India. Galbraith was eager to take this opportunity 'by the ears',[97] but the Department of State was less forthcoming. It wished to make no commitment and leave it to the Commonwealth to take the lead. All that was immediately done was to send a military mission to India. When, a few weeks later, Kennedy and Macmillan met at Nassau, the British were no more responsive.

So, from the viewpoint of the Western Powers, an opportunity to utilize the Chinese action to bind India firmly to the Western bloc was thrown away. The United States was unwilling to do any more than provide immediate military assistance worth 60 million dollars and help with aircraft and radar. India's request for military assistance worth 500 million dollars spread out over five years was by no means exorbitant, considering that the United States had already provided Pakistan with military assistance worth over 800 million dollars. Chester Bowles, appointed once again as Ambassador to India in succession to Galbraith, urged that the request be considered favourably and India built up, in place of Pakistan, as the predominant partner of the United States in South Asia. Kennedy agreed; but the Departments of State and Defence prevailed on him not to annoy Pakistan. Not only was India offered but half of what she had sought but pressure was put on her to make concessions to Pakistan on Kashmir.[98]

Nehru, on his part, now played down suggestions of an American 'air umbrella'. Apart from the fact that, in case of an air attack by China, much damage would have been done before the air force of the United States came into operation, it would make the Indian people complacent and dependent on others. Such a renouncement of self-reliance meant 'permanent cold feet', a loss of moral fibre and a failure of independence and of every basic value for which India had stood since the time of Gandhi; and this would be a far greater defeat than any reverse on the battlefield. If a country's backbone were broken, not all the arms in the world would do her much good; but if the national spirit held, even without arms life could be made hell for any enemy who came into India. He, therefore, laid stress on the United States helping India to defend herself, and insisted that India still held to non-alignment, which was an attribute of sovereignty. It was one thing to secure help from friendly countries; it was quite another to hand over the nation's defence, and all that this implied, to powerful military blocs. Alignment meant acceptance of decisions taken by others and carried with it the practical drawback of throwing away the advantages which accrued to India from Sino-Soviet differences. Kardelj of Yugoslavia came to Delhi in December and asserted that these differences were irreconcilable.[99] Khrushchev later spoke of China's 'madness' in attacking India and, while urging a settlement between India and

[97] 1 December 1962. *Ambassador's Journal* (London, 1969), pp. 504–5.
[98] C. Bowles, *Promises to Keep* (Indian edn, 1972), pp. 438–40.
[99] A.Z. Rubinstein, *Yugoslavia and the Nonaligned World* (Princeton, 1970), p. 298.

China, assured India that the Soviet Government would never support China's aggressive policy against India.[100] The Soviet authorities, in other words, had been going out of their way to show their friendly feelings to India; and for India to spurn this friendship would be folly.[101] Only the Swatantra Party, 'a mixture of the rottenest ideas imaginable',[102] favoured such a step.

Responsible opinion in even the United States and Britain saw advantage, both in the context of the immediate crisis and from the viewpoint of world peace, in India adhering to the concepts of non-alignment. But Kennedy was still hopeful of closer ties with India. He believed that the preservation of Indian democracy and freedom against the onslaught of Chinese communism was the most important problem facing the world. India should be supported in both defence and development so that she could stand up to China militarily, politically and ideologically, for her security and independence were vital to the survival of the freedom of the states of Asia.[103] He informed Macmillan that the United States had better perhaps 'go it alone' if Britain were unwilling to be involved,[104] and he inquired from Krishnamachari, on a visit to Washington in May, if India would be able to accept, from a political viewpoint, a visit of American and Commonwealth aircraft on familiarization and training exercises. They would cooperate with the Indian air force on the basis of mobile radar and communication facilities which would be left behind and later replaced by more permanent installations. Krishnamachari assured him that there would be no objection if the training of Indian pilots and technicians were given emphasis.[105] Agreement was reached with the United States and Britain for the supply of radar and related communications equipment, for the training of Indian technicians to man these installations and for joint training exercises in air defence.[106] Such exercises took place in November; the United States would have preferred a second round but Nehru was unwilling.[107] Indeed, he informed Parliament categorically that there was no question of any foreign ships, troops or aircraft participating in the defence of the country. India would be defended only by her own armed services and people.[108] Kennedy was prepared also to provide more military assistance, but was assassinated four days before the meeting of the National Security Council convened to reconsider military assistance to India; and then Lyndon

[100] Nehru's note on S.A. Dange's account of his visit to the Soviet Union, 11 January 1963; record of Khrushchev's talks with Mrs Indira Gandhi at the Kremlin, 27 July 1963.

[101] Nehru to Chief Ministers, 1 January 1963; address to Congress Parliamentary Party, 27 January 1963, Tape 68 (i); speech in the Rajya Sabha, 25 February 1963, Debates, Vol. 42, pp. 915–42; Nehru to Thimma Reddy, 1 March 1963; speech in the Lok Sabha, 19 March 1963, Debates, Third Series, Vol. 15, pp. 4,814–48; speech at the A.I.C.C., 6 April 1963, A.I.C.C. papers Box 5, F. No. 0D9(i)/1963.

[102] Speech at the A.I.C.C., Delhi, 6 April, *National Herald*, 7 April 1963.

[103] Lester Pearson's report of conversations with Kennedy, recorded by M.J. Desai in Ottawa, 12 May 1963.

[104] H. Macmillan, *At the End of the Day* (London, 1973), pp. 234–5.

[105] M.J. Desai's record of talks between Kennedy and Krishnamachari in Washington, 22 May 1963.

[106] Nehru's statement in Lok Sabha, 19 August 1963. Debates, Third Series, Vol. 19, pp. 1,213–18.

[107] Despatch from Delhi in *Chicago Daily News*, 23 November 1963.

[108] Statement in the Rajya Sabha, 21 December 1963. Debates, Vol. 45, pp. 4,510–16.

Johnson's Government, guided by the Departments of State and Defence, procrastinated.[109]

Despite such inadequate military response from the United States, Nehru sought to strengthen political ties between the two countries, even though his hands were tied to some extent by the need to maintain a public posture of non-alignment. Recognizing publicly that relations with the United States had seldom been so close and cordial, he committed India to doing all she could to support the efforts of the United States to defend the countries of South-East Asia if attacked by China; but about this even Kennedy was sceptical.[110] Nehru also allowed his Government to be persuaded to sign an agreement whereby, in return for the United States providing a high-powered radio transmitter, the Voice of America would be permitted to relay its broadcasts from India to South-East Asia for three hours every day. When the announcement of this agreement was received with sharp criticism in India, Nehru looked, for the first time, at the full text of the agreement and advised the Cabinet, which was also considering the matter for the first time, to reject the agreement as being counter to India's basic policies.[111] 'Mistakes occur even in the best regulated families.'[112]

At about the same time, Nehru also, in face of opposition in the United States Congress and from a desire to avoid embarrassment to Kennedy, withdrew the request for assistance for setting up a steel plant at Bokaro.[113] Kennedy acknowledged this with a firm commitment: 'Rest assured that, whatever the ups and downs, the United States continues to stand squarely behind the development and security of India.'[114] The general belief that the decisions to jettison the Voice of America agreement and withdraw the request for assistance for Bokaro marked clear reassertions by India of the principles of non-alignment was obviously not shared by the Governments of India and the United States; for simultaneously, unknown to the people, in two matters of far greater consequence Nehru had moved beyond statements of intent to positive support for clandestine aspects of American policy. Facilities were granted to U-2 planes to land and refuel in India on their way into Tibetan airspace.[115] Nehru also permitted the United States, in the early months of 1964, to attempt to install a remote sensing device operated by a nuclear battery near the peak of Nanda Devi, in the Hima-

[109] Bowles, *Promises to Keep*, pp. 481–3; S. Mansingh, 'India and the United States: What Price Partnership?', *Towson State Journal of International Affairs*, Spring 1979.

[110] J. Nehru, 'Changing India', *Foreign Affairs*, April 1963; Bowles, *Promises to Keep*, pp. 475–6; J.K. Galbraith, *A Life in Our Times* (London, 1981), pp. 441–2.

[111] M. Brecher, 'India's Decisions on the Voice of America; a Study in Irresolution', *Asian Survey*, July 1974, pp. 637-50; Nehru to A.N. Vidyalankar, 7 August 1963; Nehru's statement in Lok Sabha, 14 August 1963, Debates, Third Series, Vol. 19, pp. 410–11.

[112] Press conference at Delhi, 9 October, *National Herald*, 10 October 1963.

[113] Nehru to J.F. Kennedy, 28 August 1963.

[114] Kennedy to Nehru, 5 September 1963.

[115] *The Times*, 22 May 1978.

layas, to secure information about the development of missiles by China.[116] In short, Nehru was so convinced of continued Chinese hostility and of India's dependence on the support of the United States that he was willing to involve India in activities which were unthinkable but a few months before.

EIGHT

India's relations with the United States had a close bearing on her relations with Pakistan. In the autumn of 1962, Ayub probably attached more importance to his grand strategy of applying pressure on India through better relations with China and influence with the United States than to bilateral discussions. On his part, Nehru restated in public India's view that no decision based on religion could be taken regarding Kashmir for it would make untenable the position of the large number of Muslims in India and of the remaining Hindus in Pakistan; nor was there any longer room for holding a plebiscite.[117]

When the Chinese launched their major attacks in October 1962, the press in Pakistan made no secret of its bias against India. Nehru was criticized for not acceding to China's terms and accused of pursuing 'expansionist and atavistic policies'.[118] Some leading personalities also spoke of the need to take advantage of the situation. Reports were prevalent about an agreement between Pakistan and China, and Pakistan's ambitions were now believed to extend beyond Kashmir. Yet the United States persuaded Nehru to authorize them to inform Ayub that he would respond immediately to assurances that there would be no threat from Pakistan;[119] and Ayub did not exploit the occasion to attack India even though he would give no assurance to this effect.[120] To Nehru he pointed out the dangers of 'induction of new war potential' into the sub-continent and the need to resolve the outstanding disputes between India and Pakistan.[121] Kennedy wrote to him as well as Nehru inviting them to 'bury the hatchet' and seek a settlement on Kashmir. Nehru in turn wrote to Ayub that, whatever the differences between India and Pakistan, Chinese expansionism was a matter of common concern; and he added the assurance that the assistance given by friendly countries would be utilized solely in resistance to Chinese aggression. 'The idea of any conflict with Pakistan is one which is repugnant to us, and we on our part will never

116 Statement of Morarji Desai, Prime Minister, in the Lok Sabha, 17 April 1978. Debates, Sixth Series, Vol. 13, pp. 307–17.

117 Press conferences at London, 20 September, and at Lagos, 26 September 1962, *National Herald*, 21 and 27 September 1962 respectively.

118 Editorial in *Dawn* (Karachi), 27 October 1962.

119 Galbraith, *Ambassador's Journal*, p. 442.

120 Ayub to Kennedy, 5 November 1962. M. Ayub Khan, *Friends not Masters* (Oxford, 1967), pp. 140–3.

121 Ayub's letter to Nehru, delivered on 6 November 1962.

initiate it. I am convinced that the future of India and Pakistan lies in their friendship and cooperation for the benefit of both.'[122] Then, after the cease-fire, Harriman and Sandys, shuttling between Delhi and Rawalpindi, secured from Nehru and Ayub agreement to start talks to reach an honourable and equitable settlement on the outstanding differences on Kashmir and other related matters.[123] 'This is an historic moment,' Nehru is said to have remarked.[124] A few hours later, under pressure from Sandys, Nehru added that no formula for settlement had been arrived at, nor were there any preconditions or restrictions on the talks.[125]

Dependent on the United States and Britain for military assistance, India could not refuse to talk to Pakistan. Harriman and Sandys argued that public opinion in their countries would only favour generous aid to India if it were linked with a settlement on Kashmir; and they claimed to fear the possibility of Ayub being replaced by 'wilder men' who would draw closer to China. But Nehru, though searching genuinely for a solution on Kashmir,[126] let it be known that he had no great hopes of the talks being successful. Kashmir was not the cause but the result of Pakistan's ill-will and Nehru believed that, even if a settlement on Kashmir were reached, it would be followed by further demands. But no such settlement seemed possible. A plebiscite was at this time out of the question because it would revive communal feelings; and India could not consider any settlement on Kashmir which directly impeded her handling of Chinese aggression.[127] This meant that no concession was feasible in the valley, through which lay the lines of communication to Ladakh. So India could consider neither a transfer of the valley to Pakistan, nor an independent valley guaranteed by the great powers nor any kind of supervision of the valley by the United Nations. Pakistan was adopting an attitude of blackmail and the Western Powers, perhaps unknowingly, were to some extent parties to this. Only if they contained such blackmail by diplomatic action could the talks have any chance of success.[128]

So India's position was declared to be firm and no pressure tactics would lead her to yield more than rectification of the cease-fire line and more trade and wider contacts between Kashmir and Pakistan. Nor did the Ayub Government provide India with incentives to consider major concessions. When the first round of talks between the Ministers of India and Pakistan was due to start; it was announced that China and Pakistan had reached agreement in principle on the location and alignment of the boundary 'actually existing' between the two countries. They hoped to sign a boundary agreement on this

[122] Nehru to Ayub, 11 November 1962, published in *National Herald*, 3 December 1962.

[123] 30 November 1962.

[124] Duncan Sandys in *The Times*, 2 September 1969.

[125] Statement in the Lok Sabha, 30 November 1962, Debates, Third Series, Vol. 10, pp. 3,973–8; remarks to press at Delhi, 1 December, *National Herald*, 2 December 1962.

[126] Galbraith after a long talk with Nehru, 9 December 1962. *Ambassador's Journal*, p. 517.

[127] Television interview in London, 13 December 1962; interview with Kingsley Martin, *New Statesman*, 22 December 1962.

[128] Nehru to Kennedy 8 December 1962; Nehru's interview in *Washington Post*, 19 December 1962.

26 In a forward area on the eastern sector, December 1962

27 *Above left* Ahmedabad, 6 November 1963
28 *Above right* With Sheikh Abdullah, Delhi, April 1964

29 In Dehra Dun with Indira Gandhi, 26 May 1964

basis as soon as possible; but it would be a provisional agreement, to be replaced by a final treaty after the Kashmir problem had been settled.[129] It was a contemptuous rejection of Nehru's suggestion that all India wanted from Pakistan was that she should not support China while India was having trouble with China.[130]

This was no auspicious start, but India did not use it as an excuse for breaking off the talks. The fact that talks were held was in itself of some advantage in lowering the barriers of suspicion and distrust; but otherwise there was no achievement. India was prepared to discuss any issue that was raised by Pakistan, but on Kashmir was willing to go no further than modifying the cease-fire line to give Pakistan an extra 1,500 square miles and to treat the new alignment as the international boundary. This, of course, did not satisfy Pakistan, whose appetite had grown in the changed circumstances. Apart from her leverage with the United States and her new ties with China, she was seeking a better relationship with the Soviet Union;[131] and India seemed in a much weaker position than ever before. As Zulfikar Bhutto, the leader of the Pakistan delegation and the rising star in his country's politics, remarked to the Indian side, 'You are a defeated nation, don't you see?'[132] The Foreign Secretary of Pakistan went on a lengthy tour of European countries urging them not to grant military assistance to India as she was building up her army, utilizing the excuse of Chinese aggression in order to be better prepared to fight Pakistan.

Although Nehru had ruled out a plebiscite or any other approach which gave emphasis to the communal element,[133] in January Ayub, after accusing Nehru and his colleagues of being tricky and short-sighted, clever in making a deal but lacking in statesmanship and large-heartedness,[134] demanded a commitment to hold a plebiscite in Kashmir within a year. Galbraith agreed with the Indian position that a plebiscite was no longer feasible; but the United States and Britain asked India what she was prepared to give Pakistan in the valley. Kennedy suggested that, to refute Pakistan's allegations that India was not serious about the talks, India make some public gesture placing a settlement on Kashmir and reconciliation with Pakistan in the context of the long-term need of the sub-continent for security and economic development. But he thought it even more important that India bring forward some concrete proposals which took account of Pakistan's viewpoint. As Ayub was weaker than Nehru and Pakistan a lesser power than India, the first step should come from India. If the Kashmir issue was settled, India's role on the world stage

129 26 December 1962.

130 Nehru's interview with Japanese correspondents, 22 December, *National Herald*, 23 December 1962.

131 Nehru's note to Foreign Secretary about conversation with Soviet chargé d'affaires, 27 November 1962.

132 Y.D. Gundevia, 'Outside the Archives' (unpublished).

133 Statement at press conference, 31 December 1962, *National Herald*, 1 January 1963.

134 Television interview in New York, 10 January, *The Hindu*, 12 January 1963.

would gain new perspectives and 'a painful diversion' complicating India's relations with the United States in a way disadvantageous to both countries would be removed.[135]

Galbraith believed that there was a fair chance of India responding and giving Pakistan some position in the valley.[136] But, as the climate appeared to be growing more favourable to Pakistan, at the session in Karachi in February 1963, Bhutto asked for the transfer to Pakistan of the whole state of Kashmir barring a small area on the south-eastern border with Himachal Pradesh, which was left to India, 'in a forgotten moment of generosity.'[137] It was now Nehru's turn to complain that Pakistan was not wholly serious and not anxious to come to an agreement.[138] The talks had obviously lost all meaning and Pakistan probably hoped that India would break them off. Had this happened, a military attack by Pakistan on India to synchronize with a renewal of Chinese aggression could not be ruled out.[139] A visit by Bhutto to Beijing and the conclusion of a boundary agreement between China and Pakistan lent strength to this surmise. But India was shrewd enough not to provide the occasion for joint aggression and continued to combine firmness with patience. Pakistan's 'lack of good intentions' suggested caution, and there could be no settlement at the cost of principles.[140] Yet, though unwilling to accede to Kennedy's suggestion that Pakistan be given 'a substantial portion' in the valley,[141] India kept the meandering talks alive. As the next round was to be in Calcutta when, apart from Kashmir, the problems of East Bengal would be discussed, Nehru advised the Assam Government not to resume the deportation of Pakistani infiltrators.[142]

However, the pitch was queered by the British, who came up suddenly with a proposal for internationalization of the valley – a suggestion which even the Americans saw to be impractical, as it played into the hands of the Chinese, who would work on any Asian and African powers concerned. But the proposal helped to make Pakistan even more intransigent and the talks 'just barely avoided being ridiculous'.[143] The problem, as Nehru saw it, was not that of Kashmir but of Pakistan's basic attitudes; even if there were a settlement on Kashmir, as long as these attitudes continued, differences between India and Pakistan would develop in some other shape. The almost complete lining up of Pakistan with China and the incidents which occurred almost daily on Pakistan's borders with India seemed to Nehru to

[135] Kennedy to Nehru, 7 February 1963.

[136] See Galbraith's record of his impressions, 22 January and, after interview with Nehru, 6 February 1963. *Ambassador's Journal*, pp. 538 and 543 respectively.

[137] Nehru's statement in the Rajya Sabha, 13 August 1963. Debates, Vol. 44, pp. 95–104.

[138] Nehru to Kennedy, 16 February 1963.

[139] Nehru to B.K. Nehru, 8 March 1963.

[140] Speeches at Hanumangarh, 1 March, and Amritsar, 3 March, *National Herald*, 2 and 4 March 1963.

[141] Kennedy to Nehru, 9 March 1963.

[142] To B.P. Chaliha, Chief Minister of Assam, 16 March 1963.

[143] Galbraith, 15 March 1963. *Ambassador's Journal*, p. 556.

corroborate this analysis.[144] But the Western Powers would not agree, and the proposals given by them in April, first to Pakistan, and then, belatedly, to India, dashed whatever hope there might have been of Pakistan toning down her demands. It was suggested that Pakistan as well as India should have, in the phrase used earlier by Kennedy, a 'substantial portion' in the valley with freedom of access to civilians and armies of both sides, and that the Indus waters treaty be reopened in order to provide Pakistan with facilities on the Chenab river for the storage of water. These proposals, though 'totally unacceptable'[145] to India, encouraged Pakistan to demand that, the valley being indivisible, it be transferred to her as a whole; temporary arrangements, for six to twelve months, would be made for an Indian presence in the valley and Ladakh for handling the 'trouble' with China. While India shared the view that the valley was, 'economically and psychologically',[146] a unit which could not be partitioned, she refused to consider its transfer to Pakistan. Indeed, instead of urging India to make concessions to Pakistan, logic would suggest that Pakistan be asked to permit a substantial Indian presence in that part of Kashmir occupied by Pakistan, particularly as the Chinese, towards whom Pakistan was making such demonstrations of friendship, were poised on that border and a pincer movement against India from the north and the west could start at any time. Intervention by third powers, if quiet, unobtrusive and objective, might have been helpful; but public and semi-public efforts at pressure had only worsened the situation. 'I am convinced that these ill-considered and ill-conceived initiatives, however well-intentioned they may be, have at least for the present made it impossible to reach any settlement on this rather involved and complicated question.'[147]

The gulf between the positions of the two countries was unbridgeable. Bhutto's revised proposal was internationalization of the valley for a limited period, to be followed by a plebiscite. The British, in particular, continued to press for a 'realistic' settlement which faced up to the 'real' issues, that is, Pakistan's demand for a share of the Kashmir valley. It was hinted that, while Pakistan's conclusion of a boundary agreement with China was 'monstrous', British military assistance to India might be affected by the failure to reach a settlement with Pakistan.[148] But there still seemed to Nehru to be no real desire on the part of Pakistan for a settlement and only a wish to take advantage of India's poor relations with China. 'For the present, both these countries [Pakistan and China] feel that the major impediment in their way is India; therefore both have the common objective of doing injury to India and

144 Nehru's note to Secretary-General on conversation with W.W. Rostow and J.K. Galbraith, 1 April 1963. File 2(42)/56-71 P.M.S.

145 Nehru's telegram to M.C. Chagla in London, 20 April 1963.

146 Nehru's interview with T.F. Brady, 16 April, published in *New York Times*, 17 April 1963.

147 Nehru to Kennedy, 21 April 1963.

148 Telegram from M.C. Chagla, High Commissioner, to Nehru, reporting interviews with Lord Home, Foreign Secretary, 22 April, and D. Sandys, Commonwealth Secretary, 25 April 1963; H. Macmillan to Nehru, 26 April 1963.

humiliating her so that in future they can proceed towards realizing their aims without this major obstacle.'[149] The talks wound up with Pakistan refusing to sign a no-war declaration and declining disengagement on the cease-fire line with both sides pulling back their troops. Even so, Nehru expressed his abiding anxiety to reach a settlement with Pakistan as it had been for long a part of India and 'not politically but emotionally, linguistically, culturally, in every way' there was more affinity between India and Pakistan than any other two persons or countries. But he regarded as 'outrageous' and beyond the pale of consideration any proposal to hand over the defence of Ladakh to Pakistan or anyone else[150] – which meant that the valley would have to remain with India. Justification, if needed, for this position came only two days later, when Pakistan disclosed its defence arrangements with China.[151] Nehru reacted promptly. It seemed to him that Pakistan now regretted not having attacked India along with China and was now providing 'one of the worst examples of blackmail'. But there was no question of India agreeing to the division or internationalization of the Kashmir valley.[152]

In response to suggestions of mediation made by the two Western Powers, Nehru consented, if Pakistan also agreed, to utilize the good offices of a competent person who would consider all matters of dispute between the two countries and generally assist in bringing about friendly and cooperative relations – a concession which he had been unwilling to make a year before and which even now he accepted with reluctance and probably under Mountbatten's pressure. But Pakistan laid down conditions for mediation which she knew India could not accept – its restriction to the Kashmir issue, the placing of a fixed time-limit and freezing of aid to India till the mediation had been accomplished. Obviously Pakistan wished the discussions to fail so that she could again resort to other measures.

Britain and the United States urged Nehru not to leave matters at this stage and again pressed for the acceptance of mediation. But to the Government of India there seemed little hope of any such mediation succeeding, so long as the essential prerequisites of a peaceful climate were lacking. Pakistan was now, in addition to infiltration and sabotage in Kashmir, collaborating with the Chinese in providing assistance to the Naga rebels. Her only object seemed to be to damage India in every way. The Chinese were making a bid for the leadership of Asia and the communist world as a first step in a bid for world leadership and exploiting Pakistan for this purpose. The suggestion of mediation only served to weaken India's defence effort and it would be more useful if the Western Powers helped with quiet diplomacy in creating the

149 Nehru to Chief Ministers, 21 May 1963.

150 Press Conference at Delhi, 15 June, *National Herald*, 16 June 1963.

151 'In the event of war with India Pakistan would not be alone. Pakistan would be helped by the most powerful nation in Asia. War between India and Pakistan involves the territorial interests and security of the largest state in Asia.' Z.A. Bhutto on 17 June 1963.

152 Nehru's speech at Srinagar, 18 June, *National Herald*, 19 June 1963.

appropriate atmosphere for better relations between India and Pakistan.[153] Kennedy, who probably did not share Nehru's assessment of China's policy, expressed surprise at his 'negative' attitude and argued that an impasse in India's relations with Pakistan increased his own difficulties in getting Congress to sanction aid to India. But Nehru thought resumption of talks or acceptance of a mediator would, far from being helpful, prove 'suicidal', for it would be regarded by Parliament and public opinion in India as the first step to yielding to pressures from China and Pakistan and a prelude to political surrender to China as well. One could, therefore, only await a suitable opportunity for any further initiative.[154] If Britain and the United States could persuade Pakistan to adopt at least a neutral, if not a pro-Indian attitude in the conflict between India and China, then mediation could be considered.[155] As it was, it almost seemed as if Pakistan and China had come to some private arrangement based not on any principle but on common hostility to India; and the possibility of a simultaneous attack could not be ruled out.[156] No effective effort towards a settlement between India and Pakistan seemed possible as long as Pakistan and China were so closely linked together in 'an alliance of animus against India'.[157] 'Our problem is that Pakistan looks at every issue from the point of view of its possible effect on India, of how they can harm India. They regard India as an enemy. But I feel that we should, while protecting our rights, try not to quarrel with Pakistan.'[158]

That Nehru was sincere in his desire for a general improvement in relations with Pakistan and was searching for a long-term settlement encompassing all matters and not just Kashmir becomes clear from his serious consideration once again of the idea of a confederation. Talking to the correspondent in Delhi of the *Washington Post* on the eve of the first round of talks between the Ministers of the two countries, he suggested that a confederal relationship between India and Kashmir could lead to a similar arrangement between the two halves of Pakistan and enable in due time a large confederation of India, Pakistan and their neighbours. The advantages to Pakistan would be a link with Kashmir as well as a safety-valve for the growing irredentist feeling in East Bengal. To India the idea was attractive because it gave up the communal approach, moved away from the 'two nation' theory and opened out vistas of peace and cooperation with Pakistan. 'Confederation remains our ultimate goal. Look at Europe, at the Common Market. This is the urge

[153] Conversation of Y.D. Gundevia, Commonwealth Secretary, with J.K. Galbraith, 1 July 1963; Nehru to Kennedy, 11 August 1963; Nehru's statement in the Lok Sabha, 13 August 1963, Debates, Third Series, Vol. 19, pp. 158–65.

[154] Nehru's notes to Secretary-General on interviews with British High Commissioner and message from Macmillan, and with American Ambassador with letter from Kennedy, both on 16 August 1963.

[155] Nehru to Kennedy, 27 August 1963.

[156] Address (in Hindi) to Congress Parliamentary Party, 12 August 1963. Tape M-70/C (ii).

[157] R.K. Karanjia, *The Philosophy of Mr Nehru* (London, 1966), p. 124; statement at press conference at Delhi, 9 October, *National Herald*, 10 October 1963.

[158] Address (in Hindi) to Congress Parliamentary Party, 17 November 1963. Tape M-72/C.

everywhere. There are no two peoples anywhere nearer than those of India and Pakistan, though if we say it, they are alarmed and think we want to swallow them.'[159]

For this reason, Nehru had hoped that his remarks would remain off the record;[160] and, when published, as Nehru had expected, there was shrill criticism in Pakistan of what was described as India's ambition to dominate South Asia, for she would obviously be the dominating member of any confederation. So, although logically and reasonably the only right course for India and Pakistan still appeared to Nehru to be to pull together while retaining considerable autonomy,[161] he let the idea lie dormant. But the idea was not out of his mind. The trend in the world appeared to him to be in favour of large groupings or confederations of independent countries; and, while not elaborating on the possibility of such a grouping in South Asia because it would irritate Pakistan, the idea to him remained attractive.[162] To the end, while not concealing his view that both Pakistan and China seemed to have 'larger objectives' in mind with regard to India, he continued to cherish the hope that India and Pakistan would be able to come together, much closer, 'even constitutionally closer'.[163]

NINE

With the failure of the talks with Pakistan, interest had shifted to events within Kashmir. These had for some time caused Nehru considerable uneasiness. Abdullah and his senior lieutenants were still in prison and their trial on charges of conspiracy dragged on interminably. The administration of the state by Bakshi Ghulam Mahomed did not sustain the normal standards of democratic government. The elections in 1962 were clearly rigged to enable the ruling party to win almost all the seats. 'In fact', commented Nehru drily, 'it would strengthen your position much more if you lost a few seats to bonafide opponents.'[164] He conceded that all that could be said for the Bakshi ministry was that it was better than the autocratic rule of the Maharaja in the years before 1947. 'It is true that political liberty does not exist there in the same measure as in the rest of India. At the same time, there is much more of it than there used to be.'[165]

At the time of the Chinese invasion, Abdullah wrote to Nehru that,

[159] *Washington Post*, 19 December 1962; S.S. Harrison, 'Nehru's Plan for Peace', *The New Republic*, 19 June 1971; S.S. Harrison, *The Widening Gulf* (New York, 1978), p. 275.

[160] See Nehru to Pyarelal, 2 January 1963.

[161] Nehru to General Habibullah, 20 February 1963.

[162] Interview with H. Bradsher of the Associated Press, 9 September, *The Hindu*, 26 September 1963.

[163] Speech in the Lok Sabha, 24 April 1964. Debates, Third Series, Vol. 29, pp. 10,705–22.

[164] To Bakshi Ghulam Mahomed, 4 March 1962.

[165] To P.N. Bazaz, 7 August 1962.

freedom being indivisible and jointly to be preserved for the whole sub-continent, the first step to take was the settlement of the Kashmir dispute.[166] This proved impossible, with Pakistan moving close to China and India unwilling to make any major concession. But the failure of the rounds of talks with Pakistan increased Nehru's concern about the internal situation in Kashmir and he was more eager to improve relations with Abdullah than with Ayub. As he later remarked, he could see no reason why Abdullah had had to be arrested and deplored that they did not have the courage to release him.[167] His effort in April 1962 to secure Abdullah's release had been thwarted by the Bakshi ministry and the Intelligence Bureau;[168] but by the end of 1963 Nehru was able to take the initiative and not leave matters to the state Government. The replacement of Bakshi Ghulam Mahomed as part of the process of implementing the Kamaraj Plan helped to improve the tone of the state administration; and the incident of the loss and quick recovery of the Prophet's hair in the Hazratbal mosque gave the central Government moral leverage. Nehru utilized this, after his serious illness at Bhuvaneshwar in January 1964, to secure, as a valedictory act of policy, the withdrawal of the conspiracy case against Sheikh Abdullah. 'If a damned thing can't be proved in four years, in six years, there is obviously nothing to be proved.'[169]

On 8 April, Abdullah was released and given an invitation from Nehru to come to Delhi as his guest. Abdullah accepted and had long talks with the Prime Minister. He was bitter with Nehru for having allowed his arrests and long detentions, and contended that now almost everyone in Kashmir disliked India and was in favour of Pakistan. If the conflict between India and Pakistan continued, not only would normal life be impossible in Kashmir; there would be far-reaching consequences in the form of communal tension in other parts of India as well as in East Bengal. It was for Nehru, who understood Abdullah's position 'as an old friend and colleague and blood-brother', to settle the problem of Kashmir by reaching some agreement with Pakistan which would create a sense of peace and cooperation.

At these talks, Nehru put forward no suggestion but pressed Abdullah to say whether he had any specific formula in mind. Abdullah gave no clear reply. All he would say was that he favoured a secular approach, that Kashmir's accession to India was not irrevocable and that the problem should be discussed in secret in India by leading members of the Congress Party as well as others – meaning, presumably, Vinoba Bhave, Rajagopalachari and Jayaprakash Narayan.[170] Nehru had said nothing to him about a confederation but Abdullah must have known that this idea was alive in Nehru's mind. So Abdullah now brought forward as his own proposal the possibility of a confederation of India, Pakistan and Kashmir. This was more limited in scope

166 To Nehru, 5 November 1962.

167 Address (in Hindi) to Congress Parliamentary Party, 3 April 1964. Tape M73/C.

168 B.N. Mullik, *My Years with Nehru: Kashmir* (Delhi, 1971), pp. 97–8.

169 Nehru's comment reported in Gundevia, 'Outside the Archives'.

170 Nehru's notes on his talks with Sheikh Abdullah, 29 April, 30 April, and 1 May 1964.

than Nehru's idea, for it did not envisage the autonomy of East Bengal; and Nehru was not happy about it, believing it to be both premature and lacking in balance. But he permitted Abdullah to propose it to Ayub when he went to Rawalpindi in response to Ayub's invitation. His attitude to Abdullah at this time was a blend of guilt at having allowed him to have been kept so long in detention and of concern at the consequences of his activities. To Nehru's relief, Ayub rejected what he thought an 'absurd' suggestion, certain to lead to the enslavement of Pakistan and the disintegration of both India and Pakistan by encouraging separatist trends among Sikhs, Tamils and – what really worried Ayub – the people of East Bengal. Indeed, Ayub saw in the proposal, without justification, the plotting of Nehru.[171] But Abdullah's visit to Pakistan was fruitful to the extent that he persuaded Ayub to agree to come to Delhi for talks with Nehru on relations between India and Pakistan and not to reject any proposals till they had been discussed with Nehru.[172] At Abdullah's request a formal invitation was sent to Ayub. It reached the Indian High Commissioner for transmission on the morning of Nehru's death on 27 May 1964.

TEN

In a sense, the question of Kashmir was part of the general problem of the Muslim community in India. In 1964, with outbreaks of violence in East Bengal, the influx of refugees into India increased; and this sparked off riots in Calcutta, Jamshedpur and other parts of eastern India. To Ayub Nehru suggested a meeting of Ministers.[173] But it was the behaviour of sections of the Indian people which pained him, for it made clear that the communal virus had not been exterminated. To compete with Pakistan in hatred and barbarity was to accept defeat and sink below the human level.[174] 'Somehow people have got so terribly excited that they do not see the consequences of their actions. We must try our best to make people see correctly. Otherwise, I agree with you that our freedom and independence are in danger.'[175] Instances of communal rioting, which had been decreasing in the 1950s, again began to grow in number; from 26 in 1960 they rose to 92 the next year, fell to 60 in 1962, mounted to 61 in 1963 and rose sharply in 1964.[176] It looked as if India were heading back to the

171 *Friends not Masters*, p. 128; G. Parthasarathi to the author, 8 February 1980. Parthasarathi was Indian High Commissioner in Pakistan at this time.

172 See Abdullah to Ayub, 1 September 1967, printed in *The Testament of Sheikh Abdullah* (Delhi, 1974), pp. 81–2.

173 19 March 1964.

174 Broadcast, 26 March, *National Herald*, 27 March 1964.

175 To Gunada Majumdar, 5 April 1964.

176 M. Ghouse, 'Nehru and Secularism', *Journal of the Indian Law Institute*, 1978, pp. 104–16.

attitudes and tensions of the months immediately after the partition of the country.

> This was the thing that nearly had us mastered,
> Do not rejoice in his defeat, you men;
> Although the world stood up and stopped the bastard,
> The bitch that bore him is in heat again.[177]

There were again 'a good deal of madness' and bloodthirsty ideas about and the atrocities committed in India suggested an organization behind them. One result was the weakening of the Government's hands in dealing with Pakistan.[178] In one of his last major speeches in the Lok Sabha, Nehru urged the country to adhere to Gandhi's approach and force Pakistan 'psychologically' into friendship by evincing goodwill and providing an example of decent behaviour. India was not free from wrong-doing and should not become too self-righteous.[179] Echoes of the events and the speeches of the first months of India's freedom returned in the last months of Nehru's life and darkened his last days.[180]

[177] Bertolt Brecht.

[178] To J.P. Jyotishi, 5 April, to Mrs Habibullah, 7 April, to Suresh Ram, 22 April, and to S.B. Ahmad, 2 May 1964.

[179] 24 April 1964. Lok Sabha Debates, Third Series, Vol. 29, pp. 10,705–22.

[180] Padmaja Naidu to the author, 28 July 1969, on her conversations with Nehru a few days before his death.

12

Full Stop

ONE

Nehru had always taken pride in his clean glow of health and 'a singularly unmedicated body'.[1] In 1957 he appeared to a sharp observer to have defeated time.[2] Two years later, when he was seventy, he boasted that it had been a long time since he had had 'a really first-class illness'.[3] But three years after, in the spring of 1962, a viral infection of the urinary tract brought on low intermittent fever. The accumulated fatigue of years delayed full recovery and, further weakened by large doses of antibiotics, Nehru spent most of April in bed. Accepting the warning with reluctance and forced to recognize that his reserves of energy were not inexhaustible, Nehru resigned himself to a slacker regimen: a siesta in the afternoon, retirement to bed by 11 p.m. and more frequent, if shorter, vacations. He also took to a more spartan diet, virtually giving up meat and milk and living mainly on fruit and vegetables varied with a little fish and eggs. But he never fully shook off the infection and, from this time, a slight puffiness round the eyes was always noticeable. His face was at last, in Auden's phrase, beginning to agree with his age.

Then, on 6 January 1964, at the Congress session at Bhuvaneshwar, Nehru suffered a mild stroke on the left side. After a short period of rest, he sought to carry on with his work as before. Informed that Soviet doctors advised a longer convalescence, he exploded: 'Let them go to hell. If I lie down in bed for even a week, I know I will not get up.'[4] He had never been afraid to die. Long years before, while languishing in prison, he had recorded that he had no particular desire for a long life. 'When life approaches its end, slow or sudden, it will not find me, I think, afraid or unready.'[5] Rather, he had wished to be 'willing and

[1] Comment to K.P.S. Menon in 1947, quoted by Menon, 'My Memories of Jawaharlal Nehru', *Akashvani* (Delhi), 1975.

[2] A.J. Toynbee, *Acquaintances* (Oxford, 1967), p. 300.

[3] V. Sheean, *Nehru: The Years of Power* (London, 1960), p. 259.

[4] T.N. Kaul, *Diplomacy in Peace and War* (Delhi, 1979), p. 153.

[5] Diary entry, 22 September 1941. *Selected Works of Jawaharlal Nehru*, Vol. 11 (New Delhi, 1978), p. 702.

prepared for the full stop when that comes';[6] and now, knowing that the end could not be far off, he drove himself to do his work as usual in the time which was permitted him. 'My lifetime', he told the press when they raised the question on every mind about the succession,[7] 'is not ending so very soon.' This was an assertion more of determination than of confidence. The lines of Robert Frost, which he had copied out and kept on his table, indicate equally his tiredness, his equanimity and his sense of duty to his people:

> The woods are lovely, dark and deep,
> But I have promises to keep,
> And miles to go before I sleep,
> And miles to go before I sleep.

In this mood of acceptance, Nehru spent one or two hours every week with Radhakrishnan, the President, not only discussing affairs of state but listening to Radhakrishnan talking on philosophical subjects. Nehru had not religious belief or faith but a religious feeling and he responded, as the years passed, more and more to the teachings of the Vedanta, the *Gita* and Buddhism. Political gossip-mongers, unaware of these meetings, spread the rumour that relations between the President and the Prime Minister had become strained. Radhakrishnan, a non-party man and a philosopher outside the bustle of politics, regarded his role as President to be one of both giving friendly advice to the Prime Minister in private and speaking out in public even if this implied criticism of the administration. On 8 November 1962, for example, in a pause between the waves of Chinese aggression, he acknowledged that 'our credulity and our negligence have caused us some initial reverses'. Nehru's outlook was not so cramped as to resent such outspokenness; indeed, he would have agreed with Radhakrishnan that India had placed too much trust in China and therefore not spent enough on defence. He appreciated that the dimensions of Indian democracy were expanded by having in the office of President a figure of stature and independence; and in their own personal relations there was now a fresh element of philosophical discourse. Never had Nehru and Radhakrishnan been closer than in the early months of 1964.

In earlier years, alarmed by the 'horrible prospect' of slowly fading away,[8] Nehru had often proclaimed his desire, when the time came, for a quick departure. 'What I want is that I should not become sick and weak and lie in bed ailing. I want to be able to work until the sudden end.'[9] Now his wish was fulfilled. Going to bed after clearing all pending papers and dealing with his correspondence, he suffered, in the early hours of 27 May, a rupture of the abdominal aorta. Pain-killing injections were required to induce a sleep from

6 To Krishna Hutheesing, 28 October 1941. Ibid., p. 718.
7 Press conference at Delhi, 22 May, *National Herald*, 23 May 1964.
8 To Jal Naoroji, 24 June 1937. A.I.C.C. file G 5/1937. N.M.M.L.
9 Speech at Bombay, 21 January, *The Hindu*, 22 January 1957.

"Give me the supreme faith of love, this is my prayer, the faith of the life in death, of the victory in defeat, of the power hidden in the frailness of beauty . . ." —Rabindranath Tagore

Vicky's cartoon in the *Evening Standard*, 27 May 1964

which he did not awake.[10] 'We all', he had written,[11] 'have to die sometime or other, but it is given only to few of us to die nobly.' His own passing did not fall below his hopes. He had been spared the slow agony of a prolonged illness and crossed over, without sad leave-takings, after a full day's work.

The death of Nehru was mourned, not only by leaders of government who came to Delhi, as demanded by protocol, for the cremation but by persons of emancipated understanding throughout the world. As Vicky's cartoons show, by his death mankind felt diminished. In a world of bigotry and belligerence, he had stood, above all else, for humaneness and rationality. But the grief was naturally the most intense in India. No such shock of national bereavement had been witnessed since the death of Gandhi over sixteen years before. Vast crowds spontaneously moved into Delhi for the last sight of the man who had, for the span of a generation, brought together the aspirations of diverse sections of Indian society; and the need to bring in large numbers of troops from outside the capital to control this deep tide of emotion even led to fears of a military coup.[12] Even after the cremation, the high pitch of popular feeling was sustained and even intensified by the publication of Nehru's will. Drafted in 1954, it appealed as much to the educated by its sensitivity as to the

[10] For details of the final illness, I am indebted to a note by his personal physician, Col. M.S. Rao, written on 8 October 1974.

[11] To R.K. Pandeya, 23 July 1960.

[12] General J.N. Chaudhuri, *An Autobiography* (Delhi, 1978), p. 186.

ordinary man and woman by its provision of one more testimony of Nehru's total commitment to the Indian people. He thanked them for the affection with which they had overwhelmed him and asked that, after his cremation, the major portion of the ashes be scattered from the air over the countryside, so that they might mingle with the dust and soil and become an indistinguishable part of India. Only a small remainder he wished to be disposed of in a different way; and the reasons for this he elaborated in sparkling prose.

> The Ganga, especially, is the river of India, beloved of her people, round which are intertwined her racial memories, her hopes and fears, her songs of triumph, her victories and her defeats. She has been a symbol of India's age-long culture and civilization, ever-changing, ever-flowing, and yet ever the same Ganga. She reminds me of the snow-covered peaks and the deep valleys of the Himalayas, which I have loved so much, and of the rich and vast plains below, where my life and work have been cast. Smiling and dancing in the morning sunlight, and dark and gloomy and full of mystery as the evening shadows fall, a narrow, slow and graceful stream in winter and a vast, roaring thing during the monsoon, broad-bosomed almost as the sea, and with something of the sea's power to destroy, the Ganga has been to me a symbol and a memory of the past of India, running into the present, and flowing on to the great ocean of the future. And though I have discarded much of past tradition and custom, and am anxious that India should rid herself of all shackles that bind and constrain her and divide her people, and suppress vast numbers of them, and prevent the free development of the body and the spirit; though I seek all this, yet I do not wish to cut myself off from the past completely. I am proud of that great inheritance that has been, and is, ours, and I am conscious that I too, like all of us, am a link in that unbroken chain which goes back to the dawn of history in the immemorial past of India. That chain I would not break, for I treasure it and seek inspiration from it. And as witness of this desire of mine and as my last homage to India's cultural inheritance, I am making this request that a handful of my ashes be thrown into the Ganga at Allahabad to be carried to the great ocean that washes India's shore.[13]

TWO

Even to those who attach little importance to personalities, Jawaharlal Nehru is clearly one of those individuals of whom E.P. Thompson has said they are of importance in history because they may exhibit values with which we can

[13] Nehru's will and testament, 21 June 1954.

"There could be no more fitting memorial to him than a world without war..."
—President Johnson

Vicky's cartoon in the *Evening Standard*, 28 May 1964

identify or by which we may be inspired.[14] He has, of course, not been without his critics. A few did not find his personality congenial. For a man who, in the 1930s, had believed that the 'fundamental thing of life from which all else springs is the relation of human beings to each other',[15] too often, as Prime Minister, he put off persons eager to be friendly with a self-absorption which evaded even normal civility. Pablo Neruda, for example, has described an interview in 1950 from which Nehru emerges as not a likeable person. 'He rose and shook my hand without any trace of a welcoming smile . . . He replied in monosyllables to everything I said, scrutinizing me with his steady, cold eyes . . . There was something high and mighty about him, something stiff, as if he was accustomed to giving orders but lacked the strength of a leader.'[16] To Malcolm Muggeridge he was 'rather a conceited second-rate person';[17] and Hugh Gaitskell did not like him at all.

> He is a very arrogant man; I think that is one reason why he makes such long speeches. He really thinks everyone wants to listen to them. He is a complete aristocrat and although of course he accepts, no doubt genuinely, democratic institutions, nevertheless he certainly does not behave

[14] *The Poverty of Theory* (London, 1978), p. 234.
[15] Quoted by Shiela Grant Duff, *The Parting of Ways* (London, 1982), p. 108.
[16] *Memoirs* (Penguin edn, 1978), p. 202.
[17] 12 May 1950. *Like It Was*, the diaries of M. Muggeridge (London, 1981), p. 388.

> in what you would call a democratic way when it comes to mixing with other people. He is most aloof and almost unfriendly.[18]

Such personal criticisms of a hard-worked Prime Minister tormented by foreign interviewers can be brushed away as trivial. They do not mitigate from his known commitment to his fellow men and are surpassed by the many more accounts which bear witness to his quality. Patrick Blackett's reaction can be taken as representative: 'His extreme informality and charm, his physical presence was extremely attractive; he was very engaging, with a shy sort of smile . . . He was sort of light-hearted. I liked this about him. He was the opposite of pomposity. He was extremely friendly.'[19] Those who did not know him well also could not, for the most part, resist his appeal: 'he was rather an English gentleman but there was a kind of blazing quality about him'.[20] Even Muggeridge paid tribute, some years after his caustic comment in his diary, to Nehru's fastidiousness of mind and spirit.

> We who survey with (speaking for myself) growing distaste the spectacle of the pursuit of power, may be compared to a pianist in a brothel. When a client, driven by necessity, comes into the establishment and looks round at the girls provided with a distaste almost equal to our own, we are naturally drawn to him. Such a client is Mr. Nehru.[21]

Weightier than the stray personal antipathies are the adverse reports based, not on isolated and momentary impressions, but on assessments of his life, his work and his policies as a whole. Even after Nehru's death Zhou could not rise above pettiness. National policy no doubt required him to revise his earlier posture of friendship; but he cloaked his volte-face in a denunciation of Nehru as the vainest man with whom he had ever to deal. 'I have met many leaders of the world throughout my career. I met Khrushchev. I met Chiang Kai-shek. I've met American generals. But I have never met a more arrogant man than Nehru. I am sorry to say this but this is true.'[22] Bhutto of Pakistan assessed Nehru more impersonally but thought him to be no more than a successful politician whose myth and image were greater than himself. 'Although he committed aggression, alienated his neighbours, suppressed his opponents, made mock convenience of his ethics, he was Nehru the redeemer of 400 million people, a valiant fighter who led his people to freedom and, for the first time in six hundred years, gave them a place in the sun.'[23]

18 Diary entry 14 July 1956. P.M. Williams (ed.), *The Diary of Hugh Gaitskell 1945–1956* (London, 1983), p. 538.

19 Oral testimony of P.M.S. Blackett, 22 February 1972. N.M.M.L.

20 Shirley Williams in the *Observer* (London), 22 March 1981.

21 *Sunday Telegraph* (London), 19 May 1963.

22 Report of Zhou's meeting with some members of the Parliament of Sri Lanka, *Ceylon Observer*, 11 October 1964.

23 'Nehru', a confidential note written by Z.A. Bhutto a few days after Nehru's death and circulated to a few persons. Many years later, the author was permitted to see this note.

Can these opinions, too, be set aside as the prejudice of political enemies? In the final analysis, every democratic leader has to be judged by his hold on his own people; and this test poses Nehru no problem. From the mid-1920s till his death nearly forty years later, he could draw on the abundant love of the Indian masses, born of their unshakable awareness that this man, born to wealth and comfort, had been willing to discard all in their cause and had worked in their service to the last moment of his conscious life. They were, therefore, easily possessed by the glamour which attached to his personality. If romance always surrounded his name, it was because there was always a strong romanticist element in him. In prison in Ahmednagar Fort in 1943, during one of the dark periods of Indian nationalism, Nehru noted in the privacy of his diary a sentence of the Buddha, 'I would enter a blazing fire, but I would not enter my home with my goal unattained'; and Nehru added that when he had come across this sentence by chance, 'a thrill passed through me, almost an electric shock'.[24] This youthful intensity which never left him, the nakedness of spirit that had no vulgarity about it, rendered his whole life an affirming flame and roused in many who knew him, or even only knew of him, what his old friend Edward Thompson described in 1939 as 'maternal instincts'.[25] The magnetism of Nehru cannot be conveyed on the printed page; but its core was a blend of sensitivity and intellectual passion.

THREE

Nehru was not born to politics and the early years suggested a motiveless life of privilege. There was nothing particularly remarkable about the dandified dilettante who held aloof from the overpowering earnestness of a formidable father as a strategy for survival and was content with cosseted emptiness. The massacre at Jallianwala Bagh in 1919, when Nehru was thirty years of age, was the decisive, liberating moment in his life. It focused his energies and clarified his mind, made 'action urgent and its nature clear'. Thereafter he was caught up in the emotional logic of the national movement and his consuming singleness of vision gave him heroic and symbolic force. But, even as he threw himself into the struggle and never shirked prison, he began after a time to worry about the future and gave unceasing thought to the policies which a free India should follow. The progress to political renown was paralleled by an intellectual journey from moderate nationalism to an understanding of economic systems and an awareness of the international scene. His special position, from the late 1920s, was that he, of all the nationalist leaders of the front rank, understood most clearly that the campaign for freedom required an economic orientation. The fear which he roused in British authorities derived from the fact that in him converged the strands of nationalism and socialism.

[24] 11 November 1943. *Selected Works of Jawaharlal Nehru*, Vol. 13 (New Delhi, 1980), p. 282.
[25] Quoted by his son, E.P. Thompson, *Writing by Candlelight* (London, 1980), p. 143.

The Mahatma had brought the peasants into politics without alienating other classes of Indian society and had converted an elite organization into a multi-class front. At this point Nehru, in a sense, took over and gave the movement a bias towards socialism. This seemed to him necessary not only in itself, for socialism in some form was the only answer to India's problem of poverty, but also to retain the peasantry in the national movement and to bring that movement in line with progressive forces in the world.

The commitment to socialism and the international perspective gained Nehru the support of large sections of educated and left-wing opinion in India and abroad. The romantic and the rational aspects of the revolutionary spirit seemed in him to have been harmonized. Ardent, spontaneous and attractive in his robust and assertive vitality, he constantly and at great length searched for a philosophy and programme which would be appropriate to India. The merger of image and ideology seemed irresistible. Only the communists criticized him for 'petit-bourgeois phrase-mongering', all the more vehemently perhaps because they saw the inroads he was making, on behalf of the Congress, into what should have been their own recruiting ground. In fact, Nehru was serving both the present and the future of India by projecting the national movement as an anti-imperialist struggle of all classes in which the least privileged should have the greatest weight, committing the movement, at least in principle, to the goal of socialism and placing it in a world setting as part of the general struggle of humanity. Palme Dutt did not think that Nehru understood Marxism, but he could discern that Nehru had a feeling for and understanding of the new forces that were represented by socialism, communism and the Soviet Union and this was 'a great plus'; and he was very strong against fascism.[26] One can see why it is sometimes said that the 1930s were Nehru's best days.[27]

Certainly to Nehru these years of the freedom movement, even though deaths in the family were 'punching black holes' in his life, formed the happiest and most unclouded period of his public career. He was steeped in the exhilaration which results from functioning in a landscape of noble action, with abstract issues translating themselves spontaneously into human terms. But, after the magic comradeship and the heady involvement in sacrifice, came the stretch when he had to lead his people in hard, prosaic effort to build on political freedom the structure of an open, self-reliant society. Brave deeds and creative thought had to be followed by constructive statesmanship. An obvious aspect of this was the formulation of a foreign policy which, without indifference to the major issues of the world, would establish an independent role for India, free from commitment, let alone subordination, to either side in the cold war. The concept of non-alignment was formulated as an assertion of national independence and of the rational man's duty to criticize and to pose

[26] R. Palme Dutt's oral testimony, 12 October 1971, N.M.M.L.

[27] e.g., by S. Kaviraj, 'Apparent Paradoxes of Jawaharlal Nehru', *Mainstream* (Delhi), 15 November–13 December 1980.

long-term values against immediate ends. It was a question of trying to do what one thought right and, in the process, seeking to be friendly and cooperative with other countries even if in disagreement.

As Prime Minister, Nehru could not ignore the demands of national interest and security, though at no time, not even when engaged in a struggle to repel the invader, did he shed his concern for the way in which civilized nations should behave. In 1962, hard-pressed by the aggressor, India necessarily developed close links with the Western Powers; and the practice of non-alignment wore thin. But the enduring element of non-alignment, which India under his leadership did not forsake, was a mental outlook, a particular approach to world problems. Of Nehru's many contributions to the international scene, the most lasting has been the insistence, in fair weather or foul, on India's right, untrammelled by the viewpoints of the great powers, to frame her own policies so as to safeguard her independence, defend and promote her national interests and work for progressive causes such as anti-colonialism, anti-racism and disarmament. Non-alignment does not function in a vacuum and needs constant adaptation to changing circumstances; and there is much in non-alignment as it has evolved and as it is practised today which Nehru and the other founding fathers would undoubtedly find strange. It has been stretched out almost to the point of losing recognizable shape; and the criteria laid down in the early days, of rejection of military alliances in the context of the cold war and of refusal to have foreign military bases on one's territory, have occasionally been submerged in the enthusiasm to increase membership. Yet the general sense of non-alignment had, by the time of Nehru's death, become an integral part of the international pattern and entered into the climate of world thought. It is now part of the conventional wisdom of the Third World and has even seeped into the political atmosphere of Western Europe.

To have resisted imperialism, denounced fascism, promoted the emergence of an African personality and shown the way for not only India but other countries to steer clear of the cold war, while being both concerned with the problems of the world and defining and safeguarding the country's specific interests – these are no mean achievements and place Nehru among the leading statesmen of the twentieth century. The shadows on his conduct of foreign policy are more in the sphere of India's own concerns; the failure to stabilize her relations with Pakistan and the deterioration of her relations with China. On Kashmir Nehru's hands were, from the start, tied by circumstances. Working to build up a consciousness of India held together by bonds other than those of religion, he could not be expected to concede that Kashmir should be a part of Pakistan merely because the majority of its inhabitants were Muslims. Pakistan's attempt to decide the matter by force precluded quiet consideration of the problem; and the idealism which prompted Nehru's reference to the United Nations soon soured when the issue was swamped in power politics. The dismissal and arrest of Sheikh Abdullah a few years later weakened Nehru's confidence that the majority in Kashmir preferred secular India to the Islamic state of Pakistan and he was prepared for the transfer of the Kashmir valley to Pakistan on the basis of a plebiscite.[28] But the opportunity was lost when Kashmir was dragged into cold war politics by the military alliance between the United States and Pakistan. A second chance of a settlement on Kashmir came in 1963 when Nehru, in his last years, was anxious not to leave the problem to his successors; but again Pakistan, believing that India had been brought to her knees by China, destroyed hopes of an equitable solution by laying claim to virtually the whole state. A few months later, Nehru was in the middle of another effort when he died. Even had he lived, it may not have come to much; for no Government of Pakistan, civilian or military, seems to have been keen, in Nehru's time at any rate, on a settlement on Kashmir; the issue was a symptom rather than the cause of poor relations, which had a long history going back beyond the years of independence and which could not easily be improved. It should be added that, with the people of Pakistan, as against their Governments, Nehru had a special relationship; and they generally grieved at his death as if he were their own national hero.[29]

If past sentiment worked against cordial relations with the Governments of Pakistan, the opposite was true of relations between India and China. Nehru repeatedly stressed the close ties which had existed for centuries between these two peoples of Asia; but it was not such shallow nostalgia which inspired his desire for friendly cooperation with the Government of China. He was among the first to realize that the People's Republic would function, sooner or later, as an independent factor in the balance of world forces; and this convinced him that it was necessary that the Chinese should not be left, in de Gaulle's phrase, 'isolated in their own rage'.[30] He also grasped that the traditional expansionism of China had been strengthened rather than deflected by a radical ideology. He attached importance to what Henry Kissinger much later termed 'the geopolitical tradition' – the concept of the world consisting not of warring ideologies but of powers pursuing their own interests according to their best perception of them. He grasped that there could be no genuine friendship with a country which, particularly in the later 1950s, was pursuing a foreign policy lacking in flexibility and based on intense nationalist pride and expectation from other countries of political tribute. But he thought that the communist regime would have enough problems at home to engage its full attention for some years to come, and he believed that, if other nations adopted a friendly approach, it would help to keep China in the ways of international peace. 'I firmly believe that what one gives others, one gets back.

[28] This attitude of Nehru, now established by documents, was no secret even at that time and was known, for example, to the Canadian, Australian, and Pakistani High Commissioners in Delhi. Escott Reid, *Envoy to Nehru* (Delhi, 1981), p. 123.

[29] See I. Malhotra's articles in *Illustrated Weekly of India*, 12 November 1972, and the *Guardian* (London), 28 May 1979. Malhotra was in Pakistan at the time of Nehru's death.

[30] Quoted in H. Kissinger, *The White House Years* (London, 1979), p. 107.

If our approach to others is friendly, others are friendly to us.'[31] To India this would have the advantage of enabling concentration on internal development and the gradual strengthening of her presence in the border areas rather than enormous, self-mutilating expenditure on the defence of the Himalayas. By following a course of patience, courage and pragmatism he hoped to maintain the uneasy peace. As he described his foreign policy to Nasser in 1955: 'always take the first step . . . then take the second step . . . then take the third step . . . .'.[32] It was a rational policy which proved not to be the right one in that India was overtaken by events. China, in her drive to recover the place among the nations which she felt was her due, saw in Nehru's India an obstacle on the path; and she saw too, more clearly than Nehru did, that India's prestige and influence could be damaged severely without involving China herself in hostilities with other powers.

FOUR

In domestic affairs, the long years of hard thinking had enabled Nehru to reach firm conclusions as to the paths along which free India should move. The ideological shape of the nationalist struggle, the influence of Western liberal thought and the more recent attraction of Indian (as against materialist) philosophy all mixed in Nehru to form a granite core of intellectual and moral commitment to democratic values. For him democracy was an end in itself and not just a means to an end. He hated every form of forced conformism and attached prime importance to the human personality. 'Nothing can be worse for the world, I think, than a deprivation of human freedom of the individual.'[33] Also, though he professed no belief in Hindu faith, he felt the appeal of the old Hindu idea that, if there be a divine essence in the world, every individual possessed a part of it. Democracy was the most acceptable form of government because, in the final analysis, it promoted the growth of human beings and of society. Freedom of thought and expression was to him a principle on which even the demands of public safety should not normally encroach. Within India he ensured a limited and cautious exercise by public authorities of their prerogative; and it was a relief to him that, before his own death, he could secure the release of Sheikh Abdullah. Abroad he virtually functioned, in his heyday, as a one-man Amnesty International. At the request of the International P.E.N., he pressed the authorities in Hungary to adopt a more lenient attitude towards writers and intellectuals.[34] On hearing from Mrs Djilas that her husband was being treated harshly in prison, Nehru

31 Address to the general assembly of the World Council of Churches, Delhi, 4 December, *The Hindu*, 5 December 1961.

32 Quoted in M.H. Heikal, *The Cairo Documents*, (New York, 1973), p. 291.

33 Nehru in the United States 1949. *Visit to America* (New York, 1950), p. 136.

34 Nehru to David Carver, Secretary, International P.E.N., 3 July 1957.

asked his Ambassador to raise the matter informally with the Yugoslav authorities if an opportunity arose and tell them that such conduct did their reputation no good; and Tito was persuaded not to keep Djilas in solitary confinement.[35]

When the Soviet Government refused to allow Boris Pasternak to receive the Nobel Prize, Nehru, claiming to act more in his capacity as the Chairman of the Sahitya Akademi (the Indian Academy of Letters) than as Prime Minister, conveyed, again informally, to Moscow his feeling that the injustice which was being done to Pasternak would damage the prestige of the Soviet Union.[36] In whatever capacity Nehru professed to function, his views carried weight and the Soviet authorities assured him that there was no reason to fear for Pasternak; he was free, if he wished, to leave the Soviet Union 'to experience the delights of the capitalist paradise'.[37] Thereafter Nehru declared publicly that the Soviet attitude towards Pasternak 'pained us somewhat' because it was entirely opposed to India's position; a noted writer, even if he expressed views which conflicted with the dominant ones in his country, should be respected rather than subjected to any kind of restrictions.[38] Word of Nehru's interest in him had reached Pasternak, who expressed his gratitude in broken English. 'A legend (rather than rumour) is afloat that Prime Minister Nehru should have interfered during my misadventures, should have had heard of me, should have had of me a notion. Even in a case of a legend I lay my great great gratitude to his feet.'[39] Pasternak also heard rumours that Nehru had offered him political asylum and, planning to leave the Soviet Union, relied on Nehru to secure the release of his companion, Olga Ivinskaya. He later abandoned ideas of exile; but the friendly contacts between Nehru and Pasternak continued. A few months before his death, Pasternak declared that the 'personal, modern, undogmatical, heroic distinguishable trait in Mr. Nehru is for me the most precious and though it be immodest congeric [congenial?]. His understanding that the spiritual is more real as an individual caprice and grace than as a general trite affirmation.'[40] Nehru in turn sent Pasternak on his seventieth birthday the present of an alarm clock in defiance of the fact that he was in official disgrace.[41] So too, at a time when China's aggressive postures made improved relations with the Nepal Government of great importance to India, Nehru wrote to King Mahendra on a purely personal level about B.P. Koirala, the Prime Minister whom the King had placed in detention. He told the King that a humanitarian approach

[35] Nehru to Ali Yavar Jung, 1 July 1958; W. Jovanovich, *Now Barabbas* (London, 1965), pp. 151, 182–3.

[36] Telegram to K.P.S. Menon, 30 October 1958.

[37] K.P.S. Menon's telegram to Nehru, 3 November 1958; K.P.S. Menon, *The Flying Troika* (Bombay, 1963), p. 223.

[38] Press conference at Delhi, 7 November, *National Herald*, 8 November 1958.

[39] B. Pasternak's letter to Amiya Chakravarty, 15 September 1959, Sahitya Akademi files, New Delhi.

[40] B. Pasternak to A. Chakravarty, 12 January 1960. *Indian Literature* (New Delhi), April–September 1960, pp. 27–8.

[41] Olga Ivinskaya, *A Captive of Time* (London, 1978), p. 337.

demanded that Koirala, who was very ill, should be given all medical facilities and his own doctors, if necessary, should be allowed to attend on him.[42] His intervention, as Nehru expected, had no effect; but neither that anticipation of Mahendra's obstinacy nor the pressure of India's security requirements deterred Nehru from speaking his mind.

Institutionally, this commitment to democratic principle took shape in India, under Nehru's guidance, in the establishment of cabinet government and a parliamentary system. The forms of representative government which the British had constructed lacked life and Nehru, who once described himself as the last Englishman to govern India,[43] could have easily continued the autocratic tradition and allowed the legislatures to remain moribund. The experience of other countries, where the first generation of nationalist leaders themselves became dictatorial or were succeeded by military rulers, shows to what extent the entrenching of democracy in India is the exception rather than the norm. Nehru was always keenly aware of both the importance and the fragility of this effort. When he met Nkrumah for the first time in 1957, his immediate reaction, ignoring protocol, was to rebuke him for promoting a personality cult in Ghana. 'What the hell do you mean by putting your head on a stamp?'[44] An instinctive arrogance, as some have charged, may have lain just below the surface; but in public life Nehru submitted to a rigorous, self-denying ordinance. He did not project himself as a means of aggregating power or permit his personal ascendancy to be institutionalized. Of the multi-track revolution which he initiated in free India, it is the political side which has been the most successful and has proved enduring. Taking advantage of the political mobilization achieved during the freedom movement, Nehru introduced adult suffrage; and one primary purpose of his ceaseless touring of the country as Prime Minister was to teach the people to cherish this privilege and exercise it with responsibility. Education and leadership were at the core of democratic government. His speeches made hard issues vivid and plain to a people who for the most part were illiterate. He saw himself as a schoolmaster, trying to explain matters to his audiences in as simple a language as possible and getting them to think and to understand.[45] Asked once what his legacy to India would be, he replied, 'Hopefully, it is four hundred million people capable of governing themselves.'[46]

This effort at establishment of political rights has been a striking success. The value of the vote has been appreciated and the system of elections has taken deep root. India has proved that political literacy is not synonymous

42 Nehru to King Mahendra of Nepal, 7 July 1961.

43 J.K. Galbraith, *The Age of Uncertainty* (London, 1977), p. 332.

44 Vijayalakshmi Pandit, *The Scope of Happiness* (Indian edn, 1979), p. 307. It is said that Nkrumah never forgave Nehru this snub. W. Scott Thompson, *Ghana's Foreign Policy 1957–1966* (Princeton, 1969), p. 51.

45 Talks with M. Brecher, 6 and 13 June 1956. M. Brecher, *The New States of Asia* (London, 1963), Appendix, p. 214.

46 Interview with Norman Cousins, *Saturday Review of Literature* (New York), 27 May 1961.

with the ability to read and write.[47] By the time of Nehru's death, 'a moderately stable constitutional culture'[48] had been firmly established. Experts debate whether this culture is modern, traditional or mixed; no one doubts that it is widespread and permanent.

The corollary of this culture is the sovereignty of Parliament. Even as Nehru campaigned regularly round the country to embed the significance of the franchise in the national consciousness, he also took every care to see that the dignity of an elected legislature was never dimmed. The non-official Bills passed by the Indian Parliament belong entirely to the Nehru era. Even during his last months, though patently stricken, he missed no session and in order, as he said, to preserve the decorum of the House,[49] struggled to his feet every time he had to answer a question or make an intervention despite repeated suggestions from the Speaker and every section of the House that he speak sitting. There is tragic appropriateness in the fact that, on the day of his death, the two Houses of Parliament were scheduled, at his instance, to meet to consider a Bill to amend a clause in the Constitution. An earlier effort to pass it had failed for lack of a two-thirds majority and Nehru, rejecting the suggestion that the rule be suspended, had asked for a special session. 'Even as he died,' a political opponent has commented,[50] 'Jawaharlal Nehru gave a salute to Parliament, the bedrock of our democratic system.' Achieved against daunting odds, democracy in India – adult suffrage, a sovereign Parliament, a free press, an independent judiciary – is Nehru's most lasting monument. With all that it connotes, the transformation of India from a traditional into an open, participant and non-passive society is a major development in the history of the world.[51]

FIVE

The establishment of such a democratic system in a vast and crowded country with so many fissiparous pulls was not only a stupendous achievement in itself; it was perhaps the only way of holding India together. The 'Daedalian social and cultural structure',[52] with divisive religious, linguistic, regional, caste and tribal allegiances, might have split apart, despite its recent administrative

[47] Nor, it may be added, does ability to read and write carry with it political awareness. A survey in Britain in 1977 showed that 25 per cent of school-leavers associated nationalization with the Conservative party and 44 per cent thought the I.R.A. was a Protestant organization. *The Economist*, 22 July 1978.

[48] J.P. Nettl, *Political Mobilization* (London, 1967), p. 89.

[49] 28 April 1964. Rajya Sabha Debates, Vol. 47, pp. 845–8.

[50] H.V. Kamath, *Last Days of Jawaharlal Nehru* (Calcutta, 1977), p. 26.

[51] 'The biggest democracy the world has ever known is now preparing to hold another general election. The mere fact that this is possible is one of the most heartening features of the present international scene. Only a minority of mankind has ever won the right to decide its political fate peacefully by a free vote; and of those who hold that right today, nearly half are the citizens of India.' *The Economist*, 1 September 1979.

[52] C. Geertz in *Old Societies and New States* (New York, 1963), p. 139.

unity, long before economic integration developed sufficiently to bind the country together, if Nehru had not imposed a parliamentary framework held in place, till it took root, by the virtually unbroken dominance, in his time, of one party subordinate to himself. As, in his time, no right-wing party was in power and left-wing parties accepted his credentials in an overall sense, Nehru could function as a national leader without breaking away from the Congress Party. In fact, to strengthen the party and enable it to function as a cementing force, he kept both its flanks open and gained it wider support. The middle ground was Nehru's base.

However, despite the parliamentary network, the unity of the country was still brittle and national integration a live concern. The problem of linguistic differences was sought to be set aside by the continued use of the English language, the creation of linguistic provinces and the general disinclination of the central Government to lean too heavily on the states. Nehru allowed (except in the case of Kairon) whoever had the support of the majority in the Congress legislative party to become Chief Minister and then limited himself to good advice – to develop the human approach, to provide the provincial Cabinets with a sense of functioning together, to call party meetings frequently and to carry all groups by rising above them. On matters of administration he rarely went beyond admonition. Provincial autonomy was allowed to become a reality even to the extent of jeopardizing vital programmes such as education and land reforms.

An even greater barrier to national cohesiveness was the hierarchy of Indian society. 'What is wrong with us?' Nehru once asked, and answered, 'We have no sense of equality.'[53] For the gradual elimination of class differences Nehru looked to the spread of socialism. Caste to him was something worse than class; it was 'petrified class'.[54] But he believed that caste would be weakened by the political franchise and was certain that it was a rapidly disappearing phenomenon which would fade out even if it took a little time. He conceded that politically it was not fading out but even this he believed was a temporary phenomenon.[55] A year after the enactment in 1955 of untouchability as a criminal offence, he was optimistic enough to claim that untouchability had broken up, had no life in it and, except in odd areas, had gone.[56] This was certainly a 'capacity for self-delusion' even if not 'amounting almost to deliberate self-deception'.[57] The spirit of over-confident Benthamism was still strong in India. The Prime Minister underestimated the resistance to economic and social change and believed too much in the power of reason, the strength of the law and the leverage of the vote. This was too naïve a theory of modernization, which ignored the rigidity of tradition, the endurance of

[53] Quoted by Krishna Menon in an article in the Malayalam newspaper *Mathrubhoomi* (Calicut), 14 November 1964.

[54] Nehru to Chief Ministers, 25 October 1957.

[55] Speech at Allahabad university, 1 December 1961. A.I.R. Tapes.

[56] T. Mende, *Conversations with Mr. Nehru* (London, 1956), p. 112.

[57] The phrases are Professor Hugh Tinker's, *Times Literary Supplement*, 4 July 1975.

conservatism and the propensity to violence. In India, in Nehru's time as today, law, belief and fact are all divergent from each other. Perfect codes and the widest catholicity of outlook go with the narrowest and most bigoted forms of social behaviour.

Nowhere was this clearer than in what Nehru regarded as the chief problem of Indian unity, the need to foster among the Muslims the feeling that they were not second-class citizens in India. For this purpose he made secularism the national policy. There would be no official religion and belief was a private matter for each individual. The tolerance at the heart of the Hindu faith (whatever the practice) could form the base for the Western concept of separation of the state from religion. Secularism would be the cement of a new social contract binding together the inhabitants of India into one political community, with religious faith having no bearing on civic rights. This, of course, was the only civilized position possible for any state in the twentieth century; and Nehru strove incessantly to ensure implementation of this policy. The need, for example, to recruit to the civil services a sufficient number of Indians belonging to faiths other than Hinduism was one of his perennial concerns. The rejection of the outrageous thesis that a good Muslim cannot be a good Indian coloured even his foreign policy and strengthened his resolve not to hand over Kashmir to Pakistan. But a secular society had not become established beyond question in India by the time of his death. Communal riots are still not a past phenomenon.

Paradoxically, in his efforts to make the Muslims feel at home in India, Nehru declined to enact a common civil code and insist on monogamy and rights of divorce, property and inheritance for all Indians of whatever faith. Nehru prided himself on what he had done for the emancipation of women, which was to him the test of a civilization; but he had to reconcile himself to the denial of equality, proclaimed by the Constitution, to Muslim women. In the interests of unity and integration, this aspect of the social revolution, on which Nehru laid great store, was deliberately held back from completion.

SIX

There were weaknesses too in the working of the democratic system. Nehru assumed that, as in the years of the national movement, politicians in India would be, by and large, honest, intelligent, conscientious and public-spirited. In fact, in a different setting, they have generally turned out to be selfish and narrow-minded; and they have been able to secure control of the political and party machinery. With the lack of simultaneous economic and social transformation, the unequal society has subdued adult suffrage to its own advantage. As Marx had noted, universal suffrage may give the right to govern but does not give the power to govern. Despite the growing spread of politicization, as of today the major beneficiaries of democracy in India are the most prosperous sections of society, the dominant landowning castes and the individuals who can derive influence from the wide network of traditional caste, kinship and economic ties. Nehru sought to arrest this development by promoting participatory democracy as a support to the base of the parliamentary system. This is no new idea in recent times. Marx spoke vaguely of self-organized communities of workers while John Stuart Mill expected cooperatives of producers to bring about a moral revolution in society. In modern Britain there is a fresh emphasis on the need to reduce the intervention of the state even in the cause of socialism[58] while the community programme is widely regarded as the essence of the American ideology of development.[59] In line with such thought, Nehru, with a faith in human nature which was never weakened, looked to local initiative for mitigating the distortions of the parliamentary system in a country of such size and sprawl. He was more of a moral than a mechanistic revolutionary and sought the proper blend of spontaneous voluntary effort, legislative impetus and official interventionist activity. But the ambitions of politicians combined with bureaucratization to smother 'decentralized democracy' in all the forms in which it was tried. The millennial promise of these programmes has petered out. Had Nehru not waited till the 1960s to place great emphasis on the primacy of education, the villagers might have secured sufficient self-confidence and intellectual alertness to ensure the better functioning of *panchayat raj*. It might also have been more rewarding if Nehru's Government had encouraged landless labour to organize itself so that greater pressure could have been brought to bear on the landlords and other influential elements in the rural areas. More attention should also have been given to the creation of cadres suited for community development and other local institutions. Administrative reforms generally were neglected. The failure to dismantle the civil services inherited from the raj and to replace them with a new machinery of administration suited to the objectives of free India set up unnecessary hurdles. Even more, the retention of a conservative bureaucracy fostered a climate in favour of the status quo.

The other hope was that political democracy would settle down on an even keel once planning had made its impact and enabled production adequate to meet the needs of all in society. Obviously industrialization, particularly in the public sector, would require decisions from the central and state Governments and the planning authorities; but in all other spheres Nehru hoped for popular initiative and consent. He would have agreed with the words of a Menshevik which Trotsky quoted against Stalin: 'You cannot build a planned economy in the way the Pharaohs built their pyramids.'[60] The objective was to provide India with economic self-reliance, based on a strong

[58] See e.g., E. Luard, *Socialism without the State* (London, 1979).

[59] E.S. Mason, *Economic Planning in Under-developed Areas: Government and Business*, quoted in G. Myrdal, *Asian Drama*, Vol. 2 (New York, 1968), p. 1,152.

[60] I. Deutscher, *The Prophet Armed Trotsky 1879–1921* (Oxford, 1970 edn), p. 500.

public sector in heavy industry, a regulated private sector and cooperative farming. These would, apart from increasing production and thereby enabling a more just distribution, produce a climate of modernization and a social revolution by persuasion. Disparities should be lessened and social justice promoted by public pressures and a friendly approach even if it slowed down the pace of change; and the whole process would be carried through in a democratic way. 'I want to change the "vested interests". I do not want to destroy them.'[61] He was coming round to Gandhi's position that a revolution is not necessarily a break, and drastic change without loss of continuity could be attained by forming connecting links between conflicting elements.

Committed even from the early 1930s to fundamental changes in the economic and social structure of India, Nehru was by 1947 confident as well as determined that these changes should be brought about by peaceful methods. In the 1930s he had believed that a measure of coercion was necessary. In the mid-1940s he was in two minds: if conflict were inevitable it would have to be faced, but there was an obvious gain in avoiding or minimizing it. But as Prime Minister he had no doubt that persuasion was the only possible way. Too much of the democrat by now to consider any other means, he had also come under the spell of traditional Indian philosophy. In Ahmednagar prison, 'almost unawares, a vague idealist approach would creep into my mind, something rather akin to the Vedanta approach. It was not a difference between mind and matter but rather of something that lay beyond the mind.'[62] At first supporting Gandhian non-violence for tactical reasons, as Prime Minister he accepted it on ethical principle as well as being, because of the horrendous dimensions of nuclear weapons, without an alternative. Nor did he think that armed struggle was indispensable for the recasting of society. The class war no doubt existed but it could be resolved, in India at any rate, without the use of force. Nehru was not committed to Gandhi's doctrine of trusteeship. His forecast was that in India, where the princely states had been integrated and the *zamindari* system abolished without much even of a murmur, the propertied classes would accept the unavoidable as production increased so that there was enough for all, distribution became more equitable without hardship to anybody, the country moved steadily towards modernization and the vote was cast by vast numbers with full freedom. In the *Autobiography* Nehru had quoted with approval Tawney's observation that you cannot skin a live tiger paw by paw;[63] but he now clearly believed that the remark was not applicable in free India. Socialism not rigidified by definition and adapted to the Indian context was the logical consequence of democracy. Discarding ideological slots, the people of India would move peacefully in their own way towards a social pattern where equality of opportunity would be provided and the economic power of classes and individuals controlled; the

[61] Mende, *Conversations with Mr. Nehru*, p. 40.

[62] *The Discovery of India* (Calcutta, 1946), p. 18.

[63] p. 422.

country 'may wake up some morning to find that socialism has come'.[64] India, he claimed in 1956 when everything was going well, had a capacity for winning over people rather than fighting them; and the persuasive approach, which was proving so effective politically, could be applied to economic and social matters. The benefits of higher technological and industrial experience could be obtained without going through a phase of capitalism.[65] It was a grand dream of a modern, democratic, socialist India, achieved with as much importance attached to the means as to the end. Nehru's hope was for a society where decisions would be made on the basis of popular will and rational discourse, human improvement would be achieved by education and social progress promoted by general consent. He could not believe that socialism required the discarding of liberal values. His strategies, both political and economic, arose coherently out of his fundamental belief in liberty. He had a harmonic conception of society, of an India finding her own peaceful path to modernity without suppressing her individuality. There need be no tension in reconciling commitment to progress with allegiance to the past. 'We are trying to evolve a modern state within the framework of India's culture.'[66] In one of his last writings, two days before his death, he emphasized that India should benefit by modern technical processes and increase production; 'but in doing so we must not forget that the essential objective to be aimed at is the quality of the individual and the concept of *dharma* underlying it'.[67]

It can, of course, be argued that the very premiss of Nehru's philosophy of democratic socialism was wrong and that a parliamentary system is inseparable from capitalism. His ideas, formulated in the 1930s when liberal democracy seemed the only alternative to fascism and communism, have been condemned as unfitted to India and a cloak for capitalist stabilization and the perpetuation of the ascendancy of the middle class. The belief that there need be no conflict between poverty and property is part of the myth of 'bourgeois universalism'. The shattering by one class of the authority of another can be brought about by dispossession from below or confiscation from above but never by persuasion and voluntary surrender. To right a wrong, insisted Mao, one has to exceed the proper limits.

> The blue eyes of the Revolution
> Shine with a necessary cruelty . . .[68]

In certain situations, to act justly is to act brutally. Many harsh episodes, Lukács has said, were unavoidable in the ultimately humane logic and libertarian dynamics of the French Revolution. Class society cannot be

[64] Keir Hardie.
[65] Address to the Standing Committee of the National Development Council, 7 January 1956.
[66] To T.A. Nizami, 6 May 1964.
[67] 25 May 1964. Preface to Shriman Narain, *Socialism in Indian Planning* (Delhi, 1964).
[68] Louis Aragon.

reconstructed by rational methods. Bourgeois parliamentarism is bound, in Rosa Luxemburg's phrases, soon to lose its stimulating fire and move logically in a descending line. From this viewpoint, Nehru is seen, whatever the rhetoric, as anchored securely to his own class and being no more than 'a hole-and-corner reformer'[69] with the political and moral outlook of a British Edwardian liberal – an Asquith in *khaddar*. With 'the false consciousness of the radical bourgeoisie',[70] he managed to have it both ways, combining the comforts of a privileged class with the intellectual pleasure of rejecting it. Conscience-stricken members of exploiting elites prove powerful advocates for a few concessions which ensure the continuance of a steady flow of benefits to their own class.

However, a humane and democratic socialism is not necessarily fated to futility. There can be more to it than ethic and rhetoric. Weaknesses and illusions are neither innate nor unavoidable in a country like India. The right of all individuals to develop their capacities need not be confined to market societies; nor need it be given a racist tinge and believed to be possible only in North America and Western Europe.[71] Nehru was courageous enough to seek to extend this particular European tradition to India. Though heavily influenced by Marxist writings in his younger days, basically Nehru was in the line of William Morris, who was repelled by the vulgarity and the squalor of capitalism, and of those European radicals who saw in socialism the result of a purely rationalist conception of society seeking to diminish the obscure and evil forces. The revolution could not be hastened by violence but should come only when the people willed it after their minds had been trained for it by experience of elections and by education. Nehru's socialism, as that of the French socialists, Jaurès and Blum, was above all 'a humanistic creed, placing its major emphasis on the fulfilment of the individual'.[72] But, unlike the European radicals, who looked down on nationalism, Nehru thought a love of country could inspire revolutionary change. It could inspire authority to coherent activity and sustain popular initiative as a liberating force.

Are such attitudes, lofty and noble as they are, suited to India, where poverty and hunger are the norms of daily life? A developing society's need for law, security and economic growth would seem to take priority over individual rights. It has recently been suggested that the two principles of justice, namely the basic liberties and no inequality in distribution unless it works for the benefit of the least advantaged group in society, should be introduced once a society has reached a certain measure of economic development so that there is enough to feed everybody.[73] Nehru accepted the second part of the formula and worked on the basis that differences in wealth should

[69] Marx and Engels, *The Communist Manifesto*.

[70] P. Clarke, *Liberals and Social Democrats* (Cambridge, 1978), p. 4.

[71] C.B. Macpherson, *The Life and Times of Liberal Democracy* (Oxford, 1977), argues the first point convincingly but restricts his discussion almost wholly to the Western world.

[72] T. Zeldin, *France 1848–1945*, Vol. 2 (Oxford, 1977), p. 1,081.

[73] J. Rawls, *A Theory of Justice* (Oxford, 1972).

be tolerated till production was sufficient; but he insisted on civil liberties even before a certain level of economic growth had been attained. He did not think that the price of democracy was necessarily the neglect of the true interests and aspirations of the Indian people; rather, the first could make the second more stable even if slower of attainment.

The experience of various models of development in the last seventy years strengthens the view that Nehru's model for India, however unprecedented, is a practical one. Stalin modernized the Soviet Union with authoritative measures and succeeded because he could insulate his country in the 1920s from the outside world. Mao tried to do the same in China in the 1950s and 1960s with less success; and now China is willing to compromise with capitalism. In fact, one can hardly talk any longer of a distinctive Chinese model, for in that country the revolution has lost its way and her rulers have come round to the view that class struggle is subservient to production, that, in a socialist country, at each period of history, those relations of production which best promote the development of the forces of production are the best for that period, and that growth must come first for without growth there will be very little to distribute.[74] Ideology has sunk out of sight while the party hurries down the capitalist road. In contrast, the Indian effort, at development with participation as an integral factor and openness to the outside world, has, over the years, gained credibility in comparison with other parallels.

SEVEN

For the great increase in industrial and agricultural production which he planned for India, Nehru placed his hopes in science and technology. Deeply influenced by the writings of Russell, Bernal, Haldane and the radical scientists of the 1930s, Nehru saw science as the natural agent of progress and the obvious servant of socialism. The world had now both the resources and the means, if properly utilized, to make every person prosperous. Laws of scarcity need no longer apply; and that there was enough and more to go round for everybody was 'the real meaning of socialism'.[75] Liberation would come through knowledge. A scientific outlook would lead to rational decisions; and the fuller development and wider application of science would themselves create the preconditions for socialism. This was scientific socialism not in the Marxist but in a much narrower sense; a planned economy producing goods and services sufficient for all and equitably distributed.[76] Science was the ability to change the world. It could take society without violence across the

[74] See the essays, especially those of J. Gray, T. Saich and A. Watson, in J. Gray and G. White (eds), *China's New Development Strategy* (London, 1982).

[75] Speech at the A.I.C.C., Nagpur, 9 January, *The Hindu*, 10 January 1959.

[76] G. Werskey, *The Visible College* (London, 1978), pp. 210–11.

threshold to a world of prosperity and full control of resources. These ideas lost support in Western Europe after the Second World War; but, thanks to Nehru, they became a part of establishment thinking in India. In an official resolution sponsored by the Prime Minister, the Government of India laid down that the key to national prosperity, apart from the spirit of the people, was to be found in the effective combination of technology, raw materials and capital, and of the three the first factor was the most important, for modern scientific techniques could make up for a deficiency in natural resources and reduce the demand on capital. So scientific research in all its aspects, pure, applied, and educational, would be encouraged.[77] In fact, public expenditure under this heading rose from Rs 2·4 crores in 1947 to Rs 55 crores in 1964. Symbolic of India's achievements was the completion of the construction at Trombay, just before Nehru's death, by Indian scientists and engineers, of a plant for the extraction of plutonium. Indeed, it was generally accepted that India could make an atomic bomb, though clearly she had no intention of doing so.

Scientists were also treated with special respect. Apart from encouraging Indian scientists, when Robert Oppenheimer was disgraced in the United States Nehru invited him to India, for a brief visit or a long stay or permanent migration – as he wished. Oppenheimer declined for he felt that, till he had been cleared, his place was in the United States; and he feared that permission to go to India would not only be refused but the very act of seeking it would increase suspicion of him.[78] But Haldane was anxious to work in India and was welcomed and provided with the facilities he required.

The encouragement of science and scientists was expected to help not only in improving the material environment but in influencing even the mental conditioning. In India 'we live with every century surrounding us, not only in our external lives but in our minds'. The spread of scientific knowledge would reveal the absurdity of such mental co-existence by strengthening the scientific attitude, which to Nehru was basically open-mindedness, the effort to search out the truth by experiment, not to believe anything that could not be proved to be true nor to disbelieve anything unless proved wrong.[79] But, while enthusiastic about the capacity of science and technology to make India an advanced economy and strengthen the rational outlook, Nehru did not forget that science should be a servant and not the master of man. Scientists should look beyond their technical achievements and 'gradually develop something of the wisdom of the sage, something even of the compassion of the saint'.[80] He was particularly anxious that scientific progress should not be at the cost of the consensus of basic values which had developed in India over the centuries. The

[77] Resolution of the Government of India on scientific policy, 4 March 1958.

[78] Consul-General of India in New York to Prime Minister after meeting with R. Oppenheimer, 19 July 1954; Nehru to H.J. Bhabha, 26 July 1954.

[79] Speech in the Lok Sabha, 1 May 1958. Debates, Second Series, Vol. 16, pp. 12,764–75.

[80] Speech at the inauguration of the Indian Science Congress at Madras, 6 January, *The Hindu*, 7 January 1958.

aim should be 'a marriage between ancient Indian thought based on a spiritual approach and modern scientific endeavour based on experimentation in search of truth'.[81] He was struck by a remark of Vinoba Bhave that 'the days of politics and religion are gone and the days of science and spirituality have come'. Science was organized knowledge and without it India's problems could not be solved; but it was for the human mind and spirit to control science and steer it in the right direction.[82] That would enable a synthesis between modernity and the individuality of India, between all that was valuable in the past and worthwhile in the present.[83] The atomic reactor at Trombay and the massive image of Trimurti, the three-faced god, in the Elephanta caves, facing each other across a strip of sea at Bombay, symbolized for him not only the contrast between physical and spiritual power but the importance for both of them to be present on the scene and work together, neither by itself being enough.[84] All the science and industry in the wide world could not save or help a nation unless it followed certain basic standards and human values.[85] To harmonize the two was the great problem of the age; and the way could only be one of slow growth.

> So let science grow, as it must and will. Let the arts and humanities grow also. Behind it all let there be that dynamism, that vibrant message, that creativeness without which life for the individual becomes drab and dull, and a community gradually weakens and plays no effective part.[86]

EIGHT

Science and technology were to be employed, in Nehru's view, immediately and on a massive scale for the purpose of the industrialization of India. Britain's exploitation of India as an agricultural dependency being to him one of the worst aspects of imperialism, Nehru moved away from Gandhi's aversion to industrialization and was convinced that its promotion at all levels was of primary importance. As he said to Gandhi in 1940, if you sit on your large-scale industries, then other countries will sit on you.[87] There was to him no hope of India coming into her own and consolidating her independence without industrialization. Few now dispute that this was the right policy. In an economy of the size of India's, with a very large market, abundant natural

[81] Speech at Calcutta, 30 November, *The Hindu*, 1 December 1958.

[82] Speech at Bangalore, 15 September 1960. A.I.R. Tapes.

[83] Address to the Congress Parliamentary Party, 19 April 1963. Tape M-70/C.

[84] Speech to the Central Advisory Board of Education, 17 January 1961. A.I.R. Tapes.

[85] Speech at Teheran university, 20 September 1959. A.I.R. Tapes.

[86] Speech at Punjab university, Chandigarh, 27 February 1959. A.I.R. tapes.

[87] See Amrit Kaur's notes of a discussion at Wardha sometime in 1940, *Selected Works of Jawaharlal Nehru*, Vol. 15 (Delhi, 1982), Appendix, p. 647.

30 With a young visitor, Dehra Dun, 26 May 1964

31 27 May 1964

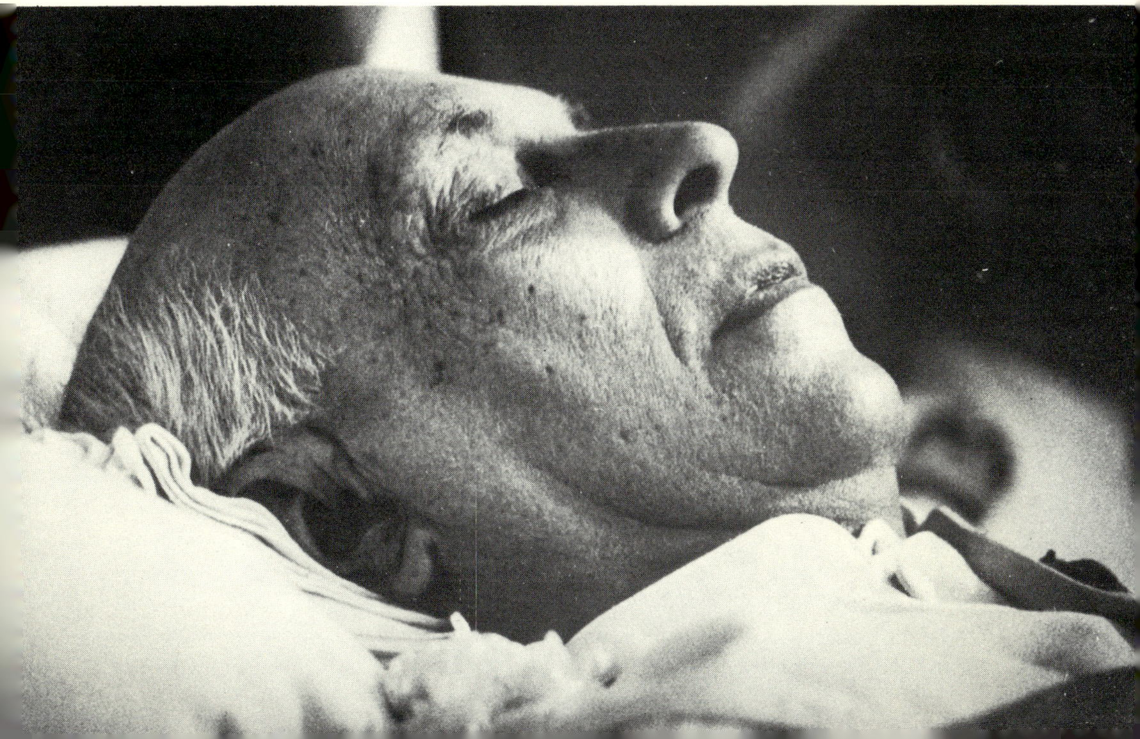

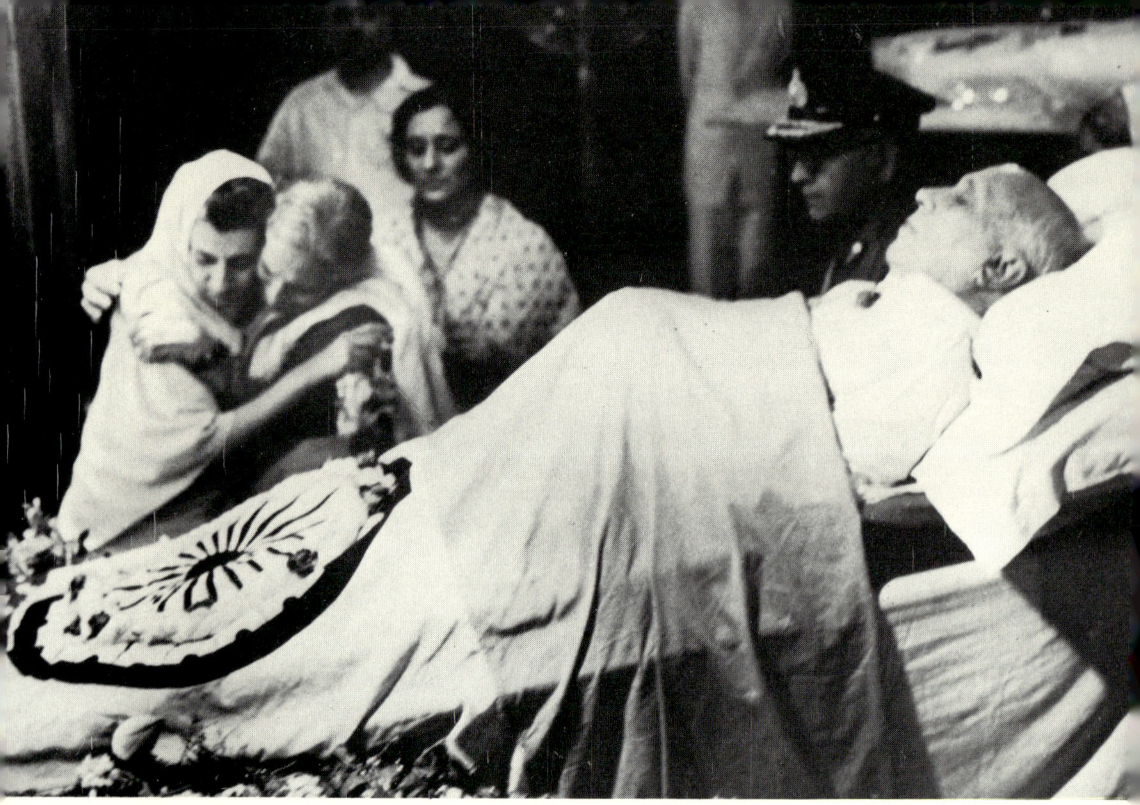

32 Lying in state, 27 May 1964

33 The funeral procession, 27 May 1964

resources of every kind and vast reserves of skilled and unskilled manpower, a strong and diversified base of capital goods is 'a historical necessity',[88] indispensable for self-reliance, defence, technology for investment in agriculture, adequate production of consumer goods and development in other sectors. The advance attained, during the Nehru years, in the metallurgical, mechanical, chemical, power and transport sectors has provided India with the broad foundations of a modern economy. Electric power capacity increased fourfold, the freight-carrying capacity of the railways more than doubled and the length of surfaced roads increased nearly twofold. Particularly spectacular was the development of the production of machine tools, iron ore, aluminium, petroleum products and fertilizers. The country has today, because of Nehru's policies, the basic facilities required for almost every branch of modern manufacture, the capacity to look after her own conventional defences in the long run and a large corps of scientists, engineers and technicians. Between 1951 and 1965, the index of industrial production registered an average growth rate of about 7 per cent per annum, a rate respectable even by the standards of capitalist countries. The index (using 1956 as a base line) rose from 74 in 1951 to 182 in 1966. Alongside, there was admittedly an increase in the country's indebtedness, for, after the rapid exhaustion in the 1950s of the sterling balances accumulated during the Second World War because of the disproportionate import by the private sector of consumer goods and equipment, India ran short of foreign exchange and became dependent for this on Western countries and, in the 1960s, on an 'aid India' consortium.[89] Yet, of all the countries of the Third World, India has the strongest industrial base.

Nehru did not think it necessary that the state should be in charge of the whole industrial process. His experience of the work of the planning committee before 1947, where capitalists and industrialists had joined with others in drawing up a blueprint of national production, and the fact that a few major industralists had drafted in 1944 the 'Bombay Plan' for accelerated industrialization, led him to believe that a joint effort on similar lines was possible in a free India. A mixed economy, with both public and private sectors, could lead to growth in every sphere. Obviously the state would have to be responsible for the construction and development of the heavy, machine-building, 'mother' industries. Apart from the necessity of public control of such industries in a socialist society, there was also the practical aspect. The relatively small capitalist class in India could not possibly supply large capital investment and provide the high level of technology over long periods which these industries required. The state could afford to take a long view as well as preclude monopoly gains and ensure public accountability in vital areas.[90] The growth of the public sector is not by itself the growth of socialism; but it

[88] Raj Krishna, 'The Nehru–Gandhi Polarity and Economic Policy', in B.R. Nanda, P.C. Joshi and Raj Krishna, *Gandhi and Nehru* (Delhi, 1979), p. 59.

[89] D. Thorner, *The Shaping of Modern India* (Delhi, 1980), pp. 136, 144–5; P. Patnaik, 'Industrial Development in India since Independence', *Social Scientist*, June 1979, pp. 3–19.

[90] S. Chakravarty, 'Nehru and the Public Sector', *Mainstream* (Delhi), 29 November 1980.

would help to lay the foundation of socialism by enabling the material basis for a socialist management of the economy.

So long as the state controlled the basic industries, Nehru was willing to leave private enterprise in the remainder. Seeing no inherent conflict between the public and the private sectors and deprecating 'grousing, nibbling and squabbling' about priorities between them,[91] Nehru was willing to place the Finance and Commerce Ministries, right through his years of office, in the hands of men who did not conceal their right-wing views. He did not think that this in itself would hinder the movement towards socialist objectives, for socialism was to him not a code of dogma but a pragmatic endeavour leading to higher production, more even distribution and greater equality of opportunity. Nehru was heavily influenced from his undergraduate days by Bernard Shaw; as he wrote to Shaw much later, 'like many of my generation, we have grown up in company with your writings and books. I suppose a part of myself, such as I am today, has been moulded by that reading.'[92] His ideas of socialism were certainly very akin to those of Shaw: sufficiency of means, equality of opportunity and national intermarriageability for everybody, and poverty, not wealth, as the evil to attack and abolish. He frequently quoted Shaw's analysis of socialism: 'the economist's hatred of waste and disorder, the aesthete's hatred of ugliness and dirt, the lawyer's hatred of injustice, the doctor's hatred of disease, the saint's hatred of the seven deadly sins.'[93]

These tenets of socialism in practice Nehru believed would emerge more rapidly, and with less violence and conflict, from the accommodating ethos of a mixed economy than from a rigid and dogmatic adherence to orthodox socialist doctrines. He even accepted that a mixed economy was based on a 'mixed ideology'.[94] He was a confirmed believer in the application of Liddell Hart's doctrine of the indirect approach to political and economic problems. 'Avoid a frontal attack on a long established position; instead seek to turn it by a flank movement, so that a more penetrable side is exposed to the thrust of truth.'[95] To Nehru the mixed economy was, in the context of India's under-development, such an indirect approach towards the fact of socialism even if not in accordance with any theory.[96] A capitalist economy with considerable state control and a public sector directly under the state would gradually transform itself into a socialist economy. He envisaged the private sector helping in increasing the national wealth even while the public sector gradually expanded, overlapped and finally overwhelmed the private sector. Meantime, India would have been modernized, would be producing more

[91] Speech at the A.I.C.C., Nagpur, 8 January, *The Hindu*, 9 January 1959.

[92] 4 September 1948. Nehru, *A Bunch of Old Letters* (Bombay, 1958), p. 500.

[93] *Everybody's Political What's What?* (London, 1945), p. 78.

[94] Address to the Congress Parliamentary Party, 27 November 1961. Tape M-61, Parts I and II.

[95] Liddell Hart's preface to 'The Strategy of Indirect Approach' (1941). Quoted in *The Discovery of India*, p. 542.

[96] Cf. Keynes: 'The true socialism of the future will emerge, I think, from an endless variety of experiments directed towards discovering the respective appropriate spheres of the individual and of the social and the terms of fruitful alliances between these sister impulses.' *The Nation*, 24 May 1924.

than enough for her requirements and would have become self-reliant; and there would be enough for all.

None of this, as we know, has happened. The public sector has yielded results in that production has steadily risen in sectors such as oil, steel, transport, power and heavy chemicals; and, but for the initiative of the state, these results could not have been attained. Whatever the deficiencies in the working of enterprises in the public sector, the general achievement is impressive. But this sector has not been as successful in slowly spreading so as to squeeze out the private sector. Rather, it has served the private sector and helped it to maintain itself. Before 1951, the private sector was responsible for 92 per cent of India's gross national product; the corresponding figures were over 90 per cent during the 1950s and over 86 per cent in the 1960s.[97] Even the representatives of British capital in India have expressed satisfaction at the new opportunities given to the private sector by the activity of the state in basic and heavy industries.[98] After 1957, the Government encouraged foreign collaboration to ease the problem of foreign exchange and to secure technical and managerial skills. If Nehru had been more committed to nationalization, such developments might have been curbed. Public ownership is not, of course, an objective in itself and is only one possible means to an end. Socialism is more than economic organization; but it is also more than a public sector with a certain amount of moralism. The mere play of economic forces in a mixed economy, even with official encouragement, has proved inadequate to tilt the balance in favour of the public sector. A rich business class nullified the intentions of the Government.[99]

NINE

The development of heavy industry was also expected to provide collateral advantages in agriculture. By the mid-1950s Nehru had begun to comprehend that, unless there were an increase in agricultural productivity, there could be no real 'take-off' of the economy. But it was thought that such an increase could be achieved by mechanization. The application of scientific methods to agriculture has resulted in a considerable increase in production and, indeed, alone made it possible. Even a 4 per cent rate of growth in agriculture requires a high rate of industrial growth supplying electric power, fertilizers and other necessary inputs. Better techniques certainly help to raise the yield; and in

[97] S.A. Kochanek, *Business and Politics in India* (University of California Press, 1974), p. 91.

[98] See the comments of leading British businessmen in 1957 and 1960, quoted in *The Bengal Chamber – 125 Years of Service* (published by the Bengal Chamber of Commerce and Industry, Calcutta, 1978), pp. 92, 94.

[99] See A.K. Bagchi, 'Long-Term Constraints on India's Industrial Growth 1951–1968', in E.A.G. Robinson and M. Kidron (eds), *Economic Development in South Asia* (London, 1970), pp. 170–92.

India, where the yield per acre, even in 1964, was among the lowest in the world, there was considerable scope for such investment.[100]

The rise in agricultural productivity, while perhaps not as great as it should have been, is still considerable. During the years 1961–5, production rose by 65 per cent. The compound rate of annual increase of food production from the early 1950s to 1964–5 was about 3 per cent.[101] In the three Plans, apart from the investment in the industries serving agriculture, almost a fifth of the outlays in the public sector was consistently allocated for agricultural development. Nehru's strategy was plural; his 'chronic eclecticism'[102] led him to work for simultaneous progress in all sectors of the economy. Yet the Plans did not provide sufficient funds to agriculture. The First Plan allotted 15·5 per cent of the total outlay to agriculture and community development and 16 per cent to major irrigation projects; these were reduced to 11 per cent and 9 per cent respectively under the Second Plan; and the figures under the Third Plan were 14 per cent and 9 per cent. The amounts become even lower when it is realized that community development did little for agricultural production. The allocations for agriculture in the Plans were not raised even higher because of the belief that industrialization would serve as a lever for agricultural growth, thereby dispensing with the need for greater direct inputs into rural development. But in a country like India both are needed with equal emphasis.

More worrying is that, even with the increase achieved in productivity, there has been no consequential widespread distribution of the agricultural yield. Neither political democracy nor local voluntary effort nor the achievement of growth has resulted in a revision of the basic structure of society. Whereas in China, in 1946–7, after the war with Japan had ended, Mao instituted a policy of radical land reform in the liberated areas,[103] in India the triumph of nationalism was primarily political; and even after 1947 Nehru's Government did not eliminate, to use Marx's phrase, 'medieval rubbish'. Indeed, with landlords with medium-sized estates and the richer peasantry taking advantage of better techniques and greater facilities, a new elite has developed in the countryside. The ownership of land by a few and the improved methods of agricultural operations have worsened the position of the rural poor. By 1964, with continuous shortfalls in agricultural production and growing stress on the need to increase it by greater irrigation and more intensive methods of cultivation, land reforms fell into the background.

It has now become common to fault Nehru for these false priorities and to

[100] Cf. Sir Arthur Lewis: 'Far too much emphasis is placed in current discussion on other institutional matters — especially fragmentation, size and marketing — and much too little upon other means of increasing efficiency — especially water supplies, seed farms for improved seed, fertilizers and agricultural extension services . . . The present institutional framework is in most under-developed countries (but not all) quite adequate for an enormous advance in productivity by means of the introduction of improved technology.' *Theory of Economic Growth*, (London, 1963), p. 136.

[101] Thorner, *The Shaping of Modern India*, pp. 146–7.

[102] Raj Krishna, 'The Nehru–Gandhi Polarity and Economic Policy', p. 52.

[103] T. Skocpol, *States and Social Revolutions* (Cambridge, 1979), p. 261.

suggest that, having little interest in economics,[104] he was misled by his belief in industrialization and faith in science to give agriculture a low importance and allow it to develop distortions in growth. It is perhaps true that Nehru, whose first-hand experience of the peasantry was derived from Awadh, an area dominated by *talukdars*, was prone to believe that once the *zamindari* system had been abolished the main barrier to economic and social change in the rural areas had been removed and thereafter progress would build up its own momentum. He was not sharply conscious of differentiation within the peasantry and placed stress only on two catagories, the rich landlords and the poor peasantry. At the Congress session in Nagpur in 1959, when the draft resolution on cooperative farming proposed the vesting of surplus land in *panchayats* of 'landless labour and small peasants', Nehru had the reference to small peasants deleted. But it should be remembered that the Second Plan, which elaborated the strategy of the importance of machine-building industries and the ancillary development of agricultural productivity, was not the brain-child of Nehru alone. Apart from Mahalanobis, who was Nehru's chief adviser, the drafting of the Plan benefited from the expert opinions of distinguished economists from both Western and Eastern Europe – and they all agreed that industrialization should be the main thrust of India's economic programme.[105]

That the intensification of inequality was not the result of stagnation but the paradoxical consequence of greater economic growth – this had become clear by the late 1950s. Nehru, of course, knew that a democratic and socialist society implied the reduction of class differences; but he was confident that these would be gradually eroded, even if not immediately ended. Socialism would come in phases and economic development had to precede social justice. He knew that socialism was redistributive growth. It was not accumulation by itself as sought after by capitalism;[106] but distribution without a sufficient quantity to distribute is meaningless. A socialist is not a voyeur of poverty. India had, with socialist objectives, to initiate a major programme of capital accumulation, invest vast resources in building up a large infrastructure in such areas as energy and transport, move away from dependence on a few agricultural commodities for exports, improve agricultural yields and develop skilled manpower. But Nehru did not grasp sufficiently that production and distribution must be simultaneous, that technological productivity and structural changes in society need to go together, that growth and equity are parts of a single model. The consequences for India of such dichotomy in planning have been increased growth with sharper inequity. During the years of Nehru's Prime Ministership, India

[104] For example, J.K. Galbraith, *A Life in our Times* (London, 1981), p. 331.

[105] P.C. Joshi, 'Dimensions of Agricultural Planning: Reflections on the Mahalanobis Approach', *Man and Development* (Chandigarh), Vol. IV, pp. 23–31.

[106] cf. Marx: 'Accumulate, accumulate! That is Moses and the prophets! . . . Accumulation for accumulation's sake, production for production's sake; by this formula classical economy expressed the historical mission of the bourgeoisie . . .' *Capital*, Vol. 1 (Moscow edn, 1959), p. 595.

maintained a steady annual growth rate – 3 per cent during the First Plan, (1951–6), 4 per cent during the next five years and 17·6 per cent during the first four years of the Third Plan. Investment was stepped up from less than 5 per cent before 1951 to 14 per cent by the end of the Third Plan. The rate of savings rose from 5·7 per cent of the national income in 1950–1 to 11·2 per cent in 1963–4. The gross national product went up by 70 per cent over the years 1951 to 1966 and the per capita income rose, despite an increase in population of 135 millions, by 20 per cent. Prices were virtually stable for the first seven years and sometimes even fell below the base level of 1950–1. They began to rise only after 1960 and then by very little. The average rise in prices during these thirteen years was 1·7 per cent. Despite the concerns about Pakistan and China, the percentage of the national income spent on defence during these years was not more than 1·9 per cent.

Yet this planned development did not pave the way for socialism but promoted capitalist enterprise in both industry and agriculture. Growth has resulted in a greater concentration of economic powers. The failure to distribute land, and its utilization to meet the wants of a few owners rather than the needs of the majority of the rural population, have continuously increased the extent and levels of poverty among the landless peasantry.[107] Nehru placed his hopes for reversing this process in cooperative farming. This was an idea he had for long favoured. In 1936 he had spoken of 'collective and cooperative enterprises' as the obvious way of reforming the land system;[108] but as Prime Minister he rejected the concept of collective farming because it involved regimentation, and was an advocate of peasants with small holdings coming together voluntarily. But cooperative farming could not solve the problem of the large numbers of landless labour; and even as a means for greater productivity it would have been more pertinent if land reforms had come first, for viable cooperatives cannot be firmly based on unequal holdings.[109] Nor did the other institutions set up in the rural areas prove more effective. It was even hoped by some that community development would discourage the reorganization of property relations by stressing a commonalty of interests.[110]

Moreover, the effort at cooperative farming, such as it was, was made too late and too weakly to have a decisive impact. The farmers who had taken over from the *zamindars* had no intention of merging their newly acquired estates in any joint enterprise. By October 1964, out of the 80 million acres of tenanted land in the country, only about 384,000 acres, with about 69,000 members, were covered by 1,806 'pilot' societies set up by the Government, and 1,651 societies, organized by local initiative; and in many even of these societies

[107] C.T. Kurian, *Poverty, Planning and Social Transformation* (Delhi, 1978), pp. 112 ff; P.C. Joshi, 'Contradiction between Vision and Emerging Reality: Dynamics of Rural India' (cyclostyled paper, 1980).

[108] *An Autobiography* (Indian edn, 1962), p. 524.

[109] J.P. Mencher, *Agriculture and Social Structure in Tamil Nadu* (Delhi, 1978), pp. 236, 289.

[110] See S. Saberwal, 'Sociologists and Inequality in India', *Economic and Political Weekly*, Annual Number, 1979.

there was no joint farming. A small number of families often exploited cooperation to private advantage.[111] It would have been far better if Nehru, in the earlier years of full power and influence, had quickly followed up the abolition of the *zamindari* system with drastic measures of distribution of land and security of tenure rather than allowing the smaller landlords and the richer peasants to replace the traditional landowners of large estates. By 1954 the trend was towards land reforms; but the optimistic anticipation that once begun it could not be stopped[112] has been belied. Nehru did not stress sufficiently the urgency of land reforms. He was fully aware of the importance of such measures not only for a marked improvement in agricultural productivity but for the deeper reason, which indeed was for him its main object, 'to break up the old class structure of a society that is stagnant'.[113] The peasant, as he once said, had to be placed in the centre of the piece, because 'if we don't do it, they will'.[114] But the legislation passed in the various states to restrict the size of agricultural holdings was hardly enforced and there was consequently little change in the lower levels of the class structure. Rather, because of the expansion of growth, these levels have become more firmly entrenched. Instead of embarking simultaneously on political democracy and economic equality, hope was placed in adult suffrage as the instrument for effecting revolutionary change once there had been sufficient production to enable fair distribution. Nehru did not realize that the structure of Indian society made this impractical. He constantly gave voice to the essential values of political participation and saw in representative government the defence of the weak and the scourge of the rich rather than a mean-spirited system for the benefit of the privileged.

But it has not worked that way. Because civil liberties were not underpinned by a widespread distribution of property, from Nehru's efforts to build by stages a socialist utopia has emerged an India safe for businessmen to make profits in and for a new class of landlords to preserve its property and enforce social subordination. The effort at revolution carried out from above with the support of all sections of the people has been transformed into the protection of conservatism festooned with socialist trappings. There has been no permanent and irresistible shift in power and wealth to the lowest rungs of society. The smaller landowners have used their control of the voters to protect their own interests and the Congress Party became 'a socialist head with a conservative body',[115] Nehru taking the initiative in land reforms and his leading supporters in the rural areas thwarting them. After years of planning, development in India is associated as much with an overall increase in poverty, inequality and unemployment as with a steady growth. All the measures introduced by

111 Tarlok Singh, *Towards an Integrated Society* (Delhi, 1969), p. 94.

112 W. Ladejinsky, 'Report on India', August 1954, reprinted in *Agrarian Reform as Unfinished Business* (Oxford, 1979), pp. 202–3.

113 Note 13 July 1958, printed as 'The Basic Approach', *A.I.C.C. Economic Review*, 15 August 1958.

114 'They' meaning the Communists; quoted in Ladejinsky, 'Report on India', p. 209.

115 D. Warriner, *Land Reform in Principle and Practice* (Oxford, 1969), p. 139.

Nehru were found compatible with the maintenance of capitalist relations of production and the preservation of middle-class hegemony. It seemed that he had stood for no more than a verbal socialism of soft vagueness which fitted the facts of increasing class differentiation and growing control by new elites. To his credit, Nehru saw this distortion of his efforts and sadly commented, as his time was running out, that the process of development in any real sense had not taken root in India, except perhaps in some parts.[116]

TEN

Whatever success was achieved in agriculture also paled in contrast with the incessant increase in population. This was not so at the start. Under the first two Plans, the production of foodgrains rose at the rate of 3·39 per cent per annum while population expanded at the rate of only 1·97 per cent per year.[117] But, during the years of the Third Plan, which has been described as 'a dismal failure' in the matter of agricultural production,[118] output stagnated while the population grew by over 2·3 per cent annually instead of the estimated 1·25 per cent. Nehru gave relatively little attention to this problem. Economic progress rather than family planning was to him the primary need and he believed, in the mid-1950s, that, apart from small areas here and there, India was not an over-populated country.[119] This optimism was confirmed by the grossly inaccurate estimates of the Planning Commission. In 1951 it reckoned that the population in 1976 would be 500 millions and was proved wrong by 120 millions; and in 1956 it calculated that the population was going up by 4·6 millions every year whereas the figure was 7·5 millions. The Prime Minister compounded these errors by placing the Health Ministry in the hands of disciples of Gandhi, who regarded contraception as moral degradation and failed to utilize even the limited funds earmarked for family planning. Nehru ordered in 1958 that encouragement in every effective way be given to the development of an oral contraceptive and that community development blocks be instructed to take up family planning programmes.[120] The next year the Government of India openly supported all recognized means of controlling births.[121] But even thereafter Nehru continued to insist that India, taken as a whole, was not very heavily populated and family planning

[116] Address (in Hindi) to the Congress Parliamentary Party, 3 December 1963. Tape M-72/C.

[117] A. Mitra, 'Population and Foodgrain Output in India', in Robinson and Kidron (eds), *Economic Development in South Asia*, pp. 21–8.

[118] Myrdal, *Asian Drama*, Vol. 2, p. 1,255.

[119] See, for example, interviews to M. Brecher, 6 and 13 June 1956, M. Brecher, *The New States of Asia* (London, 1963), Appendix, p. 203; press conference at Stockholm, 24 June 1957, *Nehru in Scandinavia* (Information Service of India, Stockholm, 1958), p. 137.

[120] Nehru's note and letter to Health Minister, 23 April 1958. File 28(50)/58-60-P.M.S., Vol. One, Serials 9A and 10A.

[121] 'Family Planning Policy in India', Myrdal, *Asian Drama*, Vol. 3, Appendix 12.

was only a part of the larger movement for raising the people's standards of living. With the spread of education, especially among women, and the success of the Plans, he expected the increase of the population to be automatically controlled.[122]

A few years later, however, Nehru recognized that, whether India be over-populated or not, all efforts at development could be jeopardized seriously by the pressure of growing numbers. He warned the people that if the rise in population were not restricted, then living conditions would not improve.[123] He also recognized that they had 'not succeeded remarkably'[124] in controlling the birth rate. But to the end he did not fully comprehend the gravity of the problem and retained the comforting belief that the increase in numbers was a result of progress, of the reduction in the death rate and of the higher expectation of life.[125] He was confident too that, as education spread and development accelerated, the birth rate would automatically go down; meanwhile, it was no good just getting a pill and making everybody swallow it.[126] Long-term trends more than offset, in his view, what he regarded as short-term alarms.[127] His whole attitude was summed up in his remarks that 'it is a conceivable possibility, and some people threaten us with that, that this growth of population may overwhelm us in India and upset all our calculations. It is a possibility. I do not think it is a probability. But it is a possibility.'[128] He has proved to be over-optimistic. The inadequacy of family planning programmes and the unbroken rise in population have been among the chief barriers to India's progress. This was one of the areas of vital importance where Nehru's sense of priorities faltered.

ELEVEN

Though Nehru has been dead now for nearly twenty years, his influence is still a vital force in India. As his hopes remain valid, the controversy round his personality, work and plans continues to rage. Events since his death too colour attitudes towards him. As François Furet says of the French Revolution, scholarship is never sufficient in itself to modify the conceptualization

[122] Speech at the International Conference on Planned Parenthood, 14 February 1959; P.I.B.; Foreword dated 26 October 1960 to S. Chandrasekhar, *Population and Planned Parenthood in India*, 2nd edn (London, 1961).

[123] Address to the Central Council of Local Self-Government, 6 September 1962, *Speeches*, Vol. 5, *1963–4* (Delhi, 1968), p. 98.

[124] Address to the Asian Population Conference at Delhi, 10 December 1963, *Speeches*, Vol. 5 p. 117.

[125] The expectation of life was about 32 in the years 1941–51, 37·5 in 1951–6, 42 in 1956–61 and then 47·5.

[126] Interview to H. Bradsher of the Associated Press, 9 September, *The Hindu*, 26 September 1963.

[127] Speech in the Lok Sabha, 11 December 1963. Debates, Third Series, Vol. 23, pp. 4,201–22.

[128] Address to the Andhra legislature, Hyderabad, 27 July 1963. A.I.R. tapes.

of a problem or an event[129] – and, one may add, of a person. His critics have consistently depicted him as a weak and unrealistic Prime Minister, who has been proved a failure in all spheres of policy, domestic and foreign. It is charged that unquestioned control for years of the levers of political power had not been utilized by him to secure enduring benefit for the millions of the Indian poor, while abroad his empty flourishes had finally invited humiliation. The angry prejudice which insinuates that he was a hypocrite or no more than an ambitious politician does not merit serious treatment.[130] But attention is demanded by such assessments as that his long tenure of office 'was in many ways a premiership of character rather than accomplishment',[131] or that, as unchallenged Prime Minister, he set out to build socialism and in effect consolidated capitalism, and thus was 'a political success and at the same time a historical failure'.[132]

Character there certainly was in the Prime Ministership. Nehru was important as much for what he was as for what he strove to do. He wandered far and wide in India bearing testimony that politics was not all meanness and there was a beneficent motive in administration. No one who lived in India during the enchantment of the Nehru years needs to be reminded of the positive, generous spirit, the quality of style, the fresh and impulsive curiosity, the brief flares of temper followed by gentle contrition and the engaging streak of playfulness, all of which went along with an unrelenting sense of duty, a response to large issues, an exercise of reason and unaffiliated intelligence in human affairs, an intense, but not exclusive, patriotism and, above all, complete and transparent integrity. If Gandhi imbued the national movement with a moral tone, Nehru gave the first strivings of free India a noble purpose. To a whole generation of Indians he was not so much a leader as a companion who expressed and made clearer a particular view of the present and vision of the future. The combination of intellectual and moral authority was unique in his time.

The handling of Patel, the victory over Tandon in the early 1950s and the promotion of the Kamaraj Plan in the last year of the Prime Ministership are sufficient evidence of Nehru's tough and professional political skills. But there was another side to him, that of the withdrawn and sensitive intellectual. Yet, though he did not permit trespassers on the private enclosures of his spirit, he was keenly aware of all that was going on round him. With the press he always enjoyed a quiet rapport based on understanding and good humour; and his monthly press conferences were events of the Delhi season. Literature and the use of language were an abiding interest and he wrote in English with exquisite grace. He followed the current literary trends in India and abroad and sought out interesting and talented persons in fields outside politics. In

129 F. Furet, *Interpreting the French Revolution* (Cambridge, 1981), p. 9.

130 P. Chatterji, 'Jawaharlal Nehru and the Decade after Freedom', *Indian Historical Review*, July 1979–January 1980.

131 T.H. Beaglehole in *Dictionary of National Biography 1961–70* (Oxford, 1981).

132 Kaviraj, 'Apparent Paradoxes of Jawaharlal Nehru'.

his time Indians in all walks of life found through him a meaningful relation to the conduct of public affairs. To Nehru himself, his other interests seemed to provide him with a capacity for renewal in politics. The detachment, and the thrall to other worlds, helped to make him a more captivating leader.

Nehru's strength was ideas, not in the sense of original or rigorous conceptualization but in reading widely, thinking hard, listening to all who seemed to have something to contribute and trying to work out both ends and means that would incorporate the values and principles in which he believed and which would be suited to India and her people. 'So in this rather curious world of ours today, all one can do is to pose questions. It is only a very, very wise man or a very, very foolish man who would attempt to answer them. I am not very wise and I hope I am not very foolish.'[133] He took a broad view of events, noted historical parallels and looked for deeper explanations. The touch of the universal was never absent from his thought; and his policies were organized within a framework of some firm ethical convictions. He was admittedly prone to be taken in too easily by glib thinking – community development, *panchayat raj*, the 'take-off' stage of economic growth, the two cultures; and all too often his mind appeared in the grip of cliché. Professor Hanson had justifiably accused him of setting 'some bad intellectual fashions'.[134] But he was successful beyond measure in formulating the goals in every sphere as well as the ways by which they could be reached. He knew what India required and how it could be achieved. He was a visionary as well as a planner; and the combination imbued his vision with realism and gave a wide sweep of perspective to his planning.

The fondness for ideas, taken with his attractive failings – the agonizing continually in public over all aspects of every question, the open-mindedness carried to excess, the over-developed democratic instinct to carry all shades of opinion with him, the civilized self-doubt – have together clouded Nehru's reputation as an administrator. Doubts, as he once observed,[135] are perhaps never resolved, and all one can do is to choose that which is less evil than the alternatives. But from such hard choices he persistently retreated and was addicted to over-scrupled hesitation and delay in action. 'Well, if you like you may call me weak, I have no objection to being called weak. I do not like the dictatorial tendency in any person or any government.'[136] So he drifted to decisions on such important and thorny questions as the formation of linguistic provinces, the survival of the communist regime in Kerala and the ending of colonialism in Goa.

Even when Nehru's ideas were sound and decisions prompt, they were never as effectively and forcefully pushed through as they should have been and as he

[133] Speech at the symposium on the prospects of democracy in Asia, 12 December, *The Hindu*, 13 December 1958.

[134] *The Process of Planning* (Oxford, 1966), p. 259.

[135] Shiela Grant Duff, *The Parting of Ways*, p. 115.

[136] Speech at the A.I.C.C., Durgapur, 28 May 1961. A.I.C.C. papers, Box 19, File G-22/1961. N.M.M.L.

would have liked them to have been. For example, he repeatedly urged his colleagues in the central Government, the Chief Ministers of the states and the members of the Congress Party that a national effort was required to replace the old plough and provide the tillers with a more efficient one. He wanted the production to be undertaken in the community development blocks and the new plough given to the peasants, if necessary, on credit. This would seem a simple operation; but Nehru could only express his bewildered unhappiness that nothing was done.[137] Nehru took a deep interest in every aspect and level of the administration; but the brisk interventions which followed were not, and, given the vastness and complexity of India, could not be, continuous. Perhaps too the cast of Nehru's mind, alert but darting, was not suited to the enforcement of decisions and an unbroken watch on implementation. Blackett thought he had 'too much of intellectualism' to solve any problem. 'He just chatted. He liked chatting about the world in general . . . When I was consultant to the Defence Ministry, when I stayed with him, he just chatted. It was curious. I was surprised. He chatted.'[138]

The administration was further clogged by Nehru's frequent choice of the wrong persons to do what he wanted done; and even when he discerned their inadequacies – or had them pointed out to him – he was not prompt in dispensing with their services. He had a weakness for flamboyant buccaneers and was easily led to regard as dash and enterprise what was frequently no more than crooked manipulation. He went out of his way, for example, to secure official assistance for a shady financier to launch a shipping company; and Dharma Teja's activities were to involve the Government of India in the loss of crores of rupees. But even when his protégés were found out, Nehru was loath to discard them or take punitive action. Lack of care in selection was matched by lack of promptness in dismissal. His fidelity to his friends admitted of no question. Pushed against the wall, he dismissed Mathai and accepted Krishna Menon's resignation but persisted in believing, against all evidence, that they had been unjustly treated; and in the case of many others where disclosed facts were not so overwhelmingly against them, Nehru stoutly defended them and gave them the benefit of every doubt.

However, despite these drawbacks, the achievements of Nehru are substantial enough. The rooting of democracy in India and the formulation of a foreign policy new in concept, adapted to national interest and yet helpful in fostering a world community, in themselves ensure Nehru's position as one of the few great men of the age. In addition, there is the governance of a large and uneven country like India, keeping political life healthy and giving the extra nudge to every branch of administration and 'the right push in the right direction', as he modestly described it,[139] to the economy and society. As his

[137] Speech at the A.I.C.C., 6 January, *National Herald*, 7 January 1961.

[138] Oral testimony of P.M.S. Blackett, 22 February 1972. N.M.M.L.

[139] Address to the annual session of the Federation of Indian Chambers of Commerce and Industry, Delhi, 24 March 1962. A.I.R. tapes.

Prime Ministership drew to an end, Nehru could claim that, under the Plans, national income had increased by 42 per cent, food production by 46 per cent and industrial production by 94 per cent. Despite an increase of 21 per cent in the population, food consumption had risen from 1,800 to 2,100 calories per capita and use of cloth from a little over 9 yards per year per head to 14.5 yards.[140] It is only since the mid-1960s that there has been a noticeable deceleration in the process of growth.[141] Above all, Nehru made certain objectives so much a part of the general consciousness of India that they can today be taken for granted even if they have not been as yet fully attained – unity, democracy, civil liberties, secularism, a scientific and international outlook, planning to realize the vision of socialism. He provided India with a rich and many-sided social morality.

If, even so, Nehru seems a prophet frustrated and with his hopes unfulfilled, the cause lies in the failures to follow up the courageous introduction of adult suffrage with a speedy enforcement of land distribution and tenancy reforms, a proper emphasis on education, a revision of the administrative apparatus and control of the population. Had these steps been taken, democracy would have been accompanied by basic changes in society and the 1950s would not now appear more and more of a faded golden age. With Nehru ended the first phase of free India and events since his time make it seem increasingly remote. It is as if, when he died, he took a whole epoch with him. The Nehru age, of confident assumptions, high aspirations and considerable achievements, seems today a vanished world. There is a sickening sense of lost ideals and missed opportunities. Public service is no longer a selfless pursuit, politics in India has become dispirited and the objectives which he gave his people, then so challenging, now seem tired and muddled. Even socialism seems to have lost its spirit and become a dead residue while liberal humanism has a crumpled look. The collective self-confidence of India has received severe jolts, making the people less optimistic and economically self-assured and more fragmented socially and politically.

Nehru's career would seem, then, to underline the melancholy truths that, in public affairs, sincerity, decency and high-mindedness are not enough, and that nobility without force, statesmanship without strength, are invitations to disaster. But the revolution, which he did not believe in carrying through instantly, has, even if it has lost some of its shine, not aborted. There is a limit to the achievement of an individual and even of a generation. An elephant, says the Indian proverb which Nehru was fond of quoting, takes time to stand up. Nehru was so right about so much and what he did was so considerable, that those who function in a world he changed are apt to be critical about what he left unfinished. His very achievements demand that he be judged by standards which one would not apply to the ordinary run of Prime Ministers;

140 Nehru in the Lok Sabha, 11 December 1963. Debates, Third Series, Vol. 23, pp. 4,201–2.

141 S.D. Tendulkar, 'Economic Inequality in an Indian Perspective', in A. Beteille (ed.), *Equality and Inequality* (Delhi, 1983), p. 98.

and disappointment stems from the force of our expectations. He had the foresight to insist that democratic socialism is feasible in an under-developed society and the ability to frame a model which made this practical. It avoided centralization, gave a proper role to the political franchise and set for the first phase the right priorities. Execution was not adequate to the scheme, the authority of the state was not fully brought to bear, the political will was not often strong enough. But popular pressures were also weak. Nehru could have achieved more if his hands had been strengthened, or even forced, by left-wing forces in the country;[142] if, instead of licking the wounds which Nehru, to some extent, had helped to inflict they had assisted him in breaking down conservative resistance by promoting the mobilization of the masses. Nehru himself was only too conscious of the compromises and complexities which the exercise of power entails and of the consequent slowing down of the pace. 'We go on, a step at a time, and do the best we can.'[143] But he started India on the right road. Nehru's India was a half-made society, to use Naipaul's phrase; but it is not, therefore, destined to remain half-made for ever. When he was at Nagarjunasagar in October 1959 to inaugurate a dam, a worker came up to him and said in Telugu, 'Here you have lighted a lamp.' Nehru was greatly moved, for this seemed to him a proper test of a person's work. 'Do we, in the course of our lives, light lamps, or do we snuff out the lamps or candles that exist?' In India in his time innumerable lamps had been lit, but the field was vast and great parts of it were still in darkness.[144] The task of the generations after Nehru is to continue where he left off along the lines which he laid down. He consolidated a nation, trained it for democracy, constructed a model for economic development and set the country on the path to growth. His permanent achievements have stood out more clearly after his death. But it remains to fulfil what he envisaged – social justice – so that the pattern can be complete. India's major problem even today is the failure to reduce inequality, exploitation, elitism, illiteracy, class divisions, sexual discrimination and social backwardness.[145] Rousseau described the maker of a Commonwealth as one who toils in one century so as to reap in another.[146] Nehru was of that category. He is India's once and – we may hope – future king.

[142] Though Nehru had little in common with Bismarck, he could have considered Bismarck's effort to work out a relationship with the socialist leader Lassalle in order to exert pressure on the middle classes.

[143] To V. Sheean in 1959. Sheean, *Nehru: The Years of Power*, p. 274.

[144] Nehru to Chief Ministers, 16 October 1959.

[145] Amartya Sen, 'How is India Doing?' *New York Review of Books*, Christmas number, 1982, and 'India: The Doing and the Undoing', *Economic and Political Weekly*, 12 February 1983.

[146] *The Social Contract*, Book 2, Ch. 7.

Appendix: The Northern Boundary of India

The crucial fact in the Sino-Indian border problem is that, whatever the vagaries and ambiguities of earlier maps, from 1954 the Survey of India was showing a precise and clearly delineated northern boundary. It follows the watershed as well as the highest ranges in the areas – the Kuen Lun and the Himalaya mountains. The boundary of Kashmir with Sinkiang and Tibet (the western sector) is about 1,100 miles of which the frontier of Ladakh (a part of Kashmir) forms nearly two-thirds. At least from the tenth century, important points on the present alignment were recognized as the traditional limits of Ladakh on the one hand and Tibet on the other. This whole area of the Aksai Chin plateau and the Lingsi Tang plains was administered by the Governments of Ladakh and Kashmir and utilized for grazing by the people of Ladakh. A regular sequence of official records, stretching over many years, provides testimony on such matters as revenue assessment, police jurisdiction, public works' projects, census returns, control of trade routes and survey and mapping operations. Throughout this century, officials of the Kashmir Government and Indian traders and hunting parties have been moving freely in this area. In contrast, the Chinese authorities (and their supporters elsewhere) have been unable to produce any evidence that the Chinese were ever, before 1954, at any time in these areas; and indeed the southern limits of Sinkiang reached up to the Kuen Lun mountains only towards the end of the nineteenth century.

The boundary between Tibet and the states of Punjab, Himachal Pradesh and Uttar Pradesh (the middle sector) lies along the major watersheds; and its delimitation by tradition secured confirmation by the recognition, in the treaty of 1954 between India and the People's Republic of China, of six border passes. The frontier between Sikkim and Tibet is a watershed defined in the Anglo-Chinese Convention of 1890 and partially demarcated five years later on the ground. The northern frontier of Bhutan also lies along the highest Himalayan ranges in this area.

The frontier east of Bhutan to the tri-junction of India, Burma and China (the eastern sector) also follows the major watersheds. Tibetan influence in the

Tawang area has led to suggestions of 'dual suzerainty'; but such Tibetan jurisdiction was that of the local monastery and ecclesiastical in nature. Otherwise, there is no evidence to justify the Chinese claim to an alignment along the foothills, incorporating about 36,000 square miles of Indian territory in China. There are no documents to prove that the area was at any time under Chinese or Tibetan administration. At one stage in the 1960s the Chinese Government promised to supply the Government of India with information concerning the ways of Tibetan administration of this area; this information has yet to be received. In fact, the alignment on Chinese maps is no more than a line depicting the limit of administration of the Indian state of Assam.

The international alignment in this sector, along the highest watershed ranges, was formalized by the Indian and Tibetan representatives at the Simla Conference of 1914. The McMahon Line, as it was called after the representative of the Government of India, was not defined verbally but was drawn on 'rough compilation' maps in two sheets on the small scale of one inch to eight miles. This boundary was also marked on the map of the draft Convention presented at the Simla Conference and initialled by the Chinese representative. The Chinese Government later repudiated this treaty map because of objections to the boundaries as drawn between Tibet and China. But no objection was raised to the India–Tibet border; and, even if China had objected, it would not have mattered, for Tibet was in these years exercising treaty-making powers with the full knowledge and sanction of the Chinese Government. To give but a few illustrations: the Indo-Tibetan Convention of 1904 was formally accepted by the Anglo-Chinese Convention of 1906; and on 7 August 1913 the Chinese Foreign Office informed the Government of India that its plenipotentiary would open negotiations for a treaty jointly with the Indian and Tibetan plenipotentiaries and on an equal footing. Even the People's Government of China have acknowledged this special status of Tibet, for by the treaty with Nepal in 1956 they explicitly abrogated the treaty between Nepal and Tibet signed a hundred years earlier.

This traditional boundary of India, along its whole length, as shown by the official Indian maps of 1954, was known to the People's Government of China when, by the treaty of 1954, they explicitly undertook to respect India's territorial integrity. India had no reason to suspect *malafides*, for the Chinese were, at this time, nowhere south or west of the Indian alignment. The intrusion of some Tibetan officials and Chinese troops at a few points across the middle sector in the months after the conclusion of the treaty could be brushed off as minor disputes. In the eastern sector, the Chinese respected the Indian boundary alignment. Even in the Thagla sector, which in 1962 they questioned as not conforming to the McMahon Line, in 1953 the Chinese official at Tsona complained that the customary permission for Tibetans to utilize the pastures in the Namkha Chu valley had not been given by the Indian authorities at Tawang. This practice of giving permission to Tibetans to use the pastures continued till 1959 when, for the first time, the Chinese disputed the alignment. In the western sector, an Indian patrol to Aksai Chin and Lingzi Tang in 1951 encountered no Chinese. But major incursions began in 1955, when the Chinese authorities, with full knowledge of where India delineated the limits of her territory, started levelling a caravan route across the uninhabited plateau of Aksai Chin and completed it in about two years. But they were still not to be found west of this road; and regular Indian patrols, to Lanak La in 1952, 1954 and 1956, to Qaratagh pass via Shamal Lungpa in 1957, to Sarigh Jilganang and Amtoghar lake and to Qizil Jilga in 1958, and to Lanak La along the Chang Chenmo valley in June 1959, did not come across any Chinese. But between June and October 1959, when they attacked an Indian patrol at Kongka La, they had moved well beyond the road. A line linking up these furthest posts by November 1959 would show them in occupation of about 6,000 square miles of Indian territory. Between November 1959 and October 1962 they occupied another 5,000–6,000 square miles; and in the major assaults that began on 20 October 1962 they occupied another 2,000 square miles.

So, in the western sector, the Chinese started the occupation of Indian territory from 1955, had reached certain positions by June 1959, and thereafter constantly pushed forward the 'line of actual control' and claimed that the traditional and customary boundary lay wherever they happened at the moment to be. In 1956 an official map of China delineated the boundary in the western sector incorporating in China about 12,000 square miles of Indian territory; but the map carried a legend that the boundaries as shown on the map were yet to be revised. However, Zhou informed Nehru in December 1959 that the alignment on this map was the correct delineation. At the talks of the officials in 1960, the Chinese presented a map advancing their claims to take in another 2,000 square miles; and the Chinese Government claimed that the two lines, of 1956 and 1960, were identical. In 1962 they occupied even more territory than the furthest claims on their maps. They would seem in fact to be in search of a new alignment suited to their needs and ambition rather than defending a traditional one.

The Chinese, therefore, are imprecise about their alignments, can produce no evidence even faintly substantiating their demands and base their case solely on occupation of territory which they knew India regarded as hers. But, curiously, efforts have been made by non-Chinese writers to damage the strength of the Indian case on the border while ignoring the hollowness of the Chinese version. Much has recently been sought to be made, for example, of when and in what circumstances the McMahon Line agreement of 1914 was printed in the official collection of treaties published by the Government of India. This may be of interest to nit-pickers of historical research; but it makes no difference to the validity of the agreement. The details about the printing of the agreement of 1914 cannot affect the fact that the Chinese Government have all along been aware of the treaty and have had the McMahon Line maps in their possession. Indeed Zhou produced one of the original copies in his discussions with the Indian Ambassador in 1959. In an official publication of 1962 of the Chinese Government, 'Select Documents on Sino-Indian Relations', the McMahon Line is shown on a map as the alignment along 'the Himalayan mountains'. So even the Chinese do not regard it as an arbitrary line drawn in 1914 but as the natural frontier along the highest watershed ridge in this area.

Again, frequent reference is made to a number of old maps published by the British Government which do not show a border tallying with the Indian boundary alignment; and more weight is given to this than to the fact that there are several old Chinese maps which depict the boundary as shown by India. But the issue is a broader one than a comparison of nineteenth-century maps. To set aside the considerable and varied evidence of tradition, custom and administration stretching over centuries and look solely at some odd maps of the last hundred years is to miss the wood for some of the nearest shrubs. To assume that nothing mattered in India before the arrival of the British, to revel in the details of policy-making during the raj and to recommend compromise alignments whose sole claim to consideration is that they were suggested by Englishmen is to exhibit intellectual shallowness. The inclination of some British officials at the end of the nineteenth century to relinquish Indian sovereignty over parts of the Aksai Chin plateau does not provide China with traditional rights to this area.[1]

[1] The assumption that there was no India before British rule still lingers. Cf. 'Robert Clive, the Man Who Founded India', a broadcast in London, quoted in the *Listener*, 14 April 1983.

Biographical Notes

Abdullah, Sheikh Mahomed (1905–82). Organized the National Conference in Kashmir State in 1938; President of the All-India States Peoples Conference 1946; Prime Minister of Kashmir from 1948 to 1953, when he was dismissed and arrested; thereafter served long terms in prison; Chief Minister of Kashmir again from 1975 till his death.

Ali, S. Fazl (1886–1959). Chief Justice of the Patna High Court 1943–7; judge of the Federal Court 1947–50 and of the Supreme Court 1950–2; Governor of Orissa 1952–4; Chairman of the States' Reorganization Commission 1954–5; Governor of Assam 1956–9.

Ayub Khan, General (1907–74). Commissioned in the Indian army 1928 and transferred to the Pakistan army 1947; Commander-in-Chief 1951–4; Minister for Defence 1954–5; chief martial law administrator 1958; soon after proclaimed himself President of Pakistan; obliged to resign after widespread rioting in 1969.

Azad, Maulana A.K. (1888–1958). Scholar and nationalist who served long terms in prison; President of the Congress 1923 and 1940–6; Minister for Education from 1947 till his death.

Bakshi, Ghulam Mahomed (1907–72). Leading member of National Conference in Kashmir; Deputy Prime Minister 1947–53 and Prime Minister of Kashmir 1953–63.

Bandaranaike, Felix (b. 1931). Politician of Sri Lanka; Minister in charge of various portfolios 1960–5 and 1970–7.

Bandaranaike, Sirimavo (b. 1916). Married S.W.R.D. Bandaranaike, Prime Minister of Sri Lanka (d. 1959); Prime Minister of Sri Lanka 1960–5 and 1970–7.

Bevan, Aneurin (1897–1960). British politician; Minister in the Labour Government in charge of Health 1945–50 and Labour 1950–1.

Bhabha, Homi (1909–66). Fellow of the Royal Society; Chairman of the Indian Atomic Energy Commission; Chairman of the international conference for peaceful uses of atomic energy 1955.

Bhave, Vinoba (1895–1982). Disciple of Mahatma Gandhi, who chose him to inaugurate civil disobedience in 1940; after 1947 started the movement to donate land to the poor.

Bhutto, Z.A. (1928–79). Pakistani politician; Minister for Commerce 1958–60, for Minority Affairs 1960–2, for Industries 1962–3 and Foreign Minister 1963–6; President of Pakistan 1971–3 and Prime Minister 1973–7; deposed in 1977 and hanged on a charge of murder 1979.

Blackett, P.M.S. (1897–1974). Professor of Physics, London University 1953–65; Nobel Prize 1948.

Bowles, Chester (b. 1901). United States Ambassador to India 1951–3 and 1963–9; Under-Secretary of State 1961.

Bulganin, N.A. (1889–1975). Chairman of Moscow Soviet 1931–7; given rank of Marshal 1947; Deputy Chairman of Council of Ministers 1949–55; Prime Minister of the Soviet Union 1955–8.

Chagla, M.C. (1900–81). Chief Justice of the Bombay High Court 1947–58; Ambassador to the United States 1958–61; High Commissioner in Britain 1962–3; Minister for Education 1963–6 and for External Affairs 1966–7.

Chaliha, B.P. (1912–71). Leading member of the Congress Party; Chief Minister of Assam 1957–70.

Chaudhuri, J.N., General (1908–83). Commissioned in the Indian army 1928; commander of police action in Hyderabad 1948; overall commander of Goa operation 1961; Chief of Army Staff 1962–6; High Commissioner in Canada 1966–9.

Chavan, Y.B. (b. 1913). Chief Minister of Maharashtra, 1956–62; Minister for Defence, Government of India, 1962–6, and in charge of other portfolios 1966–77.

Chen Yi (1901–72). General in the Chinese army; Mayor of Shanghai 1949–58; Minister for Foreign Affairs 1958–72.

Dalai Lama (b. 1935). Recognized as the fourteenth incarnation; temporal and spiritual leader of Tibet; left Lhasa for refuge in India, March 1959.

Dayal, R. (b. 1909). Joined Indian Civil Service 1933; Permanent Representative at the United Nations 1952–4; Ambassador in Yugoslavia 1954–8; High Commissioner in Pakistan 1958–62; United Nations Representative in the Congo 1960–1; Foreign Secretary 1967–8.

Desai, M.J. (1904–67). Joined Indian Civil Service 1928; Commonwealth Secretary 1955–61, Foreign Secretary 1961–3 and Secretary-General, Ministry of External Affairs, 1963–4.

Desai, Morarji (b. 1896). Resigned from Bombay provincial service and joined civil disobedience movement 1930; Minister in Bombay Government 1937–9 and

1946–52; Chief Minister of Bombay 1952–6; Minister of Commerce 1956–8 and Finance 1958–63; Deputy Prime Minister 1967–9 and Prime Minister 1977–9.

Deshmukh, C.D. (1896–1982). Joined Indian Civil Service 1918; Governor of Reserve Bank 1943–9; Minister of Finance 1950–6; Chairman, University Grants Commission 1956–61.

Dhebar, U.N. (1905–77). Leading member of the Congress Party; Chief Minister of Saurashtra 1948–54; President of the Congress 1957–9.

Diefenbaker, J. (1895–1979). Leader of the Conservative Party in Canada from 1956; Prime Minister of Canada 1957–63.

Dulles, J.F. (1888–1959). American lawyer; consultant to Secretary of State 1950; Special Representative 1950–1; Secretary of State 1953–9.

Eisenhower, D.D. (1890–1969). Supreme Allied Commander in Europe 1943–5; President of Columbia University when Nehru received a degree 1949; President of the United States 1953–61.

Galbraith, J.K. (b. 1908). Professor of Economics at Harvard University 1949–75; United States Ambassador to India 1961–3.

Gandhi, Indira (b. 1917). Daughter of Jawaharlal Nehru; married in 1942 Feroze Gandhi (died 1960); President of the Congress 1959–60; Minister for Information and Broadcasting 1964–6; Prime Minister of India 1966–77 and since 1980.

Ghosh, A. (1909–62). Involved in the terrorist movement; joined Communist Party of India 1933; General Secretary of the Party 1951–62.

Gopalan, A.K. (1904–77). Member of the Congress 1927–39, when he joined the Communist Party; member of Lok Sabha 1952–77; member of politbureau of C.P.I. (Marxist) from 1964 till his death.

Graham, F. (1886–1972). Professor of History at North Carolina University; United Nations mediator in Kashmir dispute.

Gundevia, Y.D. (b. 1908). Joined Indian Civil Service 1931; Ambassador in Switzerland 1953–4; High Commissioner in Sri Lanka 1957–60; Commonwealth Secretary 1961–4; Foreign Secretary 1964–5.

Hammarskjöld, D. (1905–61). Swedish official and economist; Secretary-General of the United Nations 1953–61; killed in an air accident in central Africa.

Harriman, A. (b. 1891). United States Ambassador to the Soviet Union 1943–6; Governor of New York 1955–9; Assistant Secretary of State for Far Eastern Affairs 1961–3.

Home, 14th Earl of (b. 1903). Disclaimed peerage 1963, created life peer 1974; Secretary of State for Commonwealth Relations 1955–60; Foreign Secretary 1960–3; Prime Minister 1963–4; Foreign Secretary 1970–4.

Iyer, V.R. Krishna (b. 1915). Minister for Law in Kerala 1957–9; judge of the High Court of Kerala 1968–71 and of the Supreme Court 1973–8.

Jain, A.P. (1902–77). Congressman from Saharanpur in Uttar Pradesh; Union Minister for Rehabilitation 1950–4 and for Food and Agriculture 1954–9.

Jarring, G. (b. 1907). Swedish Permanent Representative to the United Nations, 1956–8.

Jayaprakash Narayan (1902–79). One of the founders of the Congress Socialist Party 1934; member of Working Committee of the Congress 1936; after 1947 was for some time a leading member of the Socialist Party; in detention 1975–7.

Kairon, P.S. (1901–65). Joined the Congress in 1929; President of Punjab provincial Congress Committee 1950–2; Minister in the Punjab 1947–9 and 1952–6 and Chief Minister 1956–64.

Kamaraj, K. (1903–75). Congressman from Madras; President Tamil Nad Congress Committee 1940–54; Chief Minister of Madras 1954–63; President of the Congress 1963–7.

Kasavubu, J. (1910–69). President of the Congo 1960–5.

Katju, K.N. (1887–1968). Lawyer and Congressman of Allahabad; Minister in the United Provinces 1937–9 and 1946–7; Governor of Orissa 1947–8 and of West Bengal 1948–51; Union Minister for Law 1951–2, for Home Affairs 1952–5 and for Defence 1955–7; Chief Minister of Madhya Pradesh 1957–62.

Kaul, B.M., General (1912–72). Commissioned in Indian army 1933; Chief of the General Staff 1961; coordinator of Goa operation 1961; corps commander in North East Frontier Agency 1962.

Kaul, T.N. (b. 1913). Joined Indian Civil Service 1936; Ambassador to the Soviet Union 1962–6; Foreign Secretary 1968–73; Ambassador to the United States 1973–6.

Kennedy, J.F. (1917–63). Member United States House of Representatives 1947–53 and of the Senate 1953–60; President of the United States from 1961 till his assassination in November 1963.

Khrushchev, N.S. (1894–1971). Elected to Central Committee of the Communist Party of the Soviet Union 1934; member of the Praesidium 1949; First Secretary of the Central Committee 1953–64 and Chairman of Council of Ministers of the Soviet Union 1958–64.

Koirala, B.P. (1914–82). Educated in India; Prime Minister of Nepal 1959–60; thereafter served long terms in prison and spent many years in exile.

Krishnamachari, T.T. (1899–1974). Businessman of Madras; joined Congress in 1942; Union Minister for Commerce and Industry 1952–6, for Finance 1956–8, without Portfolio 1962, for Economic and Defence Coordination 1962–3 and for Finance 1963–5.

Krishnamachari, V.T. (1881–1964). Entered Madras Civil Service 1908; Dewan (Prime Minister) of Baroda 1927–44 and of Jaipur 1946–9; Deputy Chairman of Planning Commission 1953–60.

Lal Bahadur Shastri (1904–66). Congressman from the United Provinces; Minister in the United Provinces 1947–51; Union Minister for Railways 1952–6, for Communications 1957–8, for Commerce and Industry 1958–61, for Home Affairs 1961–3 and without Portfolio 1964; Prime Minister from June 1964 till his death in Tashkent, January 1966.

Lumumba, P. (1925–61). Founder of the national movement in the Belgian Congo 1957; Prime Minister of the Congo from 1960 till his murder in 1961.

Macmillan, H. (b. 1894). British Conservative politician; Foreign Secretary 1955; Chancellor of the Exchequer 1955–7; Prime Minister 1957–63.

Mahalanobis, P.C. (1893–1972). Physicist and statistician; Fellow of the Royal Society; member of the Planning Commission 1955–67.

Mahendra, King of Nepal (1920–71). Succeeded his father as King 1955; dismissed the ministry and assumed full powers 1960.

Malaviya, K.D. (1904–81). Congressman from the United Provinces; Deputy Minister in the Union Government 1954–7; Union Minister for Oil and Mines 1957–63 and 1973–7.

Mao Zedong (Tse-tung) (1893–1976). Chairman of the Chinese Communist Party 1935–76; proclaimed the People's Republic of China on 1 October 1949; Chairman of the People's Republic of China 1949–59.

Mathai, M.O. (1909–81). Member of Nehru's personal staff 1946–59.

Medhi, B.R. (1888–1981). President of the Assam Congress Committee 1930–9; Minister for Finance in Assam 1946–50 and Chief Minister 1950–7; Governor of Madras 1958–64.

Menon, K.P.S. (1898–1982). Joined Indian Civil Service 1921; later seconded to Indian Political Service; Ambassador to China 1947; Foreign Secretary 1948–52; Ambassador to the Soviet Union 1952–61.

Menon, V.K. Krishna (1896–1974). Secretary of India League in London 1929–47; High Commissioner in London 1947–52; member of Indian delegation to the United Nations 1952–62; Minister without Portfolio 1956–7 and for Defence 1957–62.

Menzies, Sir R. (1894–1978). Prime Minister of Australia 1939–41 and 1949–66.

Mirza, Iskandar (1899–1969). Joined Indian army 1921 and selected for Political Service 1926; Defence Secretary in Pakistan 1947; Minister for Home Affairs 1954; Governor-General 1955 and President of Pakistan 1956–8.

Mobutu, General (b. 1930). Chief of Staff Congo army 1960; assumed supreme power in name of army 1960; President of Congo (now Zaire) since 1965.

Mountbatten of Burma, 1st Earl (1900–79). Chief of Combined Operations 1942–3; Supreme Allied Commander South-East Asia 1943–6; Viceroy of India March–August 1947; Governor-General of India August 1947–June 1948; First Sea Lord 1955–9; Chairman Chiefs of Staff Committee 1959–65.

Nagy, I. (1906–58). Prime Minister of Hungary 1953–5; reinstated after demonstrations in Budapest in October 1956 and overthrown by Soviet intervention the next month; arrested and executed in 1958.

Namboodiripad, E.M.S. (b. 1909). Joined the Congress Party 1930; one of the founders of the Congress Socialist Party 1934; joined the C.P.I. 1941 and was its General Secretary 1953–6, 1962–3 and 1967–9; Chief Minister of Kerala 1957–9.

Nasser, G.A. (1918–70). Deputy Premier of Egypt 1953; Prime Minister 1954–6 and President 1956–70.

Nehru, B.K. (b. 1909). Joined Indian Civil Service 1934; Ambassador to the United States 1961–8; High Commissioner in Britain 1973–7; Governor of Assam 1968–73 and of Kashmir since 1981.

Nehru, R.K. (1902–81). Joined Indian Civil Service 1925; Ambassador to Sweden 1949–52; Foreign Secretary 1952–5; Ambassador to China 1955–8 and to Egypt 1958–60; Secretary-General in Ministry of External Affairs 1960–3.

Nkrumah, K. (1909–72). Leader of the freedom movement in Ghana (formerly the Gold Coast); Prime Minister 1952–7 and President from 1957 till his deposition in 1966.

Noon, Feroze Khan (1893–1970). Member of Viceroy's Executive Council 1942–5; Minister of Foreign Affairs in Pakistan 1955–7 and Prime Minister 1957–8.

Nu, U (b. 1907). Joined Nationalist Party in Burma 1938; Prime Minister 1947–58 and 1960–2; a devout Buddhist.

Palit, D.K., General (b. 1919). Commissioned in Indian army 1939; Director of Military Operations 1961–3; Commandant Indian Military Academy 1966–9; author of books on military strategy.

Palme Dutt, R. (1896–1974). Member of executive committee of British Communist Party 1922–65; editor of *Labour Monthly* from 1921 till his death.

Panchen Lama, second in Tibetan hierarchy after the Dalai Lama; after the Dalai Lama went into exile in March 1949, the Chinese Government dealt with the Panchen Lama as the leader of Tibet.

Pant, G.B. (1887–1961). Advocate of Allahabad; Chief Minister of United Provinces 1937–9 and 1946–55; Union Home Minister 1955–61.

Parthasarathi, G. (b. 1912). Ambassador to China 1958–61; High Commissioner in Pakistan 1962–5; Permanent Representative to the United Nations 1965–9; Vice-Chancellor of Jawaharlal Nehru University 1969–74.

Pasternak, B. (1890–1960). Soviet poet and novelist best known for his novel *Doctor Zhivago*; awarded Nobel Prize for Literature in 1958 but declined it.

Phizo, Z.A. (b. 1900). Leader of the Naga rebels; wanted on charges of murder, he fled to Pakistan and then to Europe and Britain.

Prasad, Rajendra (1884–1963). Lawyer from Patna who joined Mahatma Gandhi in 1917; President of the Congress 1934, 1939 and 1947–8; President of the Constituent Assembly 1946–50; President of India 1950–62.

Radhakrishnan, S. (1888–1975). Professor of Philosophy at Calcutta University 1921–41 and of Eastern Religions at Oxford University 1936–52; Ambassador to the Soviet Union 1949–52; Vice-President of India 1952–62; President of India 1962–7.

Rajagopalachari, C. (1878–1972). Leading Congressman of Madras; Chief Minister of Madras 1937–9; Governor of West Bengal 1947–8; Governor-General of India 1948–50; Union Minister without Portfolio and then for Home Affairs 1950–1; Chief Minister of Madras 1952–4; founder of the conservative Swatantra Party.

Rao, B. Ramakrishna (1899–1967). Congressman from Hyderabad; Chief Minister of Hyderabad 1952–6; Governor of Kerala 1956–60 and of Uttar Pradesh 1960–2.

Roy, B.C. (1882–1962). Physician and Congressman of Calcutta; Chief Minister of West Bengal from 1948 till his death.

Rusk, D. (b. 1909). United States Secretary of State 1961–9; Professor of International Law at University of Georgia since 1970.

St Laurent, L. (1882–1973). Lawyer of Quebec; Minister of External Affairs of Canada 1946–8; Prime Minister 1948–57.

Sampurnanand (1891–1969). Congressman from the United Provinces; Chief Minister of Uttar Pradesh 1955–60; Governor of Rajasthan 1962–7.

Sandys, D., now Lord Duncan-Sandys (b. 1908). British Minister of Defence 1957–9; Secretary of State for Commonwealth Relations 1960–4.

Scott, Michael (1907–83). Anglican priest; sponsored case of Hereros at the United Nations 1947–55; member of Nagaland peace mission 1964–6.

Sen, L.P., General (1910–81). Commissioned in Indian army 1931; prominent in Kashmir operations 1947–8; Chief of the General Staff 1958–61; in charge of the Eastern Command 1961–3.

Singh, Harbaksh, General (b. 1913). Commissioned in Indian army 1955; Chief of Staff at Western Command 1961; in charge for a while of the corps in the eastern sector during the fighting in 1962.

Sri Prakasa (1890–1971). Contemporary of Nehru at Cambridge; Secretary of the Congress 1927 and 1931; after 1947 served as High Commissioner in Pakistan, Union Minister and Governor of Assam, of Madras and of Maharashtra.

Srinagesh, S.M., General (1903–77). Commissioned in Indian army 1923; Chief of Army Staff 1955–7; Governor of Assam 1959–62, of Andhra Pradesh 1962–4 and of Mysore 1964–5.

Stevenson, A. (1900–65). Governor of Illinois 1949–53; Democratic candidate for presidency of United States 1952 and 1956; visited India 1953; United States Ambassador at United Nations 1961–3.

Suhrawardy, H.S. (1893–1963). Leader of Muslim League in Bengal; Minister in Bengal 1943–5 and Chief Minister 1946–7; Prime Minister of Pakistan 1956–7.

Sukarno, A. (1901–70). Leader of nationalist movement in Indonesia; President of Indonesia 1949–67.

Thapar, P.N., General (1906–75). Commissioned in Indian army 1926; Chief of Army Staff 1961–2; Ambassador to Afghanistan 1964.

Thimayya, K.S., General (1906–65). Soldier with distinguished service in Second World War and in Kashmir operations 1947–8; Chairman of neutral nations' repatriation commission in Korea 1953; Chief of Army Staff 1957–61.

Tito, Marshal J.B. (1892–1980). Led the uprising in Yugoslavia against Nazi occupation during the Second World War; President of Yugoslavia from 1953 to his death.

Tshombe, M. (1919–69). Leader in Katanga in the Congo; Prime Minister of the Congo 1964–5.

Vijayalakshmi Pandit (b. 1900). Sister of Jawaharlal Nehru; married in 1921 R.S. Pandit (d. 1944); Minister in the United Provinces 1937–9 and 1946; Ambassador to the Soviet Union 1947–9 and to the United States 1949–51; President of United Nations General Assembly 1953–4; High Commissioner in Britain 1954–61; Governor of Maharashtra 1962–4.

Zhou (Chou) Enlai (1898–1976). Founded Chinese communist youth group in Paris 1922; chief negotiator for communists 1946; Prime Minister of the People's Republic of China from 1949 till his death.

Glossary

Bhai: brother

Crore: ten millions or one hundred lakhs

Dharma: moral duty

Holi: spring festival

Khaddar: cloth woven of handspun yarn

Kisan: peasant

Kismat: fate

Lakh: one hundred thousand

Lok Sabha: House of the People; lower house of Parliament

Panchayat: village council

Panchayat raj: administration by village councils

Rabi: spring harvest

Rajya Sabha: House of States; upper house of Parliament

Talukdar: a landowner, particularly in Avadh

Wakfs: Muslim charitable foundations

Zamindar: a landowner, particularly in Bengal

Zamindari: landowner's estate

Bibliography

Manuscript Sources

Jawaharlal Nehru papers
In the custody of Shrimati Indira Gandhi

Radhakrishnan papers
In the custody of the family

Nehru Memorial Museum and Library

The files of the All India Congress Committee

Tape-recordings of the proceedings of the Congress Parliamentary Party

Krishna Menon papers

All-India Radio
Tape-recordings of important speeches of Nehru

Press Information Bureau
Verbatim texts of Nehru's press conferences and important speeches not covered by All-India Radio

Official Records

Some files of the Prime Minister's Secretariat
Some files of the Planning Commission

Published Sources

Third Five Year Plan (Delhi, 1961)
Parliamentary (Lok Sabha and Rajya Sabha) Debates 1956–64
Notes, Memoranda and Letters Exchanged and Agreements signed between the Governments of India and China 1954–65. White Papers I to XI (Ministry of External Affairs Delhi 1959–65).
Report of the Officials of the Governments of India and the People's Republic of China on the Boundary Question (Delhi, 1961).
Karanjia, R.K. *The Mind of Mr. Nehru* (London, 1960). Text of interviews with Nehru in 1960.

Karanjia, R.K. *The Philosophy of Mr. Nehru* (London, 1966). Text of interviews with Nehru 1961–3.
Nehru, J., *India Today and Tomorrow* (Delhi, 1959).
Nehru, J., *Speeches*, Vol. 4, *1957–63* (Delhi, 1964); Vol. 5, *1963–4* (Delhi, 1968).
Nehru, J., *India's Foreign Policy*, Selected Speeches (Delhi, 1961).
Nehru in America (Information Service of India, New York, 1950).
Nehru in Scandinavia (Information Service of India, Stockholm, 1958).

Newspapers and Journals
Series consulted

The Economist (London)
The Guardian (London)
The Hindu (Madras)
Mainstream (Delhi)
National Herald (Lucknow)
The Times (London)

Oral Testimony
Nehru Memorial Museum and Library
P.M.S. Blackett
R. Palme Dutt
R. Sankar

Author's interviews with persons are mentioned in the footnotes.

Secondary Sources
Only books and articles involving more than a passing reference are listed.

Ayub Khan, M., *Friends not Masters* (Oxford, 1967).
Bowles, C., *Promises to Keep* (Indian edn, 1972).
Brecher, M., *India and World Politics* (London, 1968).
Brecher, M., 'India's Decisions on the Voice of America: A Study in Irresolution', *Asian Survey*, July 1974.
Brecher, M., 'Non-Alignment under Stress: The West and the India–China Border War', *Pacific Affairs*, Winter 1979–80.
Crocker, W.R., *Nehru* (London, 1966).
Dalvi, J.P., *Himalayan Blunder* (Bombay, 1969).
Damodaran, K., 'Memoirs of an Indian Communist', in K.N. Panikkar (ed.), *Prospects of Left Unity* (Delhi, 1979).
Dayal, R., *Mission for Hammarskjöld* (Delhi, 1976).
Eisenhower, D.D., *Waging Peace* (London, 1966).
Erdman, H.L., *The Swatantra Party and Indian Conservatism* (Cambridge, 1967).
Frankel, F.R., *India's Political Economy 1947–77* (Delhi, 1978).
Galbraith, J.K., *Ambassador's Journal* (London, 1969).
Galbraith, J.K., *A Life in Our Times* (London, 1981).
George, T.J.S., *Krishna Menon* (London, 1964).
Gittings, J., *Survey of the Sino-Soviet Dispute* (Oxford, 1968).
Gittings, J., *The World and China 1922–72* (London, 1974).

Gore-Booth, Lord, *With Great Truth and Respect* (London, 1974).
Gundevia, Y.D., 'Outside the Archives' (unpublished).
Hanson, A.H., *The Process of Planning* (Oxford, 1966).
Harrison, S.S., 'Nehru's Plan for Peace', *The New Republic*, 19 June 1971.
Harrison, S.S., *The Widening Gulf* (New York, 1978).
Hoskyns, C., *The Congo since Independence* (Oxford, 1965).
Kaul, B.M., *The Untold Story* (Delhi, 1967).
Kaviraj, S., 'Apparent Paradoxes of Jawaharlal Nehru', *Mainstream*, 15 November–13 December 1980.
Ladejinsky, W., *Agrarian Reform as Unfinished Business*, (Oxford, 1979).
Lieten, G.K., *The First Communist Ministry in Kerala 1957–9* (Calcutta, 1982).
Macmillan, H., *Riding the Storm* (London, 1971).
Macmillan, H., *Pointing the Way* (London, 1972).
Macmillan, H., *At the End of the Day* (London, 1973).
Maddick, H., *Panchayati Raj* (London, 1970).
Maxwell, N., *India's China War* (London, 1970).
Mullik, B.N., *My Years with Nehru: The Chinese Betrayal* (Delhi, 1971).
Mullik, B.N., *My Years with Nehru: Kashmir* (Delhi, 1971).
Myrdal, G., *Asian Drama* (New York, 1968).
Nanda, B.R., Joshi, P.C., and Raj Krishna, *Gandhi and Nehru* (Delhi, 1979).
Nossiter, T.J., *Communism in Kerala* (Delhi, 1982).
Palit, D.K., 'A Summary of Events and Policies *vis-à-vis* the Chinese Attack 1961–2' (unpublished).
Prasad, N., *The Fall of Towang 1962* (Delhi, 1981).
Reid, Escott, *Envoy to Nehru* (Delhi, 1981).
Robinson, E.A.G., and Kidron, M. (eds), *Economic Development in South Asia* (London, 1970).
Rubinoff, A.N., *India's Use of Force in Goa* (Bombay, 1971).
Rustomji, N., *Imperilled Frontiers* (Delhi, 1983).
Schlesinger, A.M., *A Thousand Days* (Boston, 1965).
Schram, S. (ed.), *Mao Tse-Tung Unrehearsed* (Penguin edn, 1974).
Sheean, V., *Nehru: The Years of Power* (London, 1960).
Sulzberger, C.L., *The Last of the Giants* (London, 1971).
Tendulkar, S.D., 'Economic Inequality in an Indian Perspective', in A. Beteille (ed.), *Equality and Inequality* (Delhi, 1983).
Thorner, D., *The Shaping of Modern India* (Delhi, 1980).
Urquhart, B., *Hammarskjöld* (London, 1972).
Weissman, S.R., *American Foreign Policy in the Congo, 1960–1964* (Cornell University Press, 1974).
Whiting, A.S., *The Chinese Calculus of Deterrence* (Ann Arbor, 1975).
Wilson, D., *Mao the People's Emperor* (London, 1979).
Yahuda, M.B., *China's Role in World Affairs* (London, 1978).

Index